RESEARCH IN
FINANCIAL SERVICES:
PRIVATE AND PUBLIC POLICY

Volume 10 • 1998

BANK CRISES: CAUSES,
ANALYSIS AND PREVENTION

EDITORIAL BOARD

RESEARCH IN FINANCIAL SERVICES: PRIVATE AND PUBLIC POLICY

BANK CRISES: CAUSES, ANALYSIS AND PREVENTION

Editor: GEORGE G. KAUFMAN
School of Business
Loyola University Chicago

VOLUME 10 • 1998

 JAI PRESS INC.

Stamford, Connecticut   London, England

CONTENTS

PART III

LIST OF CONTRIBUTORS

James R. Barth

Lowder Eminent Scholar in Finance
College of Business
Auburn University

Philip F. Bartholomew

Senior International Advisor
  Office of the Comptroller
  of the Currency
(Washington)

Harald Benink

Limburg Institute of Financial
  Economics
Maastricht University (Netherlands)

R. Dan Brumbaugh, Jr.

Senior Finance Fellow
Milken Institute (Santa Monica, CA)

Gerard Caprio, Jr.

Lead Economist
  Development Division
The World Bank

Thomas F. Cargill

Department of Economics
University of Nevada

Douglas Evanoff

Vice President
Federal Reserve Bank of Chicago

Gillian Garcia

Senior Economist
  Division of Bank Supervision
International Monetary Fund

R. Alton Gilbert

Vice President
Federal Reserve Bank of St. Louis

Benton E. Gup

College of Business Administration
University of Alabama

Paul M. Horvitz   College of Business Administration
                                   University of Houston

George G. Kaufman   John F. Smith Professor of Finance
                                   School of Business
                                   Loyola University Chicago

Randall S. Kroszner   Graduate School of Business
                                   University of Chicago

Thomas S. Mondschean   Department of Economics
                                   DePaul University

Richard Nelson   Vice President
                                   Wells Fargo Bank (San Francisco, CA)

Lalita Ramesh   Research Department
                                   Milken Institute (Santa Monica, CA)

Paolo Marullo Reedtz   Director
                                   Banking and Financial Supervision
                                   Bank of Italy

Anna J. Schwartz   Research Associate
                                   National Bureau of Economic
                                       Research, Inc

Mark D. Vaughan   Senior Manager and Economist
                                       Banking Supervision & Regulation
                                   Federal Reserve Bank of St. Louis

Gllenn Yago   Director of Capital Studies
                                   Milken Institute (Santa Monica, CA)

INTRODUCTION

The papers in this volume were presented at three invited sessions at the annual meeting of the Western Economic Association in Lake Tahoe, Nevada on June 30 and July 1, 1998. The comments of the discussant at each of these sessions are also included.

The papers focus on the widespread banking and financial crises that have recently plagued or are currently plaguing many countries worldwide. Indeed, a recent study by the International Monetary Fund (Lindgren, Garcia, & Saal, 1996) reported that banking crises had been experienced by nearly three-quarters of its 180-plus member countries since 1980. And this was before the current problems in Korea and Southeast Asia. Only the African continent, where banking systems are generally quite primitive, appears to have been bypassed by this plague.

The costs of these banking crises have been high both in terms of increased unemployment, lower output, misallocation of resources, depreciation in exchange rates and resulting higher rates of inflation, and general uncertainty that often led to political repercussions and in terms of transfer costs from the use of public (tax-payer) funds to protect the par values of some or all deposits at banks and banking-type institutions whose assets had declined in market value of some or all deposits at banks and banking-type institutions whose assets had declined in market value below this amount. Such transfer costs totaled between 2 and 3 percent of GDP in the United States to resolve the thrift debacle of the 1980s and have exceeded 10 percent of GDP in a number of countries. Thus, preventing such crises in the future, or at least minimizing their adverse fallout, is a high current public policy concern worldwide.

The IMF and other earlier studies also identified a large number of common factors that appear to precede almost all crises and may reasonably be identified as common causes. The papers in this volume amplify on the evidence in this area for additional countries; expand the earlier analyses; describe, discuss, and evaluate alternative procedures for resolving bank insolvencies and recapitalizing the banking system, and suggest ways of maintaining bank solvency and preventing reoccurrences of these costly crises. The papers are timely, add considerably to our storehouse of knowledge, and are likely to be of particular value to policy makers, bankers, and fellow researchers.

George G. Kaufman
Series Editor

REFERENCES

Lindgren, C., Garcia, G., & Saal, M. I. (1996). *Bank soundness and macroeconomic policy.* Washington, DC: International Monetary Fund.

PART I

BANKING ON CRISES:
EXPENSIVE LESSONS

Gerard Caprio, Jr.

I. INTRODUCTION

Since the writings of John Stuart Mill, an illustrious group of economists have
argued either that finance is unimportant or that it matters most when it gets out of
order. As evidence of its neglect, generations of economists constructed models
without money or a financial sector, and development texts, though routinely men-
tioning savings and investment, did not feature chapters on the financial system.[1]
With the explosion of banking crises around the globe in the last two decades of
the twentieth century, finance is back in fashion. The turbulence and spread of
financial crises in the East Asian "miracle" economies—and in Japan—has raised
concerns about the stability of financial systems in many countries, as well as
inquiries as to the lessons of this experience. Authorities around the world are concerned about financial crises: how do they happen, why are there more and more
costly crises, and what steps can be taken to minimize vulnerability.

   This paper will address these issues. Section II will summarize briefly the volu-
minous literature on proximate and more distant causes of crises. Although both

Research in Financial Services: Private and Public Policy, Volume 10, pages 3-20.
Copyright © 1998 by JAI Press Inc.
All rights of reproduction in any form reserved.
ISBN: 0-7623-0358-1

micro and macro factors are associated with crises, beyond lobbying for changes in the international financial system, national authorities are left with following sound macro policies, improving financial sector infrastructure, and upgrading regulation and supervision as means of minimizing the likelihood and costs of financial crises. Is there a payoff to improving the regulatory framework? Tentative evidence presented in section III, which compares the broad regulatory environment in 12 selected Asian and Latin American countries, suggests that the answer is affirmative. This comparison both reveals how some countries have been progressing, in some cases beyond the BIS minimum standards, and can help as a guide, indicating weak areas of regulation that should be a target for further improvement. Generally, those countries that have higher scores on their regulatory systems appear to have weathered the latest crisis well, suggesting that improving the regulatory environment, broadly interpreted, should be a goal for countries that have not thus far made much headway in this area. The predominance of Asian countries at the bottom of the regulatory ranking (and the jump in interest rates there) provides another explanation of the mostly regional focus of the latest crisis. An added advantage of this scoring system is that it offers a game plan for the authorities in improving the regulatory environment.

A plausible hypothesis then is that authorities are learning—at great cost—from the last two decades of crises and are moving to raise the cost or otherwise tighten the safety net supporting the banking sector. Section IV will conclude with unresolved issues and suggestions for future research.

II. CRISES: CAUSES NEAR AND FAR

Panics do not destroy capital; they merely reveal the extent to which it has been previously destroyed by its betrayal into hopelessly unproductive works.
—John Stuart Mill (1867).

The literature on banking crises has grown exponentially with the boom in bust banks in recent years. Indeed, the Asian crisis has spawned several websites, one of which lists, as of June 3, 1998, 43 pages of citations of research papers, country reports, news, and other websites with related information.[2] This section, after clarifying what we mean by crisis, briefly reviews some of the latest contribution to the literature on proximate causes of financial (here, mostly banking) crises, before turning to some of the fundamental causes. Understanding the proximate causes may help with predicting crises, but an understanding of the fundamental factors is necessary to help with their prevention.

Any review of the "crisis" literature should commence with the warning that not all of the crises discussed are the same; a key issue thus is what constitutes a crisis. In the last few years, as economists have tried to model crises, there has been a tendency to distinguish two types: currency crises and financial crises. The former involve a sudden movement of the exchange rate and sharp change in capital flows.

Financial crises regularly originate in or induce insolvency in the banking system, and feature a collapse in asset prices, most often in equity and securities markets. Banking system insolvency has various manifestations, such as a run on the banks, large bailout programs or bank nationalization (Demirguc-Kunt & Detragiache, 1997) or a large nonperforming loan problem (Caprio & Klingebiel, 1997).

Still, these categorizations require some judgment for determining when a country is in a crisis of either type.[3] Either of these crises may be mild or severe. But a financial crisis usually involves a corporate debt problem in the nonbank financial sector—in other words, banks and other intermediaries usually do not get into trouble if borrowers can easily service their debt. Financial crises can occur without any currency crisis, as witnessed in many cases in Africa and in transition countries (though the crisis here, when no run was involved, was rather the insolvency of the banking system). Mild currency crises usually involve neither a corporate debt problem nor a banking crisis, as in the case of the 1992 ERM episode, whereas severe currency crises usually do trigger one or both. That is, severe currency crises usually entail a crisis in the banking and nonbank sectors.

This paper focuses on financial crises, regardless of whether a currency crisis is deemed to be involved.[4] A search for causes can be divided along two lines: more proximate causes, in the sense that they may provide indicators of incipient crises, and more distant, or fundamental factors. Demirguc-Kunt and Detragiache (1997, 1998) look at determinants in the former sense, using a multivariate logit analysis of the likelihood of a banking crisis, based on the following indicators:

- macro (GDP growth, change in terms of trade, real interest rate, inflation, depreciation of the exchange rate, and government surplus/GDP);
- financial (M2/ foreign exchange reserves, credit growth/GDP, bank cash/ bank assets, and private credit/GDP);[5] and
- institutional indicators (GDP per capita, the presence or absence of explicit deposit insurance, and in index of law and order, which is a proxy for the ability to enforce contracts).

This model, originally estimated up to 1994, performs quite well in prediction, explaining about 70 percent of the crises that occurred, and within sample only predicting a crisis when none occurred in 15 percent of the cases. Interestingly, in their research thus far, exchange rates or the terms of trade are not that significant in most specifications, though their original data did not include the Mexican and Asian crises. Slower output growth, increases in real interest rates, declining liquidity, faster credit growth, explicit deposit insurance, poor legal systems, and low per capita GDP are found to be associated with a greater likelihood of banking crises.

Previous research had debated whether macro or micro and institutional factors "caused" banking crises, and Demirguc-Kunt and Detragiache reveal that both play a role in the drama, consistent with the finding of Caprio and Klingebiel

(1997) that out of 80 cases, both macro and micro factors regularly were cited as causes of systemic crises.[6] More recent attempts to explain crises have focused on the Asian episodes, which stand out in a number of respects, not least because the countries most directly involved—Thailand, Indonesia, and Korea—for several decades had seen such rapid growth of real incomes and living standards, and all appeared to have relatively favorable macro indicators, especially low inflation, fiscal balance or surpluses, and exceptionally high savings rates.[7] Krugman (1998) focuses on the links between moral hazard and overinvestment: implicit guarantees that governments would stand behind financial intermediaries led to investment based not on expected returns but on those likely in a "Panglossian" state (best of all possible worlds). Cronyism, here interpreted to be close links between the government and the owner/managers of intermediaries, is featured in this explanation. Although applied to E. Asia in the 1990s, this description fits a number of other financial crises, including the U.S. Thrift institutions in the 1980s and, as Brad De Long has pointed out, the 1873 U.S. financial crisis (DeLong, 1998).

McKinnon and Pill (1997, 1998) highlight the other side of this relationship, overborrowing, which occurs when the non-bank private sector becomes "...euphoric or triumphalist about the success of reform because of the overly optimistic implicit signal about macroeconomic developments contained in loose credit decisions" (McKinnon & Pill, 1998, p. 14). Both these explanations are reminiscent of the debt-deflation literature (Fisher, 1936; Kindleberger, 1978; Minsky, 1982; Bernanke, 1983), and in the East Asian context apply with particular force to Korea, which had debt-equity ratios in 1997 of 3, 4 or higher, depending on when measured, well above those of OECD countries. With such high ratios, firms are vulnerable to the slightest downturn in earnings, since most earnings are committed to paying interest on their debt.[8]

Certainly either version rings true. Excessively high leverage, a reliance on short-term debt, and property market bubbles were featured in East Asia. Private credit grew substantially in excess of GDP throughout the 1990s, which is consistent with this hypothesis, but as Corsetti et al. (1998) note, this explanation fits Thailand better than Korea and Indonesia. In Korea debt-equity ratios had been excessive for some time, making it difficult to highlight a period of demonstrably excessive growth. Consistent with (and encouraged by) the real exchange rate appreciation of their currencies, there was a sharp increase in investment in non-traded goods, especially construction. By 1997, it became clear that much of the new office space—in Bangkok and Jakarta, capacity reached 5-8 times the level of the early 1990s—was a misallocation of resources. Indeed, the property boom appears to have collapsed well in advance of any foreign exchange panic, as property indexes on the stock exchange by the end of 1996 were off their peaks of 1993 in Indonesia (by about one-third) and Thailand (by three-quarters). Property booms, of varying magnitudes, figured prominently in the Scandinavian, U.S., and Japanese crises, among others.

Radelet and Sachs (1998), again on the Asian crisis, argue that the panic by foreign investors caused the crisis, but given the warning signs of problems in the financial sector, including the declining property market, it is more likely that the panic exacerbated the problem. In other words, John Stuart Mill (above) was only partly right: panics both reveal pre-existing resource misallocation and, to the extent that asset markets overshoot, can significantly deepen the crisis as well. Corsetti, Pesenti, and Roubini (1998) argue that the crisis occurred because investors became aware of the fundamental problems about banking and corporate debt. In this regard, Burnside et al (1998) develop a model in which a currency crisis can be caused by foreigners awakening to the fiscal costs of the financial sector crisis; that is, even if stated fiscal positions are in balance or surplus, the actual position, when there are large contingent liabilities of the banking sector, can be in large deficit. This approach admits the possibility of self-fulfilling crises: if the market decides that banks are weak and run the currency, banks with direct (on balance sheet) or indirect foreign exchange exposure (on their customers' balance sheets) can be rendered insolvent. Thus a panic by investors might be rational or irrational. In addition, the Asian crisis featured a number of policy errors that compounded what might have been a smaller crisis (Corsetti et al., 1993).

Last, not just related to East Asia but on financial crises more generally, Stiglitz (1998) and Demirguc-Kunt-Detragiache (1998) note the role played by premature financial sector liberalization, especially where existing institutions—regulation, supervision, and other parts of the infrastructure that would support incentive-compatible behavior—are absent. This view stresses the need for sensible pacing and sequencing of financial reforms.

More Fundamental Factors Behind Crises

The debate among most of the aforementioned authors on the prime cause of the crisis is interesting, but those searching for a single cause of crises miss or at least de-emphasize, a key point, namely that multiple factors were featured most of the time. Thus, of the 86 episodes of bank insolvency (1980-1994) in the Caprio-Klingebiel dataset, at least 20 of these featured "cronyism," meaning excessive political interference, connected lending, or similar labels, and at least 30 featured overborrowing. Panics by foreign investors played a role in Latin American crises of the 1980s and in East Asia in the 1990s, and premature liberalization could be cited in virtually all cases. And of course, macro factors are common in bank insolvency, especially terms of trade declines or recessions.

But rather than emphasize these proximate factors, it is helpful to realize that crises are manifestations of deeper characteristics of the financial sector, which make it prone to such events. Indeed, as Rodrik (1998) has noted, it is distressing that whenever crises occur the economics profession tends to come up with a new generation model to explain the events, only to find that the next crises do not fit the model. Focusing on more proximate factors makes this continual chase almost inevitable.

8

GERARD CAPRIO, JR.

Instead, it is useful to consider the fundamental characteristics of finance: information asymmetries, intertemporal trade, and (some) demandable debt. Providers of funds have difficulties monitoring intermediaries, who in turn face the same problem with users of funds. Those receiving funds know better how they will utilize them than the providers, while the exchange of money today for money in the future further complicates the monitoring problem. This information asymmetry affects bank owners, market participants—depositors and other creditors—and bank supervisors.[9] Thus most bank loans are illiquid and not easily marked to market, making banking, with demandable debt, especially vulnerable to a revaluation of expectations and contributing to its inherent fragility.[10] Indeed, this feature of banking makes it particularly susceptible to multiple equilibria.

Information asymmetries and intertemporal trade foster incentive problems in finance. Bank managers in a perfect information world would find it more difficult to take risks in excess of shareholders' comfort level, and supervisors could intervene in time if they always knew the true net worth of banks.[11] Thus looting, gambling for resurrection or Ponzi schemes could not occur with perfect information and any reasonable form of corporate governance. Information and incentive problems worsen during the crisis itself, as markets may not distinguish between better and worse banks, and asset prices, which may have been inflated before the crisis, can overshoot their equilibrium level as investors rush for the door.

While countries are in a "good" equilibrium, it is perhaps understandable that authorities are not disposed to deal with the weaknesses in their financial systems, even though this is likely the best time to do so. Once the economy slips into crisis—the bad equilibrium—it is likely easier to muster political support for reform, though the long delays in responding in the United States and Japan, among other countries, suggest that the process is neither automatic nor necessarily rapid.

III. BANK REGULATION AND OPERATING ENVIRONMENT

In response to the wave of banking crises of the last two decades, authorities in some countries have begun raising the cost and limiting the extent of the safety net supplied to banks. Enacting and tightening the regulations that banks confront is a key way to achieve this goal, and cross-country comparisons of bank regulation can help reveal the relative strengths and weakness of the operating environment for banks, as well as keep track of progress made in this respect. Yet it is difficult to compare regulatory environments, much less the way in which the regulations are supervised. This section attempts the former task, comparing bank regulation, adapted from the CAMEL framework employed by bank supervisors, variations of which have been used for this purpose by JP Morgan (1997) and Ramos (1997) precisely for rating regulations.[12] Just as individual banks can be assessed by their capital, asset quality, management, earnings, and liquidity, regulatory systems can be compared by using similar criteria, assessing not how these measures compare for all the banks in a country, but rather how the country's requirements and overall environment compares with those of others. Unfortunately, data needed to do these assessments were readily available only for a dozen East Asian and Latin American countries, but a current World Bank research project is extending this information to a wider variety of countries and also quantifying some supervisory variables.

Capital here is assessed here by the minimum required capital-asset ratio, as well as its definition; the more restrictive the allowances for recognizing asset revaluations as part of capital, or the more that risk taking is explicitly accounted for in constituting minimum ratios, the higher the ranking. Asset quality is proxied by the definition of non-performing loans—the number of days till a loan becomes nonperforming—and the provisioning required once this judgment is made. Management quality is the most difficult to compare, but the arbitrary assumption made here is that countries with more assets in foreign banks enjoy better managed assets; foreign ownership also brings better diversification. Management quality could be regarded as separate from regulation, but is included in an index of the regulatory environment as indicating the types of owners that are allowed into the industry.[13] Earnings are not included, as they relate only partly to regulations or the environment, but more to cyclical considerations (as well as to accounting conventions). Minimum liquidity requirements, the inclusion of foreign exchange as a separate reason for liquidity, and the extent of its remuneration are included in the liquidity indicator.[14]

The environment in which banks function is affected by their operating environment and the degree of transparency, which here are included as part of the broad regulatory environment. The overall operating environment is proxied by measures of property rights (the poorer these are defined, the more difficult it becomes to secure credit), creditors' rights, which indicate the ability of creditors to secure repayment, and a measure of the enforcement of the laws (LaPorta et al., 1998; Levine, 1998). Finally, transparency is perhaps the most difficult to gauge. The ranking here is based on whether bank ratings are required, the number of top 10 banks with ratings from international firms (judged to be superior in emerging markets to local counterparts and less susceptible to corruption), and an index of corruption. The latter is included because the greater the extent of corruption, the less likely it is that disclosed information will be accurate.[15] Appendix A contains the details behind each category.

Several caveats are in order. These measures are as of late 1997, before most of the crisis countries made any significant changes in their regulations, however, the components of the operating environment and the corruption index (part of the transparency measure) are from the early 1990s. Since the latter variables only change slowly, this lag is not likely be a significant drawback. Most importantly, each category is equally weighted, clearly an arbitrary rule of thumb. Each category has its proponents: some argue that management is key, others that loan classification and provisioning matters most, and in the wake of the Asian crisis, transparency is receiving a much emphasis. Or, proponents of narrow evaluations of regulations alone would prefer to include only capital, assets, and liquidity, which would change the rankings somewhat, as noted below. Only further research, once a broader dataset is available, will possibly settle this issue. Although capital standards, liquidity ratios, and the share of (majority owned) foreign banks in total assets admit to relatively straightforward measurement, with some scope for interpretations of definitions, the other variables are more difficult to measure. Last, until data on or proxies for supervisory effort become available, it is not possible to determine how the regulations are enforced. With these caveats, Table 1 shows the overall "CAMELOT" rankings, with lower numbers indicating a higher rating.

As readily apparent several clusters of economies stand out, with Singapore showing the strongest regulatory environment, followed in the order shown in Table 1. Note that it is unlikely that differences in total scores of a few points will be significant. Also, the rankings may understate the present health of various systems; for example, in Hong Kong, official regulations do not require a given amount of provisioning even once a loan is in arrears by 180 days (hence a lower score here), yet the authorities encourage provisioning, and Hong Kong Shanghai Bank, a very large part of the "Hong Kong" banking system, may have much stricter standards and a first-rate market and credit risk management system. Still, the comparison in Table 1 is on bank regulation systems, which may only correspond to the health of the banks in the long run. Also, note that some countries, such as Peru, the Philippines and Colombia, score quite well on narrow CAMEL

Table 1. Summary Measures of the Bank Regulatory Environment

Country	Total Score	Capital Position	Loan Classification	Foreign Ownership (Management)	Liquidity	Operating Environment	Transparency
Singapore	16	1	6	2	5	1	1
Argentina	21	1	4	3	4	7	2
Hong Kong	21	3	9	1	2	2	4
Chile	25	5	1	4	8	5	2
Brazil	30	7	3	4	3	8	5
Peru	35	5	2	6	1	11	10
Malaysia	41	5	9	8	8	3	8
Colombia	44	3	4	11	6	10	10
Korea	45	7	9	10	11	3	5
Philippines	47	4	6	7	7	11	12
Thailand	52	7	12	12	8	6	7
Indonesia	52	7	8	9	12	8	8

criteria, but have a lower ranking due to their relatively lower scores on the operating environment and transparency.

These regulatory environment rankings are potentially useful for several purposes. First, for the authorities in each country they show areas in which improvements are more important. For example, authorities in the Philippines might find efforts to improve the legal system and transparency, where they have a low score, to be of higher priority than encouraging higher capital the latter already being a strength. And Colombian authorities apparently do not need to make improvements in capital or loan classification, but other criteria would appear to need attention. Again, however, it is important to note that these recommendations assume that further research—only possible once a broader database is available—bears out the importance of these criteria. Also, the ratings should not be used as simple "minimum standards," in that they are no substitute for the commitment of the political and financial elite of a country to avoid the costs of bad banking. Rather, these ratings could be used as a tool by an already committed elite to effect change in their banking system.

Second, it should be no surprise when economies with poor scores are hit by crises. Those at the top or middle of the range in Table 1, which may have tighter regulations either because they experienced crises in the 1980s (Argentina, Chile, Hong Kong) or due to concerns about the vulnerability associated with being small, highly open economies (Hong Kong, Singapore), tend to have been less affected by the recent crisis. By early 1998, interest rates in a variety of emerging markets had risen significantly (Table 2), as did the rates at which they borrowed

Table 2.   Money Market Interest Rates

Country	1995	1996	1997	Latest 1998	Change Dec. 96 to Spring 1998	Regulatory Score
Singapore	2.56	2.93	4.35	5.38	2.45	16
Argentina	9.46	6.23	6.63	7.02	0.79	21
Hong Kong	6.00	5.13	4.50	4.50	−0.63	21
Chile	15.7	14.03	13.49	14.16	0.13	25
Brazil	53.37	27.45	25.00	34.32	6.87	30
Peru	16.3	13.9	11.7	15.8	1.90	35
Malaysia	na	7.30	10.32	10.95	3.65	41
Colombia	22.40	28.37	23.83	26.38	−1.99	44
Korea	12.57	12.44	13.24	23.53	11.09	45
Philippines	11.76	12.34	12.89	17.79	5.45	47
Thailand	10.27	9.16	na	20.57	11.41	52
Indonesia	13.64	13.96	27.82	57.18	43.22	53

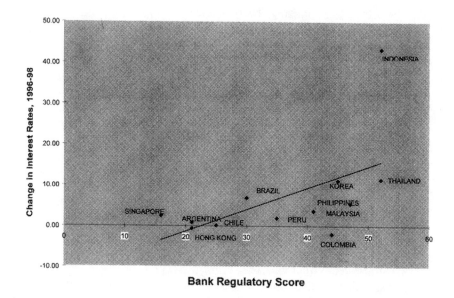

Figure 1. Bank Regulatory Environment and Interest Rates

in international markets. As seen in Figure 1, domestic interest rates between the end of 1996 and the spring of 1998 have widened most for economies with the weakest (i.e., highest) regulatory scores, though to be sure with only a dozen observations the sample is insufficient for more formal testing.[16] Still, an evaluation of bank regulation may help in understanding the vulnerabilities of financial systems. Strengthening the regulatory environment likely pays off: thus, Argentina was more seriously affected in the wake of the Tequila crisis than by the Asian "flu," having in the meantime substantially strengthened capital regulations and loan classification procedures, allowed the percentage of foreign banks to rise significantly, and markedly improved transparency.

Third, in the emerging debate on contagion, some effort is being devoted to explaining why the Mexican and Asian crises appeared to be largely regional. This literature almost exclusively focuses on "real" sector explanations (Diwan & Hoekman, 1998; Glick & Rose, 1998), an approach that fits particularly well in Asia, where trade links are larger than in other emerging market regions. Another explanation, by no means mutually exclusive, is that shocks or dislocations come along regularly, and those countries that are the most susceptible to a significant financial crisis are those in which the incentive and information systems are the weakest. This view also helps explain why Singapore and Hong Kong, both with strong real sector links in the East Asian region, were less affected by the crisis.

IV. CRISIS LESSONS

What lessons can be learned from the crises of the last two decades? The main candidates for explaining the boom in bank failures and the unprecedented fiscal cost of these episodes are that:

- with the demise of colonialism and rise of nation-states, there has been more local banking—more countries attempting to have banks that specialize in lending to the home market, leading to greater bank fragility and more banks to fail;
- macro volatility, post-Bretton-Woods, has increased or shocks are transmitted more readily; and/or
- government safety nets are encouraging greater moral hazard, without commensurate improvements in the information and incentive environment.

Although the first factor likely matters, it is not plausible that it alone explains the phenomenal surge in systemic banking problems. Also, while it is evident that interest rate and exchange rate volatility and capital mobility are greater in the 1980s and 1990s than during the Bretton Woods period, the same statement would not be true for a comparison with the nineteenth and early twentieth century, particularly if real interest rates and real GDP volatility were compared. Moreover, the work of Demirguc-Kunt and Detragiache shows that macro factors alone do not explain banking crises. Thus the third factor likely plays an important role in this story.

Correcting information and incentive problems then stands out as a key area for national authorities' attention, and some tentative evidence was presented suggesting that those economies with the most conservative regulatory environment have best weathered crises. Once more systematic information is available to score a wider variety of regulatory and supervisory systems, this tentative evidence can be subjected to more formal econometric testing. Although improving information should be a clear goal, authorities need to realize that they will never eliminate information asymmetries—or financial crises! Even the best information environments have banking crises—notwithstanding the views of some Texans, this state in the 1980s was part of the United States, and shared its accounting, auditing, and corporate governance systems.

Given the nature of information problems, having bank surveillance by "multiple eyes" is a recommended approach, meaning that owners, markets, and supervisors all need to be given clear incentives and information to monitor banks. Merely increasing capital ratios in the hope that it will induce better bank performance may not be successful: the quality of bank capital, and of bank balance sheets, is difficult to monitor, and higher required capital ratios could induce more risk taking (Hellmann, Murdoch, & Stiglitz, 1997; Berger et al., 1995). In Argentina, the required capital ratio most clearly is a function of the risks being taken: banks are required to have higher minimum ratios the lower their individual

CAMEL rating, the more they lend in excess of 200 basis points above prime rates, and the greater the market risks they undertake. Also, with the requirement that banks issue subordinated debt, there is now the ability to use both market and supervisory input in making decisions as to their riskiness. Moving to forward-looking risk models as a way to ensure better behavior among bankers should be effective but only if significant penalties are assessed when bankers violate the assumptions of their risk models. Making sure that there are some uninsured debt holders in the market will help with monitoring from this source.

Owners of banks also can be motivated by increasing their franchise value, such as through limiting entry. Both U.S. and Japanese banks got into difficulties after several decades of declining franchise value (Weisbrod, Lee, & Rojas-Suarez, 1993; Keeley, 1990). But enforcing entry limits will be difficult in higher income economies given that nonbanks can start up banking functions at low cost.

Last, supervisors also need incentives. In many countries there are disincentives to monitor when: supervisory agencies have little political independence, pay is a fraction of that in the industry being supervised, supervisors face personal legal liability for their official actions, and former supervisors are allowed to take jobs in banking, in effect raising the possibility that they enjoy deferred compensation for not doing their job well. Calomiris (1997) has documented well examples from the nineteenth century, when deferred compensation for supervisors was used to induce effective supervision, and Kane (1997) actively makes a case for a "bonded regulator," arguing that least-cost supervision will not be attained until supervisors are given better incentives.

Governments are not moving significantly on this last point, but instead there is growing support for requiring "prompt, corrective action" as a way to ensure that supervisors act in a timely fashion. Unfortunately, these rules can be re-written in times of crisis (Caprio, 1997), and whether such rules are more or less likely to be overturned than a bonded regulator is an unresolved issue. Still, the fact that a number of both high and middle income countries are making improvements in the information and incentive environment in banking suggests, that after some of the costliest financial crises in history, authorities are learning. To the extent that authorities raise the cost or limit the coverage of the safety net for banking, fewer banking crises may be expected. However, with a more limited or more expensive safety net, the nonbank industry will grow rapidly, as it has in Argentina in the last 2 years, in part to escape the costs.

As the Thai authorities discovered most recently, nonbank finance company problems can infect the banking sector, and a cardinal rule of financial regulation should be that all institutions that take deposits and make loans, regardless of what they are called, should be regulated as banks. The challenge for authorities, then, will be to ensure that financial intermediation, wherever it occurs, is well (not over-) regulated. With an improved regulatory environment, governments can more realistically expect that financial intermediation will be more likely to absorb, rather than magnify, shocks.

Appendix A.   Components of the CAMELOT Ratings for
Banking System Regulation[17]

Capital Country	Definition	Minimum Ratio	Ranking
Singapore	Only Tier 1 eligible	12	1
Argentina	Capital ratio geared to CAMEL rating and interest rates; capital req. for market risk added, with bonds of duration over 2.5 years requiring higher capital	11.5	1
Hong Kong	70% of revaluation reserves eligible for inclusion. Minimum can be raised up to 12% for licensed banks, 16% for restricted license or deposit-taking company; institutions required to observe a "trigger" 1% above the minimum. Capital requirement for market risk as of late-97.	8	3
Chile	Only LT sub debt, up to 20% of capital; risk weight for mortgages above Basle norm.	8	5
Brazil	Reval. reserves, loss reserves, included tier 2	8	7
Peru	No revaluation accounts, sub. debt permitted; min. capital ratio raised by 150-200% for overdue loans.	8	5
Malaysia	Only tier 1 in 8%	8	5
Colombia	150 % risk weight for loans, only 50% of revaluation assets.	9	3
Korea	Up to 45% of revaluation gains included in tier 2 capital	8	7
Philippines	No tier 2, unweighted (all at 100%)	10	4
Thailand	Tier 2 includes revaluation accounts, provisions, unrealized securities profit/loss, subordinated debt	8.5	7
Indonesia	Sub. debt up to 50%,	8	7

Loan Classification

Country	Days to NPL status	Min. initial provision[*]	Comments	Ranking
Singapore	sub. risk	loan value- .8[*] collateral (50% min.)		6
Argentina	90	25%	1% provision on normal loans, Max. single, 15%	4
Hong Kong	180	no general rule	Max. single, 25%	9
Chile	30/90	60%/n.a.		1
Brazil	60	100		3
Peru	60/90	50-60%		2
Malaysia	180	0/1% gen. provisions		9
Colombia	90	50%		4
Korea	180	20%		9
Philippines	sub. risk	25%		6
Thailand	360	15%		11
Indonesia	90	10%		8

Note: [*]On unsecured balances.

Appendix   (Continued)

Management (Foreign Ownership)

Country	% of assets in foreign banks	Rank
Singapore	61.6	2
Argentina	42.9	3
Hong Kong	65.6	1
Chile	33.1	4
Brazil	33.6	4
Peru	28.0	6
Malaysia	14.6	8
Colombia	5.3	11
Korea	8.0	10
Philippines	15.0	7
Thailand	1.8	12
Indonesia	10.8	9

Liquidity

Country	Ratio(s)	Forex	Remuneration	Ranking
Singapore	24%	Watched closely		5
Argentina	20% on liabilities up to 89 days, 15% for 90-179; 10% for 180-365; and 0 for over 365 days. Approx. 9.7% additional as Repos.	Watched closely	Mostly remunerated, half offshore	4
Hong Kong	25% of liabilities	Watched closely	Mostly remunerated	2
Chile	9% on demand, 3.6% on time			8
Brazil	78/15/20			3
Peru	9%	36% added required	Mostly dollar deposits, so 45%	1
Malaysia	13.5%	No restrictions		8
Colombia	21%, 10%			6
Korea	5% on demand, 2% on time			11
Philippines	13%			7
Thailand	7%			8
Indonesia	3%			

Note: Note that in ranking for operating environment, those with a "1" on property rights, get ranked first (hence a 4-way tie); those with a 2.5 get a 5 (2-way tie), and those with a 2 come next, etc. Creditors' rights are ranked in the same manner (except that ratings range from a low of -2 to a high of 1, and enforcement of the legal system is ranked linearly from the high of Singapore to the low of the Philippines.

Appendix (Continued)

Operating Environment

Country	Property Rights[*]	Creditor Rights[**]	Enforcement[**]	Ranking
Singapore	1	1	8.715	1
Argentina	2	1	5.13	7
Hong Kong	1	1	8.52	2
Chile	1	1	6.91	5
Brazil	3+	2	6.31	8
Peru	3	2	3.59	11
Malaysia	2	1	7.105	3
Colombia	3	2	4.55	10
Korea	1	1	6.97	3
Philippines	2	2	3.765	11
Thailand	2.5	1	6.91	6
Indonesia	2.5	1	5.035	8

Notes: [*]1998 Index of Economic Freedom.
[**]Levine (1997) and La Porta, Lopez de Silanes, Shleifer and Vishny (1997).

Transparency

Country	Bank Rating Required[*]	Top 10 Banks with Int'l Ratings[*]	Corruption[**]	Ranking
Singapore	No	All	8.22	1
Argentina	Yes	10	6.02	2
Hong Kong	No	3	8.52	4
Chile	Yes, 2	10	5.3	2
Brazil	No	9	6.32	5
Peru	Yes	6	4.7	10
Malaysia	No	2	7.38	8
Colombia	No	5	5.0	10
Korea	No	10	5.3	5
Philippines	No	8	2.92	12
Thailand	No	9	5.18	7
Indonesia	No	10	2.15	8

Notes: [*]BIS Annual Report, 1997, and World Bank data.
[**]Laporta et. al.

For transparency, those countries requiring banks to be rated get a 1, those without this requirement get a 0; the number of top 10 banks and the corruption measure are ranked as above, and rankings then totaled in the same manner, with the lowest score getting a first place, and so on.

ACKNOWLEDGMENTS

Comments from Philip Bartholomew, Philip Brock, Asli Demirguc-Kunt, Paul Horvitz, Patrick Honohan, Daniel Lederman, Ross Levine, and Guillermo Perry, participants at a

World Bank conference on International Financial Integration and participants at the Western Economic Association Meeting are gratefully acknowledged. Anqing Shi provided competent research assistance. Still, the findings, interpretations, and conclusions expressed in this paper are entirely those of the author. They do not necessarily represent the views of the World Bank, its Executive Directors, or the countries they represent.

NOTES

1. I am indebted to Ross Levine for the point on development texts.

2. The web page is Nouriel Roubini's at www.stern.nyu.edu/~nroubini/asia/AsiaHomepage.html. Paul Krugman, in an observation on the extensive nature of this website, raised the question of whether Roubini "had a day job." For discussions of the Asian crisis, see in particular The World Bank, 1998; Krugman 1998, Goldstein, 1998, and Corsetti, Pesenti, and Roubini, 1998.

3. That is, it is not clear what constitutes a "sudden" move of the exchange rate, a sharp change in capital flows, when a bank run is systemic (or merely represents a flow of deposits from weak banks to strong ones).

4. In the Kaminsky-Reinhart (1996) database, in 38 cases there was an exchange rate crisis without a banking crisis. The time from a banking crisis to an exchange rate crisis was minus (i.e., the banking crisis led the exchange rate crisis by) 5 years to plus six years (if one omits the plus 14-15 year cases!).

5. Since thus far there are no comparable cross-country data on domestic private debt or debt equity ratios, the model could not include such indicators.

6. They found that terms of trade shocks, recessions, or credit booms, on the macro side, and deficient management, faulty supervision and regulation, government intervention, or some degree of connected or politically motivated lending, on the micro side, were cited as causes of most systemic crises.

7. Yet macro indicators were not uniformly strong. Thailand, Indonesia, and Korea all lost some competitiveness from the Chinese devaluation of 1994 and the slide of the yen in 1996-1997; by the end of 1996, the real exchange rate in Indonesia, Malaysia, and Thailand had appreciated by 30-40 percent since the early 1990s. Thailand in particular kept its exchange rate fixed and interest rates above international levels since the early 1990s; given the boom in domestic credit, only rising fiscal surpluses would have been consistent with the pegged exchange rate. The problem, of course, was that capital inflows continued regardless of this inconsistency.

8. With high debt equity ratios, raising interest rates will only worsen insolvency. The only solutions are: injecting equity (unlikely in crisis environments), reducing the real value of debt through higher inflation, or a debt-equity swap, which means wiping out existing equity holders and telling (some) debt holders that they now have an equity claim.

9. Mishkin (1997) and Wyplosz (1998) elaborate on these information problems.

10. When a sufficient information becomes available on a firm so that its credit can be easily priced, the firm graduates to direct market finance. Information technology may reduce the cost of disseminating information on firms, but small and medium-size firms still rely on banks for most of their credit, even in industrial economies.

11 In fact, with perfect information, there would be no need for supervision—everyone would know what risks banks were taking!

12. Note that this effort is distinguished from that of Morgan in including the operating environment and transparency as part of the broad regulatory environment, and from Ramos in quantifying and ranking the countries, as well as on the content of the various indicators.

13. There is no intention to suggest that authorities should admit more foreign banks regardless of the initial conditions in banking and at a rapid pace, as foreign banks in some settings could be a source of instability. There are solid banks in developing countries that are domestic banks. But it is at least

arguable that foreign banks, the majority of which are from OECD countries, have better banking and in particular risk management skills. Claessens, Demirguc-Kunt, and Huizinga show that foreign bank entry leads to lower profits and overheads for domestic banks, increases the stability of the financial system and promotes long term growth. If this variable were dropped, it turns out that only the positions of Colombia and the Philippines are reversed, and Thailand moves from eleventh to tied for ten place with the Philippines.

14.   If liquidity requirements are not well-remunerated, then bankers will do their best to avoid them.

15.   Thus this ranking goes beyond what was attempted in Morgan (1997) and is more rigorous that Ramos (1997). A more thorough classification of financial sector regulation will be attempted in a World Bank research project, which is just beginning, and which will be compiling more extensive information on how financial systems are regulated and supervised. Note, the LaPorta et al. measure of accounting was not used as no data were available for Indonesia, and the indicator for Argentina, which dated back to the early 1990s, is known to be out of date.

16.   Spreads on sovereign borrowing would be more informative but are not available for all these countries.

17.   In addition to various national sources and those noted following various tables, sources included: JP Morgan (1997), Ramos (1997), Hong Kong Monetary Authority (1997) and IMF (1997).

REFERENCES

Bernanke, B. (1983). Nonmonetary Effects of the Financial Crisis in the Propagation of the Great Depression. *American Economic Review, 73*(3).

Berger, A. (1995). The Relationship between Capital and Earnings in Banking. *JMCB, 27,* 432-456.

Burnside, C., M. Eichenbaum, & S. Rebelo. (1998). *Prospective Deficits and the Asian Currency Crises,* mimeo. The World Bank.

Calomiris, C. (1997). *The Post-Modern Bank Safety Net: Lessons for Developed and Developing Countries.* Washington, DC: AEI Press.

Caprio, G. Jr. (1997). Safe and Sound Banking in Developing Countries: We're Not in Kansas Anymore. In *Research in financial services: private and public policy.* Stamford, CT: JAI Press.

Caprio, G. Jr., & Klingebiel, D. (1997). Bank Insolvency: Bad Luck, Bad Policy, and Bad Banking. In M. Bruno & B. Pleskovic (Eds.), *Annual Bank Conference on Development Economics 1996.* The World Bank.

Corsetti, G., Pesenti, P., & Roubini, N. (1998). *What Caused the Asian Currency and Financial Crisis.* Paper presented at the CEPR/World Bank Conference, May 8-9, London.

DeLong, B. (1998). *Asia's flu: A history lesson.* mimeo, Jan. 11, http://econ161.berkeley.edu/.

Diwan, I., & Hoekman, B. (1998). *Financial crises: Contagion and market volatility.* Paper presented at the CEPR/World Bank Conference, London, May 8-9.

Demirguc-Kunt, A., & Detragiache, E. (1997). *The determinants of banking crises: Evidence from industrial and developing countries.* World Bank Policy Research Working Paper 1828, September, www.worldbank.org/html/prddr/prdhome/IBNNewsletter.htm.

Demirguc-Kunt, A., & Detragiache, E. (1998). *Financial liberalization and financial fragility.* Paper presented at the April 1998 Annual Bank Conference on Development Economics, The World Bank, www.worldbank.org/html/prddr/prdhome/IBNNewsletter.htm.

Fisher, I. (1997). *The works of Irving Fisher: Vol. 10. Booms and depressions and related writings.* London: Pickering and Chatto.

Glick, R., & A. Rose. (1998). *Contagion and trade: Why are currency crises regional?* Paper presented at the CEPR/World Bank Conference, May 8-9, London.

Goldstein, M. (1998). *The Asian financial crisis: Causes, cures, and systemic implications.* Washington, DC: Institute for International Economics.

Hong Kong Monetary Authority. (1997). Prudential Supervision in Hong Kong, December.

International Monetary Fund. (1997). *International capital markets: Developments, prospects, and key policy issues, appendix 2.* Washington, DC: International Monetary Fund.

J.P. Morgan. (1997). Latin American Banks: How Conservative Regulations Help Create Profits. *JP Morgan Equity Research,* January 22.

Kane, E. (1997). Comment on Understanding Financial Crises: A Developing Country Perspective. In M. Bruno and B. Pleskovic (Eds.), *Annual Bank Conference on Development Economics 1996.* The World Bank.

Keeley, M. C. (1990). Deposit Insurance, Risk, and Market Power in Banking. *American Economic Review, 80*(5).

Kindleberger, C. P. (1978). *Manias, panics, and crashes: A history of financial crises.* New York: Basic Books.

Krugman, P. (1998). *What happened to Asia,* mimeo, January.

Kaminsky, G. L., & Reinhart, C. M. (1996). *The twin crises: The causes of banking and balance of payments problems,* mimeo. Board of Governors of the Federal Reserve System and University of Maryland, September.

LaPorta, R., Lopez-do-Silanes, F., Shleifer, A., & Vishny, R. W. (1998). Law and finance. *Journal of Political Economy.*

Levine, R., N. Loayza, & Beck, T. (1998). *Financial intermediation and growth: Causality and causes,* mimeo. The World Bank.

McKinnon, R., & Pill, H. (1998). *International overborrowing: A decomposition of credit and currency risks,* mimeo. Stanford University, February.

Minsky, H. P. (1982). *Can "it" happen again: Essays on instability and finance.* New York: M.E. Sharpe.

Mishkin, F. S. (1997). Understanding financial crises: A developing country perspective. In M. Bruno & B. Pleskovic (Eds.), *Annual bank conference on development economics 1996.* The World Bank.

Peek, & Rosengren. (1997). *Collateral damage: Effects of the Japanese real estate collapse on credit availability and real activity in the United States,* mimeo. Federal Reserve Bank of Boston.

Radelet, S., & Sachs, J. (1998). *The onset of the east Asian financial crisis.* Harvard Institute for International Development, mimeo.

Ramos, R. (1997). *A comparison of prudential norms across Asia and in the U.S. using the CAMELOT framework.* Goldman Sachs Asia Banking Research, January 8.

Stiglitz, J. (1998). *Sound finance and sustainable development in Asia: Keynote address to the Asia development forum,* mimeo. The World Bank, March 12. Available at: http://www.worldbank.org/html/extdr/extme/speech.html.

Weisbrod, S., Lee, H., & Rojas-Suarez, L. (1993). *Bank risk and the declining franchise value of the banking systems in the United States and Japan.* IMF Working Paper 92/45. Washington, DC: International Monetary Fund.

Wyplosz, C. (1998). *Globalized financial markets and financial crises,* mimeo. Geneva: Graduate Institute of International Studies.

World Bank. (1998). *Global development finance.* Washington, DC: The World Bank.

THE EAST ASIAN FINANCIAL CRISES

Gillian G. H. Garcia

I. INTRODUCTION

This paper examines events in five East Asian countries: Indonesia, Korea, Malaysia, the Philippines, and Thailand in 1997 and 1998. It divides the happenings into five phases: (1) pre-crisis until July 2, 1997, (2) deterioration into dual currency and banking crises to mid January 1998; (3) stabilization to late April 1998; (4) the Indonesian reversal that began then and is still ongoing at the time of writing in July 1998, and (5) time to take the opportunity that crises offer to engineer a long-term recovery.

II. PHASE 1: THE TIGER YEARS

The East Asian countries most visibly affected by financial crisis in 1997 and 1998 appeared to be thriving right up to July 2, 1997, when the Thai baht was allowed to float, despite some fundamental weaknesses that are discussed in the next section. Four of these countries (Indonesia, Korea, Malaysia, and Thailand) had enjoyed a number of advantages. They had, for example, experienced high rates of

Research in Financial Services: Private and Public Policy, Volume 10, pages 21-32.
Copyright © 1998 by JAI Press Inc.
All rights of reproduction in any form reserved.
ISBN: 0-7623-0358-1

GDP growth without interruption (at 9.5, 12.1, 12.2, and 14.7 percent, respectively) over the 10 years through 1996. Growth in the Philippines was slower—4.3 percent over this period. These growth rates compared favorably to Japan's 3.5 percent and the United States' 2.5 percent over the 10-year period. The four countries had enjoyed political stability, which had been less evident in the Philippines, had young populations with high rates of saving and investment, exhibited fiscal prudence, and had opened their economies to international trade and investment.

The Asian economies also benefited from a period of peace in which world trade was growing, capital flows were setting records, inflation was under control, and world interest rates were relatively low.

III.   PHASE 2: THE TWIN CRISES

For the 7 months beginning in July 1997, the five countries began to experience twin banking and currency crises (Kaminsky & Reinhart, 1996). Whether currency crisis is defined narrowly as sharp depreciation or, as is now commonly accepted, as a broad index comprised of changes in exchange arrangements, introduction of capital controls, loss of foreign reserves, and increases in interest rates, all five countries experienced it. As is shown in Figure 1, Indonesia's currency hit "rock bottom" on January 23, 1998 with a decline of 84 percent from its value at the end of June 1997. Thailand's currency had fallen 56 percent by January 12, 1998, Korea?s 55 percent by December 24, 1997, Malaysia's 47 percent by January 7, and the Philippines' 42 percent on January 6, 1998.

At the same time, stock markets plummeted. By January 12, 1998, Malaysia's main board had declined by 57 percent compared to the end of June 1997 level, Indonesia's and Korea's markets had fallen 53 percent by December 12 and 15, respectively, the Philippines' by 46 percent and Thailand?s by 40 percent (see Figure 2). In fact, the stock markets in these countries, particularly Thailand's, had already been declining earlier in 1997.

Banking stocks were particularly had hit, because analysts anticipated a recession that would harm both banks and their borrowers. There is less agreement in the literature over the definition of a banking crisis. It can be defined narrowly as a t bank run or failures that lead banks to suspend convertibility. Kaminsky and Reinhart (1996) describe banking crisis broadly as occurring in a set of circumstances where: (1) "bank runs lead to the closure, merging, or takeover by the public sector of one or more financial institutions or (2) if there are no runs, to the closure, merging, or takeover, or large scale government assistance, for important financial institutions (or a group of financial institutions)." The definition used here is an intermediate one—that of Lindgren, Garcia and Saal (1996, p. 20)— where there are runs or other substantial portfolio shifts, collapses of financial firms, or massive government intervention.

Table 1.   Survey of Banking Problems: 1980-Spring 1996[1]

Country	Problem	Measure of Extent
Indonesia (1992-97)	Significant	Nonperforming loans, which were concentrated in state-owned banks, were over 25% of total lending in 1993 but declined to 12% in 1995. A large private bank was closed in 1992.
(1997-present)	Crisis	Nonperforming loans escalated and 54 banks have been placed under the control of the Indonesian Bank Restructuring Agency.
Korea (Mid 1980s)	Significant	Nonperforming loans of deposit money banks rose significantly in the first half of the 1980s, exceeding 7% of total assets in 1986. The ratio of nonperforming loans to total assets declined subsequently to 0.9% in 1995.
(1997-present)	Crisis	Nonperforming loans rose and 14 merchant banks were suspended.
Malaysia (1985-88)	Crisis	The largest domestic bank wrote off nonperforming loans equivalent to approximately 1.4% of GDP in 1983. Nonperforming loans were estimated at 32% to total loans in 1988.
(1997-present)	Significant	Bank Negara has announced that nonperforming loans rose to 7.6 percent of commercial bank loans (and 13.5 percent for finance companies) in March 1998, but that only two banks and three finance companies were undercapitalized at the end of 1997. The finance company industry is being restructured to reduce the number of companies from 39 to 8.
Philippines (1981-87)	Crisis	...Through the mid-1980s, a number of institutions failed or were taken over by government financial institutions. Nonperforming assets of two state-owned banks were transferred to a government agency. These assets accounted for 30% of total banking assets. In 1986, 19% of loans were nonperforming.
(1997-present)	Significant	Two thrifts have been excluded from the clearing system and one commercial bank is to be sold because it is experiencing problems.
Thailand (1983-87)	Crisis	Fifteen percent of bank assets were nonperforming. There were runs during the crisis of 1983-85 and 15 finance companies failed. More than 25% of the financial system?s assets were affected.
(1997- present)	Crisis	56 finance companies have been closed and 4 commercial banks have been intervened, but not closed.

Note: Lindgren, Garcia, and Saal (1996) and press reports.

In fact, it is difficult in Asia to distinguish the true depth of the banking problems that have occurred from published information about banks? condition and the authorities? intervention in troubled banks. What published information is available is summarized in Table 1 where the entries in regular type are taken from Table 1 of Lindgren, Garcia, and Saal (1996) and those in italics are updates from information released to the press by the authorities in these countries.

Despite the lack of hard evidence, bank analysts have been competing with one another to forecast the depth of the non-performing loan problem. Goldstein (1998, Table 5) summarizes five analysts' estimates of non-performing loans in the early months of 1998 as a percentage of total loans as ranging between 9 and

Table 2. Representative Academic Models

Factor	Balance of Payments Crises			Banking Crises		
Domestic	K&R	K,L&R	K	K&R	K	E&R
Index of Production	x		x	x	x	
Money Stock	x					
Deposits at commercial banks				x	x	
Bank credit to the private sector		x		x		
Credit to the public sector		x				
Inflation—CPI		x				
Ratio of debt to GDP		x			x	x
The money multiplier			x	x	x	
M2/M0				x		
The real interest rate				x	x	
Stock price index			x	x	x	
External						
Foreign exchange reserves	x	x	x	x	x	
Foreign reserves/monthly imports						x
M2/ foreign reserves	x		x		x	
Terms of trade	x			x	x	
Real exchange rate	x	x	x	x	x	x
Value of exports	x		x		x	
Vakue of imports	x					
Current account/GDP						x
Domestic/foreign interest rate differential	x				x	
World or northern interest rates			x		x	x
Real growth in OECD countries						x
Exchange rate regime	x					

Notes: Kaminsky and Reinhart (1996); Kaminisky, Lizondo and Reinhart (1997); Kaminisky (1998); Eichengreen and Rose (1998).

25 percent for Indonesia, 14 and 34 percent for Korea, 6 and 25 percent for Malaysia, 3 and 15 percent for the Philippines, and 18 and 36 percent for Thailand.
Clearly, however, Indonesia, Korea and Thailand have already experienced bank
runs and crises both in the broad and the intermediate senses. The Malaysian
authorities have engineered a major consolidation among finance companies in an
attempt to forestall major deterioration in the condition of the weakest ones. Only
time can tell whether Malaysia and the Philippines will escape the full rigors of
banking crisis.

Table 3. Common Vulnerabilities

Country	Over-heating	Inflation CPI	Asset Price Inflation	Capital Inflows	High Real Exchange Rate	Banking Problems
Indonesia	X	x	X	X	X	X
Korea	X	x	X	X	X	X
Malaysia	X		X	x	x	x
Philippines	X	x	X	x	x	x
Thailand	X	x	X	X	X	X

Note: "X" indicates a serious problem and "x" suggests a lesser problem.
Source: IMF, International Financial Statistics; Goldstein (1998).

Much has been learnt in the past few years about the causes of banking and currency crises. Researchers have tried to find a parsimonious set of variables that explain and predict such crises. Table 2 summarizes the factors that have been found by a number of researchers to be empirically useful for explaining and/or predicting currency and banking crises. There is a noticeable overlap between the explanatory variables relevant to the two kinds of crises. The real exchange rate, the level of foreign exchange reserves or their ratio to the stock of money, and indebtedness explain both crises.

Table 3 shows the vulnerability of these countries to overheating from fast growth of money and credit (often exacerbated by rapid capital inflows) that resulted in inflation in the goods and asset markets, from a high and rising real exchange rate, and from weaknesses in the banking sector. With the exception that the consumer price index in Malaysia had not risen rapidly, all five countries showed vulnerability to all of the factors to a greater or lesser extent.

Economic researchers at the Fund have focused particular attention on the ability of just three factors to predict currency crises: (1) an over-valued exchange rate; (2) credit growing much faster than GDP; (3) and a high and rising ratio of M2 to international reserves (World Economic Outlook, 1998). Table 4 shows that these countries were exposed to each of these factors (with the exception that Korea's exchange rate was not overvalued). For example, the consumer price index, while not inordinately high, rose by an average of 8 percent per annum in Indonesia, 5.4 percent in Korea, 3.2 percent in Malaysia, 7.3 percent in the Philippines, and 5.8 percent in Thailand. With the exception of Malaysia's, these rates of inflation were well in excess of the three-year average increase of 2.6 percent in the United States.

As these countries were pegged to the dollar formally or informally, their real exchange rates appreciated as inflation exceeded that in the United States. This appreciation reduced the competitiveness of their exports whose growth rates then declined. The loss of competitiveness led to large current account deficits which

Table 4. Applying the WEO Factors

Country	Over-Valued Exchange Rate (Percentage)	Ratio of Credit Growth to GDP Growth	Ratio of M2 to International Reserves
Indonesia	4.2	5.0	6.2
Korea	−7.6	0.8	6.2
Malaysia	9.3	11.6	4.0
Philippines	11.9	29.5	4.9
Thailand	6.7	8.5	4.9

Source: IMF, International Financial Statistics; Goldstein (1998).

averaged 3.1 percent of GDP in Indonesia, 3 percent in Korea, 6.6 percent in Malaysia, 4.5 percent in the Philippines, and 6 percent in Thailand over the three-year period. These percentages are higher than those of the United States (1.9%), that infamous accumulator of current account deficits.

In short, these countries were vulnerable. In the same way that a disease does not infect every person that is exposed to it, but only those that have weakened immune systems and have become susceptible to it, the crisis proved to be contagious to vulnerable economies not only within the region but also outside it. The almost parallel movements of the five countries' exchange rates and stock market indices are a telling indicator of the power of contagion over their economies.

IV.   PHASE 3. STABILIZATION

The IMF intervened rapidly to assist these countries. The Fund's Executive Board approved a program for Thailand on August 20, 1997, for Indonesia on November 5, and for Korea on December 4, 1997. The Philippines extended and augmented its existing IMF program late in 1997. The Fund's mandate to assist countries experiencing currency/balance of payments crises is clear. Among "the purposes of the International Monetary Fund" is Article 1 (v):

> To give confidence to members by making the general resources of the Fund temporarily available to them under adequate safeguards, thus providing them with opportunity to correct maladjustments in their balance of payments without resorting to measures destructive of national or international prosperity.

That the IMF came to the assistance of these countries is understandable, but the amounts of the aid were unusually large (see Table 5), particularly as four of the countries are small in economic terms. Even Korea's GDP, the world's 11th largest, was only 5.1 percent of U.S. GDP in 1996. Moreover, four are small in terms of population, while Indonesia has the world's fourth largest population. The countries? shares of world GDP and population are shown in Table 6. These

Table 5. Assistance form the International Community
(In billions of U.S. dollars)

Country	Commitments				IMF Disbursements
	IMF	Multilateral*	Bilateral	Total	as of 6/10/98
Indonesia	9.9	8.0	18.7	36.6	4.0
Korea	20.9	14.0	23.3	58.2	17.0
Philippines	1.4			1.4	
Thailand	3.9	2.7	10.5	17.1	2.8
Total	36.1	24.7	52.5	113.3	23.8

Note: *World Bank and Asian Development Bank.

Source: IMF, June 15, 1998.

Table 6. Shares in World GDP and Population in 1996

Country	Percentage of World GDP	Percentage of World Population
Indonesia	0.4%	3.4%
Korea	1.1%	0.8%
Malaysia	0.3%	0.4%
Philippines	0.2%	1.2%
Thailand	0.5%	1.0%
United States	22.2%	4.7%

Source: International Financial Statistics Yearbook (Vol L, 1997).

countries were probably judged to be important beyond their size because of their orientation toward international trade, their historic ties to important members of the Fund (the Netherlands, Japan, the United Kingdom, and the United States), and the fear of spillover and contagion to the rest of the world.

The programs that conditioned financial aid were centered around financial reform in general and strengthening the banking system in particular. The IMF?s role in banking is relatively new. It was only in 1996 that the Executive Board formally acknowledged that a strong banking system was essential to the conduct of good macroeconomic policy and conversely that sound macroeconomic policies were a necessary condition for strong banks (see Lindgren, Garcia, & Saal, 1996). In March 1996, the Board decided to make an examination of the financial system an integral part of IMF surveillance. That decision has required that the IMF adjust its schedules and practices, train its existing staff in financial sector surveillance, hire additional expertise, and cooperate more closely with the World Bank and with international regulatory bodies such as the Basle Committee, the

International Organization of Securities Commissioners (IOSCO) and the International Accounting Standards Committee (IASC).

During the first four months of the year, IMF assistance was interpreted as a vote of confidence in the recipients' determination to recover. The markets stabilized and the road to recovery seemed to be at hand, but that confidence proved to be short-lived.

V.   PHASE 4. THE REVERSAL

The reversal began with rioting in Indonesia in April that led to the downfall of President Suharto. That the exchange rate and stock market in Indonesia would react negatively is not surprising, but markets declined throughout the region. Possibly investors noticed that political regimes that had previously seemed stable had already been replaced in Thailand, Korea, and the Philippines. Only Malaysia had avoided a change in government. Moreover, recession was in progress and was proving to be worse than had been hoped.

As shown in Figure 1, by June 1998, the exchange rates of Indonesia and Thailand had fallen below their nadirs in January, while those in Korea, Malaysia, the Philippines and neighboring countries fell sharply. The stock markets in four of the five countries (the Philippines being the exception) plummeted below their January bottoms. The press began to debate Russia's need for additional international financial assistance and the Fund began to arrange further assistance for Indonesia. The markets waited to see whether China, including Hong Kong, would continue to resist devaluing the yuan and the Hong Kong dollar, and whether Japan could reverse its economic ills.

VI.   PHASE 5: CHALLENGES AND OPPORTUNITIES

While the challenges of achieving economic recovery remain to be met, the current period of difficulty provides opportunities to strengthen the financial system in emerging markets. It typically takes a serious setback to call into question accepted ways of doing things. People see no reason to make changes when things are going well. Conditions attached to Fund lending in Asia have required measures aimed to strengthen the financial system.

A sound financial system begins with strong internal governance by owners and managers. These parties need accurate and timely management information systems in order to make the good decisions that will protect their bank. That requires the adoption of strong accounting principles, such as those recommended by the Internationally Accounting Standards Committee (IASC) for banks and their customers. The Fund and the World Bank are working together with the international accounting bodies to persuade the Big Six accounting firms to adopt the IASC's standards in these countries. Given that local laws typically require use of local

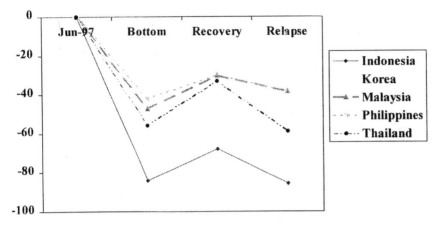

Source: IMF (June 15, 1998).

Figure 1. Declining Exchange Rates

accounting standards, either the law will need to be changed or two sets of accounts will be needed—one for the use of the international agencies and the other to conform to local law. This dilemma still needs to be negotiated to resolution.

To the extent that operators in some financial systems lack expertise in modern techniques of risk management, the current environment provides new opportunities to acquire it. Countries needing to recapitalize their banking systems may allow greater foreign participation in ownership and management of ailing institutions. That can bring additional expertise to the country. The international agencies can offer technical assistance and training where countries request them and indeed such assistance is an integral part of the IMF program to the crisis countries.

Market discipline is the second strand of sound banking. That too requires accurate and timely information, but also its dissemination to depositors, other creditors, borrowers, supervisors and politicians. Progress is being made in modernizing standards for loan classification and provisioning in all of these five Asian crisis countries. Without it, published capital levels are misleadingly exaggerated. But countries remain reluctant to reveal the full extent of their banking problems. Effective market discipline, however, demands that the authorities solve problems and not try to hide them.

Much has been written about the inadequacies of bank supervision and regulation—the third strand in sound banking—in the troubled countries. Supervisors need freedom from political interference while being held accountable for their actions. Politically directed and/or insider lending had weakened bank portfolios in these countries. Supervisors need good information and reliable early warning systems to enable them to foresee problems ahead. They need a system of prompt

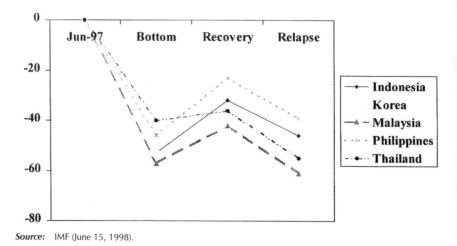

Source: IMF (June 15, 1998).

Figure 2.   Plummeting Stock Markets

corrective actions in place to tackle and resolve problems as they arise. The IMF and the World Bank are providing technical assistance to this end. In fact, improvements in supervision are under way in these countries being a condition for financial assistance in the program countries.

All three sources of strength for banking (internal governance, market discipline, and supervision and regulation) need a good incentive structure if they are to serve the public good. That structure will require both sticks and carrots. The compulsive components of the incentive system include a strong legal system with modern and effective laws and regulations, impartial and efficient courts, and swift and firm enforcement. The economic environment needs to offer broad and robust financial markets that include an efficient and reliable payments system, provide opportunities to insure and hedge so that risks are appropriately shared and realistically priced. A good incentive structure also requires a stable political system and one that the public supports. Above all it must rest upon a system of recognition and reward that encourages agents, both public servants and private parties, to do what society needs. For example, a system of limited deposit insurance to replace the comprehensive guarantees that have been offered to bank creditors would remove some of the political obstacles to dealing firmly with failing banks and thus improve the incentive structure.

The international agencies need to play their part in providing the right incentives to governments and markets. To this end, a number of analysts (Barry Eichengreen and Richard Portes, Morris Goldstein, Alan Greenspan, Henry Kaufman, Prime Minister Mahathir, Professor Meltzer, the Shadow Regulatory Committee, and Professor Tobin) have made suggestions to strengthen the international financial system. Their suggestions range from increasing regulation in the international capital markets to reducing moral hazard in international lending by abolishing the IMF. Perhaps the most practical suggestions would have the IMF revise its program of lending to result in greater exposure to loss for the international creditors of banks through an enhanced ability to reschedule debts. The intention of such proposals is to reduce the moral hazard threatened by large financial aid packages that protect from loss the creditors of the banks in crisis countries.[1]

VII. CONCLUSIONS

The outlook in the near term remains uncertain. Markets are concerned about the deteriorating economic situation in east Asia and about the possibility of further depreciation in the Asian currencies—a depreciation permitted in order to stimulate the economy though higher exports.

Despite the economic concerns, however, the crises offer an opportunity to strengthen the financial sectors in the crisis countries. While it may be many years before economists learn how to prevent international crises, it is hoped that financial sector will reduce their frequency and severity.

ACKNOWLEDGMENTS

The information presented in this paper is drawn entirely from published sources. The opinions expressed are those of the author, not the International Monetary Fund.

NOTE

1. Morris Goldstein's, Henry Kaufman's, Professor Meltzer's, the Shadow Regulatory Committee's, and Professor Tobin's proposals were presented at the Brookings Institution's Symposium on Moral Hazard on June 4, 1998.

REFERENCES

The Brooking Institution. (1998). *Economic symposium: Limiting moral hazard in international financial rescues.* Washington, DC.

Goldstein, M. (1998). *The Asian financial crisis: Causes, cures, and systemic implications.* Washington DC: Institute for International Economics.

Greenspan, A. (1998). *"Remarks" in Proceedings of 34th Annual Conference on Bank Structure and Competition.* Chicago: Federal Reserve Bank of Chicago.

International Monetary Fund. (1998). *International financial statistics.* Washington, DC: International Monetary Fund.

International Monetary Fund. (1998). World economic outlook. Washington, DC: International Monetary Fund.

International Monetary Fund. (1998). *The IMF's response to the asian crisis.* Washington, DC: International Monetary Fund.

Kaminsky, G., & Reinhart, C. (1996). *The twin crises: The causes of banking and balance of payments problems.* Board of Governors of the Federal Reserve and the International Monetary Fund, International Discussion Paper No. 544. Washington, DC: Board of Governors of the Federal Reserve System.

Lindgren, C., Garcia, G., & Saal, M. (1996). *Bank soundness and macroeconomic policy.* Washington, DC: International Monetary Fund.

THE POLITICAL ECONOMY OF BANKING AND FINANCIAL REGULATORY REFORM IN EMERGING MARKETS

Randall S. Kroszner

I. INTRODUCTION

Economists have devoted much effort to analyzing the causes of banking and financial sector troubles and to proposing solutions. Problems of moral hazard, adverse selection, lack of market discipline, conflicts of interest, time inconsistency, and information asymmetry have been thoroughly studied in the context of banking and financial markets, both empirically and theoretically. A wide range of policy alternatives for minimizing the impact of these problems in developed, emerging, and transition economies have been carefully constructed. Academic economists, however, have given little attention to analyzing how to implement durable and effective banking and financial sector reform. This weakness arises from the tradition of emphasizing normative welfare evaluations of institutions

Research in Financial Services: Private and Public Policy, Volume 10, pages 33-51.
Copyright © 1998 by JAI Press Inc.
All rights of reproduction in any form reserved.
ISBN: 0-7623-0358-1

and regulations and ignoring the question of why they exist and why they have the forms they do. Rather than take regulations as given, the political economy approach attempts to provide a positive analysis of how and why regulations evolve as they do and what forces can lead to durable policy change.

The goal of this paper is to provide a framework for understanding why particular banking and financial regulations arise in particular circumstances and what causes them to change. This subject thus far has received relatively little study, and this paper is an exploratory first step toward developing a systematic framework. The positive analysis of how regulatory change has evolved can ultimately provide normative guidance for those who wish to implement lasting policy reforms.

Factors relating to the demand for and supply of regulation will play a major role in the positive framework. The first concerns the role of interest groups that pressure the legislators and regulators to pursue policies that tend to promote their private interests rather than promote social welfare. Rival interest groups compete in the political marketplace for alternative regulatory policies. The second factor concerns the incentives associated with the regulatory structure itself. The incentives given to the regulators have a powerful impact upon how policies are implemented and, often, which policies are chosen. In some settings, the regulators may constitute a separate interest group and pursue their own self-interest which might include maximizing the agency's budget, and so on. In addition, the structure of the regulatory institutions also will have an important impact upon the incentives of different groups to organize and, in turn, which groups may be the most effective lobbyists. In other words, the relative strength of competing interest groups is not simply exogenous but can be affected by the institutional incentives.

The next section reviews alternative theories of regulatory change. I then examine the technological, legal, and economic shocks that the political economy approach would suggest are the primary factors that disturb a regulatory equilibrium in banking and financial markets. A case analysis of the world-wide reforms in government securities markets then illustrates the motivations for and outcomes of financial regulatory change. I then consider the "crisis" theory of regulatory change and argue that it is a branch of the political economy approach, since crises typically involve a dramatic change in the fortunes of different interest groups. Obstacles to implementing welfare-enhancing reforms are considered in the next section.

Taming the political economy process to promote "good" policies is a key challenge for policymakers interested in lasting beneficial reform. In using the positive political-economy framework to understand how and why regulatory reform has come about in banking and finance, the paper will also have normative implications of how to achieve socially beneficial regulatory reform. The concluding section explores how to make more likely the "incentive compatibility" of "incentive compatible" regulation.

II. ALTERNATIVE APPROACHES TO REGULATORY REFORM IN BANKING AND FINANCE

Public Interest versus Private Interest Theories

The traditional approach that economists took to explaining the existence of regulation emphasized that regulations exist to correct market failures and protect poorly informed consumers from harm.[1] From this perspective, regulatory intervention occurs primarily to maximize social welfare. This is why this approach is often called the "public interest theory" of regulation. The main challenge to the public interest view is that many forms of regulation have little or no redeeming social value. The geographic restrictions on bank expansion, portfolio restrictions that hinder diversification by financial institutions, and entry restrictions that protect banks from competition provide examples in financial services that are very difficult to rationalize on public interest grounds. Examples outside of financial services also are ubiquitous (see Stigler, 1988).

Virtually all regulation, regardless of whether it may have a public interest rationale, has significant distributional consequences. The parties affected by the regulation thus have an incentive to try to ensure that the government structures the regulation in such a way as to benefit them. Public interest rationales may be used to mask the private interests that the intervention serves. The economic theory of regulation, also called the private interest theory, characterizes the regulatory process as one of interest group competition in which compact, well-organized groups are able to use the coercive power of the state to capture rents for those groups at the expense of more dispersed groups (e.g., Stigler, 1971; Peltzman, 1976, 1989; Becker, 1983). Regulated groups may be sufficiently powerful that they influence the regulatory bureaucracy to serve the interests of those subject to the regulation. In other words, the regulated group "captures" the regulators, hence this is sometimes called the "capture theory" of regulation.

The incentives for such regulatory behavior may be direct or indirect. Pressure may be exerted directly on politicians, though campaign contributions or votes, who then pressure the regulators to act sympathetically towards the interest group. Indirect incentives may come through regulators understanding that cooperative behavior may be rewarded with lucrative employment opportunities in the industry after leaving the government, a practice the Japanese euphemistically call *amakudari* or the "descent from heaven."

While the public and private interest theories are not necessarily mutually exclusive nor exhaustive,[2] they do have different implications for regulatory reform. The private interest theory leads us to look behind the public interest rationales to understand which groups are the winners and losers in the struggle for rents. This focus can then help us to understand why certain types of regulation are so difficult to change. A sound economic argument concerning social welfare thus is neither necessary nor sufficient to bring about regulatory change, although it can reduce the costs and increase the effectiveness of lobbying for policy reform. The emphasis is instead upon the costs and benefits of the regulation to different interest groups and the costs and benefits of the groups organizing and lobbying in the political process.

The effectiveness of the interest groups, hence the likelihood and nature of regulatory change, depends upon a number of factors. First, cohesive groups will find it easier to organize and overcome free-rider problems in lobbying for regulations that may benefit them. Producers of goods and services tend to be more compact and better organized than consumers, for example, so there is a tendency for regulation on net to benefit producers more than consumers (Stigler, 1971). The ability of a group to organize is often inversely related to its size, but many labor unions and trade organizations have been able to develop effective lobbying bodies through carefully crafted incentives that provide a variety of information and support services in return for membership (see Olson, 1965).

Second, groups tend to be more effective not only when the benefits are concentrated among group members but also when the costs of the regulation are relatively diffuse. The more concentrated are the costs of the regulation, the less effective will a group be in obtaining regulation to benefit itself. A compact group of losers each of whom would experience high losses associated with the regulation will be likely to form a lobby that will try to counteract the original interest group's pressure. Interest groups most directly affected by the regulation may join forces to lobby for or against a regulation. In addition, groups with completely unconnected interests may form "support trading" or "log rolling" coalitions. Two groups may agree to support each other even if the members of one group are not affected by the regulations that the other wants. Tariffs are a classic case of "log rolling" in which, say, lumber and glass producers support each other's call for higher protection, thereby providing greater support for higher tariffs than otherwise would be (Irwin & Kroszner, 1996).

Third, in addition to the diffusion of the costs across different groups, the level of the costs relative to the benefits obtained by the interest group play an important role (Becker, 1983). Deadweight loss is defined as precisely the difference between the winner's benefit minus the loser's cost from the change in output generated by the regulation. Factors affecting the "efficiency" of the regulatory or transfer mechanism thus may have an important impact on political outcomes. As the deadweight loss of grows, for example, the losers are losing more for each peso of the winner's gain. When this gap widens, losers have a greater incentive to fight each peso of the winner's gain and the winners have less incentive to fight for each peso of the loser's loss. In other words, when deadweight losses are high, an interest group faces greater opposition to its protective regulation on the margin and hence is less likely to be successful.[3]

Similarly, politicians in electoral democracies are concerned about finding an optimal support coalition to promote their re-election chances, so they take into account the marginal costs and benefits to different groups. The rents generated by regulation in an electoral democracy thus are likely to be spread among different groups, even though one group may be the primary beneficiary (Peltzman, 1976).[4] The combination of (implicit or explicit) government deposit insurance and directed credit illustrate such rent-sharing. If the deposit insurance premia are not high enough to cover the risks, which is almost always the case, banks are being subsidized. The distribution of that subsidy, however, will depend upon the structure of the insurance scheme and requirements to allocate credit to targeted groups, such as those embodied in the Community Reinvestment Act. Flat rate deposit insurance, which again is typical, tends to subsidize the smaller and riskier banks at the expense of the larger, better diversified, and safer banks. Lobbying for flat rate deposit insurance historically has been consistent with this pattern of relative benefits (e.g., Calomiris & White, 1994; Hubbard et al., 1996).

Political-Economy Factors Driving the Recent Trend Toward International Financial Liberalization and Regulatory Reform

The framework outlined above suggests a number of factors to explore when trying to understand how financial reform can become politically feasible. In this framework, technological, legal, and/or economic shocks must occur in order to change the relative strengths of interest groups that would then alter the previous political-economy equilibrium. Identifying and analyzing these factors can provide a basis for facilitating and perhaps shaping future reforms.

Technological change is often cited as a key force behind the innovations in financial markets and institutions during the last two decades. In the political-economy framework, technological improvement does more than simply shift the production possibility frontier for an industry. Technical change can have significant distributional consequences, completely independent of its effects on the costs and efficiency of production, that is, such change is rarely "distributionally neutral." New products and markets bring forth new constituencies. Innovations affect the pre-existing markets and institutions and cause shifts in the interests and alliances. Changing the relative strength of competing interests can then lead to regulatory reform.[5]

From the political-economy perspective, we must try to identify shocks to the old equilibrium that would lead to regulatory reform fostering globalization and liberalization (see Kroszner & Strahan, 1998). A number of shocks, for example, have increased the elasticity of the supply of depositors' funds, thereby eroding the value of regulation protecting local geographic monopolies. First, the invention of the automatic teller machine (ATM) in the early 1970s was one factor that began to reduce the value to the local banks of geographic protections. In countries like the United States, legal challenges about whether an ATM constituted a branch slowed the spread of the ATMs until the courts determined that an ATM was not a branch, thereby permitted the growth of interstate ATM networks. ATM networks then rapidly spread worldwide.

Second, consumer-oriented money market mutual funds and accounts offered by investment banks arose in the last two decades. These types of new opportunities for individuals demonstrated that banking by mail and telephone, using toll free numbers, provided a feasible and convenient alternative to local banks. Third, technological innovation and deregulation have reduced transportation and communication costs, particularly since the 1970s, thereby lowering the cost for customers to use distant and foreign banks.

Since the increasing elasticity of deposits supplied to banks reduces the value of geographical restrictions to their traditional beneficiaries, these beneficiaries had less incentive to fight strenuously to maintain them. Also, as elasticities increase, there are fewer rents to share among competing groups so regulation becomes less likely (Peltzman, 1989). While any deregulation that eliminates inefficient regulation is broadly consistent with the public interest theory, the timing of the deregulation is difficult to explain by that approach. The opening of banking markets occurs precisely when the geographic restrictions are becoming less burdensome for the public, due to the elasticity-increasing innovations discussed above.

On the lending side, increasing sophistication of credit-scoring techniques, following innovations in information processing technology, financial theory, and the development of large credit data bases, has begun to change the relationship-character of bank lending towards less personal and more standardized evaluation. As a result of these innovations, for example, securitization of mortgages, loans, and consumer credits have become commonplace in the developed countries and are becoming increasingly so in emerging markets. In recent years even banks' lending to small businesses has become increasingly automated, relying less on the judgement of loan officers and more on standardized credit scoring programs.

Technological change thus has diminished the value of specialized local knowledge that long-established local bankers might have about the risks of borrowers in the community. Such changes have increased the feasibility and potential profitability for large and foreign banks to enter what had traditionally been the core of small, local bank activities. The large and foreign banks have therefore had an incentive to increase their lobbying pressure to attain the freedom to expand into these markets. In terms of our models above, the deadweight costs of preventing the large and foreign entry is increasing, so the small, local banks are less likely to be able to maintain the restrictions. In addition, as the value of a local banking relationship declined, local firms that were the main borrowers from the local banks also would be more likely to favor the entry of large and foreign banks into local markets (Kroszner & Strahan, 1998).

The method of opening up of the banking markets also is consistent with the private interest theory (see Kroszner, 1997). Typically, new foreign entry is first permitted through investment in existing banks and mergers, rather than de novo entry (particularly in institutions that are in financial distress, as Citicorp's new entry into Mexico illustrates). By removing the geographic barriers in this way, the small, local banks have an opportunity to share in the benefits of deregulation by selling out at a premium rather than being competed out of existence. The smaller banks in the country thus would tend to lobby for foreign entry through mergers because they would prefer to have more potential bidders in the market, which tends to increase the premium paid for small banks (Brickley & James, 1987).

An increase in foreign bank penetration in emerging markets can generate a virtuous circle in that foreign banks tend to be less politically connected and less likely to be able to "capture" the regulatory authorities. In addition, they are less likely to succumb to pressure for directed lending by the government. With capture less likely and fewer direct benefits to the politicians of bank regulation (e.g., through quid pro quos for directed lending), regulatory reform becomes more likely. New Zealand, for example, began its reform process when roughly 30 percent of the banking system was already foreign owned. By the end of the reform process, a very large fraction of the banks had become foreign owned. This helps to increase the likelihood that the reforms are sustainable and not simply temporary. In sum, technological change was a shock to the old political-economy equilibrium and had important distributional consequences that are typically ignored in economists' emphasis on efficiency issues but are extremely important to a positive explanation of regulatory change.

Public Finance Motives behind Financial Reform and Globalization: The Case of Government Securities Markets Reform

In addition to the technological changes described above, financial liberalization has been fueled by a desire by governments to lower the costs of public finance. Noll (1989) has characterized conceiving of governments as distinct interest groups concerned about financing their expenditures as the Leviathan Approach (see also Niskanen, 1971; Brennan & Buchanan, 1977). This section provides an analysis of how recent international reforms of government securities markets illustrate the interrelationships among the rent-sharing, deadweight-loss-reducing, and Leviathan theories.

Since the late 1970s, there has been dramatic growth in the use of publicly-traded debt as a financing tool for both emerging as well as developed countries (Kroszner forthcoming). Before this time most countries, with the exception of the United States, typically placed a large share of their debt with domestic banks, either directly or through a bank syndicate arrangement.[6] While the banks were to some extent captive financers of the government, they typically received compensation through protective regulation, below market discount loans from the central bank, and implicit lender-of-last-resort or deposit insurance subsidies.[7] With government debt growing much more rapidly than bank assets, however, it was no longer feasible for governments to rely so heavily upon direct funding by the banks.

Motivated by a desire to keep financing costs on their rapidly mounting debt relatively low, politicians thus had incentives to broaden their sources of funding. Consistent with our deadweight cost analysis above, politicians would like to engage in their redistributive activities but must take into account the losses associated with the transfers. The worldwide reforms of the structure and operation of government securities markets during the last two decades, particularly in emerging markets, can be explained in terms of this motive. Auctions replaced or significantly supplemented the traditional placement of securities with the banks. Simultaneously, the government created or formalized a primary dealer system in which it authorizes specially designated dealers to have the exclusive right to bid directly in the auctions and to have the responsibility of distributing the securities to investors.[8]

An important feature of these reforms was that foreign-controlled financial firms were permitted to enter the market and become primary dealers, thereby encouraging the globalization of the investor base.[9] Previously, developing countries typically had shielded their domestic banking and financial markets from foreign competition. The politicians had a strong incentive to broaden their investor base to finance their growing deficits, and the percent of government debt owned by foreigners has grown rapidly during the last two decades (see Kroszner forthcoming).

The internationalization of the government debt markets also has been associated with an increase in the liquidity of these markets. The primary dealers have an obligation to the government, as well as their own private incentive, to foster the growth of a liquid secondary market in government bonds. Liquid secondary markets help to reduce the government's financing costs, by fostering demand by investors (especially foreign investors) who are more willing to hold instruments which have easily observable market prices and can be easily traded. Liquidity also facilitates the dealers' distribution of the securities to investors. The depth of the government securities markets typically has been associated with an increase in the depth and development of other securities in these countries and increased foreign involvement.

As the economic theory of regulatory reform would suggest, the changes which began the opening of domestic financial markets to foreign competition and created liquid debt markets, providing another form of competition to the banking sector, did not occur without some quid pro quo for the banking industry. In particular, the choice of auction technique illustrates a role for private interests in the details of the institutional changes.

Governments consistently adopted sealed-bid, multiple-price auctions (also called "discriminatory" or "first-price" auctions) rather than uniform-price auctions (also called "non-discriminatory" or "second-price" auctions).[10] The popularity of the multiple-price auction technique in the recent reforms contrasts sharply with the sustained academic criticism that this format has received relative to the uniform-price technique as a way to issue securities (e.g., Friedman, 1960; Smith, 1966, and more recently Rheinhart, 1992; U.S. Treasury et al., 1992; Umlauf, 1993; Tenorio, 1993; Nyborg & Sundaresan, 1996). Unlike the uniform-price auction, the multiple-price auction is subject to the winner's curse. The probability of winning is positively related to the price that one bids in both types of auctions. In the multiple-price auction, unlike in the uniform-price auction, the expected profit from winning is negatively related to the bid price, given that there is some uncertainty as to the exact value of the securities in the secondary market. As a result, bidders will tend to bid a bit less at the auction than what they estimate the secondary market value will be.

In addition, potential bidders without access to detailed information on which to base the estimates of the secondary market value would be less willing to participate directly in a multiple-price than a uniform-price auction. Consequently, the demand curve at auction using a multiple-price format will be below that in the uniform-price auction. The demand curve also is likely to be flatter, since the uncertainties generated by the "pay what you bid" format tend to make the bidders at the auction more price sensitive.

In principle, the revenue loss from the downward shift in demand at a multiple-price auction relative to a uniform-price auction could be offset by the ability to price-discriminate in the multiple-price auction. Actual and experimental evidence, however, generally indicates that the added revenue from price-discrimination is not sufficient to compensate for the lower and flatter demand curve (see, e.g., Smith, 1966). In Mexico, for example, Umlauf (1993) showed that the government's auction revenue increased in their Treasury bill market when Mexico temporarily switched from multiple-price to uniform-price format. Tenorio (1993) found similar results for Zambia.

The sealed-bid, multiple-price technique also suffers from the potential for manipulation and may foster cartel-like behavior among dealers. The potential for precisely such manipulations was widely understood, having been described by Friedman (1960) decades earlier. When Mexico briefly switched from a multiple-price to a uniform-price auction, for example, bidders' overall profits fell sharply and auction revenue rose, suggesting that the multiple-price format permitted greater scope for manipulation (Umlauf, 1993).

Given that the potential problems of the multiple-price auction were well-known, why have the reforms almost universally adopted this format? One explanation is that other countries were simply copying the U.S. which had used this format for many years. This solution, however, is unsatisfactory. Although the reforms followed the general pattern of moving in the direction of a U.S.-style market, there are enough country-specific variation that adopting a different auction technique certainly would have been feasible.

An alternative explanation is that the multiple-price technique enhances the value of the information to which the primary dealers have privileged access. The reforms initially gave primary dealers or syndicate members exclusive access to the inter-dealer brokers, consultations with the Ministry of Finance, regular dealings with the central bank through open market operations. Most trading in the government securities also is concentrated in their hands. In a uniform-price auction, information gathered from such sources and activities is less valuable since both the informed and the uninformed bidders will pay the same "consensus" price. The primary dealers, *ceteris paribus*, thus would prefer to have the government use the multiple-price technique, and governments appear to have obliged. Also, it is extremely difficult to measure the extent of this benefit for there is no line item in the government's budget to represent it. Obscure transfers are much more likely to avoid public scrutiny (as described in more detail at the end of the next section) and, hence, are a preferred means of compensation by the government. The reforms provided some benefits to the government, reducing their fiscal burden, and preserved some rents for the large financial institutions.[11] Part of the trend toward globalization and financial liberalization, thus, can be accounted for by public finance motives.

What is the Role of Banking and Financial Crises in the Political-Economy of Regulatory Reform?

Reforms are often associated with banking and economic crises, and the "crisis" hypothesis provides an alternative to our political-economy approach. Developing as well as developed countries experiencing major bank insolvencies have subsequently undertaken some reform and restructuring of their banking regulatory and supervisory systems (Caprio & Klingebiel, 1996). First on the list of sixteen hypotheses about reform drawn up by John Williamson (1994), distilled from the experiences of top policy-makers presented at a conference on "The Political Economy of Policy Reform," is that "policy reforms emerge in response to crisis."

Are crises an independent factor which can be said to "cause" reform to occur? Rodrik (1996) has been critical of the crisis hypothesis because it is almost non-falsifiable—if reform does not occur, proponents of this view will say that the crisis was not sufficiently severe—and because reforms responding to similar crises take very different forms (e.g., Caprio & Klingebiel, 1996). The United States, for example, responded to the banking and economic crisis of the early 1930s by fragmenting the financial system (Kroszner, 1998). The Glass-Steagall Act of 1933 narrowed the range of activities permissible for commercial banks, and a series of Acts starting with the Federal Home Loan Bank Act of 1932 created modern Savings & Loan institutions which narrowly focused on the financing of residential mortgages. In continental Europe, however, a number of countries responded in the oppose way by increasing the diversification of their financial institutions, by introducing or broadening universal banking.

From a political-economy perspective, crises are associated with reform because crises are likely to upset the old political-economy equilibrium. There are four reasons for this. First, crises rarely affect all parties similarly and tend to have important distributional consequences. Since the relative position of competing interests is one of the key elements to a political-economy equilibrium, it is thus not surprising that reforms often occur following crises. Powerful groups or coalitions may fragment as their interests diverge during economic trouble, and new constituencies may be created. Although smaller, less diversified banks tended to support federal deposit insurance, for example, they became politically powerful enough to enact it only in 1933 (Hubbard et al., 1996; but also see Calomiris & White, 1994).

Second, economic upheaval can change the relative costs and benefits of particular regulations. An interest rate ceiling, which may act like a price-fixing arrangement among banks to enhance their profits during normal times, for example, could lead to large outflows of funds and liquidity problems during high-interest crisis periods (see Barth, 1991; Kroszner & Strahan, 1996). Hyperinflation crises turn many of the regulations that had protected banks from competition into obstacles in the new circumstances. Innovations in financial technology may create new markets and institutions, and new constituencies with them.

Third, crisis can also affect bureaucratic incentives for regulatory change, as in the "Leviathan" theory described in the previous section. Deposit insurance, for example, commits the government to bail-out banks that have liquidity and solvency problems. During times of crisis, deposit insurance funds typically are bankrupt so an explicit taxpayer-financed bail-out would be necessary. To postpone such actions, politicians and regulators may have incentives to reduce various regulatory barriers as a quid pro quo for a financial institution using its private funds to bail out a troubled institution. Special dispensations to cross geographic or product lines have occurred in the United States, particularly during the Savings & Loan crisis (Kroszner & Strahan, 1996), in Mexico, where Citicorp recently took a large stake in a troubled local Mexican bank, which dramatically eased the expansion of its operations in Mexico, and in Japan, where "arranged" mergers have helped some banks expand into new activities.

Finally, the enormous costs of a financial crisis may serve an important educational role for the public (see Kane, 1996). During normal times, individual voters may not know the full value of the implicit or explicit guarantees that the government, that is, the taxpayer, is making. After a crisis, however, the government is likely to have to raise taxes and sell bonds in order to pay for the bail-out. This more explicit accounting will reveal the costs of policies that the public may not have known were so costly. Bank failures thus may heighten the public's awareness of the costs of regulation and may make it more difficult, that is, more costly in terms of votes, to maintain the old regulatory regime. The banks now would have to provide more support to politicians, for example, through greater campaign contributions, in order to offset the greater popular opposition. Since the banks are experiencing financial distress, they may not be in a strong position to provide the additional funds, so the likelihood of reform increases.

The reform and repeal of the Argentine deposit insurance system follows this pattern. During the 1980s, Argentina experienced two major banking crises. The first in 1980-1982 has been estimated to have required more than 50 percent of GDP to resolve and the second crisis in 1989-1990 roughly 13 percent of GDP to resolve (Rojas-Suarez & Weisbrod, 1996; Lindgren, Garcia, & Saal, 1996). With such large costs to the bail-outs, the public was now acutely aware of the costs of government guarantees of deposits. Due to the hyperinflation, there were rela-tively few deposits left in the bank system to be insured by 1990, so there were fewer depositors demanding insurance. Also, the banks were in a rather weak position. In other words, the crisis involved a dramatic shift in the relative strength of the groups supporting and opposing deposit insurance. In these circumstances, it became politically feasible to eliminate deposit insurance and Argentina did so.

This reform, however, was not completely sustained. Five years later, during the Tequila crisis, the interests in favor of deposit insurance grew and a private deposit insurance scheme was instituted (Guidotti, 1996). The deposit insurance premia are relatively high but the insurance agency is owned by the banks that contribute to it. Thus, if the system stays healthy, they earn the profits from the insurance agency but will bear the burdens when the banks require bail-outs.

The changes in geographic restrictions within the U.S. also can be understood within this framework. Kane (1996) argues that an important shock to the old equi-librium favoring branching restrictions was an increase in the public's understand-ing of the costliness of having government-insured but (geographically) undiversified financial institutions. During the 1980s, an increasing number of depository institution failures and the Savings and Loan crisis culminating in the taxpayer bail-out heightened the awareness by the public of the costs of restric-tions that make depository institutions more fragile and more likely to require infusions of taxpayer funds. The result is the 1994 Riegle-Neal Interstate Banking and Branching Efficiency Act which phases out geographic restrictions on bank expansion within the United States (see Kroszner & Strahan, 1997).

Obstacles to Implementing Welfare Improving Reforms

Will policy reforms that can make everyone better off always be implemented? There are many policies for which there is consensus that they would enlarge the economic pie sufficiently that any losers could be more than compensated by the winners. Implementation of such policies, however, can be very slow or perhaps may not occur at all.

Neither irrationality nor myopia is required to understand why Pareto-improv-ing bargains are not always reached in the political arena. Information problems and coordination problems may lead to outcomes that are inefficient even for the politically powerful groups themselves (see Rodrik, 1996). First, opposing parties may become involved in a "war of attrition" which can significantly delay reform programs (Alesina & Drazen, 1991). Such a delay can arise when the opposing factions do not know what the cost is to their rivals of continuing the current (inef-ficient) policies. Rather than implement the mutually-beneficial policy reform immediately, each group waits to see whether one of the other groups is willing to "give in" first, thereby signalling that they are experiencing very high costs of the current policies. Having revealed their high cost of the old regime, these groups will then be in a weak bargaining position in the reform process and receive the fewest benefits or bear a disproportionate share of the reform burdens. The high cost groups agree to reform only when they perceive that the net gain from reform, even though they will receive relatively few benefits, outweighs the value of waiting to see whether their rivals will give in.[12]

Second, another type of uncertainty could lead to a bias against reform and towards the status quo. Assume that voters and politicians agree that there exists a policy which will benefit a majority of the electorate. A rational electorate may reject such a reform proposal if the identity of the ex post winners cannot be determined ex ante (Fernandez & Rodrik, 1991). Without uncertainty, the reform clearly would pass. With incomplete information about which individuals will reap the rewards of a reform, however, the group of individuals who are uncertain about whether they will benefit may find it in their individual interests to vote against the proposal. This argument does not rely on any risk aversion by individuals, although risk aversion would make the rejection more likely to occur.[13]

Third, the potential for post-reform opportunism can undermine the ability to reach ex ante agreements. The compensation to minority of losers following a reform, for example, may not be credible. If a majority approves of a reform that would benefit itself, even including compensation to the losers, that reform would continue to have majority support without compensation. The minority understands this and would oppose the reform because they do not believe that the ex ante promised compensation will be forthcoming (Rodrik, 1996). In addition, compensation paid to ones' rivals today can be used by them to increase their political power in the future (Rajan & Zingales, 1997). Rather than compensation being a pure transfer, it may entail greater future rent-seeking, hence greater future costs to those paying the compensation than simply the nominal value of the transfer. Since interest groups cannot credibly commit to give up rent-seeking in the future, regulations that all parties agree are inefficient may not be altered.

III. NORMATIVE LESSONS FROM A POSITIVE POLITICAL-ECONOMY APPROACH

The positive political-economy theory of interest group competition described above has been able to account for the liberalizing and globalizing tendency of banking and financial regulatory reform during the last two decades. Drawing normative lessons from a positive approach is always a difficult task, but the political-economy considerations suggest which circumstances will make beneficial regulatory reform more likely to occur. Some tentative propositions about increasing the likelihood of welfare-improving reforms in banking and finance follow.

First, education of the public and of policymakers of the actual and potential costs of regulation plays an important role. Rather than waiting for a crisis to reveal the full costs of poor policies, cost-benefit and comparative international studies provide a valuable role. When the costs of policies are obscure and little known, the beneficiaries of such policies will face less opposition in attempting to win political support for them. Uncertainty about the policy-outcomes of regulatory reform, as noted above, can slow the building of a winning coalition in favor of beneficial reforms. While solid academic research is neither necessary nor sufficient for policy reform, it can reduce the costs of producing good policy outcomes. Armed with carefully and thoroughly researched arguments and evidence, forces promoting beneficial change are more likely to be effective.

Second, competition among rival interest groups can increase the likelihood of beneficial reform. Rival groups have an incentive to battle each other in addition to battling the consumer. If they dissipate their efforts against each other, they are less likely to be able to support narrow special interest regulation. In many emerging markets today, e.g., Russia, a major question concerns whether creating universal banks would allow one particular interest to have too much political power and thwart reform. In addition, the rival groups have an incentive to try to unmask any misinformation that the competing side is generating. This can help to inform both the policy-makers and the public.

Third, the structure of regulatory and government institutions also plays a role. A clear structure of legislative oversight of the regulatory process through, for example, specific committees in the Parliament with responsibility for banking and financial matters may provide a forum which fosters the information generation process (Gilligan & Krehbiel, 1989; McCubbins, Noll, & Weingast, 1989; Krehbiel, 1991; Austin-Smith & Wright, 1992, 1994; Kroszner & Stratmann, forthcoming, 1998). Similarly, the incentives for groups to overcome free-rider problems and organize is related to the expected benefit of them doing so. In other words, the organization of interests is endogenously related to the structure of the regulatory process (see Irwin & Kroszner, 1997). Opening the regulatory process to include clear channels for new groups that would tend to oppose narrow special interest "capture" regulation increases the likelihood of regulatory reform by increasing the costs of maintain the regulation to the special interest.

Fourth, greater transparency in government involvement in the financial system is significant. Politicians often use the financial system, either through implicit guidance or explicit through state-owned banks, to provide low-cost financing to targeted industries or groups. Directed lending leads to implicit or explicit quid pro quos in order to have the banking sector follow this direction. Problems in Korean banks, for example, stem from encouragement by the government to continue lending to troubled enterprises in return for implicit assurances of a bail-out. Privatization of state owned enterprises, for example, can reduce the benefit to politicians' of directing credit and can generate new constituencies for an efficient banking and financial sector—as long as the firm has been fully privatized and does not have special influence with the government (Kroszner, 1996b). Requiring that any such transfers or subsidies be explicitly included in the government's fiscal accounts would clarify such transactions and help to break nexus of implicit agreements and quid pro quos through regulation that support them.

Finally, as noted above, a foreign bank entry can generate a virtuous circle because foreign banks tend to be less politically connected domestically and less likely to be able to capture the regulatory authorities. Foreign banks also are less likely to succumb to pressure for directed lending by the government. With capture less likely and fewer direct benefits to the politicians of bank regulation (e.g., through quid pro quos for directed lending), regulatory reform becomes more likely. While there is no simple formula for successful and sustained banking and financial regulatory reform, a positive analysis of the political-economy of rent-seeking does suggest how process and institutions facilitate beneficial reform.

ACKNOWLEDGMENTS

Thanks to Gerard Caprio, Paul Horvitz, George Kaufman, Philip Keefer, and Guillermo Perry for comments and discussion. Presented at the Annual Meeting of the Board of Governors of the World Bank Group and the International Monetary Fund, Hong Kong, September 21, 1997, the Federal Reserve Bank of Chicago, Conference on Bank Structure and Competition, May 8, 1998, and the Western Economics Association Meeting, Lake Tahoe, June 30, 1998.

NOTES

1. Joskow and Noll (1981) call this normative analysis as positive theory.

2. There are many alternative theories of government and politics that have implications for the causes of regulation and deregulation, such as the Leviathan theory discussed below (see Noll, 1989).

3. Becker (1983) argues that competition among lobbying groups thus will lead to the most efficient (lowest deadweight cost) regulations being chosen, so there is a tendency for regulation to be "efficient" in this sense. Wittman (1995) takes this argument further to conclude that both democratic institutions and outcomes are efficient.

4. When the constraint of future elections is less binding on politicians, they may engage in less rent-sharing and provide windfalls to targeted groups. McGuire and Olson (1996), however, argue that less democratic regimes may be better able to insulate themselves from rent-seeking and might find it in their own interest to pursue economic policies the public interest.

5. Important factors behind globalization of financial markets have involved both innovation in information processing and telecommunication and their effects in reducing regulatory barriers to geographic and product lines expansion. This is particularly true in Latin America, where an increasing number of foreign banks are purchasing local banks.

6. This form of financing could be seen as a mild form of financial repression (Fry, 1997).

7. There is a long and rich history linking a government's financing desires and financial regulation. During the first fiscal revolution in the United States when state governments began to rely heavily on debt financing in the 1840s, for example, many states adopted "free banking" statutes. This legal change eased entry into banking but required the banks to hold state government securities as reserves, thereby boosting the demand for the state's bonds (see Kroszner, 1997; Kroszner & Strahan, 1998).

8. Emerging and transition countries that have recently reformed their government debt markets and adopted auctions as the distribution method for government debt include: Bolivia, Burundi, Czech Republic, Egypt, Gambia, Ghana, Guyana, Honduras, Hungary, Jamaica, Jordan, Kenya, Latvia, Lebanon, Mexico, Morocco, Nigeria, Pakistan, Philippines, Russia, Slovak Republic, Tanzania, Tunisia,

Venezuela, and Zambia (see Bartolini & Cottarelli, 1997; Fry, 1997). Note that the United States is the exception in that it has long auctioned its government debt.

9. See Drazen (forthcoming) for a detailed political-economy explanation of why governments may wish to sell their debt to foreigners.

10. In multiple-price auctions, winning bidders pay the price that they bid, so different winners may pay different prices. Winners are determined by ordering bids by price and filling bids from highest to lowest price until the total quantity of securities auctioned has been sold. In a uniform-price auction, all of the successful bidders pay the same price. Who wins is determined the same way as in the multiple-price auction, but the price that the winners pay is highest unsuccessful bidder's price, not the price each winner bid (see U.S. Treasury et al., 1992).

11. Rapid technological innovation, however, has begun to erode the information advantages associated with being a primary dealer. Proliferation of inter-dealer broker screens and the growth of organized derivatives markets, for example, are narrowing the information gap between the primary dealers and others. As this trend continues, the value to the primary dealers of the multiple-price format may fall sufficiently that they would be indifferent between the two techniques. Eventually, governments then may switch over to uniform-price auctions and relax some of the distinctions between dealers and non-dealers that no longer provide important benefits to the primary dealers (see Kroszner, forthcoming).

12. Casella and Eichengreen (1994) extend the Alesina-Drazen model to show that the prospect of external aid can increase the delay in policy reform as rival groups wait until the aid arrives before taking actions.

13. Alternatives models not relying on uncertainty include Laban and Sturzenegger (1994a, 1994b) and Mondino, Sturzenegger, and Tommasi (1992) which develop dynamic games in which access to a "financial adaptation" technology can postpone reforms. Only one group, for example, may be able to adapt to domestic financial instability by moving its banking accounts and financial activities outside of the system (at a fixed cost). In these models, as conditions worsen domestically, the rival group without the ability to adapt will eventually agree to reforms, and receive a lower share of post-reform benefits, than they would have initially.

REFERENCES

Alesina, A., & Drazen, A. (1991). Why are stabilizations delayed? *American Economic Review*, 1170-1188.
Alston, L. (1996). Thrainn Eggertsson, and Douglass North (eds.), *Empirical studies in institutional change*. New York: Cambridge University Press.
Austin-Smith, D., & Wright, J. (1992). Competitive Lobbying for a Legislator's Vote. *Social Choice and Welfare, 9*, 229-57.
Austin-Smith, D., & Wright, (1994). Counteractive Lobbying. *American Journal of Political Science 38*, 25-44.
Bartolini, L., & Cottarelli, C. (1997). Treasury Bill Auctions: Issues and Uses. In M. Blejer & T. Ter-Minassian (Eds.), *Macroeconomic dimensions of public finance* (pp. 267-336). New York: Routledge.
Becker, G. S. (1983). A theory of competition among pressure groups for political influence. *Quarterly Journal of Economics*, 371-400.
Benston, G. J., & Kaufman, G. G. (1996). The appropriate role of bank regulation. *The Economic Journal, 106*, 688-697.
Brennan, G., & Buchanan, J. (1977). Towards a tax constitution for Leviathan. *Journal of Public Economics, 8*, 255-273.
Brickley, J. A., & James, C. M. (1987). The takeover market, corporate board composition, and ownership structure: The case of banking. *Journal of Law and Economics, 30*, 161-180.

Calomiris, C., & White, E. (1994). The origins of federal deposit insurance. In C. Golden & G. Libecap (Eds.), *The Regulated Economy* (pp. 145-188). Chicago: University of Chicago Press.

Caprio, G. Jr., & Klingebiel, D. (1996). Dealing with bank insolvencies: Cross country experience. Policy Research Department Working Paper. The World Bank.

Casella, A., & Eichengreen, B. (1994). Can foreign aid accelerate stabilization? Unpublished manuscript.

Drazen, A. (1996). Towards a political-economic theory of domestic debt. In G. Calvo & M. King (Eds.), *The debt burden and monetary policy.* London: Macmillan.

Fernandez, R., & Rodrik, D. (1991). Resistance to reform: Status quo bias in the presence of individual-specific uncertainty. *American Economic Review,* 1146-1155.

Friedman, M. (1960). *A program for monetary stability.* New York: Fordham University Press.

Fry, M. (1997). *Emancipating the banking system and developing markets for government debt.* London: Routledge.

Gilligan, T., & Krehbiel, K. (1989). Asymmetric information and legislative rules with a heterogeneous committee. *American Journal of Political Science, 33,* 459-490.

Guidotti, P. (1996). Debt, monetary, and banking policy in emerging markets: Reflections from the 'tequila' effect." University of Maryland, Department of Economics Working Paper No. 28.

Irwin, D., & Kroszner, R. (1997). The roles of interests, institutions, and ideology in durable policy change: The republican conversion to trade liberalization after smoot-hawley. National Bureau of Economic Research Working Paper No. 6112.

Hubbard, R. G., Palia, D., & Economides, D. (1996). The political economy of branching restrictions and deposit insurance. *Journal of Law and Economics,* October.

Joskow, P., & Noll, R. (1981). Regulation in Theory and Practice: An Overview." In G. Fromm (Ed.), *Studies in public regulation* (pp. 1-65). Cambridge: MIT Press.

Kane, E. J. (1987). No room for weak links in the chain of deposit insurance reform. *Journal of Financial Services Research, 1,* 77-11.

Kane, E. J. (1988). How market forces influence the structure of financial regulation. Chapter 9 in Kushmeider (ed.), *Restructuring Banking and Financial Services,* AEI.

Kane, E. J. (1996). De jure interstate banking: Why only now? *Journal of Money, Credit, and Banking, 28*(2), 141-161.

Kaufman, G., & Kroszner, R. (1997). How should financial institutions and markets be structured? In L. Rojas-Suarez (ed.), *Safe and sound financial systems: What works for Latin America?* (pp. 97-122). Washington: Inter-American Development Bank.

Krehbiel, K. (1991) *Information and legislative organization.* Ann Arbor: University of Michigan Press.

Kroszner, R. S. (1996). The evolution of universal banking and its regulation in twentieth century America. In A. Saunders & I. Walter (eds.), *Universal banking: Financial system design reconsidered* (pp. 70-99). New York: Irwin Professional Publishers.

Kroszner, R. S. (1996b). An Analysis of Bank Privatization. Unpublished manuscript, Graduate School of Business.

Kroszner, R. S. (1997). The political economy of banking and financial regulation in the U.S. In G. M. von Furstenberg (Ed.), *The banking and financial structure in the NAFTA countries and Chile* (pp. 200-213). Boston: Kluwer Academic Publishers.

Kroszner, R. S. (1998). Rethinking bank regulation: A review of the historical evidence. *Journal of Applied Corporate Finance, 10,* 48-58.

Kroszner, R. S. (In press). Global government securities markets: The economics and politics of market microstructure reforms. In G. Calvo & M. King (Eds.), *The debt burden and monetary policy.* London: Macmillan.

Kroszner, R. S., & Rajan, R. G. (1994). Is the glass-steagall act justified? A study of the U.S. experience with universal banking before 1933. *American Economic Review, 84,* 810-832.

Kroszner, R. S., & Rajan, R. G. (1997). Organization structure and credibility: Evidence from commercial bank securities activities before the Glass-Steagall Act *Journal of Monetary Economics, 29*, 475-516.

Kroszner, R. S., & Strahan, P. (1996). Regulatory incentives and the thrift crisis: Dividends, mutual-to-stock conversions, and financial distress. *Journal of Finance, 51*, 1285-1320.

Kroszner, R. S., & Strahan, P. (1998). What drives deregulation? Economics and politics of the relaxation of bank branching restrictions. Stigler Center for the Study of the Economy and the State Working Paper No. 136, University of Chicago.

Kroszner, R. S., & Stratmann, T. (1998). Interest group competition and the organization of congress: Theory and evidence from financial services political action committees. *American Economic Review, 88.*

Kroszner, R. S., & Stratmann, T. (1997). *Notes on development of the congressional committee system in the twentieth century.* Unpublished manuscript University of Chicago.

Kroszner, R. S., & Stratmann, T. (1998). *Does political ambiguity pay? Corporate campaign contributions and the value of legislator reputation.* Unpublished manuscript, Graduate School of Business, University of Chicago.

Laban, R., & Sturzengegger, F. (1994). Distributional conflict, financial adaptation, and delayed stabilization. Economics and Politics, 257-276.

McCubbins, M., Noll, R., & Weingast, R. (1989). Structure and process, politics and policy: Administrative arrangements and the political control of agencies. *Virginia Law Review, 78*, 431-482.

McGuire, M., & Olson, M. (1996). The economics of autocracy and majority rule. *Journal of Economic Literature,* 72-96.

Mondino, G., Sturzenegger, F., & Tommasi, M. (1992). *Recurrent high inflation and stabilization: A dynamic game.* Unpublished manuscript.

Niskanen, W. (1971). *Bureaucracy and representative government.* Chicago: Aldine-Atherton.

North, D. (1981). *Structure and change in economic history.* New York: Norton.

Noll, R. (1989). Comment on Peltzman. *Brookings Papers: Microeconomics,* 48-58.

Olson, M. (1965). *The logic of collective action.* Cambridge, MA: Harvard University Press.

Olson, M. (1982). *The rise and decline of nations: Economic growth, stagflation, and social rigidities.* New Haven, CT: Yale University Press.

Peltzman, S. (1976). Toward a more general theory of regulation. *Journal of Law and Economics, 19*(1), 109-148.

Peltzman, S. (1989). The economic theory of regulation after a decade of deregulation. *Brookings Papers: Microeconomics,* 1-41.

Poole, K., & Rosenthal, H. (1997). *Congress: A political-economic history of roll call voting.* Oxford: Oxford University Press.

Rajan, R., & Zingales, L. (1997). The tyranny of the inefficient: An enquiry into the adverse consequences of power struggles. Unpublished manuscript.

Reinhart, V. (1992). An analysis of potential treasury auction techniques. *Federal Reserve Bulletin,* June, 403-413.

Rodrik, D. (1996). Understanding economic policy reform. *Journal of Economic Literature,* 9-41.

Sheng, A. (1996). *Bank restructuring: Lessons from the 1980s.* Washington: The World Bank.

Shepsle, K., & Weingast, B. (1995). *Positive theories of congressional institutions.* Ann Arbor: University of Michigan Press.

Stigler, G. J. (1971). The theory of economic regulation. *Bell Journal of Economics and Management Science, 2*(1), 3-21.

Stigler, G. J. (1988). *Chicago studies in the political economy.* Chicago: University of Chicago Press.

Umlauf, S. (1993). An empirical study of the Mexican treasury bill auction. *Journal of Financial Economics, 33*(3), 313-340.

U.S. Department of Treasury. (1992). U.S. Securities and Exchange Commission, and the Board of Governors of the Federal Reserve System (1992) *Joint Report on the Government Securities Market*. Washington: GPO.

Weingast, B. R., & Marshall, W. J. (1988). The industrial organization of congress; or, why legislatures, like firms, are not organized as markets. *Journal of Political Economy, 96*(1), 132-163.

White, E. (1983). *The regulation and reform of the American banking system, 1900-1929*. Princeton: Princeton University Press.

Williamson, J. (1994). *The political economy of policy reform*. Washington: Institute for International Economics.

Wittman, D. N. (1995). *The myth of democratic failure*. Chicago: University of Chicago Press.

THE ONGOING CRISIS IN
THE CZECH BANKING INDUSTRY

Thomas S. Mondschean

I. INTRODUCTION

Due in large part to the consequences of banking problems in major economies such as the United States and Japan, we have witnessed a growing awareness of the importance of sound, well-managed financial institutions in promoting economic growth in major industrial nations. In developing countries, however, banks play an even more important role in channeling funds from savers to borrowers and entrepreneurs because other institutions and markets that could provide financial services are generally underdeveloped. Thus, a poorly capitalized banking system making unsound lending decisions can cause even greater damage in an emerging economy.

This paper focuses on banking system development in the Czech Republic. Of all the so-called economies in transition, few countries began the 1990s in as strong a macroeconomic position as Czechoslovakia. Due to conservative fiscal policies maintained by the Communists in power, government budget deficits were kept low for many years, and the government debt burden was relatively

Research in Financial Services: Private and Public Policy, Volume 10, pages 53-69.
Copyright © 1998 by JAI Press Inc.
All rights of reproduction in any form reserved.
ISBN: 0-7623-0358-1

small.[1] The ratio of foreign debt to GDP in 1989 was under 20 percent, less than a third of the levels observed in Poland and Hungary. In addition to the relatively solid fiscal position, the central bank had not allowed the domestic money supply to grow as rapidly as its counterparts in Poland and Hungary had done. As a result, the degree of monetary overhang (excess money creation that would lead to inflation once price controls were lifted) was much smaller than in other transition economies.

Another point in Czechoslovakia's favor was that the election in 1990 gave the first non-Communist government in over 40 years a strong mandate for serious economic reform. In 1991, the new government, under the leadership of Finance Minister (and later Prime Minister) Vaclav Klaus, implemented many significant economic changes. Prices representing over 85 percent of the value of goods and services were immediately freed and subsidies to producers and consumers were cut. The exchange rate value of the Czech koruna (crown) was devalued in 1990 by approximately 45 percent, made fully convertible at 28 per dollar, and, on December 28, 1990, was pegged to a basket of currencies. International trade was liberalized and tariffs were reduced to an average of around 5 percent. Later policies included several "waves" of privatization of state-owned firms using various methods including vouchers, restructuring of existing firms and banks, and legal reform. In addition, Czechoslovakia was divided into two independent states at the beginning of 1993, a decision that favored the Czechs from an economic standpoint.

By 1995, the Czech economy appeared to be among the most successful of the transition economies of Central and Eastern Europe. Real economic growth exceeded 6 percent for the year, inflation was less than 10 percent, and unemployment was a remarkable 2.9 percent. The economy continued to grow in 1996; however, it was becoming clearer to many observers that the expansion was not sustainable. For example, foreign debt expanded from 29.7 percent to 39.8 percent of GDP between 1994 and 1996, indicating that economic growth in 1995 and 1996 was fueled in large part by foreign borrowing. By early 1997, the large current account deficit, which had increased to 7.6 percent of GDP in 1996, was reducing investor confidence in the government's ability to maintain its fixed exchange rate, and capital flows began to shift in the other direction. By May 1997, the central bank was obliged to let the currency float, and the crown depreciated against the dollar by approximately 20 percent during 1997, reducing investor confidence even further.

In retrospect, the exchange rate turmoil of 1997 was symptomatic of a number of structural problems in the Czech economy. One of the areas of greatest concern has been the banking industry. While many Central and Eastern European banks inherited large amounts of nonperforming loans from the Communist era, Czech banks continued to make poor lending decisions in the 1990s. As a result, approximately one third of total bank loans remain classified as substandard by the Czech National Bank (CNB) as of the end of 1997. Despite large additions to loan loss provisions, the largest Czech banks remain undercapitalized, and the CNB has been forced to resolve a number of small and medium sized bank failures in the past few years.

The performance of the Czech banking system raises a number of questions of interest to those studying banking crises. First, what were the causes of the bad loan problems in the Czech Republic? Second, why did the bank regulators allow the problems to continue as long as they did before taking action? Third, what lessons can be learned from the Czech experience that we can apply to other countries? The paper is divided into five sections. Section II presents an overview of Czech economic performance during the 1990s and compares it to Slovakia, Hungary, and Poland. Section III examines the evolution of banking reform in the Czech Republic during the transition and documents Czech banking performance in detail. Section IV explains why reforms were ineffective in improving the Czech banking system, focusing attention on the lack of incentives for banks to encourage firm restructuring and improve corporate governance. It will also discuss the consequences poorly implemented banking reform has had on other aspects of the Czech economy. The final section concludes by drawing lessons from the Czech experience that may apply to other countries.

II. CZECH ECONOMIC PERFORMANCE

Table 1 presents a macroeconomic overview of the 1990s for the Czech Republic, the Slovak Republic, Hungary, and Poland. All four countries initially experienced declining output due to economic restructuring, the collapse of trade with the Soviet Union, and a recession in Western Europe. Poland started its market reforms a year before the Czech and Slovak Republics, came out of recession earlier than the other countries and is growing rapidly, averaging over 6 percent per year since 1993. Slovakia, after a longer period of restructuring, has also appeared to move onto a high growth path. Hungary experienced declining output through 1993 and a brief spurt of economic growth in 1994. In 1995, the Hungarian government adopted an austere fiscal policy that led to a slowdown in 1995 and 1996 and recovery in 1997.

The Czech Republic experienced a similar decline in real GDP through 1992. Afterward, economic growth accelerated, peaking in 1995 before declining to 1 percent in 1997. Panel B of Table 1 shows that the Czech unemployment rate was substantially below other transition economies and it remained low even during the period when GDP was declining. However, unemployment has been rising since 1995. Panel C of Table 1 documents the inflationary performance of these four countries during the 1990s. All four countries experienced an initial spurt of consumer price increases due to price deregulation combined with monetary overhang (Poland experienced a short period of hyperinflation with prices rising over 580% in 1989). After a second jump in prices in 1993 due to the introduction of value added taxation, the inflation rate in the Czech Republic fell below 10 percent in 1995 and remained there until the beginning of 1998.

Table 1.   Macroeconomic Data for the
Czech Republic and Neighboring Countries

Year	Czech Republic	Slovak Republic	Hungary	Poland
A. Real GDP Growth Rate (%)				
1990	−1.2	−14.2	−3.5	−11.6
1991	−11.5	−11.2	−11.9	−7.0
1992	−3.3	−6.5	−3.0	2.6
1993	0.6	−3.7	-0.8	3.8
1994	2.7	4.9	2.9	5.2
1995	6.4	6.9	1.5	7.0
1996	3.9	6.6	1.0	6.1
1997	1.0	6.5	4.0	6.9
1998Q1	−0.9	6.2	4.9	6.5
B. Unemployment Rate (%)				
1990	0.8	1.6	0.4	6.3
1991	4.1	11.8	1.9	11.8
1992	2.6	11.4	7.8	13.6
1993	3.5	12.7	13.2	16.4
1994	3.2	14.6	10.4	16.0
1995	2.9	13.8	10.9	14.9
1996	3.5	12.6	9.2	14.7
1997	4.9	12.6	10.2	10.5
May 1998	5.3	12.9	9.4	9.8
C. Consumer Price Inflation (%)				
1990	9.7	10.6	28.9	585.3
1991	56.6	61.2	35.0	70.3
1992	11.1	10.1	23.0	43.0
1993	20.8	23.2	22.5	35.3
1994	10.0	13.4	18.8	29.5
1995	9.1	9.9	28.2	27.8
1996	8.8	5.8	23.6	19.9
1997	8.5	6.4	18.7	14.9
May 1998[*]	13.0	7.6	15.8	13.3

Note: [*]Percent change from a year ago.

Source: Statistical offices of the four countries.

Based on these data, the Czech economy performed rather well during the transition in terms of macroeconomic stability and especially in terms of employment. So why have economists both inside and outside the country criticized Czech economic performance? First, the economic growth during the 1994-1997 period

Table 2. Growth of Consumer Prices, Wages, and Labor Productivity in the Czech Republic (Annual Growth Rates in Percent)

Category	1992	1993	1994	1995	1996	1997
Consumer Prices	11.1	20.8	10.0	9.1	8.8	8.5
Nominal Average Wage	22.5	25.3	18.5	18.5	18.0	11.9
Real Average Wage[a]	10.0	3.7	7.3	8.8	9.0	3.1
Labor Productivity[b]	−3.9	0.7	1.8	2.1	3.2	2.1

Notes: [a]Nominal Wage index divided by the cost of living index of employees.
[b]Real GDP per employed person in the civilian sector of the national economy.

Source: Hajek et al. (1996, p. 70). 1997 data were calculated by the author.

occurred during a time when over one-third of Czech GDP was devoted to investment. Given such a high ratio of capital formation, an average growth rate of 3 to 4 percent seems low. Second, the labor market appeared to be overheating. Table 2 presents data on wage and productivity growth during the 1992-1997 period. One can observe that real wages grew rapidly and well in excess of labor productivity during the entire period. It is not surprising given the real wage growth that real personal consumption expenditures grew by 6.9 percent in 1995 and 7 percent percent in 1996.

The growth in unit labor costs (real wage growth exceeded productivity growth in every year from 1992 to 1997) also led to a reduction in international competitiveness. Figure 1 compares the nominal and real exchange rate values of the

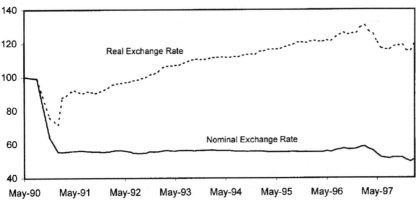

Note: Weighted averages of the U.S. dollar (35 percent) and the Deutschemark (65 percent) per Czech Koruna. Real Exchange rate was calculated using producer price indexes.
Sources: OECD, CNB, International Financial Statistics and U.S. Department of Labor.

Figure 1. Nominal and Real Exchange Rate Values of the Czech Koruna (May 1990 = 100)

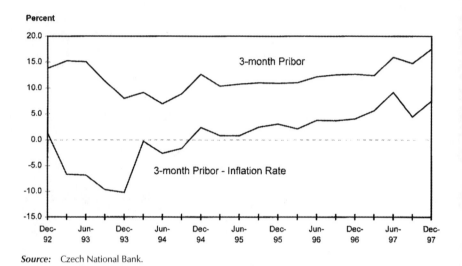

Source: Czech National Bank.

Figure 2.   Nominal and Real 3-Month Pribor Rates

Czech crown from 1990 to early 1998. One can observe the large initial devaluation in 1990, the period when the nominal exchange rate was pegged, and the
depreciation in 1997. One can also observe the real appreciation of over 50 percent
that occurred from 1991 to 1997. It seems clear that the fixed nominal exchange
rate combined with the growth in prices and unit labor costs adversely affected the
competitiveness of Czech goods on world markets. Not surprisingly, the current
account deficit grew rapidly after 1994. But large capital account surpluses (over
$18 billion over the 1993-1996 period) more than offset these deficits. The prob-
lem for the Czech National Bank during this period was to prevent the crown from
appreciating in nominal terms, which they did by sterilizing capital inflows.

But why were capital inflows so large? Figure 2 compares the nominal and real
3-month Prague Interbank Offered Rates (PRIBOR) from 1992 to 1997. Since the
end of 1994, the central bank adopted an increasingly restrictive monetary policy
to combat the growth in domestic demand. The 3-month PRIBOR rose above 10
percent and was positive and increasing in real terms as well. Given the fixed
exchange rate and no capital controls, the large differential between Czech and
U.S. or German interest rates naturally attracted large capital inflows.[2]

Figure 3 compares total bank loans outstanding with M2, both adjusted for
inflation and indexed to the end of 1992. It shows that M2 grew about 20 percent
in real terms through the beginning of 1996 and stayed relatively constant since
then. The rapid money supply growth indicates that the central bank was unable to
completely sterilize the massive capital inflows that occurred in the 1993-1995

Dec-92=100

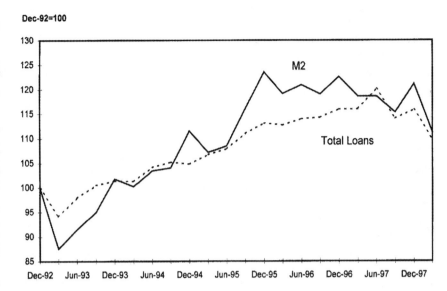

Source: Czech National Bank.

Figure 3. Inflation-Adjusted Total Loans vs. Inflation-Adjusted M2

period. The second line in the graph shows that bank loans increased steadily in real terms from early 1993 all the way until May 1997 when the exchange rate crisis occurred. It would seem that while credit may have been relatively expensive, there is little evidence of banks restraining credit growth until after May 1997. Indeed, without continued bank lending, it would not have been possible for firms to cover the large real wage increases given that the real appreciation of the crown was reducing their competitiveness vis-à-vis foreign firms. But why would the banks continue to fund this process? To understand this issue, we turn our attention to a discussion of the Czech banking system.

III. THE CZECH BANKING SYSTEM

During the period of Communist control from the end of World War II to the end of the 1980s, the banking system became highly centralized and served primarily as a conduit for transferring funds between the central government and the various state enterprises which controlled the Czechoslovak economy. The banking system was organized around four state-owned financial institutions. The State Bank of Czechoslovakia handled all central banking and domestic commercial banking functions involving enterprises. The Czechoslovak State Savings Bank offered domestic banking services to individuals. For foreign transactions, there were two banks, Ceskoslovenska Obchodni Banka (CSOB) for enterprises and Zivnosten-ska Banka (ZB) for individual foreign currency transactions and accounts.

Two laws restructuring the banking system went into effect at the beginning of 1990. Central banking functions were kept in the State Bank of Czechoslovakia. Long-term project loans were placed in a newly created Investicni Banka. The commercial banking section was moved into two banks, one in the Czech Republic (Komercni Banka) and one in Slovakia (Vseobecna Uverova Banka). The State Savings Bank was also split into separate Czech (Ceska Sporitelna) and Slovak (Slovenska Sporitelna) institutions.

To achieve the goal of a viable, modern banking system, the government had to overcome several obstacles. The most critical hurdle was the resolution of loans made to state-owned enterprises (SOEs) during the Communist era, many of which were unrecoverable. For example, Komercni Banka (KB) received the State Bank's loan portfolio of 325 billion Czech crowns, approximately three quarters of total commercial loans of all types throughout the Czech Republic, and it included a large percentage of nonperforming loans. (Snyder & Kormendi, 1997) To strengthen these large banks, the Konsolidacni Banka (KOB), similar to the Resolution Trust Corporation that managed the bailout of the U.S. savings and loan industry, was established. Between 1991 and 1993, the KOB spent CZK 45 billion (about 6% of 1992 GDP) bailing out the large banks by either recapitalization or purchase of problem loans.

A second objective was to encourage greater competition among banks to improve the quality of financial services offered to the public. One method would have been to privatize the banks by selling them to large foreign banks that had the capital, technology, and managerial expertise to modernize them quickly. However, this was ruled out as an early option because the government did not want the banking system dominated by foreign interests. Instead, the government initially offered liberal requirements to new entrants including foreign banks. As a result, the number of banks grew from 5 to 21 during 1990 and reached 56 by the end of 1994.

The policy was partially successful in the sense that foreign banks coming into the Czech market did provide competition that induced Czech banks to improve their service offerings more quickly. However, most of the small banks organized by Czech investors ran into problems due to poor lending decisions and the declining economy in the first few years of transition. In 1994, the CNB suspended licensing of new banks, a ban that would last until 1996. Not surprisingly, the number of licensed banks has been falling as operations at 12 banks representing approximately 8 percent of total banking assets, including the nation's fifth largest bank (Agrobanka), had been suspended by the Czech National Bank.[3] The Czech National Bank implemented a second bailout program in 1996 and 1997 to address the problems faced by these small and medium sized banks. The net capital cost (not including imputed interest) of this second bailout program is estimated to be around 2 percent of 1997 GDP, as reported in IMF (1998). As a result of these restructurings, the industry remains highly concentrated, with the top four banks

Table 3. Czech Banking System Performance Measures*

	1995	1996	1997
After-Tax Return on Assets	0.71%	0.39%	−0.20%
After-Tax Return on Equity	21.48%	12.30%	−6.52%
Net Interest Margin**	4.04%	3.00%	3.06%
Per Employee (000's of CZK)			
Total Assets	30,288	32,703	39,924
Net Profit	184	120	−73
Operating Costs	596	692	825
Core capital/risk weighted assets	9.24%	9.27%	8.72%
Core capital/unweighted assets	5.25%	5.43%	4.71%

Notes: *Banks with valid license as of year end 1997 excluding Konsolidacni Banka and banks under conservatorship.
**Deposits and loans of non-banking enterprises and banks excluding fees and commissions.

Source: Czech National Bank.

today (Komercni Banka (KB), Ceska Sporitelna (CS), Investicni and Postovni Bank (IPB), and Ceskoslovenska Obchodni Banka (CSOB)) controlling around 60 percent of the total assets and 75 percent of total deposits.

Despite the concentrated and protective structure of the Czech banking industry, overall profitability appears to have been mediocre. Table 3 shows that the

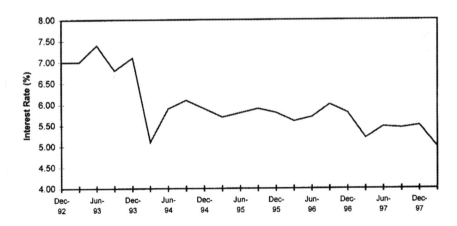

Source: Czech National Bank.

Figure 4. Net Interest Rate Margin of Commercial Banks
(Average Rate on Loans minus Average Rate on Deposits)

Table 4.   Czech Banking System Data

	1994	1995	1996	1997
Total bank assets (Kc billion)	1,449.3	1,814.9	2,008.9	2,333.3
Total bank loans	758.8	897.2	1,013.2	1,148.0
Total reserves and provisions	97.3	104.8	117.2	129.6
Bank profits	6.4	8.1	−11.2	−6.5
Without KOB and banks Under conservatorship	6.4	9.7	6.6	6.9
Distribution of credits by quality (%)				
Standard[1]	64.0	65.7	67.1	66.6
Watch[2]	7.8	6.6	6.3	6.1
Substandard[3]	5.0	4.4	3.2	2.7
Doubtful[4]	6.5	4.1	4.1	3.4
Loss[5]	16.7	19.1	19.3	21.3
Total loans/total assets	54.2	49.4	50.4	49.2
Reserves and prov./ total assets	6.0	5.8	5.8	5.6
Reserves and prov./qualified loans	30.8	34.1	35.2	33.9
Loss loans/qualified loans	46.3	55.7	58.5	63.7
Without KOB and banks Under conservatorship	36.9	51.2	55.5	55.9

Notes: [1] Payments of principal, interest, or fees paid on time or overdue for less than 31 days.

[2] (a) Payments of principal, interest, or fees are overdue for more than 30 but less than 91 days. (b) The bank has lacked sufficient information of the financial position of the debtor for more than 30 but less than 91 days since the date it should have been presented to the bank. (c) The bank, because of the debtor's financial position, changed the payment schedule more than six months ago.

[3] (a) Payments of principal, interest, or fees are overdue for more than 90 but less than 181 days. (b)The bank has lacked sufficient information on the financial position of the debtor for more than 90 but less than 181 days since the date it should have been presented to the bank. (c)The bank, because of the debtor's financial position, changed the payment schedule more than six months ago.

[4] (a) Payments of principal, interest, or fees are overdue for more than 180 but less than 361 days. (b) The bank has lacked sufficient information on the financial position of the debtor for more than 180 but less than 361 days since the date it should have been presented to the bank, or the information indicates that full repayment of the credit within its maturity is highly improbable.

[5] (a) Payments of principal, interest, or fees are overdue for 361 days or more. (b) The bank has lacked sufficient information on the financial position of the debtor for 361 days or more since the date it should have been presented to the bank, or the information indicates that full repayment of the credit within its maturity is impossible. (c) In the case of the debtor being under bankruptcy or settlement procedures, the bank records the claim as a loss.

Source: OECD (1998, p. 60). Based on end-of-year data supplied by the Czech National Bank.

after-tax return on assets (ROA) for the Czech banking industry fell from 0.71 percent in 1995 to a minus 0.20 percent in 1997. By comparison, Polish and American banks had ROAs of 2.0 percent and 1.13 percent in 1995, respectively. There appeared to be three major reasons for the relatively weak profit performance. First, as shown in Figure 4, the difference between the average interest rates on loans and deposits narrowed from about seven percentage points in 1993 to just over 5 percentage points in 1996 reflecting growing competition from foreign banks operating in the country. Table 3 indicates that the net interest margin fell from 4.04 percent of assets in 1995 to 3.06 percent in 1997. Second, operating costs per employee rose 38.4 percent between 1995 and 1997, reflecting rapid wage growth in the financial services sector and additional investment in information technology. However, the most important reason for poor profit performance seemed to be that Czech banks have had to set aside a significant portion of each year's profits to increase loan loss reserves. According to the CNB (1998, forthcoming), excluding banks in conservatorship, Czech banks set aside 1.1 percent, 0.4 percent and 1.5 percent of total assets in 1995, 1996 and 1997, respectively, to add to their loan loss reserves.

Despite the bailouts engineered by the KOB and the CNB, the nonperforming loan problem has shown little improvement in recent years. Table 4, taken from OECD (1998), reports loan data from 1994 to 1997. First, the percentage of loans classified as standard (performing) showed only a slight improvement over the period. As of the end of 1997, one third of all Czech loans are still classified as nonstandard. Moreover, the proportion classified as loss (payments overdue for over 361 days) rose from 16.7 percent of total loans to 21.3 percent between 1994 and 1997. That means that 244.5 billion crowns of Czech loans are in the loss category at the end of 1997 but banks had set aside only 129.6 billion to cover all their nonperforming loans. Thus, the gap between loss loans and total loan provisions was 114.9 billion crowns, which represents several years of normal earnings.[4]

How serious was the bad loan problem at the largest Czech banks? For Komercni Banka, total loans classified as loss at the end of March 1998 were 58.99 billion crowns (23.1% of total loans) while total provisions for all loans amounted to 29.29 billion crowns. For Ceska Sporitelna as of the end of 1996, loans classified as doubtful or loss (nonperforming for six months or more) totaled 40.38 billion crowns (one sixth of total loans) while total reserves (not including a five billion crown government guarantee) amounted to 23.05 billion crowns. Thus the combined gap for these two banks (between their problem loans and their reserves) appeared to be 50 billion crowns in 1996. Obviously the figure would have been higher if doubtful and "watch" loans had been added.

But resolution of the bad loan problem was only part of the issue. There were also the questions of why the problem had occurred and whether it might be a continuing problem. Given that the bailouts engineered by the Consolidation Bank and the National Property Fund had been expected to address pre-1990 loan problems, the "bad loan" problem existing in Czech banks in 1997 resulted in significant measure from loans made during the transition. The authors of IMF (1998) address this issue by decomposing the change in classified loans in each year into the following factors: credit growth, loan write-offs, capitalized interest on classified loans during the year, and new classified loans. They estimate that newly classified loans represented 3.3 percent, 3.4 percent and 4.2 percent of total loans in

1995, 1996, and 1997, respectively. Thus, despite government bailouts amounting to tens of billions of Czech crowns to resolve past bad loan episodes, banks continue to add to their asset quality problems.

The causes of loan quality problems at Czech banks are many. Clearly, inexperience in credit analysis and collateral appraisal are important factors, especially at the smaller banks that were started in the early years of the transition. According to IMF (1998), these banks had higher proportions of classified loans than the "big four" banks, and that their clientele consisted mainly of newly created firms, many of which subsequently failed. Many of these loans were made to finance the purchase of state-owned enterprises from the National Property Fund. Lending appeared to be based primarily on collateral rather than on the financial potential of the businesses receiving credit. As the economy was experiencing the shocks of new foreign competition, a recession in Western Europe, and the collapse of trade with the former Soviet Union, many of these newly created firms could not survive, and the banks were left with nonperforming loans. Besides these more traditional causes, outright fraud and theft also appears to have been an important source of loan losses. White-collar crime continues to be a serious problem in the Czech Republic, which has experienced severe shortages of police investigators, prosecutors and judges throughout the transition. In addition, relatively lenient laws governing financial behavior have made it easier to engage in activities such as asset stripping that would be illegal in developed countries.[5] Moreover, the difficulty of foreclosing on collateral made it hard for banks to recover part of their losses.

Besides the reasons cited above for deteriorating loan quality, the perpetuation of problem loans at the largest Czech banks was also a result of the method of privatization that existed in the Czech Republic. The government had a goal to privatize state-owned firms as rapidly as possible. It was believed that private firms would have a greater incentive to improve efficiency and customer service than state-owned banks would. Privatization was done in a variety of ways. Larger firms were sold directly to foreign investors. Small businesses were privatized by liquidation, that is, they were sold directly to individuals or firms. As stated above, banks gave loans to many entrepreneurs to finance these purchases. Finally, several waves of voucher privatization occurred. In these schemes, ownership stakes in several firms were bundled together and placed into investment funds. Vouchers representing shares in these funds were sold for a nominal fee to every Czech citizen. These vouchers could be sold for cash or converted into ownership stakes in one or more of 15 investment funds that held the shares of privatized companies.

Partial privatization of three of the four large state banks occurred through the voucher method in 1992 and 1993 (CSOB remained state-owned). However, the state retained effective control of all four because the National Property Fund (a government agency holding the state's remaining ownership shares in SOEs) possessed a significant minority stake in each bank. Because the vouchers were widely diffused, no investor could obtain a large enough position to exercise corporate control of any of the banks (although in 1998 Nomura International acquired a controlling stake in IPB). Thus, while bank privatization occurred in principle, the reality was that they remained under state control. But it goes deeper than that. Czech banks are universal banks, so they can hold equity stakes in or make loans to nonfinancial corporations. In addition, each of the four largest banks managed one or more of the 15 investment funds through their subsidiaries, and these funds typically held sizable equity stakes in major corporations throughout the country.[6] Thus, effective state control of the four largest banks meant effective control of several of these funds.

At first glance, bank control of these investment funds could aid in firm restructuring because the banks, as fund managers, would receive a bonus if the restructuring proved successful. However, the apparent success of the privatization strategy was offset by three factors. First, banks were usually both agents for the shareholders (through the investment fund subsidiary) and creditors (through loans made by the banking subsidiary). This created a conflict of interest, especially where restructuring might entail a writedown of the banks' loans. In such situations, the banks were likely to have more to gain from protecting their creditor interests by delaying restructuring. Second, to whatever extent the banking authorities represented the interests of a sitting government (due to sizable remaining stakes held by the National Property Fund or other SOEs) they might well be more concerned with potential losses in tax revenues or employment than with the longer term gains from restructuring. Finally, with banks having significant ownership stakes, it was difficult if not impossible for firms to switch banks. This reduced competition for financial services and increased the profitability of existing customer relationships to the commercial banks. Thus, the banks could maintain higher spreads and use these spreads as a mechanism for rolling over a higher fraction of doubtful loans.

IV. THE EFFECTS OF THE CZECH BANK REFORM PROGRAM

One piece of evidence supporting the view that Czech banks were behaving in an imprudent manner was that during the 1993-1996 period, total loans grew faster than inflation, especially when one excludes loans to households and governments. If banks were serious about restoring capital adequacy and building credit appraisal skills before making new loans, total loans probably would have fallen in real terms as they did in Poland between 1992 and 1995 and in the United States during the so-called "credit crunch" from 1989 to 1992. The fact that the loan growth was strong indicated that other factors, such as political pressure or the desire to maintain employment or mutually supportive relationships, might have been present.

Former Prime Minister Klaus suggested similar causes for the Czech banking problems in a 1997 speech:

While trying to expand [the banking system] rapidly we probably underestimated the need to impose sufficiently high capital requirements and, at the same time, we did not succeed in strictly dividing the financial and production sectors of the economy. We more or less accepted the German (or continental) type of banking with its strong interrelationships between banks and firms in the production sector. We see many problems with it now but I am not sure we could have started differently (Federal Reserve Bank of Kansas City, 1997, p. 190).

An implication of the foregoing argument was that lax lending standards were being condoned by lax bank supervision from the central bank. If so, this in turn implied that the behavior of bank regulators contributed to the inflationary pressures affecting the Czech economy. Lax supervisory policy on the part of the CNB would permit banks to continue to lend to favored borrowers. The additional funds would allow firms to avoid eliminating unprofitable product lines and/or branch operations and delay in "downsizing their managerial overheads," while at the same time allowing them to grant nominal wage increases in excess of inflation and productivity growth. In short, lax regulatory standards would be a major contributor in fueling rapid wage growth in an already tight labor market.

Higher real earnings of 6-8 percent per year led to growth in real consumption expenditures in 1995 and 1996 (which continued in the first half of 1997), which raised prices. To combat the price and wage pressure, the CNB tightened credit by raising interest rates. In these circumstances, high quality borrowers had to pay higher interest rates along with weaker firms. Figure 2 shows that the real interest rate had been increasing since the end of 1993 and especially since the end of 1996, confirming that monetary policy had indeed grown increasingly restrictive during the entire period. Thus, the central bank condoned a generous and indeed expansionary policy at the microeconomic level by engaging in lax supervision, a policy sometimes referred to as "bank socialism." At the same time, it was pursuing a restrictive policy in its role in managing the money supply. The restrictive monetary policy in turn led to higher interest rates that induced large capital inflows and put upward pressure on the real exchange rate.

Besides this "macroeconomic" implication of lax bank supervision, the more traditional allocative effects also occurred. Funds that were lent to prop up inefficient SOEs were not made available to other, potentially more profitable investment opportunities. The high interest rates exacerbated the adverse selection problem because the bankrupt SOEs cared more about the availability of funds than their cost. Thus, the low productivity performance of the Czech economy is explained both by the lack of hard budget constraints on state-owned firms due to the easy lending policy as well as the difficulty facing new firms in receiving credit at reasonable interest rates.

At the heart of the matter, the fact that the government controlled a large enough stake in the large banks allowed this process to continue. The prudential regulations that allowed the CNB to effectively regulate the banking system were in place by 1994. Nevertheless, the bank regulators continued to practice forbearance until the spring of 1997. Why? There is no definitive answer to this question, only speculation. Pushing genuine bank reform would have required cutting off credit to the less creditworthy SOEs, and this would have led to restructuring or bankruptcy. Either way, it would have led to greater unemployment in the short run.

Since the exchange rate crisis of May 1997, policy has changed radically. First, the CNB has forced banks to increase loss reserves even further. Second, the government decided in late 1997 that the large banks need to be fully privatized as quickly as possible, although recent election results may slow the pace of future bank privatization. IPB has already been sold to Nomura, and Agrobanka has been taken over by GE Capital. CSOB appears to be next on the list. The prospect of real bank privatization has forced the banks to reduce forbearance. The drying up of bank loans has predictably led to more rapid firm restructuring and higher unemployment. The rising unemployment rate, however, should be viewed as a healthy sign that the Czech economy is finally beginning to really restructure and productivity is growing, especially among manufacturing firms.

Third, the Parliament has passed a number of capital market reforms that will hopefully address some of the conflict of interest problems with bank relationships with its nonbank customers. Bank employees are now prohibited from serving on the supervisory boards of their customers. Stronger firewalls between commercial and investment banking were created to reduce the potential for insider trading, and rules requiring professional care in securities trading were designed to make it harder to engage in asset stripping or other harmful corporate practices. Any acquisition of more than 5 percent of a bank's stock must now be approved by the CNB, and the acquirer must satisfy the same "fit and proper" criteria as the founders of the bank. The CNB also has the power now to strip shareholders of their voting rights if they undermine the proper operation of the bank. In addition to many other statutory changes, a securities and exchange commission is now in place to regulate the capital markets. These legal reforms will help to improve corporate governance, but a better bankruptcy law is still needed to clarify the legal basis of collateral and reduce uncertainty in lending.

V. CONCLUSIONS AND IMPLICATIONS FOR BANKING CRISES

In some ways, the Czech government squandered advantages they had inherited from the previous regime. Given the low level of government debt, the government could have recapitalized the banking system quickly. They chose not to do this in part because the ability and will to enforce prudential regulation did not exist for several years. There are several lessons from the Czech experience that can be applied to other countries. First, forbearance is costly. The Czech economy, like the Japanese economy of the 1990s, practiced forbearance by not quickly addressing the asset quality problems of its banks and by allowing banking to continue to make risky loans with little real capital. It has paid the price in low productivity, sub-par economic growth, and the recognition that delaying bank reform and firm restructuring only increased the future cost of reform. Second, adopting liberal entry requirements without adequate bank supervision or regulation in place can lead to costly bank failures down the road. Stiglitz (1998) cites rapid financial liberalization without adequate bank supervisory safeguards as one of the underlying causes of the Asian financial crisis, and the Czech example provides additional evidence for this conclusion. Promoting greater bank competition is a reasonable objective, but it must come from healthy, well-managed banks that need not rely on government guarantees (implicit or explicit) to stay in business. Third, voucher privatization does not necessarily lead to improved corporate governance. Indeed, in the Czech case, it allowed the government to say that banks are privatized but still maintain significant control. Fourth, the Czech experience shows that universal banking without the proper institutional framework in place can lead to serious corporate governance and conflict of interest problems. This is important because it shows that certain legal safeguards must be in place for universal banking to work properly. Given the almost universal support among financial economists for the repeal of the Glass-Steagall Act in the United States, it is useful to have cases where inadequate laws and regulations led to undesirable consequences. Finally, the Czech case highlights the relationship between bank regulatory policy and monetary policy. Lax bank regulation makes monetary policy more difficult by requiring higher interest rates to achieve the same degree of restraint in aggregate demand growth. Stronger bank regulation, at least for banks that are undercapitalized, will lead to reduced credit growth. In addition, it should improve allocative efficiency as banks start using creditworthiness as the primary criterion for receiving credit.

ACKNOWLEDGMENT

This research is an outgrowth of a case study on Czech economic reform co-authored with Professor Bruce Scott of Harvard Business School. I would like to thank the Czech National Bank for graciously supplying data and I especially thank Board Members Miroslav Hrncir, Ota Kaftan, and Ludek Niedermeyer for explaining the intracacies of the Czech banking system. I also thank Paul Horvitz for his comments and Ellen Dawson for her research assistance. Financial support of DePaul University's College of Commerce and the Institute for Strategic Change at Andersen Consulting is gratefully acknowledged.

NOTES

1. The national debt/GDP ratio was 19.2 percent in 1992 despite falling real GDP from 1990 to 1992.

2. According to OECD (1996), the 3-month PRIBOR was approximately 600 basis points above a weighted average of the DM (Frankfurt) and Dollar (LIBOR) interest rates during 1995 and 1996.

3. On June 15, 1998, the CNB announced formal approval of the sale of Agrobanka to General Electric Capital Corporation.

4. Part of the difference is made up by loan guarantees and collateral. However, the value of collateral has been called into question because of the legal difficulty of foreclosing on real estate as well as the state of the economy and its effect on real estate values. In a June 18, 1998 press release posted on its web site, the Czech National Bank has ordered phased-in increases in provisions for classified loans secured by real estate, an action "...which was necessitated by legal and procedural problems in recovering debts and particularly by the critical situation in foreclosing on real estate collateral."

5. According to the Economist Intelligence Unit (1998), "a report produced by a Czech team investigating economic crime produced a report at the end of September (1997), cataloguing 1,420 cases of "tunneling out" in 1996. The number of cases reached 892 in the first half of 1997.

6. According to Holle (1997), voucher privatization led to the concentration of ownership of one third of all publicly traded equity in about 15 major investment funds by March 1995.

REFERENCES

Anderson, R. W., & Kegels, C. (1998). *Transition banking: Financial development of Central and Eastern Europe*. Oxford: Clarendon Press.

Czech National Bank. (1993-1996). *Annual reports*.

Czech National Bank. (1996/1997). *Banking supervision in the Czech Republic*.

Czech National Bank. *Czech National Bank Monthly Bulletin*, various issues.

Economist Intelligence Unit. (1998). *Country report: Czech Republic*, 1st Quarter.

Federal Reserve Bank of Kansas City. (1997). *Maintaining financial stability in a global economy*. Proceedings from a Symposium at Jackson Hole, Wyoming.

Hajek, M., Izak, V., Janackova, S., Kacvinsky, P., Kotulan, A., Nachtigal, V., & Prokop, L. (1997). *Macroeconomic analysis of the czech economy: 1996*. Czech National Bank Institute of Economics Working Paper, No. 67.

International Monetary Fund. (1998). *Czech Republic, IMF staff country report No. 98/37*, April.

OECD. (1998). *OECD economic surveys: The Czech Republic*.

Holle, D. V. (1997). *Czech banks: Weighed down by debt, merrill lynch research report*. New York: Merrill Lynch Research.

Snyder, E. A., & Kormendi, R. C. (1997). Privatization and performance of the Czech Republic's Komercni Banka. *Journal of Comparative Economics*, 97-128.

Stiglitz, J. (1998). *Sound finance and sustainable development in Asia*. Keynote Address to the Asia Development Forum, March 12, on The World Bank Web Site.

COMMENT

Paul M. Horvitz

This is the first of three sessions on bank crises that George Kaufman has organized for these meetings. George has been studying and writing about banking
crises for a long time. Because George is not quite old enough to have been an
observer of the U.S. banking crises of the 1930s, his first direct experience,
like most of us, was with the thrift and banking crises of the 1980s and early
1990s. George has made significant contributions to our knowledge of banking
crises and approaches to resolving and preventing them. Those problems are
about over for the United States, though some remnants live on in the courts,
and it appeared that George would have to find a new justification for hopping
around the world from conference to conference. Just in time, however, new
crises arose, and George has arranged for us to gather here to discuss the application of what we have learned in the United States to banking crises in Eastern Europe, Latin America and, particularly East Asia. It is important to
recognize that the issue for us is not simply the Asian crises which now get
daily press coverage, but the rest of the world, as well. It is particularly appropriate at this session to have a paper on Czech banking reform, since much of
U.S. banking legislation has been inspired by the work of that great Czech
economist, Franz Kafka.

Research in Financial Services: Private and Public Policy, Volume 10, pages 71-74.
Copyright © 1998 by JAI Press Inc.
All rights of reproduction in any form reserved.
ISBN: 0-7623-0358-1

The four papers in this session are very different from one another, but all are well-aimed at the general topic of the session. They also provide an interesting illustration of the value of this type of forum for consideration of these issues. Randy Kroszner, in particular, in introducing the theme of these sessions has provided me with a great opportunity to air one of my pet peeves. His paper starts out with a basic premise that I believe is very wrong. His first paragraph says, "Economists. . . have given little attention to analyzing how to implement durable and effective banking and financial sector reform." I know that economists in the banking agencies, the Federal Reserve, the Treasury, the staff of the Congressional Committees, and the international agencies have given a great deal of attention to this problem. Even some academic economists have thought about this issue—it has been a primary focus of the work of the Shadow Financial Regulatory Committee over the last ten years, and that has been the catalyst for the recent establishment of the European Shadow Financial Regulatory Committee. The reason Professor Kroszner can make the statement he does is because he has undoubtedly done a thorough search of the professional journals and found no evidence of attention by the profession to implementation of financial reform. The journals may publish empirical or theoretical papers about financial structure or reform, but they are reluctant to publish papers dealing precisely with implementation of policy. I might note that the *Journal of Financial Services Research* does have a "Policy Section" that does publish such papers subject to a somewhat different review process. The reluctance of journals to publish such papers discourages younger scholars from devoting much of their time to policy issues, and that is a loss to the cause of developing better economic policies. In any case, the attitude of the journals makes a forum of this sort, and publication of these papers, of great value.

Part of the reason for the attitude of the professional journals is our self-perception of finance and economics as like a hard science that demands solid evidence. Much of the evidence in Kroszner's paper that attempts to explain how and why financial reform comes about is anecdotal. I think we should argue about how general or meaningful anecdotes are, and should be willing to change our minds when someone comes up with more or better anecdotes. I don't think we have to exclude anecdotes from the literature. That is the value of meetings such as this, where we can debate the meaningfulness of Kroszner's anecdotes. I think some of them are convincing, and some are not, but the views of smart observers contribute to our knowledge, and they should be aired.

We might note that the medical literature includes publication of cases of individual patients, and not just studies of large samples. As these individual cases accumulate in the literature, it may be possible to see patterns. There is value, likewise, to a discussion of an individual country's experience with financial reform, as in Tom Mondschean's paper, even if he (or we) do not attempt to draw policy conclusions from it. The same can be said of Gillian Garcia's summary of the Southeast Asia experience.

One result of a reluctance to rely on anecdotes is an attempt to turn anecdotes into real data, as is done in Gerry Caprio's paper. The numbers in that paper do not convince me that the paper is an empirical one, even a casually empirical one, rather than anecdotal. That is fine with me, because I would rather rely on an experienced observer, such as Caprio, to tell me which countries have the best banking supervisory environment in his overall judgment, than to accept numerical rankings based on rather arbitrary measures. That is, I might be able to tell you how to define better the variables you are seeking to measure, but I think we would learn more from knowing how knowledgeable observers would rank these countries in terms of their supervisory environments. Drawing judgments from Caprio's numbers, with several equally-weighted variables (admittedly arbitrary) conflicts with the conclusions that Mondschean draws from the Czech experience that corporate governance and bankruptcy law may be more important than capital requirements. Again, the environment of this meeting is conducive to appropriate discussion of these issues in a way that papers in professional journals cannot be.

There is one other point I would make about the difficulty of publishing policy-oriented papers in professional journals. Editors are appropriately skeptical of whether the policy agenda of the author is influencing the economic analysis (or interpretation of anecdotes). Economists love to draw policy implications from meager factual bases. What comes first—the economic analysis or the policy prescription? The papers we have heard raise this question. Mondschean has a brief conclusion with a few implications drawn from his positive description of the Czech experience. I am all for pointing out the evidence, but the conclusions may reflect random outcomes. For example, his conclusion that "forbearance is costly" may or may not be universally true. Similarly, his second conclusion, on voucher privatization, may reflect peculiarly Czech circumstances, so I am not convinced about the generality of the conclusion. Nevertheless, it is clearly helpful to have that experience and analysis available in the literature.

In this vein, Kroszner notes, correctly, that "Drawing normative lessons from a positive approach is always a difficult task." He proceeds to attempt that task anyway. Incidentally, I am less optimistic than he is of the contribution that economic research can make. He refers to "solid academic research," but who in the public arena makes the judgment as to what is solid academic research, particularly in the situation in which it is the interest groups that finance and, perhaps more important, publicize, the research.

To summarize this issue, I believe that the best professional journals have developed a rigid pattern of what constitutes economic research at the highest level. The second tier journals, in emulation of the best, have adopted very similar approaches. This discourages publication of case studies and non-empirical papers that focus on policy and its implementation. There is great value, then, in publications comprised of collections of papers of the sort we have heard here.

All four of these papers deal with questions of assessing or measuring the effectiveness of banking supervision. It helps to identify the crucial elements of an effective regulatory system. I have argued that there are three essentials: high capital requirements; an effective monitoring system; and an effective closure policy. Based on these papers, I would add to that list a well-defined legal system with workable provisions for foreclosures and bankruptcy.

Capital requirements need appropriate levels as well as economic measurement—that is, market value reporting rather than reliance on historical costs. An effective monitoring system means examination with the ability and willingness to find overvalued assets. If a supervisory agency has capable, well-trained personnel, but is disinclined to find overvalued assets (perhaps as in Japan), there cannot be effective supervision. The closure rule is important. Forbearance has worked sometimes, but there is no evidence that supervisors can predict when it will succeed.

The U.S. system of banking supervision now meets these requirements, but it is a difficult standard to meet. The United States met the standards only as a result of a costly financial crisis and with the passage of the Federal Deposit Insurance Corporation Improvement Act. As we attempt to assess the quality of banking supervisory systems in other countries, it is only fair to remember that FDICIA was enacted over the strenuous objections of the American regulatory establishment. The papers presented at this session are extremely helpful in making those assessments of the quality of banking supervision.

PART II

FINANCIAL FRAGILITY:
THEORIES AND EMPIRICAL EVIDENCE

Harald A. Benink

I. INTRODUCTION

Recent events of financial disorder (international debt crisis, junk bond crisis, stock market crashes, bank failures) have caused renewed interest in the subject of financial fragility. Davis (1992) defines financial fragility as a state of balance sheets offering heightened vulnerability to default in a wide variety of circumstances. Heffernan (1996) notes that this heightened probability of default implied by the term financial fragility can be used for the fragility of households, businesses, or banks themselves. However, many authors specifically use financial fragility focusing their analyses on banks.

Minsky was one of the first authors to introduce the term financial fragility. Minsky (1977) discusses financial fragility as the opposite of financial robustness. In a fragile financial system continued normal functioning can be disrupted by some not unusual event. In this sense such a fragile system is more susceptible to future outbreaks of financial disorder.

Research in Financial Services: Private and Public Policy, Volume 10, pages 77-97.

In the first part of this paper we will present an overview of the various theories of financial fragility and disorder. We will argue that the crucial difference between these theories lies in the assumed framework on risk and uncertainty. In the second part of this paper we will focus our analysis of financial fragility on the fragility of the banking system, the so-called banking fragility.

Section II presents an analysis of the use of the concepts of risk and uncertainty in economics. In section III we put the various theories of financial fragility in a risk/uncertainty framework. We first present theories of financial fragility characterized by a full understanding of risk, that is, uncertainty can be reduced to the correct and objective probability distribution. These theories, being the rational expectations and efficient markets literature and the literature on rational bubbles and runs, contain a postive view on periods of financial disorder. Basically, these periods of financial disruption are not causing serious damage to financial markets and the economy since agents are fully risk aware. In this context such periods are non-events. Section III continues by discussing other theories of financial fragility, comprised of the literature on unanticipated credit rationing, irrational bubbles and euphoria, and asymmetric information. The common element of these theories is that they all analyze a financial system characterized by an incomplete understanding of risk, thereby leaving room for uncertainty. However, they differ from each other in the way they model uncertainty. The irrational bubbles and euphoria literature is extreme in the sense that uncertainty is completely untractable and invincible. The other theories take positions somewhere in between the polar cases of uncertainty and risk.

During the 1980s and first part of the 1990s the banking sector in many countries experienced a process of rapid deregulation, increased risk taking, and major banking crises. This banking fragility will be the subject of section IV. In section V we will discuss private sector (market-based) solutions in order to cope with banking fragility. In section VI we focus on regulatory solutions. Section VII concludes the paper.

II.   RISK AND UNCERTAINTY IN ECONOMICS

With respect to the measurability of probability Knight (1921) distinguishes three types of probability:

- A priori probability.   This probability is derived mathematically. An example is the probability that a coin toss will produce a particular value.
- Statistical probability.   This probability rests on an empirical classification of instances and cannot be derived from mathematical laws or principles.
- Estimates or judgements.   The distinguishing characteristic is that there is no valid basis of any kind for classifying instances. The essential and outstanding fact is that the instance in question is so entirely unique that there

are no others or not a sufficient number to make it possible to tabulate enough like it to form a basis for any inference of value about any real probability.

The first two cases of probability are called risk by Knight. The third case embodies non-measurable probability and is referred to as (true) uncertainty. Forty years later, in 1961, Muth presented the concept of rational expectations. He postulates that economic agents form their expectations on the basis of the true structural model of the economy: Expectations, since they are informed predictions of future events, are essentially the same as the predictions of the relevant economic theory. The hypothesis of rational expectations asserts that the subjective expectations of individuals are exactly the true mathematical conditional expectations implied by the model itself.

In a rational expectations world economic agents make optimal forecasts, that is, no systematic predictions or expectations errors. Put more technically: the expectations errors conditional on the available information set have zero means and the expectations errors are uncorrelated with the values of all the variables in the information set and therefore with their own past values (Pesaran, 1987). The notion of optimal forecasts crucially depends on knowledge of the objective distribution implied by the true model, that is, uncertainty is reduced to objective risk. The optimality properties of rational expectations will follow only if agents know, or are capable of learning, the true model of the economy. Meltzer (1982) observes that the stochastic process used in standard rational expectations models misses some of the principal uncertainties that most of us face as consumers and producers.

III. FINANCIAL FRAGILITY IN A RISK/UNCERTAINTY FRAMEWORK

In this section we put the various theories of financial fragility in a risk/uncertainty framework. Attention will be paid to rational expectations and efficient markets, rational bubbles and rational runs, unanticipated credit rationing, irrational bubbles and euphoria, and to asymmetric information.

Rational Expectations and Efficient Markets

In a rational expectations world economic agents know the correct and objective probability distribution, which enables them to price correctly financial assets (efficient market hypothesis). In such a world defaults represent bad outcomes ex post, rather than systematic misperception of the true ex ante odds. Applying this reasoning to the market for junk bonds, Miller (1991) argues:

> The yields expected (in the Markowitz sense of yield outcomes weighted by probability of occurrence) on junk bonds, were below the nominal or promised yields. The high promised

yields that might be earned during the good years were understood as compensation for the possible bad years in time and bad bonds in the total junk bond portfolio. The high nominal yields, in short, were essentially risk premiums. And in 1989, for many of the junk bonds issued earlier, the risk happened.

The above world can be characterized by the existence of a stable, competitive equilibrium in which financial firms make normal profits, risks are adequately covered in loan pricing, underwriting margins and capitalization. Although the system may be subject to shocks, these do not generate systemic crises. In such an equilibrium, risk premia are sufficient to cover losses over the economic cycle. The shift to such an equilibrium from an imperfectly competitive or oligopolistic market (where insufficient credit was advanced and intermediaries gained monopoly profits) should not be a cause for vigilance, but instead a pure welfare gain (Davis, 1990). The financial innovation process of the 1970s and 1980s is viewed as very positive, since as a result of this process financial markets have become more competitive, complete, and operationally efficient (Van Horne, 1985). Miller (1986) reasons:

> By the middle and late 1960s, the recovery in world wealth (and trade) had proceeded so far that the taxes, interest rate ceilings, foreign exchange restrictions, security sales regulations, and other competitive controls slapped on in the 1930s and 1940s were becoming increasingly onerous. It was not so much that new tax and regulatory burdens were being imposed, but more that the existing burdens were increasingly binding, particularly so given the surges in the level and volatility of prices, interest rates, and exchange rates that were erupting in those years. Many of the inefficient tax and regulatory structures inherited from the 1930s and 1940s will have been driven at last from the scene along with so many of the obsolete economic and political doctrines that gave rise to them.

Although the financial innovation and deregulation process went together with a rise in debt ratios during the 1980s (see section IV), this does not necessarily imply overleveraging. The increase in the aggregate debt/equity ratio reflects, seen from a macroeconomic perspective, changing preferences of households for holding wealth (Miller, 1988). Higher debt ratios and increased financial fragility can be considered as a rational choice of risk aware agents on financial markets.

The increased financial fragility may increase the likelihood of periods of financial disorder, but it should not be considered automatically as an undesirable thing and as a rationale for increased regulation by international supervisory authorities. If risks are known and correctly priced by market participants, then these periods of financial disorder are unlucky, but calculated events.

Rational Bubbles and Rational Runs

In a world of rational expectations and efficient markets one would expect asset prices to reflect market fundamentals. However, there can be rational deviations of the price from this value. These deviations are called rational speculative bubbles (Blanchard & Watson, 1982).

Standard rational expectations models relate the price variable $p(t)$ to fundamentals $f(t)$, which are determined by a linear combination of exogenous variables (intrinsic information, that is, information incorporated in the fundamentals). The possibility of a rational bubble arises by adding the bubble term $b(t)$ to the above equation, so that $p(t) = f(t) + b(t)$. This bubble term $b(t)$ follows a stochastic time path imposed on the system. Crucial is that this bubble term is determined arbitrarily by extrinsic information (not incorporated in the market fundamentals) and refers neither directly nor indirectly to any observable phenomena (Mullineux, 1990).

According to Flood and Garber (1982) a bubble can arise when the actual market price depends positively on its own expected rate of change, as normally occurs in asset markets. Since agents forming rational expectations do not make systematic prediction errors, the positive relationship between price and its expected rate of change implies a similar relationship between price and its actual rate of change. In such conditions, the arbitrary, self-fulfilling expectations of price changes may drive actual price changes independently of market fundamentals. This movement away from market fundamentals is caused by rational speculation.

The concept of arbitrary, self-fulfilling expectations can be metaphorized by the beauty contest described by Keynes in his General Theory (1936):

> Professional investment may be likened to those newspaper competitions in which the competitors have to pick out the six prettiest faces from a hundred photographs, the prize being awarded to the competitor whose choice most nearly corresponds to the average preferences of the competitors as a whole; so that each competitor has to pick, not those faces which he himself finds prettiest, but those which he thinks likeliest to catch the fancy of the other competitors, all of whom are looking at the problem from the same point of view. It is not a case of choosing those which, to the best of one s judgement, are really the prettiest, nor even those which average opinion genuinely thinks the prettiest. We have reached the third degree where we devote our intelligences to anticipating what average opinion expects the average opinion to be. And there are some, I believe, who practice the fourth, fifth and higher degrees.

An often cited example of a bubble is the appreciation of the U.S. dollar in the 1980s (see for instance Krugman, 1985). At a certain moment many people argued that the dollar was overvalued and should decrease in value back to market fundamentals. However, the dollar appreciated even further before finally falling down. Apparently, if market participants have the arbitrary, that is, not based on market fundamentals, expectation that the dollar will further appreciate, then a rational speculator will buy dollars. Since many speculators are doing so, the arbitrary expectation will become self-fulfilling with the result of an appreciating dollar. Our rational speculator has made a profit, which he would not have made with a strategy of selling dollars based on the perception of market fundamentals. Naturally, at a certain moment in time the bubble may burst. The essential difference between a rational and an irrational speculator is that the former is living in a world of risk and is capable of calculating this probability of a bursting bubble, while the latter is not because of uncertainty.

Not only bubbles, but also runs may be seen in a rational context (Flood & Garber, 1982). A run is an event that terminates a price-fixing scheme. Some economic agents (perhaps the government) may stand ready to buy or sell a particular item at a fixed price. The viability of such a price-fixing scheme depends on the agent s maintaining a stock of the item. If other agents perceive that the price-fixing regime is temporary, that is, that the price will rise eventually, then anticipating capital gains, these agents draw down the stock that back the price-fixing scheme. If the stock is depleted entirely in one final discrete withdrawal, this event is categorized as a run.

Bank collapses can be caused by a run. A bank fixes the price of its deposits in terms of government currency. If the depositors fear a capital loss on their deposits, then they will deplete bank reserves of government currency, possibly with one final massive withdrawal, forcing the bank to cease fixing the price of its deposits.

Another example of a rational run indicated by Flood and Garber (1982) may be the currency crisis prevalent in the 1960s and early 1970s. In the case of fixed exchange rates a government announces a fixed price for its currency in terms of the currency of another country and holds foreign currency reserves of this other country. However, the government s stock of foreign currency reserves may be depleted through balance-of-payments deficits. If rational speculators can see no end to the deficits, then they anticipate the eventual demise of the fixed rate regime and may draw down government foreign exchange reserves in one final massive withdrawal—a rational run.

Reasoning from the rational framework, periods of financial disorder associated with rational (bursting) bubbles and rational runs are not undesirable events. Moreover, these so-called finance-driven events cannot be blamed for causing depressions.

On the subject of the Great Depression in the early 1930s Miller (1991) remarks:

> Contrary to wide-held folk beliefs, bankruptcies did not bring on the Great Depression. The direction of causation runs from depression to bankruptcies, not the other way around. The collapse of the stock market in 1929 and of the U.S. banking system during 1931-1932 may well have created the appearance of a finance-driven disaster. But that disaster was not just the inevitable bursting of another overleveraged tulip bubble as some have suggested. Responsibility for turning an ordinary downturn into a depression of unprecedented severity lies primarily with the managers of the Federal Reserve System.

Hamilton (1987) presents evidence for this view that the Great Depression was caused by monetary factors. At the beginning of 1928 the Federal Reserve embarked on a highly contractionary monetary policy. Two reasons motivated this policy:

> While one factor in the initial decision may well have been a desire to stem the gold outflows, this cannot explain why the U.S. continued with this tight monetary policy even after higher

interest rates were generating significant gold inflows by 1929. Instead, the major factor influencing monetary policy during 1928-1929 was surely the stock market. Despite repeated public assertions by Fed officials that the System did not regard itself as an arbiter of security prices, the consensus of most researchers who have studied Fed policy during this era is that the primary purpose of the monetary contraction was to curb the stock market boom.

In the monetary view the Fed succeeded in bringing the stock market down: in October 1929 the New York Stock Exchange collapsed. The crash was followed up by banking panics beginning in 1930. Friedman and Schwartz (1963) argue in their Monetary History that the banking panics led to a frightening away of the public from checking accounts, just as banks felt forced to increase their holdings of reserves relative to deposits. These increases in the currency-deposit ratio and reserve-deposit ratio account for the simultaneous rise in the monetary base and drop in the money supply (M1 and M2) during 1931-1933. The inability of the Federal Reserve to avert these banking panics and runs and the related drop in the money supply led to an even more severe contractionary regime compared with the period 1928-1930.

Summarizing, one could say that the monetary view of the Great Depression blames the Federal Reserve for two reasons. In the first place the monetary contraction of 1928-1929 to bring the stock market down, and in the second place the failure to prevent the banking panics and the drop in the money supply as from 1930. Miller (1991) notes that the U.S. money supply imploded by 30 percent between 1930 and 1932, dragging the economy and the price level down with it (deflation process).

Furthermore, as Bernanke (1983) argues, the deflation process may be reinforced by the fact that the banking failures undermined the ability of the financial sector to perform its intermediation services of evaluating and providing loans. More and more borrowers found credit to be expensive and difficult to obtain. The resulting credit squeeze had a negative influence on aggregate demand.

Miller (1991) sees as further confirmation of the monetary view that, because of the prompt action by the Federal Reserve to support the liquidity of the banking system after the stock market crash of October 19, 1987 (and again after the mini-crash of October 13, 1989), these crashes did not have a real impact.

Unanticipated Credit Rationing

Guttentag and Herring (1984) develop a hybrid model of financial fragility and financial disorder, applying both the concepts of risk and uncertainty. Bankers lend money to borrowers undertaking real investment projects with some probability distribution. Concerning the probability of an unfavorable outcome from this project-specific distribution, Guttentag and Herring assume that the subjective probabilities of market participants converge to the objective probabilities (rational expectations and risk in the sense of Knight). The reason for this convergence is that unfavourable outcomes are sufficiently frequent, so that participants who stubbornly cling to subjective probability distributions which differ from the objective distribution, will suffer losses and be forced to withdraw from the market.

However, nature may draw from a disastrous distribution causing an unfavorable shift in the project-specific distribution of investment returns. Guttentag and Herring refer to infrequent shocks that have less-than-catastrophic direct consequences on real economic activity, but which, if not anticipated by lenders, may have serious financial consequences that substantially exacerbate the impact of the shock on real economic activity. The state of knowledge surrounding this disastrous distribution is less complete than in the case of the project-specific distribution. There is a small but finite probability that disasters can happen. Market participants do not have a priori knowledge of the parameters of the distribution that governs whether nature draws from the disastrous distribution, nor do they have sufficient evidence to infer the parameters of the distribution from the historical record. This limited knowledge or ignorance can be qualified as true uncertainty in the sense of Knight.

Since the rational expectations and efficient market axioms do not apply in situations of uncertainty, Guttentag and Herring use the work of cognitive psychologists and decision scientists in order to formulate a hypothesis regarding the subjective probability of a disaster. This hypothesis is the disaster myopia hypothesis. It consists of two components, namely the availability heuristic and the threshold heuristic. The availability heuristic implies that estimates of frequency or probability are influenced by the ease with which instances or associations can be brought to mind. Frequent events are usually easier to recall than infrequent events. The probability of an infrequent event is likely to be underestimated, particularly as time elapses since the last occurrence of the infrequent, disastrous event. The availability heuristic argues that, with the passage of time, the subjective probability of a disaster falls until it reaches a certain threshold where it drops to zero (threshold heuristic).

The disaster myopia hypothesis predicts a tendency for subjective probabilities to fall below actual probabilities of disaster during periods in which no major shocks occur. In an expanding economy with the absence of major shocks such a process may develop. Bankers will lend to borrowers against interest rates incorporating risk premia based on the subjective probabilities being lower than the objective, but unknown probabilities of disaster. Furthermore, bankers will decline their capital positions because of the lower perceived probabilities. This process of qualitative decline in credit and capital positions makes the financial system more fragile and increases the magnitude of periods of financial disorder.

When a shock occurs, the perceived probability will jump very quickly in the direction of the objective probability. The result will be bankers reconsidering their lending portfolios: prime borrowers start paying risk premia, risky borrowers will have to pay extra risk premia or get rationed, and borrowers already rationed before the shock will be rationed extra or cut off completely from bank credit. This adaptation process towards more market-conform risk premia and a higher level of credit rationing will enable lenders to improve their capital positions. Guttentag and Herring see as relevant examples of such shocks leading to financial disorder the failure of the Herstatt Bank and the collapse of the Franklin National Bank in 1974, and the Mexican debt crisis in 1982.

Irrational Bubbles and Euphoria

The irrational bubbles and euphoria approach to financial disorder covers all the subjects of the previous subparagraphs, but interprets most of them in a different way. The heart of the argument lies in a different perception of the world: uncertainty instead of risk, which precludes the framework of rational expectations and efficient markets.

According to Minsky (1980) an economic theory that is relevant to a capitalist economy cannot evade the issues involved in unidirectional historical time by assuming recontracting and the existence of universal systems of future, or contingent, contracts. The essence of capitalism is that units have to take positions in an uncertain world.

Minsky s so-called financial instability hypothesis is grounded in an alternative interpretation of Keynes General Theory (see Minsky, 1975). The essential element of this interpretation, which is an alternative to the standard Hicks-Hansen and Klein-Patinkin view, is untractable uncertainty: agents base their portfolio decisions on a very imprecise and shaky foresight of future developments, so that unexpected behavior of the economy can lead to a large change in the relative prices of assets, which is the root of a financial crisis (Delli Gatti & Gallegati, 1995).

In the theories of Fisher and Minsky periods of financial disorder are an essential component of the turning point of the business cycle—a response to finance-driven excesses.

Fisher (1933) argues that during the upswing investment increases as well as speculation in asset markets for capital gain. The process is debt-financed, mainly by bank loans, increasing deposits, the money supply and the price level. Rising prices during the upswing reduce the real value of outstanding debt, offsetting the increase in nominal debt and encouraging further borrowing. The indebtedness of economic agents increases, and hence their chances of becoming insolvent (in modern terms we would say that financial fragility increases). However, essential is that Fisher perceives this indebtedness as an overindebtedness. Apparently, increased indebtedness is not the outcome of a rational choice reflected in risk premia. If this is the case, a financial crisis can easily develop: debtors unable to pay debts and refinance positions can be forced by creditors to liquidate assets (distress selling). If this is widespread, and in the absence of lender-of-last-resort interventions by the monetary authorities, it can trigger further crises and a deep depression (debt-deflation process). Deflation increases the real value of outstanding debt. At the same time creditors see the nominal value of collateral declining with prices. The consequence of the two phenomena is that banks start calling loans, which reinforces the process of liquidating assets. Output and employment fall until bankruptcy has eliminated overindebtedness.

Minsky (1982, 1986) further develops the concept of financial fragility in order to clarify the problem of overindebtedness. An important factor determining the degree of fragility is the changing mix of hedge, speculative and Ponzi finance during the upswing. In the case of hedge finance expected cash flows are sufficient to meet contractual payment commitments now and in the future. Speculative finance involves expected cash flows being lower than the cash payment commitments in some, typically near-term, periods. Cash flow deficiencies arise because there are commitments to pay cash on the account of principal that are greater than the receipts on principal account during these periods. Speculative financing involves the rolling over of maturing debt. Ponzi finance goes further: the amount of outstanding debt increases in some, near-term, periods in order to be able to meet cash payment commitments. Minsky s point is that during the upswing there is a shift from hedge to speculative and Ponzi finance caused by an excess demand for finance and an insufficient perception of the risks involved (euphoric expectations). As the proportion of hedge units in the population of borrowers decreases, financial fragility increases. When it becomes clear that the aggregate cash flows do not validate debt any more (for instance a stream of overextended borrowers goes bankrupt), the network of financial relations collapses and a financial crisis sets in. This is the moment that fragility translates into financial instability and that, as in Fisher's analysis, a debt-deflation process starts (see also Sijben, 1993, 1994).

Carter (1989) notes that the volatility in this boom-bust cycle depends critically on the assumption that for quite some time during the upswing lenders (and borrowers too) systematically underestimate the increase in risk as borrowers' leverage rises and as near-term debt payments balloon in relation to near-term expected income flows. If lenders smoothly raised their lending rates to compensate for increased risk because of higher corporate leverage and lower balance sheet liquidity, and if borrowers smoothly raised the risk premia they added on to borrowing rates when discounting expected cash flows from highly leveraged investment, then the growth of investment and speculative credit arrangements would be slowed.

According to Minsky, modern capitalism is prone to the recurrence of financially determined booms and busts: the financial instability hypothesis implies that instability is a systemic property of economies with complex financial structures. This instability of the financial system is caused by the fact that Minsky rejects the representative agent paradigm, in which no meaningful distinction can be drawn between banks and firms and where homogeneous agents are utility or profit maximizers in a world of certainty or certainty equivalence. Both firms and banks are conceptualized by Minsky as profit seeking agents trying to do their best in a world of untractable uncertainty (Delli Gatti & Gallegati, 1995).

Asymmetric Information

The theories discussed in the last two subsections dealt with genuine uncertainty. This uncertainty is caused by incomplete information as a result of an inability to know all of the possible states of nature or the probabilities of their occurrence. However, information can also be incomplete in the sense that it is distributed asymmetrically so that some people know more than others and can exploit this informational advantage (Hester, 1994). In this way a special type of uncertainty is created.

Akerlof (1970) argued that if one side of the market knows the quality of the good better than the other, then the number of exchanges is much lower than in a context of perfect information. Under certain circumstances there will not be a market at all. Akerlof illustrates his ideas with the market for used cars where asymmetric information exists between buyers and sellers in the sense that the seller has more information about the quality of the cars than the buyer. However, good cars and bad cars (lemons) must still sell at the same price since it is impossible for a buyer to tell the difference between a good and a bad car. Because of the uniform price for all qualities, the owners of low quality cars receive a lemon premium at the cost of those who supply high quality cars at the same price. The result is that the owners of good cars will prefer not to sell and that the market for used cars is reduced to a market on which only low quality cars are traded. Moreover, it is quite conceivable that the market for used cars ceases to exist.

The aymmetric information framework has been extended to capital markets by Stiglitz and Weiss (1981). Information asymmetries exist between borrowers and lenders (banks) causing uncertainty about the quality of borrowers. Borrowers are better informed about their own credit risk than lenders. Consequently, lenders cannot differentiate between high-risk and low-risk borrowers causing them to charge an interest rate incorporating a lemon premium: high-risk borrowers are subsidized by low-risk borrowers. This creates an incentive for low-risk borrowers to leave the market and look for alternative sources of finance such as direct external financing on the capital market. The high-risk borrowers will stay. Because of this adverse selection effect the average quality of bank loans will deteriorate, thereby increasing the vulnerability of the banking system (Sijben, 1993).

IV. BANKING FRAGILITY

In a number of recent publications the International Monetary Fund (1992a, 1992b, 1993a, 1993b) analyzes the phenomenon that during the 1980s and first part of the 1990s the banking sector in many countries experienced a process of rapid deregulation, increased risk taking, and major banking crises. The crucial question is why after a long postwar period of stability banking problems became so widespread.

Before the financial liberalization and deregulation of the 1980s cartelized banking markets, in concert with a host of regulations, served to restrict competition in the financial services industry. Banks and other financial institutions thus enjoyed a financial cushion in the form of excess profits. Government-led deregulation and liberalization, with the related market-driven financial innovation process, lowered barriers to new domestic and foreign entrants, eliminated interest rate regulations, and weakened restrictions on bank activities. The resulting new financial environment can be characterized as a process of competition-driven disintermediation from banking systems—particularly from wholesale banking systems—into securitized money and capital markets. The securitization process implies a decline in the special role of banking: the need for customers to have direct access to bank-provided liquidity has diminished because many of the larger customers now have direct access to the money and capital markets. Increased competition led both to a weakening of the profitability of banks traditional activities (price effect) and to a shift of many of the larger clients to direct finance on the money and capital markets (quantity effect). Both effects weakened the traditional sources of banks income.

Faced with a potential downsizing of their operations, many banks responded to this new, less friendly environment by increasing the riskiness of their portfolios. This behavioral response of increased risk taking has been modelled in the theoretical literature. Park (1994), analyzing how deregulation increased the riskiness of U.S. banks in the 1980s, divides the literature into two main parts: the literature emphasizing the moral hazard of bank stockholders and the literature focusing on the incentives of bank managers. Both explanations are probably relevant and mutually reinforcing.

Proponents of the moral hazard view (Marcus, 1984; Keeley, 1990) argue that banks had increased incentives to take risk in the 1980s for two main reasons: losses that impaired capital and reduced charter values due to greater competition. Lower capital reduces the exposure of stockholders and, thereby, their concern about probable losses resulting from increased risk taking. In addition to tangible capital, firms have charter values, which may be defined as the economic value deriving from the opportunity to do business in the future.

Keeley (1990) analyzes under a *fixed-rate* deposit insurance system the influence of increased competition on bank charter values, risk taking and capital ratios. Following Merton (1977) he views deposit insurance as a put option on the value of a bank s assets at a strike price equal to the promised maturity value of its debt. In the case of no banking regulation, banks seeking to maximize the value of their equity will maximize the value of the put by increasing asset risk and/or minimizing invested capital relative to assets. At the same time, however, regulation limits competition which endowes banks with market power and makes bank charters valuable. In this way the potential loss of a charter in the event of bankruptcy can counterbalance the incentive for excessive risk taking due to fixed-rate deposit insurance. Deregulation changes the subtle balance between these two effects.

Because deregulation increases competition, bank charter values will decline and, consequently, banks reach earlier the point that increased risk taking becomes attractive: the expected gain to bank stockholders of the enhanced value of the deposit insurance put option exceeds the expected loss of the charter value.

Keeley's argument starts from the assumption of a fixed-rate deposit insurance which implies that increased risk taking does not lead to higher deposit insurance premiums that banks have to pay to the deposit insurance fund. In the case of risk-based deposit insurance premiums the incentive effect for increased risk taking would be mitigated because of the fact that higher expected returns in that case would have to be adjusted for the higher deposit insurance premiums.

The literature on the incentives of managers focuses on the possibility that bank managers have an incentive to take excessive risk when they are incompetent and profits are declining (Gorton & Rosen, 1992). Until the early 1980s banking was a tightly regulated industry in which incompetent managers were able to make sufficient profits without taking excessive risk. Deregulation increased competition and decreased profitability in the 1980s. This made managerial ability more important. For incompetent managers not being able to prove their ability in the new competitive environment, taking excessive risk may have been a rational strategy for the sake of survival.

The IMF mentions several dimensions in which the increased tolerance for risk showed up. The first dimension is the rapid expansion of bank balance sheets in many countries, particularly in the countries that were highly regulated until the first part of the 1980s. Bank lending as a percentage of GDP expanded in Japan from 61 to 94 percent between 1980 and 1990; in Norway from 64 to 85 percent between 1983 and 1986; in Sweden from 43 to 68 percent from 1986 to 1990; in Finland from 55 to 76 percent between 1986 and 1990; and in the U.S. from 30 to 34 percent between 1984 and 1986. The expansion in credit was generally accommodated during the 1980s by the monetary authorities. The huge credit expansion led to an acceleration of prices in asset markets, concentrated in the residential and commercial real estate markets. The result was a growing concentration of bank lending in the real estate sector. Another dimension of increased risk taking is that, because of the decline of their traditional business, banks increased the share of their assets held in highly leveraged transactions, leveraged buyouts, developing country debt, and off-balance-sheet derivative products.

The higher risk business made banks more vulnerable to cyclical developments, particularly asset price adjustments. In the late 1980s and early 1990s the increased risks were exposed and turned into bank losses by a significant shift in economic conditions—whether a tightening of monetary policy, a large sectoral shock, a decline in asset prices, a prolonged period of slow economic activity, or a combination of these factors. Major banking crises of unprecedented scale since the Great Depression of the 1930s took place in the United States, Norway, Sweden, Finland, and Japan.

In its 1991/1992 annual report the Bank for International Settlements (BIS, 1992) evaluates deregulation and financial innovation. The BIS notes that there is a widespread perception that deregulation and financial innovation have gone hand in hand with greater financial instability, be it in the form of excessive fluctuations in asset prices or distress among financial institutions. According to the BIS, with hindsight, it is clear that the observed instability has involved an element of collective bad judgement. For instance, the real estate lending crisis resulted from misplaced optimism regarding property values and hence the soundness of collateral. Furthermore, the BIS states:

> Moreover, the general euphoria which underlay many of these excesses was in part a by-product of the vigorous and long-lasting economic expansion of the 1980s. At the same time, the changes in the financial environment helped to make such collective errors of judgement more likely and their implications more serious and widespread internationally.

With its view that the banking crises involved an element of collective bad judgement, the BIS takes the position that financial markets cannot be characterized by fully risk aware agents. Bringing back into mind our discussion in section III of the various theories of financial fragility in a risk/uncertainty framework, this implies that the BIS identifies itself with the theories analyzing a financial system characterized by an incomplete understanding of risk, thereby leaving room for uncertainty.

V. BANKING FRAGILITY: PRIVATE SECTOR SOLUTIONS

In the previous section we discussed recent episodes of banking fragility. In order to cope with this banking fragility, we can distinguish between private sector (market-based) solutions and regulatory solutions. This section focuses on private sector solutions and section VI on regulatory solutions.

Horvitz (1995) notes that: the invisible hand that most economists believe in is not inconsistent with financial fragility. Most economists do have a strong preference for market solutions, though attitudes differ. The extreme view would be a belief in market efficiency and stability to the extent that we need to do nothing more to deal with the potential problem of financial fragility than rely on market forces (see also our discussion in section III on risk and uncertainty). A notable proponent of such a view is Schwartz (1995) by making the following statement:

> I believe instability of the financial services industry is attributable to destabilizing actions of monetary authorities and regulators; that the financial services industry is not inherently unstable; that the distress and failure of individual financial firms, whether owing to poor management or bad luck, is no threat to the system as a whole; that declines in asset prices indicate wealth losses, not financial crises; that a genuine financial crisis occurs only when the payments system is impaired.

Moreover, Schwartz states that there has been no genuine financial crisis during the past 15 years in the United States or globally despite stock market crashes, wide swings in prices of real estate, distress affecting individual commercial banks or banking systems, collapse of the U.S. savings and loans, failure of BCCI and the Maxwell conglomerate, and distressed insurance companies.

Horvitz (1995) notes that, even if the extreme view is rejected, the preference among most economists is for private sector solutions that minimize regulatory interference with the market and maximize so-called market discipline.

Bruni and Paternò (1995) hold the view that private sector and regulatory solutions to the problem of financial fragility are deeply connected. To some extent market discipline can replace government supervision and regulation but, according to Bruni and Paternò, the main influence of market forces is to complement the efforts of supervisors and regulators: an adequate regulatory setting is needed for market disciplining mechanisms to be effective.

Market discipline means that financial markets provide signals that lead borrowers to behave in a manner consistent with their solvency. It implies that borrowers are led to pursue sustainable policies. Effective market discipline requires that capital markets be open, that information on the borrowers' xisting liabilities be readily available, that no bailout be anticipated, and that the borrowers respond to market signals (Lane, 1993).

In a situation of enhanced market discipline as a device for coping with banking fragility, banks will be under pressure to provide appropriate external disclosure on their various risk exposures and on the way they handle these risks. A professionalization of banks internal risk management and control systems will be the result (Taylor, 1995).

Referring to Citibank's internal risk management and control systems with respect to derivatives trading, Ruding (1995) remarks that these systems include independent risk managers overseeing all trading businessses; marking the derivatives portfolio to market on a daily basis; placing strict potential loss limitations on derivatives business relative to forecasted revenues; employing independent audit and operational control units; utilizing rigorous qualification standards with potential derivatives customers; and putting into place comprehensive tracking and record-keeping functions.

VI. BANKING FRAGILITY: REGULATORY SOLUTIONS

Financial markets are characterized by informational asymmetries and frictions, thereby creating a role for financial intermediaries such as banks. At the same time, however, these informational uncertainties also generate potential instability in the form of unanticipated deposit withdrawals and premature asset liquidations. Therefore, deposit-funded banks are vulnerable to runs, and the entire banking system may be vulnerable to panics. Many banking regulations, such as a lender of last resort facility and/or deposit insurance, can then be understood as measures to reduce this form of instability (Bhattacharya & Thakor, 1993).

However, these regulatory interventions create problems of their own. In section II, following the argument made by Merton (1977), we observed that fixed-rate deposit insurance is a put option which encourages excessive risk taking. This then necessitates a regulatory response. As Merton and Bodie (1992) note, this response may include monitoring, risk-based deposit insurance premiums, cash/ asset reserve and capital requirements, portfolio restrictions, and limits on discount window borrowing.

Government regulation with respect to banking fragility aims at preventing two types of bank failures. First, the failures of individual banks, especially when these banks are large and perceived to be too big to fail. Second, and more importantly, the focus is on the prevention of individual bank failures causing other banks to fail, thereby creating a collapse of the banking and financial system (systemic failure) that spreads to the real sector of the economy (Horvitz, 1995). This aspect of regulation pursues the achievement of systemic stability.

Most of the banking crises during the 1980s and first part of the 1990s were related to credit risk, being the risk that a counterparty defaults on its position. One of the ways international regulators try to prevent new credit risk related banking problems is by strengthening credit risk solvency requirements. Within the context of the Bank for International Settlements the Basle Committee on Banking Regulations and Supervisory Practices reached in December 1987 an agreement which was published in its final form in July 1988 (Basle Committee, 1988). The agreement implies a strengthening and harmonization of solveny requirements for most banks in the industrialized countries. The harmonization comes down to the relating of uniformly defined own funds through uniform solvency ratios, to the uniformly defined risk-weighted value of assets and off-balance-sheet activities. The 1988 Basle Accord was implemented at the end of 1992.

Another way of preventing new banking problems is to set up a clear regulatory rule for closing an institution whose problems cannot be resolved before it becomes insolvent. If it is decided to let a bank with insufficient capital continue to operate in the hope that it may earn its way out of predicament, then regulatory scrutiny of its activities should be increased (IMF, 1995a). In the United States the Federal Deposit Insurance Corporation Improvement Act (FDICIA) of 1991 puts into place a system of prompt corrective action and is based, among others, on what Benston and Kaufman call structured early intervention and resolution. FDICIA strengthens the ability of regulatory agencies to take early action with respect to banks whose capital ratios are declining.

During the 1980s, with the rapid development of securities and derivative markets as well as foreign exchange contracts, banks have become much more exposed to market risk (IMF, 1995b). Market risk can be defined as the potential loss due to unexpected general market price and interest rate changes. In order to introduce capital requirements for market risk, in April 1995 the Basle Committee announced a new proposal. The proposal allows banks to use their own internal risk management models to estimate the so-called value-at-risk which is at the heart of determining the market risk capital requirements. Value-at-risk is an estimate of the maximum loss that a portfolio could generate with a given level of confidence and during a given period into the future. After a consultative phase with the international banking community the proposal was implemented in January 1998.

VII. CONCLUSION

Corrigan (1990) summarizes the trade-off between efficiency and stability as follows:

> The globalization, innovativeness, and deregulation of financial markets have proven to be very much a two-edged sword. On the one hand, there is little doubt that these developments have expanded the choices for savers and investors, reduced the cost of financial transactions, and improved the allocation of saving and investment nationally and internationally. But, and this is a very large but, there is also no doubt—at least in my mind—that these same forces have also increased volatility in financial markets and introduced new and highly complex elements of risk—possibly even increasing systemic risk.

The central argument of this paper is that globalization of financial markets, financial innovation and financial deregulation can work out in three ways (see also Sijben, 1995):

- Imperfectly competitive or oligopolistic financial markets are opened to the forces of national and international competition and are becoming more operationally efficient, thereby generating welfare gains.
- The innovation process may increase debt ratios and volatility in asset prices and as a result financial fragility in the sense of vulnerability of the financial system to future outbreaks of financial disorder. If, however, the risks involved are known and correctly priced by market participants, then these periods of financial disorder are unlucky, but calculated events. Increased financial fragility may lead to more frequent periods of financial disorder without causing serious damage to the functioning of financial markets and the economy.
- If increased financial innovation and financial fragility go together with a lack of understanding of the risks involved, then underpricing and lack of risk awareness by financial agents will aggravate the consequences of a period of financial disorder: not fully calculated events may trigger shifts in confidence, affecting markets more than appears warranted by their significance and leading to a financial crisis.

This paper first presented theories of financial fragility characterized by a full understanding of risk, that is, uncertainty can be reduced to the correct and objective probability distribution. These theories, being the rational expectations and efficient markets literature and the literature on rational bubbles and runs, contain a postive view on periods of financial disorder. Basically, these periods of financial disruption are not causing serious damage to financial markets and the economy since agents are fully risk aware. In this context such periods are non-events. The paper continued by discussing other theories of financial fragility, comprised of the literature on unanticipated credit rationing, irrational bubbles and euphoria, and asymmetric information. The common element of these theories is that they all analyze a financial system characterized by an incomplete understanding of risk, thereby leaving room for uncertainty. However, they differ from each other in the way they model uncertainty. The irrational bubbles and euphoria literature is extreme in the sense that uncertainty is completely untractable and invincible. The other theories take positions somewhere in between the polar cases of uncertainty and risk.

Taking into account the remarks made above, the financial fragility debate boils down to the debate on risk and uncertainty (see also Benink, 1993). Based upon their subjective perception of the applicability of risk, uncertainty, or something in between, academics, regulators, and practitioners will come to different conclusions with respect to the functioning of financial markets and the desirability of regulation. Recently, two well known regulators delivering speeches at the same conference, reached different conclusions with respect to the potential dangers of derivatives. Jordan (1995), president of the Federal Reserve Bank of Cleveland and member of the U.S. Federal Open Market Committee, stated:

> The point is that there seems to be no reason to believe that the potential externality of increasingly complex financial relationships has outdistanced an increasingly powerful ability to internalize that potential externality. As long as economic agents are able to estimate compound probabilities of failures, systemic risk is indistinguishable from normal credit risk. Knowing your counterparty and your counterparty s counterparties, and even your counterparty's counterparties counterparties, should lead to quality spreads in market prices, to prudent loan loss reserves and capital from which to absorb losses, and to equality of the private and social cost of risk.

During the same conference Crockett (1995), general manager of the Bank for International Settlements, came to the following conclusion:

> The ability of some derivative products to significantly increase the leverage of market participants may increase aggregate uncertainty. I would also conjecture that because of the fundamental lack of transparency of some financial products and the difficulty of evaluating risk associated with them, the resulting concentration in some derivatives markets creates uncertainty externalities in other closely related markets. As a result of the close cross-market linkages, the uncertainty externalities cannot easily be segmented in periods of market volatility and stress. As participants seek to shield themselves against the impact of an event whose timing or probability of occurrence cannot be estimated, markets may at times experience an erosion of liquidity possibly leading to difficulties in other markets.

Davis (1989) calls for a synthesis of the different theories of financial fragility. Financial markets are probably more rational than they sometimes appear. However, a fundamental uncertainty will always be prevalent, casting doubts on the indiscriminate use of superrationality as the foundation for models of financial behavior (Modigliani, 1988). This spirit is well expressed by Corrigan (1990):

> The first lesson of the 1980s could probably apply to almost any decade but may be especially relevant for the 1980s and that is the utmost need to be cautious about the extremes of economic doctrine and theory. Indeed, whether we are speaking of the Keynesian, the monetarist, the supply sider, the rational expectationalist, or any other school of thought, single-minded approaches to public policy can be very misleading, if not dangerous.

REFERENCES

Akerlof, G. A. (1970). The market for lemons: Quality uncertainty and the market mechanism. *Quarterly Journal of Economics, 85*, 488-500.

Bank for International Settlements. (1992). Structural aspects of financial markets and prudential supervision. *62nd Annual Report*, Basle.

Basle Committee. (1988). *International convergence of capital measurement and capital standards.* Basle: Bank for International Settlements.

Benink, H.A. (1993). Theories of financial fragility. *Giornale degli Economisti e Annali di Economia, LI*, 539-549.

Bernanke, B.S. (1983). Nonmonetary effects of the financial crisis in the propagation of the great depression. *American Economic Review, 73*, 257-276.

Bhattacharya, S., & Thakor, A.V. (YEAR). Contemporary banking theory. *Journal of Financial Intermediation, 3*, 2-50.

Blanchard, O. J., & Watson, M. W. (1982). Bubbles, rational expectations, and financial markets. In P.L. Wachtel (ed.), *Crises in the economic and financial structure* (pp. 295-315). Lexington, MA: Lexington Books.

Bruni, F., & Paternò, F. (1995). Market discipline of banks riskiness: A study of selected issues. *Journal of Financial Services Research, 9*, 303-325.

Carter, M. (1989). Financial innovation and financial fragility. *Journal of Economic Issues, 23*, 779-793.

Corrigan, E. G. (1990). Reflections on the 1980s. *Seventy-Fifth Annual Report.* New York: Federal Reserve Bank of New York.

Crockett, A.D. (1995). Financial fragility: Sources, prevention, and treatment. In H.A. Benink (ed.), *Coping with financial fragility and systemic risk.* Boston: Kluwer Academic Publishers.

Davis, E.P. (1989). *Instability in the euromarkets and the economic theory of financial crisis.* Discussion Paper, Bank of England, London.

Davis, E.P. (1990). *An industrial approach to financial instability.* Discussion Paper, Bank of England, London.

Davis, E.P. (1992). *Debt, financial fragility, and systemic risk.* Oxford: Oxford University Press.

Fisher, I. (1933). The debt deflation theory of great depressions. *Econometrica, 1*, 337-357.

Flood, R.P., & Garber, P. M. (1982). Bubbles, runs, and gold monetization. In P.L. Wachtel (ed.), *Crises in the economic and financial structure* (pp. 275-293). Lexington, MA: Lexington Books.

Friedman, M., & Schwartz, A. J. (1963). *A monetary history of the United States, 1867-1960.* Princeton, NJ: Princeton University Press.

Gatti, D., & Gallegati, M. (1995). Financial fragility and economic fluctuations: Keynesian views. *Economic Notes, 24*, 513-554.

Gorton, G., & Rosen, R. (1992). *Corporate control: Portfolio choice, and the decline of banking.* Finance and economic Discussion Paper, Federal Reserve Board, Washington DC.

Guttentag, J.M., & Herring, R.J. (1984). Credit rationing and financial disorder. *Journal of Finance, 39,* 1359-1382.

Hamilton, J.D. (1987). Monetary factors in the great depression. *Journal of Monetary Economics, 19,* 145-169.

Heffernan, S. (1996). *Modern banking in theory and practice.* Cichester: John Wiley & Sons.

Hester, D.D. (1994). On the theory of financial intermediation. *De Economist, 142,* 133-149.

Horne, van J.C. (1985). Of financial innovations and excesses. *Journal of Finance, 40,* 621-631.

Horvitz, P.M. (1995). Banking regulation as a solution to financial fragility. *Journal of Financial Services Research, 9,* 369-380.

International Monetary Fund. (1992a). Structural changes and related policy issues in financial markets. *World Economic and Financial Surveys.* Washington DC, September.

International Monetary Fund. (1992b). Asset price deflation, balance sheet adjustment, and financial fragility. *World Economic and Financial Surveys.* Washington DC, October.

International Monetary Fund. (1993a). Deterioration of bank balance sheets. *World Economic and Financial Surveys.* Washington DC, August.

International Monetary Fund. (1993b). Booms and bust in asset markets in the 1980s: Causes and consequences. *World Economic and Financial Surveys,* Washington DC, December.

International Monetary Fund. (1995a). Financial supervisory and regulatory issues. *World Economic and Financial Surveys,* Washington DC, August.

International Monetary Fund. (1995b). Capital adequacy and internal risk management. *World Economic and Financial Surveys,* Washington DC, August.

Jordan, J.L. (1995). Supervision of derivative instruments. In H.A. Benink (Ed.), *Coping with financial fragility and systemic risk* (pp. 239-250). Boston: Kluwer Academic Publishers.

Keeley, M. (1990). Deposit insurance. Risk and market power in banking. *American Economic Review, 80,* 1183-1200.

Keynes, J.M. (1936). *The general theory of employment: Interest and money. Cambridge*: Cambridge University Press.

Knight, F.K. (1921). *Risk, uncertainty and profit.* Chicago: University of Chicago Press.

Krugman, P. R. (1985). Is the strong dollar sustainable. In *The U.S. dollar—recent developments, outlook, and policy options.* Kansas City: Federal Reserve Bank of Kansas City.

Lane, T.D. (1993). Market discipline. *IMF Staff Papers, 40,* 53-88.

Marcus, A.J. (1984). Deregulation and bank financial policy. *Journal of Banking and Finance, 8,* 557-565.

Meltzer, A.H. (1982). Rational expectations, risk, uncertainty and market responses. In P.L. Wachtel (Ed.), *Crises in the economic and financial structure* (pp. 3-22). Lexington, MA: Lexington Books.

Merton, R.C. (1977). An analytic derivation of the cost of deposit insurance and loan guarantees. *Journal of Banking and Finance, 1,* 3-11.

Merton, R.C., & Bodie, Z. (1992). On the management of financial guarantees. *Financial Management,* pp. 87-109.

Miller, M.H. (1986). Financial innovation: The last twenty years and the next. *Journal of Financial and Quantitative Analysis, 21,* 459-471.

Miller, M.H. (1988). The Modigliani-Miller propositions after thirty years. *Journal of Economic Perspectives, 2,* 99-120.

Miller, M.H. (1991). Leverage. *Journal of Finance, 46,* 479-488.

Minsky, H.P. (1975). *John Maynard Keynes.* New York: Columbia University Press.

Minsky, H.P. (1977). A theory of systemic fragility. In E.I. Altman & A.W. Sametz (Eds.), *Financial crises: Institutions and markets in a fragile environment* (pp. 138-152). New York: John Wiley & Sons.

Minsky, H.P. (1980). Capitalist financial processes and the instability of capitalism. *Journal of Economic Issues, 14,* 505-523.

Minsky, H.P. (1982). *Inflation, recession and economic policy.* Armonk, NY: M.E. Sharpe.

Minsky, H.P. (1986). *Stabilizing an unstable economy.* New Haven, CT: Yale University Press.

Modigliani, F. (1988). MM—Past, present, future. *Journal of Economic Perspectives, 2,* 149-158.

Mullineux, A.W. (1990). *Business cycles & financial crises.* Hemel Hempstead: Harvester Wheatsheaf.

Muth, J.F. (1961). Rational Expectations and the Theory of Price Movements. *Econometrica, 29,* 315-335.

Park, S. (1994). Explanations for the increased riskiness of banks in the 1980s. In *Economic review* (pp. 3-23). St. Louis, MO: Federal Reserve Bank of St. Louis.

Pesaran, M.H. (1987). *The limits to rational expectations.* Oxford: Basil Blackwell.

Ruding, H.O. (1995). Fragility in the banking world. In H.A. Benink (Ed.), *Coping with financial fragility and systemic risk* (pp. 279-285). Boston: Kluwer Academic Publishers.

Schwartz, A.J. (1995). Coping with financial fragility: A global perspective. In H.A. Benink (Ed.), *Coping with financial fragility and systemic risk* (pp. 251-257). Boston: Kluwer Academic Publishers.

Stiglitz, J.E., & Weiss, A. (1981). Credit rationing in markets with imperfect information. *American Economic Review, 71,* 393-410.

Sijben, J.J. (1993). Credit markets, financial fragility, and the real economy. *Kredit und Kapital, 26,* 481-515.

Sijben, J.J. (1994). Financial fragility and macroeconomic performance: An overview. In D.E. Fair, & Raymond, R.J. (Eds.), *The competitiveness of financial institutions and centres in Europe* (pp. 353-379). Boston: Kluwer Academic Publishers.

Sijben, J.J. (1995). Comment on Minsky and Calomiris. *Journal of Financial Services Research, 9,* 291-297.

Taylor, C.R. (1995). Global financial fragility and the private sector. *Journal of Financial Services Research, 9,* 363-368.

KOREA AND JAPAN:
THE END OF THE "JAPANESE FINANCIAL REGIME"

Thomas F. Cargill

I. INTRODUCTION

The economic reversal in Asia has elevated Paul Krugman's 1994 analysis and prognosis for this region of the world economy published in *Foreign Affairs*. Krugman argued Asia's "miracle" of rapid real GDP growth over the past several decades was primarily the result of labor and capital accumulation (high saving rate) rather than efficiency or technological progress; that is, Asia's miracle was one of "perspiration" rather than "inspiration." He further argued Asia's rapid growth would eventually end because of diminishing returns. To avoid stagnation Asian economies at that point would need to reform their institutions to reduce reliance on government managed growth policies and place greater emphasize on open and competitive markets.

The Asian economies are now experiencing slow or negative real economic growth, deterioration of their financial systems, and in a number of cases, capital flight and currency depreciation. Korea and Japan are the most important concerns in the region given their size and relationship to world trade and in the case of Japan, to world finance. Japan was the first to show signs of slower growth when

Research in Financial Services: Private and Public Policy, Volume 10, pages 99-113.
Copyright © 1998 by JAI Press Inc.
All rights of reproduction in any form reserved.
ISBN: 0-7623-0358-1

it officially reached a peak in economic activity in February 1991. Since 1991 Japanese real economic growth has been virtually flat with predictions of negative growth for 1998 despite a series of "Big Bang" financial reforms, a series of fiscal stimulus packages since late 1997, and a Bank of Japan discount rate of 0.5 percent since September 1995.

Korea continued to grow at rapid rates in the early 1990s, but slower growth in 1996 deteriorated to negative growth in 1998. Korea was forced in late 1997 to secure a $58 billion bailout from the International Monetary Fund to remain solvent and meet short term debts, the largest bailout to a single country in the Fund's history.

The economic declines in Korea and Japan are quantitatively and qualitatively different than anything experienced in either country's history since the early 1950s. Each has been forced either internally (Japan) or externally (Korea) to consider fundamental structural reform, some of which is in the implementation stage. While both economies will require wide ranging structural changes, much of the immediate focal point of attention is directed toward the financial system.

Three considerations underlay the concern with the financial system. First, the financial deterioration needs to be reversed to restore international confidence in the won and yen. Second, structural reforms need to be made to render financial institutions and markets more efficient and transparent in the evaluation and monitoring of credit risk. Third, aside from structural reforms, policy officials need to adopt a new policy attitude that clearly rejects managed approaches in favor of market approaches to economic organization in order to secure international confidence in Korea and Japan's ability to reverse the current crisis.

Krugman's provocative paper is a useful starting point for two reasons to discuss the financial regimes Korea and Japan employed to support postwar[1] economic growth and why those regimes are no longer relevant in the current environment. Neither reason, however, has anything to do with Krugman's ability to forecast[2] the current crisis. First, the narrow set of circumstances that permitted Korea and Japan to grow rapidly in the past were not likely to continue and as such, rapid growth was not sustainable and second, the slow down in economic growth exposed the fundamental weaknesses of their financial infrastructures which in turn, fed back onto real economic activity in an adverse manner.

These issues are especially relevant to the financial systems of Asian economies and especially Korea, which are based on the Japanese model or what can be referred to as the "Japanese financial regime." The financial regime began during the Mejii Restoration in 1868 and slowly evolved over the next 80 years to a form substantially different than the financial systems of western economies. The regime in Japan and as adopted by Korea and other Asian economies in the postwar period provided a sufficient financial infrastructure as long as a special set of circumstances were maintained. These included: restraint of market forces, limited number of financial channels between surplus and deficit units, international economic and financial isolation, export oriented growth, and rapid real GDP growth that made it politically possible to achieve consensus among different sectors and avoided any serious test of the stability of the financial infrastructure. The problem was that these circumstances could not be maintained in the new economic, financial, political, and technological environment that emerged in the 1970s. These financial structures were fundamentally incompatible with market forces and internationalization of finance because of their pervasive moral hazard, lack of transparency, and mutual support between financial institutions, regulatory authorities, and politicians sometimes referred to as the "iron triangle" in Japan.

The remainder of the paper is composed of five sections. Section II briefly compares and contrasts the economies of Korea and Japan and rationalizes the need to focus on these two Asian economies. Section III discusses the characteristics of the Japanese financial regime and compares and contrasts the regime as it evolved in postwar Korea. Section IV discusses the growing incompatibility of the regime with the new economic, financial, and political environment that began to emerge in the 1970s and the missed opportunities for Korea and Japan to modify the regime. Section V discusses the policy reactions in Korea and Japan to the failures of the financial regime. A short concluding section ends the paper.

II. KOREA AND JAPAN

Korea and Japan share important economic, institutional, and historical relationships (Cargill, 1990, 1993a). They are close in geography with important bilateral trade and financial relationships as well as share a common cultural origin, though cultural similarities between Koreans and Japanese are frequently exaggerated. Korean economic institutions bear a close relationship to Japanese institutions for two reasons: first, Japan dominated Korea militarily, politically, and economically from 1910 to 1945 leaving Korea with a set of institutions that were more Japanese than Korean and second, Japan's success in the 1950s and 1960s provided a successful model for Korea to base its own growth and postwar aspirations.

Korea and Japan exhibited impressive economic growth records in the postwar period, though Japan's growth record has been more stable and less inflationary. Korea was widely regarded as Asia's next economic giant (Amsden, 1989) to follow Japan (Patrick & Rosovsky, 1976). Korea's membership in OECD in 1995 was viewed as the turning point for Korea.

Korea and Japan relied on the same fundamentals for economic growth in addition to a common real and financial infrastructure such as a strong work ethic, educated work force, reliance on external sources of raw materials, high investment and saving-GDP ratios, and a policy attitude that restrained market forces.

The external environment that made it possible for these two rigidly regulated and administratively controlled economies to function began to change in the 1970s for Japan and in the 1980s for Korea. In particular, both financial structures came under pressure to relax constraints on competition and to permit more interaction between domestic and international financial forces. Japan initiated a financial liberalization process in the second half of the 1970s while Korea initiated a similar process in the early 1980s. Neither Korea or Japan, however, fully understood the conflicts between the newly emerging market forces and the basic elements of the old financial regime. Despite the rhetoric of liberalization that emerged from policy discussions in both countries, neither country appreciated the importance of moral hazard problems of deposit guarantees nor the problems that would be generated by a policy of delay in dealing with troubled financial institutions.

There are three reasons why Korea and Japan are worth consideration in the current economic and financial crisis in Asia.

First and most obvious, their size and importance in the world economy. Korea and Japan are the eleventh and second largest economies in the world, respectively. Japan is the largest creditor nation in the world. Both have pursued export oriented approaches to economic development which in the past have generated intense opposition from both the United States and Europe. Recent depreciation of the won and yen is likely to enhance trade frictions.

Second, their postwar economic achievements have been suggested as evidence open and competitive markets are not a necessary condition for sustained economic growth. While liberalization of markets might be suitable for western economies, Asian culture and history are more compatible with less market oriented systems. To a number of Asian economies, Korea and Japan provided evidence that liberalization may not be the most appropriate policy for developing economies. This view was also shared by many Korean and Japanese officials in the 1980s and early 1990s. Much rhetoric in favor of liberalization has been offered in both Korea and Japan in the past; however, the reality is that the process has been slow and reluctant. This is especially true with respect to financial liberalization.

Despite over two decades of financial liberalization effort in Japan and in Korea, a little over a decade of effort, their financial structures and policy attitudes have not changed as much as one would have judged from the series of reform plans, "Big Bang" announcements, and legislative changes in both countries. This is not to deny substantial progress has been made in each country when the present is viewed in the context of the pre-liberalization financial structures. Unfortunately, fundamental elements of the pre-liberalization financial regime remain in place and have limited the ability and willingness of the authorities to deal with the current problems.

Third, Korea and Japan provide case studies to shed light on what has been an apparent contradiction to those who support open and competitive financial markets. The correlation between financial liberalization and banking problems experienced in Korea and Japan as well as in many other countries has led some to argue liberalization itself is the source of the problem. This view has unfortunate policy implications because it suggests an argument for slowing down liberalization and perhaps even reversing the process. To illustrate, one of the reactions to the capital flight and currency depreciation in Asian economies at the end of 1997 was a call for a Tobin-tax on exchange rate transactions to "tone down market forces."

The correlation between banking problems and liberalization in the past decade is obvious. The causation, however, is not from liberalization to banking problems, but from the *process* of liberalization to banking problems. In particular, the failure of governments to modify their extensive deposit guarantees[3] in the face of increased ability to manage and assume risk by the private market has been a fundamental source of many of the banking problems experienced in the past decade. Certainly other factors play a role such as the collapse of the bubble economy in Japan and the extensive credit allocation and micro management policies of the Korean government, but once financial problems emerge, the moral hazard inherent in deposit guarantees and the agency problems in administering the guarantees amplifies the problem.

III. THE JAPANESE FINANCIAL REGIME AND KOREA'S MODIFICATIONS

The Japanese financial regime that played a role in Japan's postwar expansion and served as a model for the rest of Asia first emerged after the Mejii Restoration in 1868. The Mejii Restoration represents a turning point in Japan's history.[4] Perceived and real threats from the western powers, especially the United States, generated an intense debate within Japan as whether to abandon the policy of isolation and open the economy to western technology. The anti-isolation forces carried the debate and argued that Japan needed to become an industrial and military power.

To accomplish this goal, Japan became more receptive to western technology and influence. A series of policies were then enacted that transformed Japan from an agricultural feudal to an industrial society in slightly less than three decades.

As part of this transformation the financial regime that came to characterize postwar Japan emerged with the establishment of a national banking system in 1872, the Bank of Japan in 1882, and a postal savings system in 1875. The financial system was further influenced by banking problems in the wake of the 1923 Tokyo earthquake which led to an expansion of government regulation and consolidation of the banking system. Mobilization for war in the 1930s and wartime finance further influenced the financial structure. Thus, the financial regime that emerged in postwar Japan with only a few exceptions represented a continuation of pre-war trends and not the influence of the Allied Occupation as is sometimes maintained.

The basic elements of the Japanese financial model can be characterized by the following points presented in Cargill (1998):

1. The financial system is viewed as an instrument of industrial policy.
2. The financial system is designed to transfer the majority of funds from surplus to deficit units through intermediation markets, especially banking channels.
3. Highly leverage nonfinancial businesses dominated by large business groups are the primary recipient of bank finance. Smaller business firms obtain credit from small banks, other types of institutions, or unofficial markets. Households as a demander of funds are largely excluded from the financial system.
4. Government financial institutions are used to satisfy infrastructural needs for credit as well as placate politically favored sectors of the economy.
5. Foreign financial institutions are prohibited or restricted to limited participation in the financial system.
6. Government credit allocation policies including extensive interest rate controls to maintain a low cost of capital play a major role in allocating funds through intermediation markets.
7. Financial regulation and supervision are designed with opaqueness and non-transparency in mind to provide an more conducive environment for political favors and concessions to be struck between politicians, government bureaucrats, and the business sector.
8. The central bank lacks independence and serves as an agent of the government to provide high powered money to the banking system.
9. Pervasive system of deposit guarantees are maintained through the discount window of the central bank.
10. A policy of "no failures of financial institutions or markets" supported by opaque financial regulation, supervision, and central bank policy.
11. Reliance on long-term multi-dimensional relationships between banks, individual borrowers, and business groups to assess and monitor risk, or what Cargill and Royama (1988) refer to as "customer relationships" that play a relatively small role in western financial systems.

The financial system is thus an instrument of industrial policy maintained and protected by mutual support, restraints on competition, and insularity between the domestic financial sector, the ministry of finance, and politicians.

There is no doubt the Japanese financial regime fulfilled its intended objective through much of the postwar period judged by economic growth and advances in real income per capital. This is definitely true for the period from 1950 to 1970 referred to as the High Growth Period so-called because during this twenty-year period, real GDP grew at annual rates of about 10 percent with moderate inflation. Whatever inefficiencies one could point to in the regime it would be difficult to argue growth would have been higher and/or more stable during the High Growth Period.

The system, however, began to experience problems in the late 1960s and early 1970s. Two problems or contradictions in the regime can be identified. The first manifested itself in the form of political pressure brought on the Bank of Japan by the Tanaka government to use expansionary monetary policy to continue the high growth rates into the 1970s and later to support the yen during the collapse of the Bretton Woods fixed exchange rate system. Instead of high growth, however, the expansionary policy generated high rates of inflation that reached 30 percent in 1973. This problem was corrected and in fact, led to enhanced political independence of the Bank of Japan that for the next decade earned itself the reputation of being one of the world's "model" central banks (Cargill, 1989; Cargill, Hutchison, & Ito, 1997) in terms of the ability to maintain price stability in the face of internal and external shocks.

The second was more fundamental and long lasting. In response to the oil price shock and downward shift in the natural growth path of real GDP Japan's flow of funds pattern changed and brought pressure on the financial regime to become more flexible (Cargill & Royama, 1988). Banks, corporations, and securities companies saw liberalization as a means to reestablish and/or enhance market share while the Ministry of Finance was willing to relax the constraints on the financial system as the price for marketing the large amounts of government debt needed to finance Japan's large central government deficits that emerged after 1973. The shift to a flexible exchange rate regime and political pressure, especially from the United States, added additional pressure on Japan to liberalize.

The Korean financial regime drew heavily from the Japanese model; however, the Korean version differed in significant ways that made it more susceptible to shocks and more resistant to reform (Cargill, 1993a and especially, 1998).

Industrial Organization

Japan's industrial structure during the prewar period was dominated by *zaibatsu* or "financial combine or groups." The business group structure reemerged after the Allied Occupation in the form of the *keiretsu* or "groups of businesses," which unlike the *zaibatsu*, relied heavily on banks as providing leadership and credit evaluation/monitoring roles in a financial system with little financial disclosure.

The Korean business group structure is refereed to as the *chaebol*, but differs from the Japanese *keiretsu* (Huh & Kim, 1993, 1994). The *chaebol* possess greater concentration of economic power and unlike their Japanese counterparts, have increased their role in the Korean economy. More importantly, banks play a passive role in the *chaebol* which have been the recipients of extensive government industrial and credit allocation policies.

These differences are reflected in the long-standing nonperforming bank loan problem in Korea officially estimated at the end of 1997 at 7.3 percent of total loans using U.S. measurement standards (Bank of Korea, 1997). Huh and Kim (1993, 1994) provide evidence that Korea's nonperforming loan problem dates from the early 1970s and can be attributed to the passive role of banks in monitoring credit and the micro management of the economy by the Korean government. Japan's nonperforming loan problem is relatively recent starting in 1990 and is the direct outcome of the collapse of asset prices rather than internal inefficiencies in the banking and corporate sectors.

Credit Allocation Policies

The Korean government has extensively influenced the allocation of credit to a much higher degree than in Japan. Banks until 1981-1983 were owned by the government and even after de-nationalization, credit allocation decisions were subject to guidance by the government. While the Japanese system has a number of government banks receiving funding through the postal saving system, these institutions did not account for the majority of funds transferred through the financial system (Cargill & Royama, 1988). The majority of credit allocation decisions were left to private banks despite the existence of "window guidance" practiced by the Bank of Japan.

Financial Repression

Korea and Japan both restricted household access to the financial system to support a high saving to GDP ratio; however, Korea's regime also excluded small and even medium sized businesses from the banking system in their efforts to support the *chaebol*. As a result, a curb or unofficial market evolved to satisfy the needs of these excluded businesses while no such market developed in Japan. Comparisons of regulated and unrelated interest rates in Korea and Japan as a measure of financial repression (Cargill, 1993a, p. 152) clearly indicate that Korea's regime was more repressed than in Japan.

Central Bank Independence

The Bank of Japan and Bank of Korea have been ranked as formally dependent central banks, though recent[5] changes in their underlying legal structure have been designed to provide more formal independence. As argued by Cargill, Hutchison, and Ito (1997), however, formal dependence in the past has not prevented the Bank of Japan from pursuing a price stabilization policy nor has it greatly limited the political independence of the Bank of Japan. The Bank of Korea in contrast has had virtually no political independence and has been under the direction of the Ministry of Finance and Economy.

External Borrowing

Japan's economic development in the postwar period was largely self-financed while Korea relied significantly on external borrowing. Japan by the mid-1980s became the world's largest creditor nation because of persistent current account surpluses. As a result, Korea's financial system is potentially more unstable because the burden of the debt is sensitive to the exchange rate and the lack of accumulated international reserve assets hinders the ability of the central bank of intervene in the foreign exchange market.

Labor Market Inflexibility, Political Institutions, and Geo-political Situation

Korean labor markets are inflexible because of the lifetime (generally age 58 or 60 years) guaranteed employment by law. Korean politics have been unstable over the years with open elections starting only since 1986. The presence of the hostile North Korea presents significant security issues.

In contrast, Japanese labor markets are more flexible and lifetime employment (generally to 55 years) is not as pervasive as in Korea. Japanese politics have been stable with open elections starting after the end of the Occupation and Japan's security issues are less prominent.

IV. CATALYSTS FOR FINANCIAL LIBERALIZATION, PROGRESS, DETERIORATION, AND MISSED OPPORTUNITIES

The catalysts for financial liberalization in Korea were generated by internal real and financial disruptions in the early 1980s. Industrial policy had directed resources to the heavy and chemical industry sector in the 1970s. This generated overcapacity, reduced the availability of resources to small and medium sized firms, and burdened the government-owned banking system with a major nonperforming loan problem. The real sector problems were compounded by inflationary monetary policy that induced a wide gap between regulated and unregulated interest rates and increased financial repression.

Officially the Korean government in the Fifth Five-Year Plan (1982-1986) announced a plan to liberalize the real and financial sectors and reduce the influence of government resource and credit allocation policies. A series of financial reforms were announced in the early 1980s, late 1980s, and 1991 each with time tables of when and what type of liberalization would occur. The majority of observers, however, viewed Korean financial liberalization as more rhetoric than action (e.g., Greenwood, 1986). De-nationalization of the commercial banking system in 1981-1983, for example, was followed by the requirement that major personnel and credit decisions by the "private" banks required Ministry of Finance and Economy approval. The rhetoric of liberalization was designed as much, if not more, to appease foreign pressure and to gain acceptance into the OECD than to achieve structural changes in Korea's financial system.

Credit allocation continued, the Ministry of Finance and Economy ignored the large volume of nonperforming loans held by the banking system, the Ministry permitted the newly established merchant banks that specialized in short term lending to the *chaebol* to expand without oversight, and continued to require the Bank of Korea to make "policy" loans to targeted sectors of the economy until the early 1990s. Korean officials knew of the large volume of nonperforming loans and resulting weak condition of the banks but choose to ignore the problem. They adopted the same policy common in the United States in the 1980s to engage in forgiveness and forbearance in the hope that high rates of real GDP growth would allow financial institutions to grow out of the problem.

This policy on the surface appeared to work as recently as 1995 as official estimates of the nonperforming loan problem were lowered and real GDP grew in the 7 to 9 percent range. Starting in 1996, however, the real GDP growth rate slowed, large numbers of *chaebol* became bankrupt, increasing numbers of merchant banks were market insolvent as were many banks, and the financial system was increasingly dependent on short term external funds. Even by Summer 1997 the situation appeared manageable to Korean officials.

A clear example of this benign neglect is illustrated by the debate over a series of recommendations made by the Presidential Commission on Financial Reform in the Spring and Summer of 1997.[6] The Commission's three reports covered many topics emphasizing the need to render the financial system more transparent, more competitive, and resolve the nonperforming loan problem. The last report published June 1997 recommended changes in the regulatory structure that would have removed the bank supervision function from the Bank of Korea and transferred it to a new super regulatory agency. The Ministry of Finance and Economy ignored the major issues raised in the Commission's reports and instead focused on those structural changes such as removing the bank supervision function from the Bank of Korea that would have elevated its relative influence in the formation of economic and financial policy. Even as late as December 1997, the Ministry of Finance and Economy and the Bank of Korea fought over regulatory turf, civil service, and life time employment.[7]

Financial transition in Japan followed a different process than in Korea. Japan initiated an official policy of liberalization in 1976 when the Ministry of Finance recognized a previously unofficial repurchase market in government securities. This started a process of administrative and some legislative changes that gradually removed interest rate ceilings, permitted some relaxation of the constraints that separated intermediation markets, permitted the establishment of money and bond markets, and reduced restrictions on the inflow and outflow of capital. The process was gradual, administratively directed, and was not characterized by the type of financial disruptions at least through the mid-1980s as occurred in other countries like the United States. Nor was the process characterized by regulatory-market conflicts. Much of the credit for this achieve goes to the Bank of Japan.

The smooth transition, however, changed dramatically after 1985 with the run-up of land and equity prices, booming economic and monetary growth characterized as the bubble economy. The collapse of the bubble economy revealed fundamental weaknesses in both the financial system and the regulatory structure (Cargill, 1993b; Cargill, Hutchison, & Ito, 1997, 1998).

The financial and regulatory structure was poorly designed for liberalization. The regulatory structure was incapable of monitoring risk taking in the emerging liberated environment, no meaningful financial disclosure framework existed, a regulatory attitude of "no failures of financial institutions or markets," and a failure to appreciate the policy errors and moral hazard of government deposit guarantees manifested by the collapse of the S&L industry and deterioration of the banking system in the United States.

V. GOVERNMENT FAILURE: REGULATORY BLINDNESS AND INERTIA AND REGULATORY FORGIVENESS AND FORBEARANCE

The regulatory response in both countries exacerbated the problem. The regulatory response was one of denial, and once denial was no longer credible, the response was one of understatement delay, forbearance, and forgiveness.

Korean officials simply ignored the build up of nonperforming loans, ignored the enhanced risk taking by bank and merchant banks, saw no contradiction in the extensive system of government deposit guarantees and the increased competitive environment of the domestic financial system, and continued to use the financial system as a means to implement industrial policies and secure political power.

Korean officials saw no reason to be concerned because real GDP growth in the early 1990s continued to be high while inflation was generally moderate. This environment, however, would have been conducive to the type of structural changes that were needed, but instead, the favorable macroeconomic performance made it easy to rationalize a policy of inertia, forgiveness, and forbearance. As a result, the suddenness of the collapse in late 1997 was a shock to Koreans. In hindsight, however, the exposure of banks and merchant banks to external funds to support financially and structurally weak *chaebol* organizations merely needed a catalyst to bring the system down. Capital flight and currency depreciation in the smaller Asian economies was the catalyst.

Japan's situation is different. First, the catalyst was the collapse of asset prices in 1990 and 1991 that exposed the fundamental weaknesses as financial institutions for the first time since 1950 were required to respond to large numbers of nonperforming loans. While Korea had a nonperforming loan problem long before the current crisis, Japan's nonperforming loan problem was of more recent origin and a response to the fall in asset prices, especially land prices. The problem was then exacerbated by regulatory denial and when denial was no longer credible after 1992, consistent understatement of the magnitude of the problem, and reliance on a return to pre-1991 asset price levels to restore financial health. The Ministry of Finance permitted banks to hold large amounts of nonperforming loans, engaged in forbearance and forgiveness, and even used government funds to support the stock market.

Second, Japan's industrial sector was not fundamentally weak since throughout much of postwar development credit was not allocated by the government and their existed a more sophistical and complex system of credit evaluation and monitoring in Japan than ever existed in Korea.

Third, the agricultural sector and agricultural credit cooperatives play a major role in the financial crisis whereas agriculture played no meaningful role in Korea's financial problem. Credit cooperatives expanded rapidly into new areas and without supervision by either the Bank of Japan or the Ministry of Finance, especially as suppliers of funds to the *jusen* industry or housing loan companies (nondepository subsidiaries of commercial banks). The political power of the agricultural sector limited and delayed action to close down the housing loan companies until 1996 and even at that point, negotiated an agreement with the Ministry of Finance that relieved the credit cooperatives of any significant burden of closing down the housing loan companies.

Fourth, the existence of three and in some cases competing regulatory authorities (Ministry of Finance, Ministry of Agriculture, Forestry, and Fishery, and the Ministry of Posts and Telecommunications) limited action. In Korea, the Ministry of Finance and Economy dominates all other financial regulatory authorities.

Fifth, Japan has a postal savings system that is the largest financial institution in the world with about $2 trillion in deposits. This postal system has the potential to destabilize the private banking system with its complete government deposit guarantee and made it more difficult for private institutions to operate in an open and competitive environment (Cargill, 1993b). Korea's postal savings system is relatively small and has played little role in destabilizing the Korea banking system; in fact, while funds have disintermediate out of private Japanese banks to the postal savings system funds have disintermediated out of private Korean banks to foreign banks.

Like Korea, the regulatory authorities minimized the problems and passed up opportunities to deal with them such as in 1992 when the Financial Systems Reform Law permitted banks and securities companies to enter each other's market (Cargill & Todd, 1993). Despite the weak foundation of Japanese finance as evidenced by the collapse of asset prices and nonperforming loans, the 1992 law all but ignored the conflicts between increasingly liberalized financial systems and pervasive government deposit guarantees.

VI. CURRENT FINANCIAL CRISIS AND OUTLOOK FOR REFORM

Despite the clear evidence of government failure in Korea and Japan we should not loose sight of the fact that major changes in the structure of Korean and Japanese finance have taken place during the past two decades. Even though these changes fall short of achieving a stable financial environment and rejecting the Japanese financial regime, they are none the less significant and have entailed both losers and winners. More needs to be done, however. More than changing the policy parameters, Korean and Japanese officials need to adopt a new attitude toward market forces that is fundamentally opposed to the basic elements of the old financial regime.

The changes enacted and those proposed for future legislation, even were they to greatly benefit the economy as a whole, will necessarily entail losers as well as winners. The potential losers, long protected by regulation from market competition in Korea and Japan's compartmentalized financial-services industry, are likely to vigorously oppose further change. Financial deregulation in Korea and Japan has been on the agenda for many years, proceeding very gradually, and some skeptics argue that a sense of deja vu surrounds the present push for deregulation as well. The simple fact is that it has taken a crisis to reveal the fundamental weaknesses of the old financial regime and the regulatory structure that administered the financial regime.

Korea and Japan, however, are at a juncture today which is not comparable to any other episode during the postwar period. Stress in the Korean and Japanese financial system, especially failure to quickly resolve the nonperforming loan problem, continues to hold back their respective economies. The shortcomings of the existing regulatory and supervisory structure, especially in the context of the large changes in financial institutions and markets during the past 15 years, is readily apparent. Market forces and competition among financial institutions make the existing financial structure incompatible with Korea and Japan's regulatory and supervisory structure. Recent legislation creating the Financial Supervisory Commission in Korea and the Financial Supervisory Agency in Japan recognizes and attempts to address this problem. These changes, however, pale in comparison to the need to change policy attitudes about market forces and the need to resist government management of the economy.

The current crisis may well offer the needed catalyst to convince Korean and Japanese regulatory authorities and politicians that change is needed. In the case of Korea the IMF provides additional pressure. Both countries simply have no choice but to make the politically difficult changes to reject the old financial regime. Korea and Japan have both shown the world they are capable of tremendous transformation in response to external shocks and those challenges were far more daunting that the current challenges.

NOTES

1. Postwar economic growth commenced in Japan with the start of the Korean War in June 1950. The take-off stage was proceeded by a number of policy changes in 1949 referred to as the Dodge Plan to end the economic and financial disruptions following Japan's defeat in 1945. Postwar economic growth commenced in Korea following the end of the Korean War in 1953.

2. In fact, Krugman did not predict the current economic and financial declines. Instead the predicted continued rapid growth into the near future. "...Barring a catastrophic political upheaval, it is likely that growth in East Asia will continue to outpace growth in the West for the next decade and beyond" (Krugman, 1994, pp. 77-78).

3. The term deposit guarantee is used in the broad sense of policies such as "too big to fail" or "no failures of financial institutions or markets." The term includes but is more broadly interpreted than deposit insurance.

4. Cargill, Hutchinson, and Ito (1997, Chapter 2) provide a brief monetary history of Japan as well as provide references to more extensive discussions of the subject.

5. The Bank of Japan Law was revised June 1997 to provide more formal independence from the Ministry of Finance. The Bank of Korea Act was also revised December 1997. Cargill (1997/1998) discusses some the elements of the revised central banking laws.

6. The Commission's three reports are outlined and evaluated in Cargill (1997).

7. Many Bank of Korea workers are members of a labor union and during the debate in the legislature over revising the Bank of Korea Act and establishing a new super regulatory agency, the Bank of Korea's labor union members demonstrated their opposition to the proposed changes.

REFERENCES

Amsden, A. H. (1989). *Asia's next giant*. New York: Oxford University Press.

Bank of Korea, Office of Bank Supervision. (1997). *News brief* (unofficial translated version). Problem loan of Korean commercial banks. November 19, 1997.

Cargill, T. F. (1989). *Central bank independence and regulatory responsibilities: the bank of Japan and the federal reserve*. Salomon Brothers Center for the Study of Financial Institutions. New York University.

Cargill, T. F. (1990). Korean financial liberalization: lessons from the japanese experience. *Japan and the World Economy*.

Cargill, T. F. (1993a). A comparative study of financial liberalization policies: Japan and Korea. *Korean-U.S. Financial Issues*. Washington, DC: Korea Economic Institute of America.

Cargill, T. F. (1993b). Deposit guarantees, nonperforming loans, and the postal savings system in Japan. *Bank Structure and Competition*, Federal Reserve Bank of Chicago, 465-472.

Cargill, T. F. (1997). *Central banking and financial supervision in korea: in search of a stable financial and monetary framework*. Institute of Monetary Studies, Bank of Korea, Manuscript.

Cargill, T. F. (1997/1998). Central bank restructuring and independence in Korea and Japan: A solution to current financial problems? *Central Banking*.

Cargill, T. F. (1998). *Korea's transition to an efficient and stable financial structure*. Presented at the conference, "Korea's Transition to a High Productivity Economy. University of Hawaii at Manoa, February 6 and 7, 1998.

Cargill, T. F., M. M. Hutchison, & Takatoshi, I. (1997). *The political economy of Japanese monetary policy*. Cambridge, MA: The MIT Press.

Cargill, T. F., M. M. Hutchison, & Takatoshi, I. (1998). The banking crisis in Japan. In G. Caprio, W.C. Hunter, G. G. Kaufman, & D. M. Leipziger (Eds.), *Preventing bank crisis. Lessons from recent global bank failures*. Washington, DC: The World Bank.

Cargill, T. F., & Royama, S. (1988). *The transition of finance in Japan and the united states: A comparative perspective.* Stanford, CA: Hoover Institution Press.

Cargill, T. F., & G. F. W. Todd. (1993). Japan's financial system reform law: Progress toward financial liberalization? *Brooklyn Journal of International Law,* 19(1), 47-84.

Greenwood, J. G. (1986). Financial liberalization and innovation in seven east asian economies. In Y. Suzuki & H. Yomo (Eds.), *Financial innovation and monetary policy: Asia and the West.* Tokyo: Tokyo University Press.

Huh, C. G., & Kim, S. B. (1993). Japan's keiretsu and Korea's chaebol. *FRBSF Weekly Letter.* Federal Reserve Bank of San Francisco.

Huh, C. G., & Kim, S. B. (1994). Financial regulation and banking sector performance: A comparison of bad loan problems in Japan and Korea. *Economic Review,* 2.

Krugman, P. (1994). The myth of Asia's miracle. *Foreign Affairs,* 62-78.

Patrick, H., & Rosovsky, H. (1976). *Asia's new giant: How the Japanese economy works.* Washington, DC: Brookings Institution.

Presidential Commission for Financial Reform. (1997a). *Financial reform in korea: The first report.*

Presidential Commission for Financial Reform. (1997b). *Financial reform in korea: The second report.*

Presidential Commission for Financial Reform. (1997c). *Financial reform in korea: The third report.*

BANK RELATIONS AND THE PERCEPTION OF A BANK CRISIS:
A CASE STUDY ON ITALY

Paolo Marullo Reedtz

I. CONCEPTUAL FRAMEWORK

The raise of a systemic banking crisis has always been feared because of the possible consequences on the payments system, on the money stock, and on the level of economic activity.

This is the reason why in all the industrialized countries that recently experienced serious and extensive banking crises the authorities intervened by shoring up deposit guarantee schemes, providing funds at subsidized rates and supplying capital to the banks in difficulty.

The losses incurred by banks in the United States in the eighties were met by the federal government at a total cost of nearly 3 percent of GDP. The budgetary cost of restoring the stability and viability of the banking system amounted to 9 percent of GDP in Finland, 4 percent in Sweden and 2 percent in Norway. State aid is expected to be of the order of 1.5 percent of GDP in France, while it is still difficult to be ascertained for Japan.

Research in Financial Services: Private and Public Policy, Volume 10, pages 115-137.
Copyright © 1998 by JAI Press Inc.
ISBN: 0-7623-0358-1

Bank failures are usually considered highly probable since banking firms are regarded as more fragile than other firms, due to some specific features of their balance sheets: (1) the high percentage of bank liabilities which can be converted into currency upon demand sets up a high potential for bank runs; (2) in such a situation the low liquidity ratio could force a fast sale of illiquid assets and increase fire-sale losses; (3) the low capital-to-assets ratio can dampen the ability of the banks to absorb such losses (Kaufman, 1996a).

Moreover, depositors choose how to allocate their financial resources in an uncertainty regime, characterized by the lack of bank-specific information. An evaluation of the banks' asset portfolios is made particularly hard by the opaqueness of their investments connected with the confidential information they require. For this reason the reaction of depositors to rumours about the soundness of their bank can be highly unpredictable and potentially ruinous.

As soon as they perceive an increase in the riskiness of their bank, depositors could decide to run on the bank in order to be first to remove their funds. Random shocks models are not interested in the source of the shock which can push depositors to line up; their behavior is considered almost irrational (Diamond & Dybvig, 1983; Waldo, 1985; Postlewaite & Vives, 1987; Cooper & Ross, 1991).

However, bank customers may have solid reasons to believe that their bank is going to run into a crisis; in some other cases their belief may stem out from the observation of indirect indicators. Macroeconomic indicators can be considered, such as the GDP variation or the failure rate of nonfinancial businesses; information about the overall bank profitability can also be used to anticipate troubles at an individual level (Gorton, 1985; Chari & Jagannathan, 1988; Park, 1991; Dale, 1992; Temzelides, 1997).

According to some authors, in the past bank runs provided the banking system with an authomatic mechanism through which the most fragile institutions could be promptly put out of the market and the overall stability of the banks improved. Due to liquidity problems, the authorities were obliged to suspend the activity of the banks that had been interested by a run in order to ascertain their viability: if the banks were insolvent, they were quickly closed and resolved (Kaufman, 1996b).

This approach implies that the *safety net* is responsible for the increased fragility of the banks and for the high breakage rate that has been recorded in the United States after the establishment of the Federal Reserve System in 1914. In particular, protecting depositors against the consequences of bank failures has enabled preventing bank panics and contagion risk (Kaufman, 1994; Schoenmaker, 1996) but it has also reduced market discipline on bank management. By cutting the amount of capital requested by the market to the individual banks, the safety net has contributed to lower the discipline connected with corporate governance and has encouraged moral hazard on behalf of the bankers.

Given the unlikeliness of a systemic crisis, regulators would have delayed the closure of insolvent banks relying on possible favorable changes in market conditions, in practice allowing banks *to gamble for resurrection* and making bank closures highly costly (Benston & Carhill, 1992; De Gennaro & Thomson, 1993; Kroszner & Strahan, 1994; Kane & Yu, 1994; Gilbert, 1994; Barth, Hudson, & Jahera, 1995).

On the other hand, international evidence shows that a lack of deposit insurance may produce even worse consequences: depositors tend to expect a full bailout on behalf of the Government and have no incentive whatever to discipline their bank (Garcia & Saal, 1996).

The stability of the banking system would benefit by a reduction in the extent of deposit protection and banking regulation and/or by a more incentive compatible structure of the safety net. One possible solution would be that of scaling down the coverage of deposit insurance, in order to protect small depositors who cannot monitor their banks and leave large depositors with the incentive to discipline the institutions which they entrust their savings to. Large customers would be induced to refuse to deposit at weaker banks or would pretend higher interest premia.

The robustness of this analysis depends on the validity of two crucial hypotheses:

Hypothesis 1. the idea that at least the largest and the most financially sophisticated customers would be able to anticipate the crisis and would promptly withdraw their deposits.

Hypothesis 2. the idea that, counting on the deposit insurance, they refrain from exerting any market discipline over bank managers, even in the presence of a clearcut indication of bank crisis.

If these hypotheses were proved to be true, adequate disclosure would increase market discipline substantially. A regulatory reform producing a regime fully relying on market forces would become an important target for domestic legislations and international harmonization. As a consequence of the reform introduced at the beginning of 1996, banks in New Zealand are required to disclose on a quarterly basis a wide range of information they were previously providing privately to the Reserve Bank (Lang, 1996).

The probability of bank contagion is widely related to the close relationships established among the banks through interbank transactions. Since interbank balances and credit extended over the interbank market are not insured against, they can ignite a chain of subsequent failures. For this reason some proposals have been made to limit the amount of interbank liabilities at an individual level (Hoenig, 1996) or to restrict interbank lending to weak institutions (Benston & Kaufman, 1997).

However, interbank relations seem to represent the ideal scenario for market discipline: banks have both the economic incentives and the ability to monitor each other. They operate on the same markets and share the same information; they also have the expertise to evaluate bank credit portfolios and can use the information provided by the evolution of their individual interbank accounts, as in the case of corporate borrowers (Calomiris & Kahn, 1996). Peer monitoring among banks would result into a safer situation of the borrowing institutions, which could even be allowed to maintain lower capital ratios than banks raising funds only at uninformed depositors (Rochet & Tirole, 1996).

Whether banks actually have the right incentives to cross-monitor is a matter of debate: on one side they are theoretically exposed to a loss, when the borrowing bank defaults; on the other they could rely on an implicit guarantee provided by the Government, especially in the case in which the borrowing bank is too big to fail. The only criterion leading to a conclusion is that of the empirical analysis, that is, testing whether the banking firms which run into trouble encountered any shortage of interbank financing.

A final source of market discipline could be represented by the corporate borrowers, whose incentive is the need not to encounter liquidity constraints. As soon as a worsening in the bank's conditions is perceived, borrowers could switch their credit relationships to other intermediaries and/or request lower interest rate to keep their business running with the deteriorating bank. Their ability to set up new business relationships or to raise funds on the financial market is a function of their creditworthiness and may be stronger for large borrowers. On the other side, the deteriorating bank could attempt to keep its credit relationships with large borrowers: they are usually safer and require low administrative costs per unit of lending.

These different sources of market discipline add on to the corporate governance of the banking firms. As for other types of productive firms, the financial market provides a continuous assessment of management strategy and is usually able to distinguish distressed banks from other, well-managed, institutions (Wall & Peterson, 1990).

II. RESEARCH METHODOLOGY

This paper investigates the intensity of market discipline on commercial banks on behalf of savers, borrowers and other banks in the framework of the Italian credit system.

This is not an easy task: since market discipline contributes to make firms safe and sound, one could argue that a low number of bank failures could be a sufficient indication of an effective market discipline. Of course, such a conclusion would take into no account the overall condition of the economy and the cyclical pattern of the credit activity and of the bank profitability. Moreover, considering well-managed intermediaries as an indication of effective market discipline would lead to weak conclusions: one should still demonstrate that an external discipline would have been necessary on those banks.

An alternative approach is to focus on banks which run into difficulties, either irretrievable or only temporary, and check whether their customer relationships have undergone significant changes. An undeniable crisis situation enables to evaluate whether bank customers and the interbank market behaved so as to prevent imprudent choices or at least force bank managers to cope with the fragility of their firms.

In practice, the statistics on the assets and liabilities of individual banks are examined to find out either a severe monitoring on behalf of the counterparties before the bank runs into a crisis or, at least, a reaction after the crisis has become publicly known.

In this approach a crucial element is represented by the moment the public opinion has been informed by the daily press about the critical situation of the bank. In Eisenbeis (1997) words, from that moment onwards "it is more rational for depositors to withdraw funds than to seek out and evaluate costly information or risk lossing their funds by not withdrawing."

In order to simplify the data mining, quarterly series have been considered, looking for significant discontinuities around the news releases. The quarter before the press articles reporting the crisis is defined as the *benchmark date*.

In principle three different empirical results could be reached:

1. bank customers could anticipate the news and scale down or interrupt their relationships with the distressed bank: they show a high propensity to monitor their bank, ability to evaluate its situation and prompt reaction. One might argue that, although the monitoring of bank counterparties may not prove sufficient in preventing failures, the banking firms are exposed to a market discipline that is presumably quite effective;
2. bank customers decide to reduce their business with the distressed bank only after its critical situation has been publicly announced: although they have not been able to detect the crisis any sooner, they show to be sensitive to the bank's situation and ready to move towards other intermediaries;
3. bank customers do not change their behavior despite the information on the crisis of their bank: they do not make any difference between distressed and sound banks. By giving up affecting the behavior of their banks, they show to be confident that the deposit insurance or an implicit Government guarantee will restore any loss they might incur into.

The time sample of the research is the 1990-1997 period, in which the Italian banking system has undergone a remarkable reduction of its profit rate due to increased competition (Figure 1), a slowdown in lending activity and a deterioration in the quality of the claims on businesses, especially those located in the South of the country. In addition bank profitability has been negatively affected by the slowness with which Italian banks have reduced staff costs in response to the narrowing of the interest margin.

The evaluation carried out by the supervisory authority on the basis of the banks' prudential reports through a rating system similar to the U.S. CAMEL

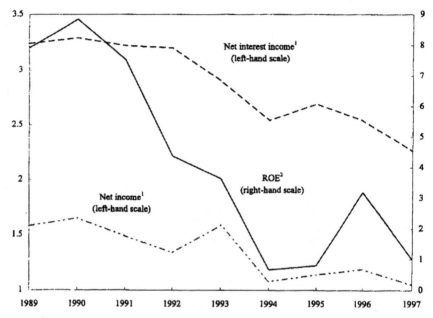

Notes: [1]As a percentage of total assets.
[2]Net profit as a percentage of capital and reserves.

***Figure* 1.**   Profit and Loss Accounts of Banks

revealed a deteriorating situation. The overall market share of the banks with serious anomalies (score of 4 or 5) increased from 17 to 19 percent between 1991 and 1997, whereas that of the banks with fully satisfactory results (score of 1 and 2) fell from 57 to 12 percent. However, the capital adequacy of the banking system on a consolidated basis was not reduced: the overall solvency ratio of banking groups and banks not belonging to groups was 11.6 percent in December 1997, well above the 8 percent minimum requirement and similar to the average of the European banking systems.

Over the 1990-1997 period 54 banks have been placed under special administration and 29 in compulsory administrative liquidation; at the beginning of the period their overall market share was 2 percent. In most cases the liquidated institutions' assets and liabilities were transferred immediately to other banks, with no interruption of operations; in a few recent cases liquidation led to the closure of the banks' branches. The resolution of the crises did not prevent the total or partial loss of capital, the replacement of the directors and the prosecution of those responsible for the losses.

Mergers and acquisitions were important both for the resolution of numerous problem cases and for the general reorganization of the banking system. Over our time sample more than 350 operations—M&As or acquisition of controlling interests—changed the ownership of banks accounting for one quarter of the system's total assets. In 40 percent of the cases the banks were in a critical situation.

In some cases the acquisition on behalf of a healthy bank was favored by the intervention of the Interbank Deposit Protection Fund (IDPF). The overall amount of these interventions was equal to .13 percent of the Italian GDP.

The Interbank Fund had been established in 1987 with the participation of virtually the whole credit system in order to provide deposit insurance. Each deposit was fully guaranteed up to 200 hundred million lire ($120,000 at the average 1997 exchange rate) and 50 percent protection was granted to the rest up to 1 billion lire ($600,000). The burden for each bank was computed on the basis of its market share on protected deposits and no risk adjustment was established. A reform of the IDPF was implemented in 1996, when the European Directive on deposit guarantee schemes was transposed into the Italian legislation. Full protection is now provided per depositor up to 200 hundred million lire and no coverage is given for higher amounts. The individual contributions to the Fund's interventions are correlated with the riskiness attachable to each bank according to a set of indicators. Interbank deposits have never been guaranted.

Remarkable improvements have been achieved in the amount and quality of information provided to the market and to the customers through legislative reforms. The European Directive on the annual accounts and consolidated accounts of banks was transposed into the Italian legislation in 1992, establishing a common layout for both the balance sheet and the profit and loss account and precise definitions for the various items. Since 1994 banks have been are required to disclose their financial statements also on a semi-annual base.

The aim of intensifying competition and protecting the weaker contractual party in financial transactions was pursued both through Law 154 of 1992 on the transparency of banking and other financial products and services and through the adoption of provisions on consumer credit.

The sample of institutions that has been used for empirical purposes in this study includes 15 banks, both publicly and privately owned, with an overall market share of 15 percent on deposits at the end of the eighties. These institutions ranged from small local banks to large-sized banks operating on the whole national territory. Most of them were southern institutions, reflecting the widespread difficulties connected with the stagnation of economic activity in the South of Italy.

They experienced serious troubles during the time sample: four of them were able to overcome their difficulties by replacing their management and reorganizing; three were placed in compulsory administrative liquidation and their assets and liabilities were transferred to other banks; eight were acquired by other institutions possessing greater financial and professional resources.

For three of them public support was decided by the Parliament, amounting to 0.4 percent of GDP. The interventions were contingent on the implementation of reorganization plans mainly aiming at reducing operating costs and restoring the market credibility of the banks involved, with a view to the banks' subsequent sale.

The variety of banking firms included in the sample will allow to qualify the statistical results under viewpoints, such as:

- are bank customers and the interbank market less reactive to the evolution of large banks, owing to the perception that the Government could not avoid intervening in the case of a major crisis?
- is the reaction of bank customers stronger in the area where the bank has its headquarter, due to informational advantages?

Three categories of bank counterparties have been considered: (1) the *savers*, both as depositors and as households entrusting their financial assets to the banks for custody and administration purposes; (2) the *borrowers*, whose size has been proxied by the amount of the individual credit lines; (3) the *banks* themselves, both domestic and foreign.

Consistently with these counterparties, the following aggregates have been considered: (1) *bank deposits* (checking accounts, certificates of deposit, other deposits); (2) the amount of *bonds held in custody* on behalf of the housedolds; (3) *bank loans* (short-term and long-term; loans to large or small borrowers); (4) *interbank transactions*.

III.   THE DISTRESSED BANKS AND THE SAVERS

The relationships between the distressed banks and the savers have been examined for the deposits and for the bonds held in custody on a separate basis.

In fact, in the case of a crisis, there is no reason why the savers should keep the same behavior with respect to the two aggregates, given the different underlying contracts: by collecting deposits the bank has taken on a liability, whereas it is only providing a service in the second case, which implies no possible losses for the customers. However, this distinction could not to be fully understood by the savers; in any case they could fear a certain degree of sluggishness in getting back their financial wealth.

Another difference is connected with the technicalities of the *flight to quality*: writing a check is sufficient to move deposits to another bank, whereas the physical transfer of the bonds trusted in custody may be required.

As for deposits it is crucially important to consider the different categories: current accounts can be transferred very quickly, whereas certificates of deposits can be decreased only at their maturity.

Table 1a.   Bank Deposits and Securities Deposited with Banks

| | BANK DEPOSITS | | | | Securities Deposited with Banks | |
| | Total | | Current Account Deposits | | | |
	Bank	Total	Bank	Total	Bank	Total
	Bank 1					
12 month before	9.8	9.3	7.6	6.3	−13.4	6.8
6 month before	9.5	9.0	21.5	12.5	−51.5	3.4
benchmark date	**3.0**	**2.2**	**10.8**	**5.7**	**−35.6**	**6.0**
6 month after	−17.9	−2.8	−21.3	−1.8	−13.8	7.9
12 month after	−19.1	0.9	−22.3	0.8	−23.8	6.9
	Bank 2					
12 month before	−9.6	−2.8	−0.3	−1.8	−36.8	7.9
6 month before	−5.1	0.9	16.6	0.8	−30.7	6.9
benchmark date	**0.1**	**3.4**	**−6.8**	**−0.1**	**1.4**	**9.0**
6 month after	−5.0	4.3	−10.4	3.4	−28.0	8.3
12 month after	−10.0	−0.6	−9.0	8.7	−41.7	12.9
	Bank 3					
12 month before	20.2	8.8	26.9	8.0	22.2	15.7
6 month before	14.7	10.3	16.1	9.2	72.1	17.2
benchmark date	**7.7**	**9.6**	**0.4**	**7.9**	**69.8**	**12.6**
6 month after	12.6	8.5	6.7	8.4	−19.7	13.4
12 month after	2.0	9.7	0.0	11.1	−34.0	13.9
	Bank 4					
12 month before	7.0	8.3	3.0	7.2	—	15.8
6 month before	6.9	11.0	−7.0	9.2	38.8	16.9
benchmark date	**7.6**	**9.6**	**0.6**	**8.8**	**33.2**	**12.5**
6 month after	9.8	9.5	13.8	11.7	37.2	13.5
12 month after	10.4	9.7	33.6	10.2	46.8	12.4
	Bank 5					
12 month before	13.2	−1.7	32.5	−1.6	−9.3	8.6
6 month before	−16.2	1.7	−26.8	0.5	29.9	5.6
benchmark date	**−7.9**	**5.3**	**−22.5**	**1.4**	**73.8**	**5.8**
6 month after	−11.0	2.4	−30.4	5.8	13.9	12.1
12 month after	..	−2.6	..	12.0	..	13.3

The evolution of deposits for each distressed bank has been considered not only at an aggregate level, but also with reference to the geographical area where they are raised.

Table 1b. Bank Deposits and Securities Deposited with Banks
(12-month percentage rates of change)

| | BANK DEPOSITS | | | | Securities Deposited with Banks | |
| | Total | | Current Account Deposits | | | |
	Bank	Total	Bank	Total	Bank	Total
			Bank 6			
12 month before	3.1	9.5	8.8	11.7	18.3	13.5
6 month before	2.8	9.7	8.5	10.2	17.5	12.4
benchmark date	**1.7**	**5.3**	**2.4**	**0.1**	**17.5**	**9.2**
6 month after	5.8	7.6	5.5	2.6	3.7	6.1
12 month after	4.5	8.2	3.5	7.3	−1.5	8.9
			Bank 7			
12 month before	10.0	7.6	6.4	2.6	9.1	6.1
6 month before	7.9	8.2	7.9	7.3	9.4	8.9
benchmark date	**4.2**	**6.4**	**7.2**	**10.0**	**1.9**	**4.7**
6 month after	−0.4	0.5	2.8	3.4	3.0	4.2
12 month after	−0.7	−1.7	0.6	−1.6	15.3	8.6
			Bank 8			
12 month before	9.4	8.5	11.6	8.4	−26.4	13.4
6 month before	4.6	9.7	11.7	11.1	−4.6	13.9
benchmark date	**3.6**	**8.2**	**3.5**	**6.3**	**16.7**	**8.1**
6 month after	6.8	8.1	−3.9	2.2	−4.7	6.0
12 month after	6.2	9.3	−1.0	6.3	5.4	6.8
			Bank 9			
12 month before	1.8	8.1	−4.6	2.2	4.3	6.0
6 month before	7.7	9.3	8.1	6.3	−2.8	6.8
benchmark date	**6.0**	**9.0**	**12.8**	**12.5**	**−6.5**	**3.4**
6 month after	−4.2	2.2	−3.1	5.7	0.6	6.0
12 month after	−11.2	−2.8	−13.3	−1.8	3.5	7.9
			Bank 10			
12 month before	−5.8	11.0	−1.3	9.5	−6.6	8.1
6 month before	−8.8	7.7	−6.0	2.4	−5.4	6.0
benchmark date	**−3.3**	**9.0**	**1.9**	**4.3**	**28.8**	**6.8**
6 month after	−2.3	14.3	10.8	11.0	−4.3	3.4
12 month after	−5.6	8.4	4.2	4.9	−13.9	6.0

As far as *deposits* are concerned, the main results can be summarized as follows (Tables 1a-1c):

Table 1c. Bank Deposits and Securities Deposited with Banks
(12-month percentage rates of change)

	BANK DEPOSITS				Securities Deposited with Banks	
	Total		Current Account Deposits			
	Bank	Total	Bank	Total	Bank	Total
	Bank 11					
12 month before	6.4	10.3	12.2	9.2	40.7	17.2
6 month before	4.3	9.6	6.1	7.9	35.1	12.6
benchmark date	**4.5**	**8.5**	**8.9**	**8.4**	**23.9**	**13.4**
6 month after	1.7	9.7	−0.4	11.1	35.7	13.9
12 month after	1.0	8.2	−1.5	6.3	17.9	8.1
	Bank 12					
12 month before	8.2	8.2	4.9	6.3	9.1	8.1
6 month before	12.6	8.1	3.9	2.2	6.7	6.0
benchmark date	**14.4**	**9.3**	**5.5**	**6.3**	**14.2**	**6.8**
6 month after	2.6	9.0	9.0	12.5	−27.5	3.4
12 month after	−6.4	2.2	5.5	5.7	−25.1	6.0
	Bank 13					
12 month before	5.3	5.3	−8.5	0.1	37.0	9.2
6 month before	6.7	7.6	−1.5	2.6	16.4	6.1
benchmark date	**13.8**	**8.2**	**17.0**	**7.3**	**7.5**	**8.9**
6 month after	9.2	6.4	19.9	10.0	23.0	4.7
12 month after	−2.3	0.5	−1.4	3.4	13.8	4.2
	Bank 14					
12 month before	2.4	8.1	0.4	2.2	1.1	6.0
6 month before	4.6	9.3	1.6	6.3	3.9	6.8
benchmark date	**0.6**	**9.0**	**2.7**	**12.5**	**0.9**	**3.4**
6 month after	−5.4	2.2	6.5	5.7	−3.8	6.0
12 month after	−11.6	−2.8	−5.8	−1.8	−1.3	7.9
	Bank 15					
12 month before	3.8	9.3	2.2	6.3	−17.4	6.8
6 month before	2.3	9.0	1.0	12.5	1.8	3.4
benchmark date	**1.6**	**2.2**	**6.6**	**5.7**	**5.1**	**6.0**
6 month after	−7.7	−2.8	−3.7	−1.8	12.8	7.9
12 month after	−7.9	0.9	−6.8	0.8	17.5	6.9

- there is almost no evidence of bank runs started prior to the *benchmark date*:
  in some cases the deposits of the distressed banks had been growing at very
  fast rates. The only cases in which bank deposits were already decreasing in

absolute terms at the *benchmark date* refer to small banks, as in the case of bank 2 and bank 5;

- the reaction after the releases of relevant news turns out to be quick and remarkable for small banks so as to depict a bank run at an individual level: in certain cases the twelve-month rate of variation became negative up to 18 percent two quarters after the *benchmark date* (bank 1);
- in the case of medium and large-sized banks the reaction is generally less timely: in some cases no significant discontinuities are recorded in the statistics after the *benchmark date*. In some other cases, the reaction lags one or two quarters, until further articles are published (e.g., bank 13). However, even among the large banks, there are cases of major contractions of deposits, up to 12 percent on a twelve-month basis (bank 14);
- as a general indication, the reduction in deposits turns out stronger for the current account component: the maximun rate of decrease, once again for small banks, is around 30 percent six months after the *benchmark date* (bank 5);
- for larger banks, the contraction of current account deposits is limited to a few percentage points, with one noticeable exception of 13 percent (bank 9); in one case the rate of variation switched from a 12 percent increase to a 4 percent decrease around the *benchmark date* (bank 8);
- in most of the cases the reduction of bank deposits is associated with a decrease of the average amount per account, signalling that the reduction has been concentrated in the deposits of a large size;
- for the banks operating at a national level, the fall in deposits turns out stronger in the geographical area where they originated and have their head offices; this factor could contribute to explain why the reduction is usually sharper for small banks operating at a local level;
- there is a mixed evidence on the banks' policies vis a vis the reduction of deposits: some banks engaged a costly interest rate policy to contrast the outflow; some others carried out a selective policy aiming at favoring the placement of CDs rather than going through a generalized increase of the interest rates.

The data regarding the *bonds held in custody* on behalf of the customers mainly confirm the indications drawn from the time series on deposits, with some important distinctions:

- the discontinuities in the time series are consistent with those recorded for deposits, but their size is even greater, probably due to the large size of the customers (e.g., banks 1, 2, 3, 12);
- a negative rate of variation more often signals a change in the customers' attitude towards the bank in advance to the press articles, especially in the case of small banks. As for example, for some of them a remarkable

decrease already took place within one year before the *benchmark date*, and
the reduction went on for some quarters after that date (banks 1, 2, 8). By
contrast, in another case a 70 percent increase at the *benchmark date* was
followed by a 34 percent reduction in one year's time (bank 3);

- for some of the largest banks the evidence is weaker or null, even in periods
characterized by negative variations of their deposits (banks 7, 11, 13, 15).
This could be consistent with a set of explanations, not mutually excluding:
(1) the customers were well aware not to incur in any possible loss; (2) they
did not consider any other bank operating nearby as well equipped to supply
that service; (3) in the presence of a *flight,* the bank persuaded the customers
to switch from deposits to the holdings of Government bonds managed by
the bank itself;

- once again the reduction of the aggregate turns out highly concentrated in
the areas where the banks have their headquarters.

IV. THE DISTRESSED BANKS AND THE BORROWERS

The perception of a crisis could induce bank borrowers to establish credit relationships with other, safer, banks in order to avoid liquidity constraints.

In fact, the purpose of hedging against a sudden reduction of the supply of loans
is considered one of the reasons for the diffusion of the multiple credit relationship
system among medium and large-sized Italian firms (Conigliani, Ferri, and Generale, 1997; Detragiache, Garella, and Guiso, 1997; D'Auria, Foglia and Marullo-
Reedtz, 1998).

Such an hypothesis would be consistent with a low growth rate or even a reduction of the loans granted by distressed firms after the *benchmark date*, or before if
the bank's difficulties had already been perceived by the borrowers.

However, it is necessary to distinguish breaks in the loan demand functions from
changes in the supply function. In fact distressed banks have several good reasons
to reduce their lending activity: they usually have to cope with deposit outflows and
to find a better equilibrium between credit risks and the degree of capitalization.

As a first approximation, a decrease in the financing to large-sized customers is
more likely to be connected with changes in the demand side of the credit relationship, given the better possibility they usually have to get financing at other
sources, whereas a reduction involving small borrowers is probably connected
with credit rationing.

This simplifying assumption has been considered with special reference to
small banks, which do not produce statistics over their interest rates. With reference to larger banks, attention has been paid to the average interest rates on short-
term lending, that are available on a ten-day basis; for some of them quarterly data
are also available referring to lending according to the size of the credit lines.

Table 2a.   Short Term Loans and Loans of a Large Amount

	SHORT-TERM LOANS[1]		LOANS OF A LARGE AMOUNT[2]
	Bank	Total	
Bank 1			
12 month before	21.7	1.0	49.6
6 month before	23.4	−6.0	54.3
benchmark date	**−6.7**	**−6.1**	**54.5**
6 month after	−30.0	2.4	55.4
12 month after	−35.8	4.5	58.2
Bank 2			
12 month before	−4.2	2.4	42.6
6 month before	3.8	4.5	47.3
benchmark date	**11.9**	**−0.8**	**50.7**
6 month after	−16.4	0.4	50.4
12 month after	−52.7	1.7	54.8
Bank 3			
12 month before	21.4	14.6	49.4
6 month before	20.1	11.1	50.7
benchmark date	**9.8**	**13.1**	**46.0**
6 month after	12.0	16.5	49.6
12 month after	−2.6	15.9	55.5
Bank 4			
12 month before	16.0	13.2	29.5
6 month before	6.0	16.0	25.4
benchmark date	**6.5**	**13.9**	**29.4**
6 month after	30.3	12.5	50.6
12 month after	45.1	13.4	55.4
Bank 5			
12 month before	13.3	5.6	68.7
6 month before	6.4	4.1	66.8
benchmark date	**−15.6**	**−0.4**	**66.1**
6 month after	−9.9	−0.1	69.9
12 month after	..	2.3	..

Notes: [1]12-month percentages rates of change of the short-term loans;
[2]Loans higher than 5 trillion lire ($ 3 million) to the corporate sector as a percentage of total loans to the corporate sector.

Of course this is only a first examination of the data. A closer study will involve the use of a rich matched bank-firm data set that provides information on the credit relationships and balance sheets of the corporate borrowers. This will allow to focus on creditworthy borrowers and to model their demand for credit at the distressed banks.

Table 2b. Short Term Loans and Loans of a Large Amount

	SHORT-TERM LOANS[1]		LOANS OF A LARGE AMOUNT[2]
	Bank	Total	
Bank 6			
12 month before	12.9	12.5	65.8
6 month before	21.6	13.4	65.4
benchmark date	**4.4**	**11.2**	**66.9**
6 month after	4.3	6.3	65.7
12 month after	−1.8	−2.2	68.0
Bank 7			
12 month before	5.2	6.3	66.5
6 month before	−12.5	−2.2	63.4
benchmark date	**−3.2**	**−6.9**	**68.0**
6 month after	−2.4	−4.3	65.3
12 month after	−12.0	5.6	66.4
Bank 8			
12 month before	65.1	16.5	49.2
6 month before	28.5	15.9	50.1
benchmark date	**10.5**	**14.6**	**51.0**
6 month after	−13.0	10.0	53.1
12 month after	−17.6	1.0	53.5
Bank 9			
12 month before	14.7	10.0	69.5
6 month before	−3.0	1.0	68.6
benchmark date	**−10.4**	**−6.0**	**70.2**
6 month after	−5.9	−6.1	70.1
12 month after	−5.1	2.4	70.0
Bank 10			
12 month before	6.5	14.6	86.8
6 month before	5.0	10.0	88.6
benchmark date	**3.3**	**1.0**	**87.7**
6 month after	−19.2	−6.0	85.9
12 month after	−2.4	−6.1	86.8

Notes: [1]12-month percentages rates of change of the short-term loans;
[2]Loans higher than 5 trillion lire ($ 3 million) to the corporate sector as a percentage of total loans to the corporate sector.

As for the moment, the main results on the relationships between banks in critical conditions and bank borrowers can be summarized as follows (Tables 2a-2c):

Table 2c. Short Term Loans and Loans of a Large Amount

	SHORT-TERM LOANS[1]		LOANS OF A LARGE AMOUNT[2]
	Bank	Total	
Bank 11			
12 month before	14.2	11.1	34.2
6 month before	9.0	13.1	35.6
benchmark date	**12.1**	**16.5**	**32.2**
6 month after	0.7	15.9	35.8
12 month after	−2.7	14.6	36.0
Bank 12			
12 month before	21.0	14.6	73.4
6 month before	11.2	10.0	73.4
benchmark date	**3.3**	**1.0**	**75.4**
6 month after	−5.6	−6.0	72.7
12 month after	−19.6	−6.1	72.8
Bank 13			
12 month before	23.6	11.2	68.7
6 month before	8.3	6.3	69.1
benchmark date	**0.1**	**−2.2**	**69.4**
6 month after	−7.6	−6.9	69.2
12 month after	−5.4	−4.3	70.0
Bank 14			
12 month before	6.2	10.0	63.4
6 month before	−4.2	1.0	62.6
benchmark date	**−25.6**	**−6.0**	**59.3**
6 month after	−30.0	−6.1	57.0
12 month after	−15.4	2.4	57.5
Bank 15			
12 month before	−9.2	1.0	61.8
6 month before	−12.8	−6.0	62.0
benchmark date	**13.1**	**−6.1**	**62.1**
6 month after	−12.8	2.4	63.4
12 month after	−12.3	4.5	66.6

Notes: [1] 12-month percentages rates of change of the short-term loans;
[2] Loans higher than 5 trillion lire ($ 3 million) to the corporate sector as a percentage of total loans to the corporate sector.

- distressed banks generally tend to limit the growth of their lending or to reduce it (the only exception is provided by bank 4);
- short-term lending is reduced by a higher amount, whereas the long-term component is linked to the maturity of the operations outstanding and is affected by the consolidation of doubtful loans;

- discontinuities in the short-term lending basically overlap with the periods of reduction of deposits. Only in a few cases a deceleration of deposits had already occurred;
- the composition of lending has almost always changed in favor of the larger borrowers. Some banks actively pursued stricter credit links with the largest customers by reducing the interest rate vis a vis the whole system.

V. THE DISTRESSED BANKS AND THE INTERBANK MARKET

Given the fine information that banks have or may easily acquire about each other and their incentive to cross-monitor, one would expect to find remarkable discontinuities in the interbank lending of distressed banks, because interbank deposits and lending receive no formal protection by the deposit guarantee scheme.

The examination of the data is hindered by the high volatility of interbank transactions and by the coexistence in the same interbank items of transactions which satisfy temporary liquidity shortages, structural imbalances between the collecting of deposits and the lending opportunities, and the needs of correspondent banking.

As for the moment, the statistics on bank balance sheets and those on bank interest rates reported at ten-days intervals[1] have been used in order to maintain the omogeneity of the data sources and of the frequency of observations.[2]

The evidence can be summarized as follows (Tables 3a-3c):

- no shortages of interbank financing is recorded for small banks prior to the *benchmark dates* : in most cases they could increase their interbank liabilities, even changing their positions from net lender to net borrower (bank 4). In the case of bank 5, in which deposits began to decrease in advance to the press articles, interbank borrowing (net) on the domestic market remained at high levels increased and a large number of foreign banks increased their lending;
- for medium- and large-sized banks no market discipline seems to have been exerted by the interbank relationships, either on the domestic or on the foreign markets, prior to the *benchmark dates*. No significant change is recorded for a few of them which were net lenders, whereas the others could increase their borrowing without paying interest rates higher than that prevailing on the market (banks 9, 10, 11, 13, 14, 15). In only one case the differential between the individual rate and the market rate widened significantly. In some cases they could also increase their interbank liabilities on the foreign market;
- after the *benchmark dates*, the banks could at least partially compensate the outflow of deposits by increasing their interbank liabilities on the domestic market, sometimes at the cost of raising interest rates. In most cases borrowing on the foreign interbank market was reduced, even though with a some lags.

Table 3a. Interbank Liabilities as a Percentage
of Domestic Fund-Raising

	DOMESTIC LIABILITIES		FOREIGN LIABILITIES	
	Gross	Net (liab.-ass.)	Gross	Net (liab.-ass.)
		Bank 1		
12 month before	2.3	−17.2	1.2	1.0
6 month before	1.9	−12.7	1.0	0.7
benchmark date	3.3	**−18.9**	0.6	0.3
6 month after	1.4	−17.5	0.7	0.6
12 month after	1.0	−25.3	0.3	0.2
		Bank 2		
12 month before	35.4	26.7	–	–
6 month before	27.3	19.0	–	–
benchmark date	15.7	6.8	–	–
6 month after	9.4	−1.3	–	–
12 month after	6.4	6.0	–	–
		Bank 3		
12 month before	13.5	2.5	3.9	3.1
6 month before	13.3	2.1	3.4	3.3
benchmark date	11.7	3.7	3.8	3.7
6 month after	10.4	0.7	3.0	2.9
12 month after	9.9	−1.5	2.8	2.7
		Bank 4		
12 month before	8.5	−5.8	–	–
6 month before	8.5	−11.8	–	–
benchmark date	4.2	**−7.7**	–	–
6 month after	10.4	2.1	–	–
12 month after	9.1	5.2	–	–
		Bank 5		
12 month before	43.3	24.2	136.2	24.7
6 month before	50.2	34.3	157.1	36.0
benchmark date	54.4	24.5	129.9	75.9
6 month after	124.1	36.6	152.6	90.1
12 month after	..	..	..	..

VI. CONCLUDING REMARKS

Free-banking economists point to insufficient market discipline as one of the
main factors behind banking crises. They argue that bank customers would be
able to monitor their banks and to influence bank management towards sound

Table 3b.   Interbank Liabilities as a Percentage
of Domestic Fund-Raising

	DOMESTIC LIABILITIES		FOREIGN LIABILITIES	
	Gross	Net (liab.-ass.)	Gross	Net (liab.-ass.)
		Bank 6		
12 month before	1.4	−4.3	14.1	8.4
6 month before	1.3	−3.6	17.4	12.2
benchmark date	**3.2**	**−3.8**	**19.9**	**13.2**
6 month after	7.6	−5.6	20.7	13.6
12 month after	11.5	−7.1	18.3	10.3
		Bank 7		
12 month before	14.1	−2.0	28.5	10.7
6 month before	20.7	−10.4	32.8	2.4
benchmark date	**19.4**	**−4.1**	**31.6**	**11.1**
6 month after	19.1	−3.8	27.7	10.2
12 month after	15.2	−10.1	24.9	11.3
		Bank 8		
12 month before	0.6	−10.1	22.8	10.7
6 month before	0.9	−9.1	28.4	27.4
benchmark date	**1.6**	**−6.3**	**32.5**	**30.3**
6 month after	1.7	−10.6	23.5	18.4
12 month after	1.2	−10.1	26.8	15.7
		Bank 9		
12 month before	25.5	2.8	42.5	6.2
6 month before	27.4	1.6	34.7	8.2
benchmark date	**34.8**	**21.3**	**31.3**	**−1.3**
6 month after	24.1	7.7	31.5	1.7
12 month after	32.2	14.2	30.5	11.1
		Bank 10		
12 month before	4.5	−6.9	5.9	4.2
6 month before	18.5	14.9	5.2	−10.3
benchmark date	**28.8**	**21.1**	**6.1**	**−17.4**
6 month after	16.3	0.3	3.8	−1.8
12 month after	6.1	−12.8	2.9	−1.9

and prudent criteria. Nevertheless, they decide not to invest their own resources
in the acquisition and processing of the necessary information because a bank crisis would imply no reduction of their financial wealth, at least up to a certain
amount of deposits.

Table 3c. Interbank Liabilities as a Percentage
of Domestic Fund-Raising

	DOMESTIC LIABILITIES		FOREIGN LIABILITIES	
	Gross	Net (liab.-ass.)	Gross	Net (liab.-ass.)
	Bank 11			
12 month before	0.0	0.0	4.4	0.8
6 month before	0.3	0.3	3.9	−0.7
benchmark date	**0.5**	**0.5**	**2.2**	**−4.7**
6 month after	0.2	0.2	3.1	−3.0
12 month after	0.3	0.3	3.4	−1.3
	Bank 12			
12 month before	25.5	12.0	5.5	3.3
6 month before	35.3	10.1	4.5	3.4
benchmark date	**29.5**	**2.0**	**5.3**	**4.0**
6 month after	21.4	10.2	2.9	−4.2
12 month after	15.2	9.2	3.2	0.4
	Bank 13			
12 month before	33.7	12.1	14.3	11.3
6 month before	28.4	1.1	13.2	9.5
benchmark date	**22.8**	**−0.1**	**11.2**	**8.8**
6 month after	21.4	−0.5	10.9	9.1
12 month after	17.8	2.9	9.8	8.8
	Bank 14			
12 month before	8.4	5.2	10.0	7.8
6 month before	7.1	2.4	7.4	6.0
benchmark date	**14.3**	**7.5**	**5.5**	**3.4**
6 month after	11.8	3.5	4.9	3.2
12 month after	4.9	2.4	6.3	2.4
	Bank 15			
12 month before	16.9	1.8	1.3	1.1
6 month before	17.8	4.4	1.0	0.8
benchmark date	**13.2**	**2.8**	**0.4**	**0.2**
6 month after	8.4	2.0	1.1	0.7
12 month after	13.3	5.5	1.2	0.9

A stronger source of market discipline should be provided by the interbank market, since interbank deposits are not covered by any explicit guarantee and banks have both the information and the ability to monitor each other. The only reason why they could decide not to go through a costly screening and monitoring of the interbank relations could be linked to the perception of an implicit guarantee on behalf of the authorities.

Looking for discontinuities in the time series referring to 15 Italian banks which became distressed in the 1990-1997 period, this study tried to ascertain whether bank depositors, corporate borrowers and other banks exerted any timely discipline on bank managers. The main empirical results are as follows:

1. bank customers rarely changed their attitude towards the distressed banks before their difficultes became openly known;
2. however, they promptly reacted to the information given by the daily press, reducing their deposits, mainly current account deposits, and the amount of financial assets trusted to the distressed bank in custody;
3. the customers' reaction was slower and less pronounced with respect to large banks; it was quicker and larger in the geographical areas where the distressed banks originated and had their headquarters;
4. the reduction of loans that is recorded for distressed banks seems to be more closely related with lending policies than with factors affecting the demand;
5. the interbank market did not play any relevant role in preventing the deterioration of individual institutions.

In conclusion, bank customers, depositors and savers, seem to be interested in the future of their banks more than borrowers or even other banks.

However, one could hardly expect them to exert any effective discipline on bank behavior, mainly due to their difficulty to evaluate the actual condition of their banks without incurring into prohibiting costs. It is not accidental that bank supervision heavily relies on on-site controls, frequent meetings with bank officers and extensive statistical reports on behalf of the banks.

On these grounds, a reduction of the coverage of deposit insurance would hardly lead to increased market discipline.

Nevertheless, since bank customers show to be quite reactive to publicly known information, bank managers have to be conscious that the effects of imprudent decisions will be made even worse by their customers' reaction, as soon as the signs of the crisis are reported by the press.

Given the prompt reaction of bank customers to the news releases, it seems worthwhile discussing over a possible improvement of market discipline through the disclosure of the ratings formulated by bank examiners.

What is really surprising is the scarce attention paid by the banks in granting interbank facilities, which makes systemic crises more probable and dangerous. Of course, this empirical result plays against the possibility of applying lower capital ratios to banks collecting a large share of their financing over the interbank market.

ACKNOWLEDGMENTS

Prepared for presentation at the 1998 Western Economic Association meetings, July 1, Lake Tahoe. The views expressed are those of the author and do not necessarily reflect those of the Banca d'Italia. The author thanks V. Cavazzino for research support and computing activity.

NOTES

1. In those statistics the interbank interest rate is defined as the maximum rate applied to the lira sight deposits of resident banks with a debit balance of more than 1 billion lire.
2. In a later work, data drawn from the screen-based interbank deposit market could be used to get a more precise timing of changes in the interbank credit relationships. For the banks that have been eventually acquired by other institutions it will also be relevant to evaluate the behavior of the acquiring bank in the most critical periods.

REFERENCES

Barth, J.R., Hudson, C.D., & Jahera, Jr. J.S. (1995). S&L closures and survivors: Are there systematic differences in behavior? In A. Cottrell, M. Lawlor, & J. Wood. (1995). *The causes and costs of depository institution failures*. Boston: Kluwer Academic Publishers.

Benston, G.J., & M. Carhill. (1992). *FSLIC forbearance and the thrift debacle*. In 28th Annual Conference on Bank Structure and Competition. Federal Reserve Bank of Chicago, May.

Benston, G.J., & Kaufman, G.G. (1997). *FDICIA After Five Years: A Review and Evaluation*. Federal Reseve Bank of Chicago, WP 97-1, July.

Benston, G.J., & Kaufman, G.G. (1994). The intellectual history of the Federal Deposit Insurance Corporation Improvement Act of 1991. In G.G. Kaufman (Ed), *Reforming financial institutions and markets in the United States*. Boston: Kluwer.

Benston, G.J., & Kaufman, G.G. (1988). *Risk and sovency regulation of depository institutions: Past policies and current options*. New York: Salomon Brothers Center, Graduate School of Business, New York University.

Calomiris, C.W., & Kahn, C. M. (1996). The efficiency of self-regulated payment systems: Learning from the suffolk system. *Journal of Money, Credit and Banking*, November.

Chari, V.V., & Jagannathan, R. (1988). Banking panics, information, and rational expectations equilibrium. *The Journal of Finance*, July.

Conigliani, C., Ferri, G., & Generale, A. (1997a). *La relazione banca-impresa e la trasmissione degli impulsi della politica monetaria*. Moneta e Credito, June.

Conigliani, C, Ferri, G., & Generale, A. (1997b). The impact of bank-firm relations on the propagation of monetary policy squeezes: An empirical assessment for Italy. *Banca Nazionale del lavoro Quarterly Review*, 271-299.

Cooper, R., & Ross, T.W. (1991). *Bank runs: Liquidity and incentives*. NBER Working Paper, No 3921, November.

Dale, R. (1992). *International banking deregulation*. Oxford: Blackwell.

D'Auria, C., Foglia, A., & Marullo Reedtz, P. (In press). Bank interest rates and credit relationships in Italy. *Journal of Banking and Finance*.

DeGennaro, R.P., & Thomson, J.B. (1993). *Capital forbearance and thrifts: An ex post examination of regulatory gambling*. In 29th Annual Conference On Bank Structure and Competition, Federal Reserve Bank of Chicago, May.

Detragiache, E., Garella, P., & Guiso, L. (1997). *Multiple versus single banking relationship*, CEPR, Discussion Paper Series, No 1649.

Diamond, D.W., & Dybvig, P.H. (1983). Bank runs, deposit insurance and liquidity. *Journal of Political Economy, 91*(3).

Eisenbeis, R.A. (1997). Bank deposits and credit as sources of systemic crisis. *Economic Review*, third Quarter.

Garcia, G. (1997). Depositor protection and banking soundness. International Monetary Fund, *Banking soundness and monetary policy*. Papers presented at the seventh seminar on central banking.

Garcia, G., & Saal, M. (1996). Internal governance, market discipline and regulatory restraint: International evidence. *Rethinking bank regulation: What should regulators do?* The 32nd Annual Conference on Bank Structure and Competition, May.

Gilbert, R.A. (1994). Federal reserve lending to banks that failed: Implications for the bank insurance fund. In A. F. Cottrell, M. S. Lawlor, & J.H. Wood. (Eds.), *The causes and costs of depository institution failures*. Boston: Kluwer Academic Publishers.

Gorton, G. (1985). Bank suspension of convertibility. *Journal of Monetary Economics, 15*(2).

Hoenig, T.M. (1996). Rethinking financial regulation. *Economic Review, 81*(2).

Kane, E.J., & Yu, M. (1994). How much did capital forbearance add to the tab for the FSLIC mess? In *30th Annual Conference on Bank Structure and Competition*. Federal Reserve Bank of Chicago, May.

Kaufman, G. (1996a). *Bank fragility: Perception and historical evidence*. Federal Reseve Bank of Chicago, WP 96-18, September.

Kaufman, G. (1996b). Bank failures, systemic risk, and bank regulation. *Cato Journal, 16*(1).

Kaufman, G. (1994). Bank contagion: A review of the theory and evidence. *Journal of Financial Services Research*, April.

Kaufman, G. (1988). The truth about bank runs. In C. England & T. Huertas (Eds.), *The financial service revolution: Policy directions for the future*. Boston: Kluver Academic.

Kroszner, R.S., & Strahan, P.E. (1994). Dividend behavior of financially distressed savings institutions. In *30th annual conference on bank structure and competition*. Federal Reserve Bank of Chicago, May.

Lang, R.J. (1996). Lessons from new Zealand—banking supervision review. In *Rethinking bank regulation: What should regulators do?* The 32nd Annual Conference on Bank Structure and Competition, May.

Park, S. (1991). Bank failure contagion in historical perspective. *Journal of Monetary Economics, 28*.

Postlewaite, A., & Vives, A. (1987). Bank runs as an equilibrium phenomenon. *Journal of Political Economy, 95*(3).

Rochet, J-C., & Tirole, J. (1996). Interbank lending and systemic risk. *Journal of Money, Credit and Banking, 24*(4).

Schoenmaker, D. (1996). *Contagion risk in banking*. LSE Financial Markets Group, Discussion Paper Series, March.

Temzelides, T. (1997). Are bank runs contagious? *Business Review*, November/December.

Waldo, D.G. (1985). Bank runs, the deposit-currency ratio and the interest rate. *Journal of Monetary Economics*, 15(2).

Wall, L.D., & Peterson, D.R. (1990). *The effect of Continental Illinois' failure on the financial performance of other banks. Journal of Monetary Economics*, 77-90.

ASIAN BANKING CRISES
IN THE 1990S:
ALL ALIKE?

Anna J. Schwartz

Discussion in the literature of the financial crises in Southeast Asian countries since mid-1997 has centered on the severe depreciation of their currencies. Less attention has been paid to the severity of problems their banks face. To stabilize their currencies and to be recipients of IMF funds, the countries have been pressured to undertake fundamental changes in their economic, political, and institutional structures. The list of required changes, said to be as many as 50 for Indonesia, but later increased to 117, includes such commitments as opening up investment in business and banking to foreigners, dismantling monopolies and cartels, eliminating restrictions on imports, and dozens of other reforms. Progress in fulfilling these reforms may be desirable, but the very multiplicity of their number detracts from the priority that should be assigned to the reform of Asian banking systems. Each of the countries has experienced a banking crisis. Until the banking crisis has been dealt with, the recovery of the economies will not occur.

Research in Financial Services: Private and Public Policy, Volume 10, pages 139-164.
Copyright © 1998 by JAI Press Inc.
All rights of reproduction in any form reserved.
ISBN: 0-7623-0358-1

Exchange rate policy may be implicated in the banking crises in the case of the Asian countries with currencies that were pegged to the dollar or to a basket of foreign currencies (Kaminsky & Reinhart, 1996).[1] Asian banking crises, however, have not been confined to countries with pegged exchange rates. The prime example of a banking crisis in a country with a managed floating exchange rate is Japan. It is of some interest to investigate why this proliferation of banking crises has happened. I propose to examine the experience of four Asian countries (Indonesia, Malaysia, Thailand, South Korea) and contrast their experience with that of Japan.

The most important propagator of banking crises in the sample of countries has been inordinate growth of financial system credit to the private sector. In four of them the growth of credit is linked to inflows of short-term foreign capital in 1993-1996. In Japan, however, it is linked to expansionary domestic monetary policy in the late 1980s.

Banking crises were festering before the onset of the currency crises that unhinged the countries with pegs. In Japan the banking crisis emerged when monetary policy tightened in 1990. It has persisted for many years since because of the government's delay in adopting measures to deal with it, although in March 1998 action to that end may finally have begun.

I begin, first, by defining a banking crisis, distinguishing it from a banking panic. Second, I review the banking experience of each of the four Asian countries and of Japan in the 1990s, and note whether steps have been taken to resolve problems. Third, I construct a checklist of features that contributed to banking crises: financial deregulation; regulatory corruption and forbearance; financial innovation; political domination of credit allocation; government guarantees of a bailout, actual or perceived; foreign capital inflows; bubbles. Fourth, I discuss contagion as a possible explanation for the simultaneous emergence of banking crises in the sample of Asian countries. Fifth, I examine the role of the IMF in helping or hindering resolution of banking problems. Sixth, I suggest what could have been done to forestall the specific banking crises covered here, and the more general case. Finally, I conclude.

I. WHAT IS A BANKING CRISIS?

Banking crises occur when insolvency threatens many institutions. Banking panics may play a role in banking crises, but not necessarily so. A panic occurs when depositors lose confidence in the ability of banks to convert their deposits into currency and therefore run on banks. A depositor run on banks unless cut short by appropriate action by monetary authorities weakens all banks. Loss of reserves by banks paying out currency leads to a scramble for high-powered money by all. Banks try to acquire high-powered money by calling loans, selling off bonds in their portfolios, and withdrawing balances with other banks, with the result that prices of assets including bonds decline for all banks. Market value of assets

Table 1.

	Total Outstanding			Short-Term Maturity[*]		
	End of		Mid	End of		Mid
	1995	1996	1997	1995	1996	1997
	A. Foreign Capital Inflows to Four Asian Countries ($ billion)					
Indonesia	44.5	55.5	58.7	27.6	34.2	34.7
Malaysia	16.8	22.2	28.8	7.9	11.2	16.3
South Korea	77.5	100.0	103.4	54.3	67.5	70.2
Thailand	62.8	70.2	69.4	43.6	45.7	45.2
	B. Short-Term External Debt as a Percentage of Foreign Exchange Reserves					
	Indonesia	Malaysia		South Korea	Thailand	
End - 1993	171	28		148	89	
Mid - 1997	182	62		214	153	

Note: [*]Omits offshore issues of commercial paper and nonbank liabilities.

Sources: BIS, 68th Annual Report, (p. 128). The Economist

declines below book value of liabilities, threatening insolvency. A panic that is not terminated by the provision of additional high-powered money by the central bank can indeed produce a banking crisis, with failures of banks that otherwise would have been solvent.

Recent banking crises, however, have not been generated by panics, although in some countries runs on specific institutions have occurred when depositors have found cause for alarm about their soundness. The problem of the banks has resulted from their own unsound performance in lending and asset acquisitions and their lack of adequate capital. Even if authorities permitted them to continue to operate, the general perception was that they were undercapitalized and that the book value of their assets was far above market value. The banks were indeed insolvent. The condition of the banks, however, was not the trigger of the financial crisis in the sample of countries. In countries with an exchange rate pegged to the dollar or another currency, the trigger was a currency crisis. In Japan the trigger was contractionary monetary policy. In both cases the upshot was the revelation of banking problems.

I now review the banking crisis in each of the four Asian countries, its relation, if any, to a currency crisis, as well as steps to resolve it, and finally the Japanese case. The origins of the banking problems were an increase in their lending power, and a decrease in the creditworthiness of the projects they financed. At the time of writing, in no country has the banking crisis been resolved.

It is not possible to provide up-to-date accurate figures that measure the Asian banking crises. At best, the published figures in official sources are

Table 2.   Growth of Bank Credit to the Private Sector Relative
to the Growth of GDP in Four Asian Countries

	1990-94	1995	1996	*1997* *Bank Credit to the* *Private Sector* *as a percent of GDP*
Indonesia	10.4	4.4	5.7	57
Malaysia	3.1	10.5	13.1	95
South Korea	2.6	2.2	−0.6	64
Thailand	10.0	11.1	5.8	105

Sources: BIS, 67th Annual Report, (p. 108); 68th Annual Report, (p. 119).

Table 3.   Number of Banking Institutions in Four Asian Countries,
July 1997, and Changes in Their Number Since Then

	Number *Of Banks* *And Finance* *Companies*	*Number* *Closed* *or* *Suspended*	*Number* *Nationalized* *or Taken* *Over by* *Restructuring* *Agency*	*Number* *Planning* *to Merge*	*Number* *with* *Foreign-Majority* *Stake*
Indonesia	228[b]	23	7[c]	11	0
Malaysia	60	0	0	41	0
South Korea	56	16	2	0	0
Thailand	108	56	4	0	4[a]

Notes: [a]2, according to New York Times, (April 16, 1998, p. D5).
[b]212, according to Wall Street Journal, (April 21, 1998, p. A23; 220, May 4, 1998).
[c]54, according to Wall Street Journal, (April 21, 1998, p. A23; 59, May 7, 1998, p. A6).

Source: The Economist, (April 4, 1998, p. 81, with some revisions).

partial and end in mid-1997. Table 1, Part A, reports the total outstanding capital inflows to the four Asian countries in each of the three years 1995, 1996, 1997, and the amount of the capital inflows that was short-term in those years. Table 1, Part B, reports for each country the percentage of foreign exchange reserves that short-term external debt constituted at the end of 1993 and mid-1997. Reliance on short-term bank borrowing made Asian countries vulnerable to reversals of private capital flows.

Table 2 reports the growth of bank credit to the private sector in relation to the growth of GDP in the sample, comparing 1990-1994 with 1995 and 1996, and the ratio of bank credit to GDP in 1997. Bank credit expansion in the 1990s was not primarily a response to profitable investment opportunities; rather the banks undertook riskier business at increasingly narrower interest margins.[2]

Table 3 lists the number of banks and finance companies in operation in July 1997 in each of the four Asian countries, and the changes in the numbers since then. The changes include the number closed or suspended, the number nationalized or taken over by a restructuring agency, the number planning to merge and the number in which foreigners have bought a majority stake. I cite other figures in my discussion, the sources of which are unpublished academic papers and press accounts.

At this juncture the figures should be regarded as illustrative rather than authoritative. In particular, the evidence on nonperforming loans in Table 4, drawn from different sources, is of uncertain value. Capitalization of interest rates on mounting nonperforming loans has added to their reported volume in some cases. In other cases banks continue to rollover loans to keep developers from default, thus camouflaging irrecoverable loans.

II. ASIAN BANKING CRISES

Indonesia

Indonesia's case exemplifies some of the causes that can account for banking crises. International banks lent short-term funds to Indonesian banks and companies. They borrowed short-term in dollars and other hard currencies and lent long-term in rupiahs. At mid-1997, outstanding capital inflows amounted to $58.7 billion, of which $34.7 billion had a short-term maturity. At the end of 1997 Indonesia had borrowed $80 billion from international banks, of which U.S. banks provided $4.9 billion, Japanese banks $22 billion, and European Union banks $21 billion.

At the end of 1997, according to one estimate, total foreign debt was 218 percent of GDP. In fact, the true size of foreign debts is not known, since banks and companies face losses as foreign exchange and derivative contracts they bought, which are not reported on balance sheets, mature.

Financial system credit to the private sector grew from 1993 on at annual rates in excess of 20 percent. Domestic debt was estimated at 66 percent of GDP at the end of 1997. Capital inflows directly into the banking system provided this funding. Bank lending predominantly was directed to nonbank corporate borrowers.

The decisions as to which industries and firms would receive loans as well as government subsidies were made by President Suharto and members of his extended family and other insiders. Large investments were made in a national car and domestic aircraft industry, neither of which was subject to a market test. Their promoters and their foreign lenders took for granted that, if they failed such a test, the government would provide additional resources.

Indonesia's financial sector comprises approximately 228 commercial banks and finance companies, some of which are owned by the state (see Table 3).[3]

Table 4.   Non-Performing Loans as a Percentage of Total Loans

	1994 (1)	1995 (2)	1996 (3)	1997 (4)	1998 (5)	1998 (6)	1998 (7)
Indonesia	12.0	10.4	8.8	15.0	9.0	12.5	11.0
Malaysia	8.1	5.5	3.9	15.0	6.0	6.0	7.5
South Korea	1.0	0.9	0.8	30.0	14.0	14.0	17.5
Thailand	7.5	7.7	NA	36.0[a]	18.0	18.0	17.5

Note: [a]Includes finance companies.

Sources: BIS (67th Annual Report, p. 107) Goldstein (1998, p. 10, based on 4 different studies).

Lack of transparency masked weakness in the financial sector. The weakness, however, cannot be attributed to deregulation, although bank supervision may have been inadequate. Improved regulations in 1993-1994 were implemented unevenly, especially with respect to limits on lending to insiders.

Depreciation of the rupiah in July 1997 as foreign funds were withdrawn jeopardized the position of bank customers with uncovered foreign liabilities, who therefore could not service their loans. Table 4 gives estimates of nonperforming loans according to diverse studies. According to other sources, nonperforming loans at state banks in mid-1997 amounted to 14 percent of total loans. Nonperforming loans at private banks were on the order of 5 percent of total credit. Nonperforming loans by the end of April 1998 were a much larger fraction of total credit, estimated at 25 percent at healthy banks, 50 percent across the banking sector. The condition of the banks aroused depositor fears. To meet withdrawal demands by depositors, the central bank printed 100 million rupiah in cash. Since it subsidized insolvent institutions, they continued to operate.

On November 5, 1997, the IMF agreed to give Indonesia a standby credit of $10.1 billion (490% of its quota), of which $3 billion was made immediately available. The total loan package including commitments from other official facilities and bilateral sources amounted to $43 billion. Lack of compliance by Indonesia led to revision of the terms of the aid agreement in January and April 1998. In July 1998, the IMF and other international lenders promised Indonesia an additional $6 billion.

With respect to the banks, in accordance with the original aid agreement, Indonesia closed 16 insolvent banks, including one controlled by the president's son, who condemned the action. He bought the license of another inactive bank and was back in the banking business in his old bank building under a new name. The closure of these banks led to a run on other banks, especially after the IMF in November 1997 proposed a deposit-insurance plan only for state-owned banks. The withdrawal of deposits from privately-owned banks by Indonesians prompted the extension of deposit-insurance to all banks, covering $55 billion in bank deposits. On December 31, a merger of four-state-owned banks was announced, their bad debts to be assumed by a new state-owned bank. Seven other banks had plans to merge. In April, 7 small banks were shut.

In late January 1998, the government created the Indonesian Bank Restructuring Agency (IBRA), which has since taken over 57 banks. Another smaller round of runs on banks occurred after closures in April. The central bank has given the restructuring agency about $13 billion that it has injected into the banking system to replace deposit withdrawals. It is not clear, however, that the central bank has succeeded in restoring depositor confidence. Deposits are still being withdrawn from the banking system.

Towards the end of May 1998, after a run by depositors, Indonesia's largest private bank was placed under the supervision of IBRA. The central bank's efforts to save the bank were fruitless. According to one report, it injected the maximum amount of liquidity allowed under its guidelines—20 percent of the bank's paid-up capital—and, according to another report, it injected double the amount of the bank's capital. The bank's chief owner is Indonesia's largest conglomerate; a Suharto son and daughter together own 30 percent of the bank. The bank will continue to operate while under supervision.

It is not known how the IBRA will administer the banks it has taken over. It is supposed to strip them of nonperforming loans. A new asset management company, to be established, is to sell salvageable assets of these banks to healthy domestic or foreign banks. At what price the company will find buyers is unclear. IBRA may be left with irrecoverable assets. At any event, by June all existing limits on foreign ownership of banks will be eliminated.

Only a dozen or so banks are expected to survive. By the end of 1998, 50 percent to 75 percent of bank loans may be nonperforming. Most banks are illiquid and insolvent. All but ten of more than 200 banks need to be recapitalized.

Merging, selling or closing unprofitable banks will lead to confrontation with Suharto's friends and his family's business partners, who are bank owners. The banks must first be audited to determine how much they owe foreign lenders. It remains to be seen whether the government will expedite auditing the banks and will proceed to dispose of them.

In July 1998 due diligence reviews of shaky Indonesian financial institutions by an international accounting firm that IBRA hired revealed that what got the institutions into trouble was complicated multicurrency derivative holdings maturing in five years or less and large amounts of loan-repurchase agreements. These transactions were not reported on bank balance sheets.

In January 1998, the government guaranteed debts the Indonesian banks owe their foreign counterparts. The banks then stopped making payments to foreign bankers. If the debts were not settled within 90 days, Indonesia would technically have been in sovereign default. The central bank, however, stated that it would indeed settle the debts, $500 million of which stem from trade-finance lines of credit.

In June 1998, a committee representing 13 U.S. and other foreign creditor banks announced a plan to restructure the $80 billion short-term foreign debt owed by Indonesian banks and as many as 800 private corporations. It is designed to deal with three categories of Indonesian foreign debt: private corporate debt, bank debt, and trade finance.

Indonesian banks will be able to exchange foreign-currency debt for new loans, guaranteed by the Indonesian central bank, with maturities of between one to four years. In exchange, Indonesian banks will repay past-due debts beginning immediately.

International banks promise to maintain trade finance lines at existing April 1998 levels, but are under no obligation to do so. The Indonesian central bank is to guarantee the lines. Clearing the arrears would clear the way for international banks to extend new credit for trade, which has ground nearly to a halt. At one-month interest rates of 50 percent, credit is scarce in Indonesia.

Companies and creditors that agree to restructure their debts would accept a fixed rate at which rupiah would be exchanged for U.S. dollars. By August 1998, the Indonesian government is to establish the Indonesian Debt Restructuring Agency to guarantee that corporations can buy dollars to repay debts, provided the creditors extend maturities of their short-term loans by eight years. The fixed rate would be based on the best of 20-day rolling averages of the rupiah's market exchange value averaged over periods that could extend through June 1999. Actual restructuring would be left to individual companies and their foreign banks. Debt forgiveness was not part of the agreement. The international banks retain the right to decide which loans to renegotiate, and which trade financings to extend to which companies. If the Indonesian company cannot reach an amicable arrangement to repay debt, the creditor bank can start bankruptcy proceedings.

Debtors will make monthly payments of interest and principal in rupiah to the Restructuring Agency from the time they enter the program. To encourage the debtors to enter the program within the first six months, those who do will get a half-percentage reduction in interest rate for the first two years; over a repayment period of eight years, the real interest rate is 5.5 percent. Debtors who agree to repay in five years pay 5 percent.

For three years the Restructuring Agency will make interest-only payments in dollars to international banks; subsequently, the agency will begin making principal payments. The hope is that: (a) during the three years when the agency is collecting rupiah, the proceeds can be invested, yielding a return to the government and (b) assuming the rupiah strengthens, the combination helps fund the foreign-exchange guarantee program. The danger is that, by assuming private sector obligations to repay U.S. dollars, when the availability of dollars is not assured, sovereign debt may ultimately become a problem for the Indonesian government. As it is, Moody's and Standard & Poor have reduced Indonesia's sovereign credit ratings several times in 1997 and 1998. The ratings in March were, respectively, B3 and B-.

In addition to foreign debt, internal rupiah debt must also be restructured. As unsettled as Indonesia's affairs were before President Suharto's resignation on May 21, they are further complicated by the appointment of his successor, whose capacity to fulfill promises to reform the economy is in question.

Malaysia

The manner in which the central bank responded to capital inflows to Malaysia is the proximate cause of the banking problems the country faces. In 1992-1993 it sterilized $12 billion of the inflow of short-term hot money and short-term bank loans, preventing expansion of domestic reserves at banks and hence the capacity to augment lending. In early 1994, however, the central bank abandoned this policy, so the banks were free to lend to the private sector the increase in their liquidity. Their loans resulted in equity and property bubbles, and a flood of consumer and capital imports.

The boom financed costly infrastructure and property projects, many of them undertaken by politically well-connected conglomerates. Financing came from banks and the stock market. The government awarded private-sector tycoons, who did not have to submit a competitive bid, large quasi-official infrastructure projects. Political patronage mattered more than technical or management skill.

The Malaysian banking system comprises 60 commercial banks, finance companies, and merchant banks. Of these, 41 are reported to be planning to merge, but it has not yet happened. The 39 finance companies were to be reduced in number to 8. Big banks are subsidiaries of conglomerates or state-owned.

The boom in lending in Malaysia, measured by the rate of growth of the ratio of bank lending to GDP, was 95 percent in 1997. The growth rate of lending by non-bank financial institutions appears to have been similar to that of commercial banks. Nonperforming loans as a percent of total loans in 1997 averaged 15 percent (Table 4).

The crisis in Malaysia was triggered by a series of conglomerate bankruptcies that had borrowed heavily to finance investment projects. In March 1997 the Bank of Negara, the central bank, restricted property and equity loans. Well before the currency crisis, it was clear that Malaysia had internal problems. After the Thai baht floated on July 2, the central bank intervened to defend the ringgit, to no avail. On September 4, Malaysia delayed several multi-billion dollar construction projects. On November 20, investor confidence in the Malaysian stock market caved. Rumors of bank runs spread. Capital outflows were massive and rapid. Despite the depreciation of the ringgit, the central bank continued a low interest rate policy to avoid monetary contraction in view of the ongoing economic slowdown, the weakness of financial institutions, and conglomerate bankruptcies.

The political situation in turn created uncertainty. A plan to support stock prices was abandoned a few days later. On December 4 the prime minister announced that the government would continue construction of an expensive land bridge and a road, rail, and pipeline project. The next day the government announced that it would cut spending on several large government projects, and tighten credit. At this point interest rates were raised.

To help relieve the debt burden of Malay-controlled conglomerates, the government will now allow ethnic Chinese to buy into troubled conglomerates, giving up the New Economic Policy adopted in 1971, after a series of anti-Chinese riots, that guaranteed preferences to ethnic Malays, 60 percent of the population, when privatizing state companies, or awarding big contracts for public facilities and services. The policy gave preferential treatment to Malays in state bank loans, property sales, university admissions, and equity ownership. The government earlier had ruled out the possibility of allowing foreigners the same right as it is now willing to grant ethnic Chinese.

Malaysia has not followed other Asian countries in seeking IMF help. A newly created National Economic Action Council is expected to devise a recovery plan. Government officials say that public funds will not be used to save the big Malay-controlled companies. They are counting on Malaysian Chinese, who control more wealth than Malays, to do so.

This pledge of abstention from government intervention initially did not apply to the banks. The use of state funds to aid Malaysia's ailing banks was occasioned by signs of increasing strain at subsidiaries of Singapore's banks. One rescued institution had a loss of 1.57 billion ringgit in the six months ending December 1997, and was said to need 1.2 billion in fresh capital to stay in business. Malaysia's second-largest banking group, a state-owned bank, was said to be short of 750 million ringgit in capital. Apparently, however, the government does not plan to bailout the entire banking system. In May 1998 the government set up an agency , the Asset Management Company, to buy nonperforming loans at market prices. The government estimates nonperforming loans at Malaysia's banks at 8.7 percent of total loans, but market observers estimate it as high as 20 percent this year. The banks are expected to immediately recognize the losses on their books when the Asset Management Company buys their bad loans to ethnic Malays who are now unable to repay them. The government hopes to finance the agency through bond sales, which, if attractively priced, could appeal to foreign investors. Foreign money, it is said, will also be attracted by the prospect of profitable resale of the loans and assets the agency acquires. At this juncture, this is speculation.

Minimum capital requirements of finance companies effective mid-June 1999 have been raised sixty-fold. Smaller firms will either have to merge with bigger ones or face closure. The full extent of banking problems is not known. In any event Malaysia will not permit foreign investment in its banks, short of capital as they are.

South Korea

South Korea's problems had emerged by the middle of 1996 after heavy borrowing by chaebols and a lending boom in the 1990s. Several chaebols collapsed in 1997 even before the won depreciated in October. Financial problems of the chaebols weakened the condition of merchant banks that had borrowed abroad to finance dubious projects of the conglomerates. In South Korea the banks were the chief borrowers from international banks.

The decline in equity market values imposed large unrealized losses on Korean banks. Instead of enforcing recognition of this condition, the central bank relaxed provisioning rules, so reserves banks had to set aside to cover equity market losses were reduced. The daily fluctuation band for the won widened from 2 1/4 percent to 10 percent.

The depreciation of the won worsened the real burden of the foreign debt. Once the condition of financial institutions became suspect, foreign banks that had in normal times renewed loans refused to roll-over lines of credit. Financial panic ensued. In November 1997 the government applied to the IMF for a standby credit. In early December, the IMF approved a record a record $21 billion over 3 years, of which it disbursed $5.6 billion immediately.

The total loan package came to $57 billion, the conditions imposed requiring radical reform of the Korean economic system. Among the changes the government agreed to introduce were the following with respect to the 56 banks: 16 of 30 insolvent Korean merchant banks would be closed; insolvent commercial banks would be merged with healthy ones or closed; 2 banks would be taken over by a restructuring agency; Korean banks would extend loans only on market considerations, not government orders.

The further collapse of the won in December, when it was freed to float, after the IMF bailout was announced, heightened the prospect of default. The political situation also contributed to the worsening of financial conditions. Kim Dae Jung, who won the presidential elections, made remarks during the campaign that left policy decisions in doubt.

A positive change occurred in January 1998 when international bank creditors agreed to negotiate an orderly renewal of short-term loans to the South Korean banks, the renewal to expire at the end of March 1998. The creditor countries then agreed to contribute immediately money they had originally intended to be a backup to the IMF bailout package.

At the end of January 1998 South Korea's international creditors made a deal to restructure $24 billion of outstanding short-term loans to banks. The creditor banks on a voluntary basis will be able to exchange loans coming due in 1998 for new loans that mature over one to three years, with South Korea government guarantees. The new loans will bear floating interest rates of between 2.25 and 2.75 percentage points over LIBOR—a lower premium than the market would have demanded.

Short-term foreign debt owed by South Korea chaebols is only one-sixth of total foreign debt, including borrowing by banks and the government, amounting to $153 billion. That debt in turn is less than half of domestic debt, estimated at $431.9 billion, owed to South Korea financial institutions by local companies. Between one-half and three-quarters of domestic debt is in the form of short-term promissory notes due in three to six months.

The chaebols are burdened with debt that is up to five times greater than equity. Seven of the top 30 chaebols have defaulted on debt payments of some of their affilates and have sought court protection for their remaining affiliates. The government has urged the chaebols to sell their low-margin earning affiliates to foreigners to bring down their debt-equity ratios. But the chaebols are reluctant to sell at prevailing low prices. Bank foreclosure would be an option if the banks themselves were solvent.

Thousands of overleveraged companies have gone bankrupt in 1998 with dire consequences for their banks. In June the government pressured South Korean banks to force out of business 55 companies, including affiliates of the country's biggest conglomerates. These companies are no longer to receive new financing from banks and existing loans to them are not to be rolled over. The 55 selected were deemed to have weak business prospects and little hope of repaying loans. These companies have until now depended on affiliates within their chaebols for funds or on emergency bank financing. The list of 55 includes only small operations that will not slim down significantly the big chaebols or change their management style.

The government bailed out two commercial banks in January that subsequently failed. Each had more than $2 billion in nonperforming domestic loans. At the heart of the problem of the financial system are nonperforming loans, estimated at 20 percent to 30 percent of total loans. Soaring interest rates have hurt both banks and their customers.

Banks' capital bases have been severely eroded. At the end of February the central bank noted that 14 of South Korea's 26 commercial banks had failed to meet capital adequacy standards required by the BIS. These banks must submit restructuring plans to shore up their capital bases. In May 12 submitted rehabilitation plans. Two banks are up for auction.

In June bank regulators announced that five of the 12, with only 7 percent of total commercial bank assets, would be closed. The remaining 7 commercial banks had their plans accepted. Of these, five stronger banks will assume the assets and liabilities of the liquidated institutions on a selective basis. The performing loans will be transferred from the liquidated institutions, and their bad loans will be acquired by a government fund. The government will provide 13 trillion won to buy the bad loans, 2 trillion to help the acquiring banks recapitalize, and 2.5 trillion to a reserve fund in case the loans that the banks acquire become nonperforming.

Although the banks had promised to stop lending to companies with little hope of survival, in May they joined with five major creditors of the tenth largest conglomerate to grant a fresh loan of $425.8 million. The conglomerate will make only reduced interest payments and no principal payments until the end of the year on its existing $2.5 billion debt. In return the main affiliate of the conglomerate must replace its management and sell some holdings.

Earlier in April, South Korea sold $4 billion in dollar-denominated bonds to investors around the globe, one-quarter in 5-year notes, the balance in 10-year securities, at yields of about 3.5 percentage points above U.S. Treasuries. How the government will spend these funds has not been announced. Presumably the money could be used to shore up the banks but that is not proposed.

In May 1998 the gove rnment committed 25 trillion won to buy bad loans from financial institutions at a 50 percent discount. That amounts to a purchase of 50 trillion bad loans, which, according to the government's estimate of nonperforming loans—loans not serviced in more than three months—total 118 trillion won. An additional 16 trillion won will be used to increase the financial companies' capital. As a result the government may become the largest shareholder in some banks. As noted above, two banks have already been nationalized. Nine trillion won will be allocated to the deposit-insurance fund.

The government expects to raise the money for the bailout by issuing bonds to the banks in exchange for bad loans or equity. Hence the plan does not provide the banks with an infusion of cash. Moreover, the government is counting on the banks to clean up the remaining bad loans on their books by the sale of collateral or calling in loans. The process will further erode the banks' capital, which, it is hoped, they will restore by issuing equity and attracting foreign investment. The government in turn will use the proceeds of privatizing state companies to service the bonds it will issue. The credibility of the entire bailout plan is doubtful. It depends on white knight rescue of the financial institutions that is fundamentally wish-fulfilling.

Nevertheless, the Korean situation was given a vote of confidence late in May by a German bank that has purchased a 24 percent stake in a merchant bank affiliated with a state-run Korean bank.

Thailand

Thailand deregulated the domestic financial system in the 1990s, liberalizing interest rates and the activities of financial institutions. As a way of liberalizing the capital account, it established the Bangkok International Banking Facility (BIBF), an offshore banking center, in 1993. BIBF-based foreign banks expanded the volume of foreign-currency denominated loans in Thailand (Kawai, 1998).

Offshore borrowing by banks and the private sector produced massive capital inflows into Thailand during the 1990s. The government gave tax breaks to banks in the BIBF, which dealt exclusively in lending and borrowing foreign currencies.

The inflows were predominantly short term (IMF, 1997), and they were not sterilized. Bank credit to the private sector expanded there to a greater extent than in the other Asian countries examined here.

Confidence in the economy sagged when it became clear that banks and finance companies had lent excessively to unprofitable real estate projects and business ventures. The stock market in the first half of 1997 fell 50 percent, and foreign investors pulled out of Thailand when their Thai partners could not raise funds for joint ventures.

Finance companies, 91 in number, were heavily exposed to commercial real estate development. The problem, however, did not end with finance company exposure. Banks, of which there were 17, held a significant share in the equity of finance companies.

In February 1997, a land company failed to make a payment due on its foreign debt, presaging property problems for finance companies. That month, when the baht was under attack and overnight interbank interest rates spiked up, the central bank raised banks' capital requirements and suspended 16 of the 91 finance companies. Through its Financial Institutions Development Fund the central bank lent about $8 billion to troubled financial institutions between February and July—about one-third of high-powered money and one-fifth of foreign reserves at the end of 1996—a sum that was largely irrecoverable. To staunch the drain on the weak condition of the finance company industry, the government promised to insure domestic deposits and liabilities. Reversing this position at the end of June, the government withdrew support from a major bank, exposing domestic and foreign creditors to losses. The action led to increased foreign withdrawals, and depreciation of the baht. On July 2, 1997, the baht was freed to float.

Thailand had $37.7 billion in foreign exchange reserves at the end of 1996, but $29.4 billion swap obligations reduced the reserve to $2 billion at the end of June 1997. Approximately $45 billion in short-term corporate debt was due foreigners. The government owed about the same amount. At the end of 1997, the private sector had an estimated $67.3 billion debt.

In August 1997 a $20.1 billion rescue package was assembled for Thailand by the IMF and Asian countries, including a $3.9 billion standby credit (505% of its quota). In return Thailand suspended 58 finance companies, of which 56 will be liquidated. Six of 16 remaining banks have been nationalized. Foreigners have bought a majority stake in 4 others. The purchase of one of the banks is not final, and the price will not be determined and paid until the year 2000, when the bank's worth will be better known. Capital shortages exist in other commercial banks. The strongest banks, however, have succeeded with enormous equity issues. The government also owns eight of thirty-five operating finance companies that are also short of cash. They had borrowed heavily from the central bank and were unable to raise capital. Seven of the eight were nationalized in May 1998. The government has been selling the assets from closed finance companies at public auction.

The IMF relaxed tax and budget targets in the March 1998 review of Thailand's economic progress. The March letter of intent outlining Thai commitments to the IMF did not include new rules that had been under discussion that would have forced the banks to declare loans as nonperforming and to provision them after three months of missed payments. The new rules would have increased the banks' need to seek funds from foreign investors. Instead the rules as of January 1, 1998, that define nonperforming loans when payments have not been made for six months, continue in force. Nonperforming loans on this rule are 25 percent of total loans. An international investment firm expects nonperforming loans at Thailand's five largest banks to peak at about 42 percent of their total loans.

A new quarterly instalment of the IMF loan that will be available in June 1998, if Thailand has fulfilled its earlier commitments, will be accompanied by a new letter of intent.

Moody's has cut the long-term subordinated debt and financial strength ratings for the big banks because of an increase in problem loans.

All banks will be required to sign agreements with the central bank by August 15, 1998, on their capital-raising plans through the end of the year. Finance companies will have until September 15 to sign such agreements.

The government said it aims to reduce its stake in four recently nationalized banks as soon as possible. The letter of intent requires it to establish a privatization secretariat, and to propose reforms to allow further privatizations.

A new bankruptcy law took effect in April. One IMF condition is that Thailand by October must pass a law making it possible for creditors to foreclose on the collateral of defaulting debtors.

In the meantime, lending activity has come to a virtual halt. Exporters can't get working capital locally, and many overseas banks no longer accept letters of credit from any Thai banks.

A government-established debt advisory committee conducted a survey of 47 domestic and foreign lenders and reported in July that respondents had completed debt restructuring in only 25 cases. An additional 505 cases are undergoing debt restructuring. The committee was set up by the Bank of Thailand in June to speed the restructuring process. The process will continue on a case-by-case basis handled by the private sector with minimal government intervention. The survey did not indicate what percent of total loans are being restructured.

Japan

The problems Japan has had with banks and other financial institutions since 1992 are unrelated to the yen exchange rate, a managed floating currency. The financial institutions include commercial and savings banks, credit unions, credit cooperatives, and life insurance companies.

Bubbles in property and stock markets in the late 1980s burst when monetary policy tightened in 1990 (Kähkönen, 1995). Banks were eager lenders until engulfed by huge problem loans. The banks counted on an implicit government guarantee to protect them. The government, however, in the years since the banks' troubles emerged has been passive, neither helping nor closing down insolvent ones. Since 1997 banks have cut back on lending even to creditworthy firms, with a resulting tide of bankruptcies and sinking equities. Banks in effect have not been functioning as credit market intermediaries.

Initially, forbearance by regulators and later the weak performance of the economy impeded solving the financial system's difficulties. Regulators are accused of accepting bribes from banks to cover up their problem loans. Full disclosure of domestic nonperforming loans on the balance sheets of the institutions, said to be $620 billion at banks, has yet to be achieved. But it is not only the internal debt problem that confronts the banks. That problem has been compounded by their exposure to the Southeast Asian banks and companies that have been unable to service their loans (said to be $271 billion) since the 1997 currency weakness in that region. For some Japanese banks, the exposure is greater than their core capital base. Fundamentally, however, it has been the Japanese government's delay in dealing with the banking situation that accounts for its persistence.

A decline in the Japanese stock market has serious consequences for the capital position of banks, which are permitted to count 45 percent of the unrealized gains on listed equities as part of their second tier capital. Life insurance companies and securities companies, which hold equity among their assets, also are vulnerable to a fall of the stock market (IMF, 1997).

The government poured over $7.5 billion in public funds into the stock market on March 31, 1998, the end of the fiscal year, to manipulate share prices, so that banks' capital base would meet international standards. The banks were given the alternative of recording their stock prices at the purchase price, instead of present market value. The equities banks hold are shares in companies which in turn hold shares in the banks.

Two brokerage firms filed for bankruptcy in November 1997. The collapse of the second one, Yamaichi Securities, revealed that it had 200 billion yen in hidden losses, which it had shifted to offshore companies, unbeknownst to regulators. Banks also failed in November. They were bailed out by the government which assembled $230 billion to rescue them. The Hokkaido Takoshuku Bank that was closed in November 1997 is the first of the 20 major banks that was not granted regulatory forbearance with respect to asset quality. Paying off its depositors will be a big drain on the Deposit Insurance Corp.

Nonperforming loans are backed by property and equity collateral whose value fell with the bursting of the bubbles. Property values are still falling, and banks pour money into weak corporations to keep them afloat. Japanese banks behave this way because they are expected to give a helping hand to struggling clients in the hope that they can be restored to health.

Stronger banks that are solvent and profitable have only lately begun provisioning for bad loans, or selling off a record $76.6 billion loans (a pittance compared to an estimated $1 trillion in bad loans) in a small but growing secondary market in the fiscal year ending March 31, 1998. One explanation for the reluctance of the banks to sell off bad loans was the imposition of a tax on sales of loans at a loss. There is now a plan by the tax authorities to exempt banks from this tax.

Problem loans are growing even as banks begin to grapple with them. If banks have set aside reserves for questionable loans, the loans still remain on their books. In addition, loans that are being fully written off were never included in the disclosed tally of problem loans. The big money center banks have recorded losses as a result of loan write offs. Loan portfolios are shrinking in view of weak corporate sales, low earnings, and rising bankruptcies.

The tally of bad loans will increase, even as write offs increase, as the change in reporting standards on loans takes effect in April 1998, limiting the banks' discretion to postpone reporting loan losses. The Ministry of Finance is offering a one-year grace period for a limited number of small banks that were supposed to meet tough new capital requirements by March 31, 1998, to enable them to replenish reserves depleted by bad loan losses.

The government, however, may finally be taking action to stabilize the financial system and end regulatory strangleholds. A Big Bang Reform program (including deregulating the scope of business activities in banking, securities, trust, and insurance industries, and the provision of innovative financial instruments) is scheduled to be spread out over five years (Suzuki, 1997). One reform that has been implemented is the complete liberalization of interest rates at banks.

In February 1998 Japan's parliament passed legislation to make available public funds amounting to $137 billion to beef up Japan's underfinanced Deposit Insurance Corp. to protect depositors. The law sets up a fund within the Deposit Insurance Corp. to issue bonds, guaranteed against default by postal savings system money backing. The proceeds of the bond sale will be used to pay depositors of banks that will be shut down. By selling assets of failed banks, the fund will acquire money to pay off the bonds.

Another piece of legislation, passed in February 1998, makes available a $102 billion bank rescue scheme. The banks are to issue either preferred shares, which carry no voting rights, or subordinated bonds, which carry fewer creditor rights than other bonds. The government is to disburse the public funds parliament allocated to buy these securities in order to strengthen the banks' capital. Since the government feared that, if only weak banks applied, depositors would regard their securities sale as a stigma and run on the banks, some pressure was exerted on the big banks to be the first to apply. Hence 21 big banks did so, but most of them chose not to sell preferred stock to avoid possible government interference in their operations. Some strong banks in fact issued preferred shares in New York to prove that they could raise funds on their own.

So far, the only banks to which funds were disbursed were banks that were not in trouble. In any event, recapitalizing the banks is only a first step. Two problems remain to be addressed. One is to cleanse nonperforming loans from the banks' portfolios. Another is to shut down many small unprofitable institutions.

Banks for too long were protected by minimal disclosure. Now they are being pressed to beef up capital to make possible writing off nonperformiing loans. Hence banks are reluctant to extend new loans. Insufficient credit is the complaint of the business sector. Until the supply of loans is restored, fiscal stimulus, which Japan is being urged from many quarters to adopt, will not solve the country's economic quagmire.

In July the government announced the Total Plan to address the banking problems at the heart of Japan's prolonged decline. The plan calls for the government to close some insolvent banks, leaving untouched the 19 largest ones. A bridge bank is to be established, with a five-year term, to arrange mergers or acquisitions of closed institutions, if possible; if not, the bridge bank will install its own managers and provide credit to creditworthy borrowers, and sort out the assets of the closed banks. Good ones will be sold, the bad ones assumed by taxpayers. A special session of the Japanese Diet is to be called to enact the Total Plan. The resignation of the Prime Minister following a poor showing of his party in the recent election of the upper body of the parliament adds to the prevailing uncertainty about the firmness of the government's commitment to financial reform.

Moody's has downgraded credit and financial strength ratings for five major Japanese banks, and put another four Japanese banks under review for possible downgrade, citing low profitability, low capital, and low reserve levels.

III. COMMON FEATURES OF THE BANKING CRISES

The basic feature of all five banking crises has been an excessive expansion of bank credit (Folkerts-Landau et al., 1995). In the case of the four Asian countries capital inflows provided the increase in bank liquidity (Corsetti et al., 1998). In the case of Japan expansionary monetary policy before 1990 was the source of the increase in bank liquidity.

In all the countries credit allocation has not been market-driven. Political influence has been exerted on the banks to lend as directed. Regulatory corruption has occurred to shield banks from penalties for not observing regulations (Table 5).

The expansion of bank credit has been channeled to loans for the creation of unprofitable industrial capacity and the purchase of equities and real estate. Banks themselves have acquired equities or have invested in other types of financial institutions that are subject to fewer restraints than they are to acquire equities and property.[4] When the bubble in asset prices eventually bursts, banks and their customers confront major difficulties. For the four Asian countries the commercial property prices bubble burst between 1990 and 1995, residential property prices between 1992 and 1997; for Japan both bubbles burst in 1990.[5]

Table 5. Contributors to Banking Crises

	Financial Deregulation	Regulatory Corruption and Forbearance	Financial Innovation	Political Domination of Credit Allocation	Government Guarantees	Foreign Capital Inflows	Bubbles
Indonesia	Yes	Yes	No	Yes	Yes	Yes	Yes
Malaysia	No	Yes	No	Yes	Yes	Yes	Yes
South Korea	No	Yes	No	Yes	Yes	Yes	Yes
Thailand	Yes	Yes	No	Yes	Yes	Yes	Yes
Japan	Yes	Yes	Yes	Yes	Yes	No	Yes

As the value of the asset collateral held by banks declines, the pressure on lever-aged investors to sell exacerbates downward pressure on prices. Assets pledged as collateral for loans or financed by bank loans can endanger the entire financial system when prices for assets collapse.

Currency crises did not bring on the banking crises in any of the Asian countries. The banking problems had already manifested themselves beforehand.

IV. DOES CONTAGION EXPLAIN THE INCIDENCE OF ASIAN BANK CRISES?

The sequence of crises beginning with Thailand, moving on to Indonesia, then to Malaysia, and on to South Korea has spawned the notion that contagion accounts for the spread (IMF, 1997). In my view these are not examples of contagious international transmission. Contagion occurs when external shocks impinge on countries independent of their condition. Instead, in the recent examples, investors recognized that the set of countries that was affected all shared the same problems. Investors then withdrew their capital. There was no contagion.

The way contagion is said to have manifested itself regionally, according to one view, is that the first country whose currency depreciated damaged the competitive position of a second country, which put pressure on its currency to depreciate, thus damaging the competitive position of a third country, and so on (Corsetti et al., 1998). This may describe the process of the diffusion of depreciation but the fundamental reason countries were vulnerable was that their economies were all riddled with problems. True, there were transitory effects on other regional countries and some at a distance, reflected in yield spreads between their sovereign debt and U.S. Treasuries, but the spreads quickly narrowed as investors differentiated their condition from that of the affected Asian countries.[6]

Implicit in the notion of contagion is the view that an individual country that has mismanaged its affairs can precipitate an international financial crisis. Thus the individual country's loss of creditworthiness is said to have a tequila effect. The supposed tequila effect is that other countries without the problems of the troubled country are unfairly tarnished as also subject to those problems. In this way, it is said, contagion spreads the crisis from its original source to other innocent victims.

But is it true that the market will withdraw its support not only from a country which has financial problems that the market has at some point become aware of but also from other countries in the region and elsewhere that do not share those problems? No one doubts that Thailand's plight that led to the plunge in the Thai baht on July 2nd was due to its own unwise policies: a growing current account deficit, excessive short-term foreign borrowing, a banking sector weighed down by speculative property loans, and corrupt government and business practices. To show that Thailand spread contagion, however, it would be necessary to demonstrate that otherwise sound economies suffered the Thai fate.

Were the sharp moves in foreign exchange markets that followed the fall of the baht, as the Indonesian rupiah, the Malaysian ringgit, and the South Korean won slipped their pegs an overreaction by investors that belied sound conditions in each of these economies? The increase after the onset of the crisis in correlations of weekly movements in equity prices in Thailand with equity prices in other stock markets is cited as indicating transmission of shocks (BIS, 1998, p. 132). To me the correlations reflect common equity market declines as features of changes in investor expectations, not transmission.

To reduce inflation and keep it low, each of these countries pegged the exchange rate at a fixed value, or within a narrow band, to that of the dollar or a basket of currencies, with the idea of achieving an inflation rate comparable to that of the dollar or the currency basket.

In today's world of highly mobile capital and deep capital markets, a pegged exchange rate signifying a low inflation policy attracts large capital inflows from abroad. That is what happened to the Southeast Asian economies. At the start, the exchange rate peg and declining inflation gave the investment climate enormous drawing power. However, while the pegged nominal exchange rate was fixed or slowly adjusted, the real exchange rate appreciated with growing capital inflows. This was the case for Indonesia, Malaysia, and Thailand, but not for South Korea. The real exchange rate of the won was undervalued even before its post-crisis drop in value. If investors did not pull out of South Korea because of misalignment of its exchange rate, there was ample reason for their concern about the health of its chaebols and banks (Willett, 1998).

Widening of the current account deficit typically accompanied an appreciation of the real exchange rate in the other Asian countries, which made imports cheap and exports expensive (Chinn, 1998). When the current account deficit mounted as a percentage of GDP, confidence in the economy deteriorated.[7] Moreover, if the capital that was attracted from abroad was not used productively, the inflow became the basis for nonperforming loans by domestic banks, some of which might be state-owned but all generally under political control.

Because local lenders harbored doubts about the future value of the domestic currency, as seen in a risk premium on domestic securities, nonfinancial firms and governments of these countries were tempted to issue interest-bearing debt denominated in foreign currencies at lower interest rates.[8] In fact, in each of the four countries, companies borrowed in dollars or yen but earned revenue in local currencies. These companies are now vulnerable to the increase in the burden of their foreign indebtedness given their limited ability to repay it.

Finally, the foreign exchange reserves of these countries were far from ample. To defend the exchange rate, the central bank would have had to tighten monetary policy to convince the market that it would not devalue. To tighten, however, would restrict economic growth, already slowing, and exacerbate the problems of distressed financial institutions.

The foreign exchange market summed up these concerns about the Asian countries by selling off their currencies. Stock market declines matched the currency declines. It was not contagion from Thailand, however, that made the countries vulnerable to a financial crisis. They were vulnerable because of their home-grown economic problems.

V. ROLE OF THE IMF

The IMF's approach to the Asian financial crises has been to offer a country requesting aid a bailout package of money in return for which it imposes programs requiring reform of financial institutions, economic structures, and political behavior. Martin Feldstein has criticized the IMF approach on the ground that the Asian countries do not need structural reforms to regain access to capital markets (Feldstein, 1998). In addition, the bailout encourages future lenders to expect that they will be bailed out, so they need not be concerned about credit risks in lending to debtor countries. This is an incentive to lenders to take reckless and irresponsible risks.

I fault the IMF on these and other grounds. One question is, for whose benefit the bailout is arranged. The bailout protects investors who lent money to governments or private sector institutions, not the people who suffer the consequences of unsound policies the Asian country has pursued. Another question is, why does the IMF rush in with a bailout, given that the fundamental solution to a situation when a country cannot meet its obligation to foreign creditors is for a workout negotiated by the debtors and creditors that restructures the debt, extending repayment dates, and reducing the contractual interest payments. The argument that creditors are too numerous and dispersed for rescheduling to occur without disbursements from the official sector has been questioned (Goldstein, 1998, p. 43).

I have already referred to my objection to the laundry list of changes the IMF demands of its Asian beneficiaries. The IMF approach does not emphasize the crucial importance of first solving the weaknesses of the banking system. The banking systems in the Asian countries are unable to lend and economic activity is frozen. Banks that can be salvaged need to be recapitalized by arranging mergers or infusions of capital from domestic or foreign sources, and some agency must be established to take over the nonperforming loans in their portfolios. Banks that are beyond salvation need to be shut down. The important aim is to revive lending so economic activity can resume. Restoring access to the world capital market is secondary to reviving the domestic banking system.

The final problem with the IMF approach is that it is weak on crisis prevention. I now turn to that subject.

VI. PREVENTING BANKING CRISES

If the main reason for the Asian banking crises has been excessive credit expansion by their financial institutions, what steps could have been taken to limit it? An effort was made to restrict specific types of lending. One measure some Asian authorities introduced was to subject real estate loans to maximum loan-to-value ratios or repayment periods. Maximum amounts were set on bank lending for the stock market and investment in property. Moral suasion was employed to deter banks from lending for property investment. Sometimes regulatory clout was used to deny authorization of new branches if the objective of moral suasion was not observed.

Another policy to limit credit expansion was directed not at specific forms of lending but at the main conduit—foreign inflows. Asian authorities imposed higher reserve requirements on foreign short-term bank deposits than on other bank deposits. This policy resembled portfolio reserve requirements by Chile in mid-1991, when it attempted to reduce a surge of capital inflows and to shift the maturity to longer term (Edwards, 1998, Table 5). Studies of the results seven years later reveal that reduction of the volume of funds entering Chile has not been achieved although the maturity of the inflows has been lengthened.

The Bank of Thailand tried to curb onlending to the domestic market by the Bangkok International Banking Facilities by limiting local banks' net foreign exchange liabilities to a percentage of assets. The banks also could not include foreign deposits in calculating statutory loan-to-deposit ratios they were required to maintain (BIS, 1997, p. 113).

These measures were ineffective. A different course is available. To prevent the rapid expansion of credit that breeds banking crises, the IMF could have urged the central banks to neutralize the capital inflow to Asian countries. The central banks could have sold their notes to the market, offsetting the rise in liquidity that the capital inflow provided.[9] This is sterilization, but its effects are not comparable to sterilization of gold inflows under the gold standard. Under the gold standard sterilization impeded the adjustment of balance of payments disequilibria, preventing expansion in the countries receiving gold, which otherwise would have experienced a decline in exports as domestic prices rose. That would have relieved pressure on countries losing gold. Sterilization in a world with independent country capital flows has no such implications for world stability. Sterilization in this world in which there are no destabilizing links of domestic financial arrangements across borders, would have prevented the credit expansion effects of a capital inflow the Asian countries could not cope with. In no way would sterilization have been damaging to the freedom of international capital flows, which is a freedom worth preserving.

Sterilization of capital inflows was attempted by some Asian countries in the early 1990s (Spiegel, 1995). Several dissertations have provided sterilization coefficient estimates ranging from -.42 to -.75 for these years, and it appears that

Thailand and Indonesia may have continued to sterilize after 1995 (Nyatepe-Coo, 1995; Rooskaveni, 1998; Sarjito, 1996). But the magnitudes for the growth of bank credit to the private sector (Table 2) could not have reached the levels recorded had sterilization been effectively and successfully pursued. There is a discrepancy between available evidence on sterilization and the outcome of the process of offsetting strong international capital inflows on the expansion of domestic liquidity in the Asian countries.

In any event, it is clear that the IMF did not monitor what Asian countries were doing in the effort to reduce the liquidity of their monetary systems, and did not offer intellectual support for their efforts. If there is a lesson to learn from the Asian banking crises, it is that prevention is preferable to post-crisis conditionality programs.

It remains to say something about how the Japanese banking crisis, which capital inflows did not produce, might have been prevented. The case is easy. The Bank of Japan should not have permitted the ratio of total private credit to GDP to increase approximately 50 percent between 1985 and 1990. Contractionary policy then was indicated. An ounce of prevention is worth a pound of cure.

VII. CONCLUSION

Banking crises are the common element of the Asian financial difficulties in the 1990s. The banking crises occurred because of excessive expansion of credit. Capital inflows were the source of the credit expansion in four Asian countries. In Japan, the source was loose monetary policy between 1985 and 1990. In each country the expansion of credit could have been prevented.

What urgently needs to be done is to speed recovery from the financial crisis in which each Asian country is, at present, mired. That will involve restoration of balance sheets of nonfinancial firms as well as of financial institutions, so that financial intermediation can resume.

NOTES

1. Kaminsky and Reinhart conclude that banking problems help predict a balance-of-payments crisis, but the converse is not true.

2. The change in net interest margins between 1990-1994 and 1995-1996 is reported in BIS (1998, p. 119).

3. In 1994, the share of assets of state-owned banks of total bank assets in financial intermediation was 48 percent (Milken, 1998, p. II-28).

4. Equity markets capitalization between 1990 and 1996 as a percentage of GDP rose six-fold in Indonesia, tripled in Malaysia, doubled in Thailand, and fell in South Korea (BIS, 1997, p. 105). Estimates of the share of bank lending in the property sector accounted for 25 to 40 percent of total bank loans in Indonesia, Malaysia and Thailand, and 15 to 25 percent in South Korea (Goldstein, 1998, p. 8).

5. See data on the trough and peak of property prices and the change since the peak (BIS, 1998, p. 140).

6. See the discussion of competitive depreciation of exchange rates in BIS (1998, p. 106).

7. See the data on the real effective exchange rate in the first half of 1997 in BIS (1998, Table 111.3, p. 38); and the data on the current account in billions of U.S. dollars and as a percent of GNP (Table V11.5, p. 130).

8. The combination of a fixed exchange rate with relatively high domestic interest rates and inflation was an incentive to residents to borrow foreign currency to finance local currency business or assets (BIS, 1998, p. 124).

9. An argument against sterilization is that, by keeping domestic interest rates higher than they otherwise would have been, the policy induced larger net inflows and a high share of interest-sensitive short-term flows (Goldstein, 1998, p. 7, note 2). Limiting the transmission of the inflows to financing private sector loans, however, would have had a countervailing effect. Would not banks and companies have been less eager to welcome inflows?

REFERENCES

Bank for International Settlements. (1997). *67th Annual Report,* 1st April-31st March.

Basle (1997). *68th Annual Report,* 1st April-31st March 1998.

Chinn, M. D. (1998). *Before the fall: Were East Asian currencies overvalued?* NBER Working Paper 6491.

Corsetti, G., Pesenti, P., & Roubini, N. (1998). *What Caused the Asian Currency and Financial Crisis?* Mimeo.

Edwards, S. (1998). *Capital inflows into Latin America: A stop-go story?* NBER Working Paper 6441.

Feldstein, M. (1988). Refocusing the IMF. *Foreign Affairs 77,* 20-33.

Folkerts-Landau, D., Schinasi,G.J., Cassard, M., Ng, V.K., Reinhart, C.M., & Spencer, M.G. (1995). Effect of capital flows on the domestic financial sectors in APEC developing countries. In M.S. Khan & C.M. Reinhart (Eds.), *Capital Flows in the APEC Region* (pp. 31-57). IMF.

Goldstein, M. (1998). *The Asian financial crisis: Causes, cures, and systemic implications.* Institute for International Economics. Policy Analyses in International Economics No. 55.

International Monetary Fund. (1997). *World Economic Outlook: Interim Assessment.*

Kähkönen, J. (1995). Movements in asset prices since the mid-1980s. In U. Baumgartner & G. Meredith (Eds.), *Saving behavior and the asset price "bubble" in Japan: Analytical studies* (pp. 51-62). IMF.

Kaminsky, G. L., & Reinhart, C. M. (1996). *The twin crises: The causes of banking and balance-of-payments problems.* Board of Governors of the Federal Reserve System. International Finance Discussion Paper 544.

Kawai, M. (1998). The East Asian currency crisis: Causes and lessons. *Contemporary Economic Policy, 16*(2), 157-172.

Milken Institute Global Conference. (1998). *Global finance: Capital access indicators.* Banks -1.

Nyatepe-Coo, A. A. (1995). Resource shocks, real exchange rate appreciation and independence of monetary policy in developing oil-exporting countries. *International Economic Journal, 9,* 91-107.

Rooskaveni, N. (1998). *The effects of monetary policy in Indonesia.* Unpublished Ph.D. Dissertation. The Claremont Graduate University.

Sarjito, I. B. (1996). *The short-run independence of monetary policy in Indonesia: Estimation of the offset coefficient and the monetary authority's reaction function.* Unpublished Ph.D Dissertation. The Claremont Graduate University.

Spiegel, M. M. (1995). Sterilization of capital inflows through the banking sector: Evidence from Asia. *Federal Reserve Bank of San Francisco Economic Review, 3,* 17-34.

Suzuki, Y. (1997). What lessons can be learned from recent financial crises? The Japanese experience. In *Maintaining financial stability in a global economy*. A Symposium Sponsored by The Federal Reserve Bank of Kansas City, 169-174.

Willett, T. D. (1998). *International financial markets as sources of crises or disciplibe: The too much, Too late hypothesis,* Mimeo.

COMMENT:
FINANCIAL CRISES AND 'MARKET REGULATION'

Douglas D. Evanoff

The devaluation of the Thai baht in July of 1997 is typically cited as the beginning of the current Asian economic crisis. This was followed by currency problems in the Philippines, Indonesia and Malaysia, and significant stock market declines in Hong Kong, South Korea, Thailand and Indonesia. The crisis is currently at a critical juncture. The means to resolve the situation are being discussed, as are "bail out" packages, and fiscal proposals aimed at stimulating domestic economic activity in order to avoid (or more realistically, dampen) the near term possibility of a recession/depression. Just as important, however, are critiques of existing regulatory arrangements and reform proposals offered to prevent similar problems from occurring in the future.

We address three basic issues. First, the events leading up to the Asian crises are reviewed, followed by a discussion of the causes of the problem. That is followed by a discussion of the economic theories and models offered to explain behavior consistent with economic/financial crises. Finally, a particular piece of evidence on the ability of market discipline to prevent crises is discussed.

Research in Financial Services: Private and Public Policy, Volume 10, pages 165-173.
Copyright © 1998 by JAI Press Inc.
All rights of reproduction in any form reserved.
ISBN: 0-7623-0358-1

I. PRECRISIS ASIA

Cargill (1998) and Schwartz (1998) review the events leading up to the crises in five Asian countries. Cargill draws upon his extensive work in this area (see e.g., Cargill, 1998; Cargill & Royama, 1988, 1998; Cargill & Hutchinson, 1977) and details the economic and financial market environments prior to the crises in Korea and Japan. He describes the "Japanese financial regime," which approximately characterizes the system in both countries, as one which stressed a strong work ethic, an educational system geared to provide a disciplined and well-trained labor force, significant external reliance on natural resources, high investment and low consumption-to-GDP ratios and, most importantly for our purpose, a public policy attitude which encouraged close corporate-to-financial sector ties and viewed the financial sector as a tool of industrial policy. There was very little reliance on market forces and market discipline. He argues that the regime was successful as long as certain non-sustainable conditions held. Inevitably, those conditions began to change, that is, the countries became less internationally isolated, the number of financial channels increased and economic growth slowed. As a result, the flaws in the system became evident. The regime which in the past had been extensively praised as a "model" for economic growth, was essentially a disaster waiting to happen.

Schwartz's analysis hones in more directly on particular near-term events leading up to the current crises in the five countries. Combining data from a number of sources she stresses the "home-grown" problems such as excessive short term bank debt, low bank capital levels, and government-directed loans. The resulting capital allocation was heavily distorted and lending standards were essentially ignored. She perceives this to have been the fundamental cause of the problem— an excessive credit expansion by financial institutions. She stresses that contagion did not play a major role in the crises; instead emphasizing the unwise domestic policies and the numerous domestic problems which riddled each country.

II. MODELING FINANCIAL FRAGILITY

The Cargill and Schwartz articles, in combination with Garcia (1998), provide an excellent review of the events leading up the Asian crises. What they do not explain, however is why the problems occurred when they did. While there were similarities with each of the five countries, (discussed in more detail later) there were very significant differences. For example, some of the countries encountering difficulties had fixed exchanged rates, while others had flexible rates. Some had state-owned banks, others did not. Agricultural loans were prevalent in some countries, but not in others. Certain countries were characterized as having tight monetary policy, others did not. The degree of credit extension and the reliance on short-term bank borrowings, while relatively high in each country, were significantly different across countries (see e.g., Schwartz, 1998, Tables 1 and 2). There were also significantly different degrees of asset bubbles across the countries; for example, contrast the difference between the situations in Japan and Korea.

In addition to there being major difference between the countries, the speed with which conditions seemed to turn sour was rather remarkable. In the period just prior to the crises, most countries in the region had budget surpluses and economic conditions that were progressing rather nicely. Inflation and unemployment were relatively low throughout the region and bond spreads between the debt of these countries and U.S. Treasuries actually fell between 1995 and 1997 (see Cline & Barnes, 1997). Recent GDP growth rates, with the exception of Japan, were the envy of the rest of the world (see Garcia, 1998). Finally, there were relatively stable political regimes and no apparent social unrest.

Then how, and why, did the crises occur so suddenly under such diverse conditions? As economists we like to have models of behavior and causal relationships which incorporate fundamental values (e.g., asset values), which we typically do not believe change as quickly as suggested by the Asian crises. The set of models capable of explaining such crises is quite limited. The standard neoclassical growth model, while probably the most commonly used to depict growth trends and transitions to new equilibrium values following a shock to the system, is poorly suited to explain crises and sudden changes in market values. Rather, shocks are typically assumed to be exogenous.

To provide background on the type of models which can be used to explain crises, Benink (1998) reviews the existing literature on growth and financial fragility. He summarizes models which may be used to explain how these apparent anomalies occur. In doing so he emphasizes the difference between risk and uncertainty.[1] Risk can be calculated, priced and managed. It can be reduced to the "correct and objective probability distribution." Parties may suffer losses, but they occur as a result of calculable risks. Uncertainty, on the other hand, involves uniqueness, and a resulting inability to form inferences about real probabilities. Benink also stresses the distinction between rational and irrational behavior. The presence in financial markets of increased irrationality and uncertainty can lead to greater opportunities for crises.

The models of market/financial fragility can be classified into three categories:[2]

- crises resulting from irrational bubbles,
- crises resulting from rational bubbles and
- cries resulting from regulatory/politically induced fragility.

Models of irrational bubbles emphasize uncertainty and postulate that economic agents base decisions on unrealistic or euphoric expectations. Standard examples include rampant speculation in foreign exchange markets and excessive optimism with irrational over-extensions of loans; for example, Minsky (1977a, 1977b), Kindelberger (1995).

I have significant problems with these types of models because of their fundamental thesis: economic agents do not behave rationally. People with economic incentives not to err, apparently make consistent, systematic errors. I also do not like, nor believe, the resulting policy recommendations. They imply that regulations need to be imposed to prevent this irrational behavior. Instead of having decisions made by those who have a vested interest in that decision, it is argued they can be made more efficiently, and should be made, by a paternalistic government bureaucrat. These models are frustrating to most economists because they challenge the fundamentals on which the discipline is based.

The second class of models associate crises with rational bubbles. These typically rely on expectations which are not based on the fundamental properties of the underlying asset. The decision to continue bidding the price of an asset upward may be entirely based on expectations that other bidders will continue to bid higher; regardless of the true value of the asset. Until this bubble bursts, there are potential profits to be realized. The potential risk involved with being "caught" in the market when it does bursts is calculable. What distinguishes this class of models is the potential for fundamentals to rationally be dominated by expectations of the actions of others. As examples, Benink discuss possible events in foreign exchange markets.

Another example of this type of model is that put forward by Marshall (1998). His model is a hybrid of the Diamond-Dybvic (1983) model and Keynes' (1936) "betting on a beauty contest" model. In this environment, external finance is required for a specific project and performance is dependent on the number of investors willing to finance it.[3] Therefore performance is dependent on an investor's perception of other potential investor's willingness to finance the project. If an investor believes that others will refrain from investing in the project then, even if it is known to be a viable project, it is rational for the potential investor to also refrain from investing. Thus beliefs are self-fulfilling and a worthwhile project has failed because of a coordination failure. Everyone would have been better off if the project had been funded. Therefore, in these models we have an equilibrium which is a function of fundamentals until this coordination failure occurs. As this threshold is reached there is a jump process as the change in the expectations of the behavior of others is sufficient to forego financing the project. I believe this is very promising work. However I think there is a long way to go before this entire line of modeling is very useful in explaining financial crises.

The final class of models imply that crises occur because of fundamental distortions to the market which result in imprudent behavior (from a societal view) and excesses of the sort typically associated with crises. A mispriced safety net, regulatory forbearance and directed capital allocation lead to less risk avoidance behavior than would otherwise occur. This results in an accumulation of lower quality assets. In this state, if a shock does occur, or if the situation is suddenly revealed to the market, a crisis can occur.

While I believe there are still problems with this being a complete explanation of financial crises, most importantly the failure to explain the timing and the suddenness of the adjustment to the new environment, I believe much of the evidence is consistent with this last model. At a minimum, the problem is made significantly worse as a result of this problem. Elements typically associated with this view were the commonalities of the Asian countries discussed by Cargill, Schwartz, and Garcia. For example, in the countries considered, nearly each had some degree of government controlled credit allocation, an aversion to market forces, opaque bank balance sheets, a poorly structured disclosure framework, some form of guarantees for depositors/investors/debtholders, rampant political patronage and a denial of banking problems typically followed by a covering up of the problem in hope it will only be transitory and self correcting. This allows a troubled institution to gamble for resurrection and potentially incur additional losses.

III. REGULATORY REFORM AND MARKET DISCIPLINE

Are these situations preventable? To the extent that they are caused by regulatory distortions, there would seem to be means to prevent them. The most topical issue currently surrounding the Asian crises is determining how to best address the existing losses and how to prevent the situation from worsening. As mentioned earlier, decisions have to be made on economic reform proposals. I would hope that simultaneously, financial regulatory reform could also be addressed. While there is generally no good time for regulatory reform—during bad times it is argued that the reforms will be too burdensome on banks, and during good times there is no groundswell for reform—it is hoped that the current crises will serve as a catalyst for governments to act.[4]

If regulatory reform is introduced, what characteristics should the new regulatory framework have? First, to the extent possible it should maximize reliance on market mechanisms. This should allow market participants, acting in their own self interest, to effectively allocate capital and reward those participants who best perform this function. It is important to insure, however, that the marketplace has the information needed and capability to regulate firm behavior. That is, the necessary infrastructure requirements must be in place. This encompasses the legal system and judiciary processes for determination of property rights and bankruptcy procedures. It requires adequate accounting standards and the assurance that accurate and useful information will be disclosed to the marketplace. Regulation can be used to insure that the infrastructure is sufficient to allow the market to function effectively. This can best be done by encouraging the dissemination of relevant information, limiting entry barriers, and promptly resolving distressed institutions.

Given a sufficient market infrastructure and heavy reliance on market forces, to the extent necessary, regulation can be used to complement market discipline.[5] It is also important that the regulatory framework have certain characteristics. For example, the agency responsible for regulation should be as independent as possible from political pressure, should pursue long-term objectives, and should have limited discretion in implementing regulatory policy (i.e., forbearance should be restricted). Additionally, the regulatory arrangements should emphasize, to the extent possible, incentive-compatible regulation which aligns the regulated firm's objectives with that of the regulator (which should align with society's objectives). This allows for regulated outcomes, but utilizes market forces instead of regulatory mandates to achieve them. By having a well-structured, incentive-compatible regulatory structure in place, banks operating in their own self interest will behave prudently. Additionally, many of the all-too-common moral hazard problems can be avoided.[6]

My recommendations suggest a greater reliance on market discipline.[7] This brings me to the Reedtz (1998) paper which evaluates the effectiveness of the market in disciplining bank behavior. As banking conditions deteriorated in Italy during the 1990s, did savers, borrowers, and other banks step in and exert timely discipline on the management of troubled banks? The basic argument typically offered by proponents of market discipline in banking relies on the presumption that market participants can anticipate problems at financial institutions, and a belief that the existence of deposit insurance will sever this discipline even if the participants are aware of problems at financial institutions. To empirically evaluate whether the market can be expected to discipline banks Reedtz evaluated creditor behavior at 15 distressed banks.

Summarily, the evidence was somewhat mixed. Reedtz found that depositors responded (via deposit withdrawals) as public information became available indicating that an institution was financially distressed. There was no response prior to this public information, thus, there was little ex ante discipline to keep the banks from encountering difficulties. The interbank market, originally thought to potentially be the best source of discipline, played essentially no role in exerting discipline.

These findings are not all that surprising. An open question is whether the findings are evidence of the failure of market discipline, or evidence of behavior consistent with moral hazard problems. While the Italian banking industry has become more competitive in recent years, has become more privatized and has recently moved to decrease deposit insurance coverage, there is still a track record of protecting creditors from failure. Thus, the lack of response by creditors, particularly interbank customers, probably results from expectations of an implicit guarantee. If this is the case, one would expect to see it most pronounced by the customers of large banks as these banks may be perceived to be too-big, or too-important, to fail. It is not uncommon for bank regulators to be much more willing to impose losses on the creditors of small banks than they are on those of larger banks. Indeed, this is supported by the findings in Reedtz. Creditors of large banks were not found to respond nearly as quickly as were the creditors of small banks which encountered difficulties. In fact, the creditors of small banks were found to respond prior to the public release of news that the bank was under duress; precisely the type of disciplining influence expected from unprotected (either explicitly or implicitly) market participants. The lack of response from the interbank market can also be explained by the expectations of counterparty-banks that they would be protected. In the past, Italian authorities have stepped in and protected failed banks and explicitly stated that this was necessary because the institution was too important to a particular region of the country to allow it to fail. In the United States there is evidence of market discipline only during the period in which losses began to be imposed and the markets became convinced that there would be no implicit guarantee (e.g., see Flannery & Sorescu, 1996).

In summary, the papers by Cargill, Schwartz, Benink, and Reedtz are worth-while additions to the current debate on the causes, and the means to prevent, banking crisis. Perhaps the most important lesson we can take from the discussion is the important role of the regulatory framework in preventing or, all too often, causing the crises. Given the paramount role played by the financial sector in determining economic activity, it is hoped that lessons will be learned. As countries are forced to allocate the losses encountered by these crises they should also move to correct the distortions in the existing bank regulatory structure. Otherwise, the topic of financial crises will be revisited all too often in the future.

ACKNOWLEDGMENTS

The author acknowledges numerous informative discussions/debates with Herb Baer, Phil Bartholomew, Charlie Calomiris, Tom Cargill, Nicola Cetorelli, Velma Davis, Gill Garcia, Hesna Genay, George Kaufman, David Marshall, Kathy Moran and Larry Mote. The views expressed are those of the author and are not necessarily shared by the Federal Reserve Bank of Chicago or the Federal Reserve System.

NOTES

1.   Knight (1921) serves as the basis for this distinction.

2.   This is the author's preferred classification. Benink provides a more detailed breakdown.

3.   The example can easily be transferred to one for a firm or a country instead of an individual project.

4.   Special care should be taken, however, to avoid a "knee jerk" reaction in an effort to respond quickly and, as a result, introduce poorly structured regulation. There are a number of cases where regulatory reforms introduced during crises may have caused more long-term problems than they resolved. In the United States potential examples include banking legislation introduced during the crises of the 1930s (e.g., Kaufman, 1994), and regulation of pharmaceutical products following the infamous Thalidomide incidents in the 1950s (e.g., Evanoff, 1989).

5.   Many would argue that the need for regulatory intervention in the market, given that the above mentioned infrastructure is in place, is quite limited.

6.   Examples of incentive-compatible regulation include elements of prompt corrective action (e.g., Kaufman, 1998; Benston and Kaufman, 1997), proposals that require subordinated debt serve as a larger component in bank capital structures (e.g., Evanoff, 1993), and the precommitment approach to bank capital level determination (e.g., Marshall & Venkataraman, 1998). It is important to emphasize the importance of the abovementioned infrastructure requirements if regulators intend to rely on market discipline and incentive compatible regulation. If it is not in place, then making adjustments to create the necessary infrastructure should be the top priority of regulators. All too often, however, it is argued that these changes and use of market discipline "will not work" in certain countries. While significant care should be taken in incorporating changes in less-developed countries, because of the lack of a fully developed infrastructure, evidence exists suggesting that even in these countries parties respond as expected to appropriately structured regulatory regimes (e.g., see Mondschean & Opiela, 1998; Moore 1997).

7.   Many of these regulatory framework characteristics are similar to those recently proposed for the new European markets by the European Shadow Regulatory Committee (1998).

REFERENCES

Benink, H. (1998). Financial fragility: Theories and empirical evidence. In G. G. Kaufman (Ed.), *Research in financial services: private and public policy.* Greenwich, CT: JAI Press.

Benston, G. J., & Kaufman, G. G. (1997). FDICIA After five years. *Journal of Economic Perspectives, 11.*

Cargill, T. F. (1988). Korea and Japan: The end of the "Japanese Financial Regime." In G. G Kaufman (Ed.), *Research in financial services: Private and public policy.* Greenwich, CT: JAI Press.

Cargill, T. F., & Hutchison, M. M. (1997). *The political economy of Japanese monetary policy.* Cambridge: The MIT Press.

Cargill, T. F, & Royama, S. (1988). *The transition of finance in Japan and the United States: A comparative perspective.* Stanford: Hoover Institution Press.

Cargill, T. F., & Royama, S. (1998). *Proceeding of a conference on preventing banking crises: Analysis and lessons from recent global bank failures.* Washington, DC: GPO.

Cline, W., & Barnes, K. (1997). *Spreads and risks in emerging markets lending.* Institute of International Finance, Research Paper No. 97-1.

Diamond, D., & Dybvig, P. (1983). Bank runs, deposit insurance, and liquidity. *Journal of Political Economy, 91.*

European Shadow Financial Regulatory Committee. (1998). *Dealing with problem banks in Europe.* Statement #1.

Evanoff, D. D. (1993). Preferred sources of market discipline. *Yale Journal on Regulation, 10.*

Evanoff, D. D. (1989). Returns to R&D, and regulation of the U.S. pharmaceutical industry. *Review of Industrial Organization, 4.*

Flannery, M., & Sorescu, S. M. (1996). Evidence of bank market discipline in subordinated debenture yields: 1983-1991. *Journal of Finance, 51.*

Garcia, G.G.H. (1998). The East Asian financial crises. In G.G. Kaufman (Ed.), *Research in financial services: Private and public policy.* Greenwich, CT: JAI Press.

Kaufman, G.G. (1998). Central banks, asset bubbles, and financial stability. In G. G. Kaufman (Ed.), *Research in Financial Services: Private and Public Policy.* Greenwich, CT: JAI Press.

Kaufman, G. G. (1994). *Reforming financial institutions and markets in the United States.* Boston: Kluwer.

Keynes, J. M. (1936). *The general theory of employment, interest and money.* Cambridge: Macmillian Cambridge University Press.

Kindleberger, C. P. (1995). Business cycles, manias, and panics in industrial societies. In C. P. Kindleberger (Ed.), *The world economy and national finance in historical perspective.* Ann Arbor: University of Michigan Press.

Knight, F.K. (1921). *Risk, uncertainty and profit.* Chicago: University of Chicago Press.

Marshall, D. A. (1998). Understanding the Asian crisis: Systemic risk as coordination failure. *Economic Perspectives,* Federal Reserve Bank of Chicago, Third Quarter.

Marshall, D. A., & Venkataraman, S. (1998). Bank capital standards for market risk: A welfare analysis. *European Finance Review.*

Minsky, H. P. (1977a) The financial instability hypothesis: An interpretation of Keynes and an alternative to "standard" theory. *Nebraska Journal of Economics and Business, 16.*

Minsky, H. P. (1977b). A theory of systemic fragility. In E. I. Altman & A. W. Samets (Eds.), *Financial crises: Institutions and markets in a fragile environment.* New York: John Wiley & Sons.

Mondschean, T. S., & Oiela, T. P. (1998). Bank time deposit rates and market discipline in Poland: The impact of state ownership and deposit insurance reform. In *Proceedings of a conference on bank structure and competition.* Federal Reserve Bank of Chicago.

Moore, R. R. (1997). Government guarantees and banking: Evidence from the Mexican peso crisis. *Financial Industry Studies,* Federal Reserve Bank of Dallas, December.

Reedtz, P. M. (1998). Bank relations and the perception of a bank crises. In G. G. Kaufman (Ed.), *Research in financial services: Private and public policy.* Greenwich, CT: JAI Press.

Schwartz, A. J. (1998). Asian banking crises in the 1990s: All alike? In G. G. Kaufman (Ed.), *Research in financial services: Private and public policy.* Greenwich, CT: JAI Press.

PART III

THE ROLE OF GOVERNMENTS AND MARKETS IN INTERNATIONAL BANKING CRISES:
THE CASE OF EAST ASIA

James R. Barth, R. Dan Brumbaugh, Jr.,
Lalita Ramesh and Glenn Yago

I. INTRODUCTION

Throughout the world there have been a large number of significant banking problems in recent years. In East Asia since 1980 there have been varying degrees of banking problems in ten countries: China, Hong Kong, India, Indonesia, Korea, Malaysia, the Philippines, Singapore, Taiwan, and Thailand. No region of the globe, however, appears to have escaped this kind of difficulty. Since 1980 nearly three fourths of the member countries of the International Monetary Fund (IMF)—133 countries in all—have experienced significant banking problems (see Lindgren, Garcia, & Seal, 1996, p. 30).

Research in Financial Services: Private and Public Policy, Volume 10, pages 177-233.
Copyright © 1998 by JAI Press Inc.
All rights of reproduction in any form reserved.
ISBN: 0-7623-0358-1

To varying degrees these problems have involved the failure of large numbers of banking institutions and the imposition of large costs to resolve the failures. In the highly industrialized United States from 1980 through 1996, for example, 5,207 federally insured banking institutions with $920 billion in assets failed, and cost an estimated $192 billion to resolve.[1] In developing and transition economies it is reported that banking problems since 1980 have collectively cost $250 billion (see Chote, 1996, p. 10). In some instances the losses as a percentage of GDP were large. Indeed, in Argentina's 1980-1982 crisis, the estimated resolution cost reached 55 percent of GDP.[2]

In many instances, particularly recently in East Asia, the losses associated with bank failures have not been limited to failure resolution costs. Banking problems in some countries have been so disruptive that they have contributed to declines in international reserves, depreciation in foreign exchange rates, and economy-wide downturns.

Our goal in this paper is to try to explain what caused the recent difficulties in several countries in East Asia and to suggest ways to prevent future problems. In doing so, we specifically focus on the banking crises in the region and attempt to explain what they have in common with other banking crises around the globe, including those in countries, like the United States, with the most well-developed financial systems in the world. An important element in understanding these issues is assessing the appropriate mix of government intervention and market forces in designing a national financial system in a global marketplace.

II. PLACING NATIONAL FINANCIAL SYSTEMS IN A GLOBAL FRAMEWORK

The General Framework

There are countless differences in financial systems among the approximately 190 countries in the world.[3] Until very recently in China, for example, all of the banks were state owned. State-owned banks are quite important in many parts of the world. In many countries, moreover, the government directly and indirectly allocates credit through state-owned and privately owned banks. Apart from central banks, state-owned banks are relatively unimportant among the financial systems of most developed countries. In the United States, for example, there are no state-owned banks, although credit is allocated in various ways through government-controlled agencies and government-sponsored enterprises. Nonetheless, all developed nations have elaborate bank and non-bank regulatory structures that directly and indirectly affect banks and the financial system more generally.

Regardless of the differences, however, the two fundamental goals of all financial systems are identical: to facilitate the flow of funds from savers to investors through a credit system and to facilitate payments through a payments mechanism.

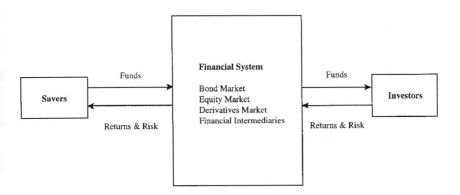

Figure 1. Designing a Financial System

This relationship is depicted in Figure 1. In facilitating the flow of funds from savers to investors and facilitating payments, every nation's financial system also attempts to address two categories of problems: minimizing transactions costs and resolving certain market failures associated with costly and imperfect information.

The ultimate goal of a financial system is to facilitate the efficient allocation of scarce economic resources in order to promote economic development and growth that improve living standards. Given technological developments there are relatively few physical or technological obstacles to capital flows anywhere in the world. The quality of information has also improved and transaction costs, including those associated with information, have declined significantly. Thus, Figure 1 can be seen as a representation of the world financial system in which increasingly savers represent all savers and investors represent all investors in the world.

At the moment different countries are at different stages of economic development and have adopted different systems of law and regulation. The stage of development, system of law and regulation, and overall institutional framework can greatly affect how well a given country's financial system works, and how well integrated it is with those in the rest of the world.[4] Nonetheless, it is significant that given the appropriate economic, legal, regulatory and institutional development, capital can now flow anywhere in the world.

The center section of Figure 1 illustrates the different institutions and financial instruments that can comprise a financial system. There are many different types of financial intermediaries, including depositories, insurance companies, pension and retirement funds, finance and mortgage companies, mutual funds, security brokers and dealers, real estate investment trusts, and issuers of asset-backed securities. In some countries these intermediaries are separate and distinct firms, whereas in other countries they are part of the same firm (see, e.g., Barth, Nolle, & Rice, 1997, Table 6a).

Each of these intermediaries functions as part of the credit or payments system, or both, and in most countries has historically tended to specialize in particular financial products and services. More recently, however, in many countries the distinctions among these different types of intermediaries have become blurred, as the emphasis by all intermediaries has been increasingly on using a wide range of financial instruments to manage the assets and to manage the risk for customers.

Not only financial intermediaries but also financial markets in equities, bonds, and derivatives, publicly and privately placed, can exist as part of the asset-management and risk-management systems facilitating the flow of funds from savers to investors. Through these markets, saving is transformed into investment. The transformation can also take place in more direct ways, such as a founder's investment in a firm or through angel and venture capital being provided to start-up or younger firms.

Not all countries employ all types of intermediaries and markets in their financial systems. In general, the lesser a given country's economy has developed the narrower and shallower will be the types of intermediaries and markets. The range of financial instruments will necessarily also be more limited. Increasingly, however, less developed countries are able to use the financial systems of more developed countries to facilitate the flow of funds from savers to investors rather than developing more extensive financial systems of their own.[5]

Economic Obstacles to Matching Savers and Investors: Transactions Costs and Market Failures

In the process of facilitating the flow of funds from savers to investors, all financial systems help resolve problems involving transaction costs and certain types of market failures, predominately involving informational asymmetries, including moral hazard (hidden action), and adverse selection (hidden information). For different types of transactions and financial institutions, attempts can be made to resolve these problems through private contracts or with government intervention.

All credit market and payment system activities involve transaction costs. An efficient financial system operates with relatively low transaction costs; both broadly and narrowly defined. An important form of broad transactions cost involves the extent to which a broad set of relationships, generally recognized in a legal system and often the focus of government regulation, exist within a society. Such well understood relationships provide a societal basis in which a financial system can operate efficiently.

In this sense, the extent to which illegal activities or the absence of enforceable property rights divert the efficient flow of resources is a broad transaction cost.[6] Custom and tradition can also involve behavior that from the perspective of financial markets raise transaction costs. Governments, furthermore, can raise transaction costs through inappropriate regulation, taxation, subsidies, corruption, or in extreme cases limiting individual economic freedom. Direct government allocation of credit, including that through state-owned banks, and indirect allocation of credit can also raise transaction costs. The availability, cost, and reliability of relevant information, and associated accounting systems may further impede the efficient flow of resources through an economy.

Narrower transaction costs can also be substantial. The U.S. government, for example, estimates that the cost is 48 cents for its own paper check transactions in contrast to two cents for electronic transactions. This is an example of how technological developments can lower transaction costs. Economies of scale also exist. Financial institutions can charge lower fees for larger transactions, thereby lowering transaction costs. A bank or mutual fund, for example, faces a lower transaction cost if one customer opens an account for $100,000 in contrast to 100 individuals opening accounts for $1,000 each.

Potential market failures in the form of information asymmetries exist in all relationships between investors and savers. Typically, for example, investors seeking and obtaining funds for specific projects have better information than lenders. This asymmetric information involving hidden information and hidden action gives rise to specific kinds of costs. One such cost involves adverse selection, for example, which refers to distinguishing good from bad borrowers before a loan is made. Another cost involves moral hazard, for example, which refers to being certain that the funds provided will be used as intended after a loan is made. In most cases, these types of market failures can be dealt with privately through contractual arrangements, which may include the use of government enforcement powers.

Forms of Government Intervention

Many forms of government intervention have developed over time in various countries. In order to protect against widespread runs on solvent depositories, most countries have established a lender of last resort.[7] These runs can occur because depositors are promised the withdrawal of their funds on demand at par value in a situation in which they have less information than depositories regarding the depositories' financial condition. Deposit insurance can serve as a backstop to a lender of last resort against widespread runs against solvent depositories, making certain that depositors never have an incentive to run and thereby disrupt the credit system or payments mechanism.[8] Deposit insurance, however, creates a need for selected regulation to control moral hazard (as well as closely related principle-agent and adverse-selection problems), which can exacerbate the risk exposure of a deposit-insurance fund.[9]

In most developed countries, the primary regulatory tools to contain risk-taking behavior of depositary institutions are the establishment of minimum capital requirements, requirements for regular consolidated financial reporting, and examination and supervision. Deposit insurance also requires a resolution mechanism in order to prevent excessively costly failures after depositories have become critically undercapitalized and subject to seizure by regulators.

Complicated and extensive restrictions on the activities, ownership, and geographic location of banks have been imposed by law and regulation in some countries. Ostensibly they have been imposed in order to limit potential conflicts of interest and those activities deemed to be excessively risky, thereby increasing the safety and soundness of banks. Some restrictions, of course, may be appropriate under certain circumstances to control the moral-hazard problem that arises with deposit insurance. Others, however, may limit the ability of banks to adapt in a prudent manner to changing market conditions.

Still other types of constraints have evolved in a variety of countries. Some laws and regulations have been enacted to promote competition. In this respect, selected antitrust actions involving bank mergers have been taken over time. Bank regulation is also used to support the provision of merit goods, such as housing, with the effect of allocating credit. Still other government regulations focus on financial issues relating to low-income individuals. Finally, other types of regulation provide protections against identifiable risks to individuals, such as specific forms of discrimination. Regulations also exist that protect banks from competition, which can arise within or from outside a country. The type and degree of constraints vary both over time within individual countries and from one country to another at a point in time.

III.   WHY ALL OF THIS MATTERS: THE WORLD'S "HAVES" AND THE "HAVE-NOTS"

There have always been "Haves" and "Have-Nots" among the world's countries in terms of financial resources. Today, unlike any other time in history, there are relatively few physical or technological impediments to the flow of funds from savers anywhere in the world to investors anywhere in the world. Thus, it is possible for the world's "Have-Nots" to fund a substantial amount of their future development and economic growth with the savings from the "Haves" of the world. As a result, the future economic development and growth of the "Have-Nots" can be much more expansive than it would be if funded only with their own internally generated savings. This is similar to a firm funding its investment projects with both internal funds (e.g., through retained earnings) and external funds (e.g., through bank loans and the issuance of bonds and stocks) by relying on financial intermediaries and financial markets.

The disparities among countries based on selected indices of overall economic and financial performance are enormous. As one can see in Figure 2 (developed from Table 1), the eleven countries of the G-10 group of countries contained only 12 percent of world population in 1995 (871 million people), but accounted for approximately 74 percent of world gross domestic product (GDP), 79 percent of world bank assets, 83 percent of world equity market capitalization, and 68 percent of world international debt securities.[10]

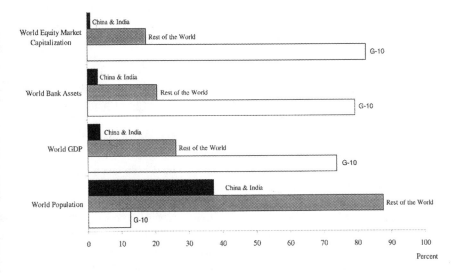

Figure 2. Comparative Population, Gross Domestic Product and
Selected Financial Information: 1995

By extension, the remaining countries in the world, numbering approximately
180, have 88 percent of the world's population (5.8 billion people) but account for
only 26 percent of world GDP, 21 percent of world banking assets, 17 percent of
world equity market capitalization, and 32 percent of world international debt
securities. As Figure 2 also shows, the world's two most populous nations—China
and India—accounted for 37 percent of world population but only 4 percent of
world GDP, 3 percent of world bank assets, and 1 percent of world equity market
capitalization.

These disparities help elucidate what the longer-term overall goal should be in
resolving the East Asian banking crisis. The disparities are also the key to understanding what the goal should be in general regarding lesser-developed countries
around the world that have experienced serious banking difficulties. The
longer-term overall goal ought to be to help these countries resolve their banking
problems in a way that enhances the efficient and stable flow of private funds from
the developed world to these countries.

Most economists have concluded that there is a positive relationship between
the depth and breadth of a nation's financial system and the rate of development
and growth of the nation's economy.[11] By extension, to the extent that nations with
relatively rudimentary financial systems can gain access to private savings from
countries with relatively well developed financial systems, it will have a positive
effect on their financial infrastructure as well as economic development and

Table 1. Comparative Population, Gross Domestic Product and Selected Financial Information: 1995 (Percent)

	Share of World Population[1]	Share of World GDP[2]	Share of World Bank Assets[3]	Share of World Equity Market Capitalization[4]	Share of World International Debt Securities[5]	Share of World Domestic Debt Securities[6]	Share of World Mutual Fund Assets[7]
Asia							
China	20.98	2.51	2.58	0.24	0.45	NA	NA
Hong Kong	0.11	0.52	0.88	1.71	0.55	NA	0.62
India	16.33	1.16	0.47	0.72	0.14	0.39	0.19
Indonesia	3.55	0.71	0.26	0.37	0.15	NA	NA
Korea	0.79	1.64	1.11	1.02	1.01	0.91	1.54
Malaysia	0.34	0.31	0.32	1.25	0.20	0.25	NA
Philippines	1.28	0.28	0.16	0.33	0.12	NA	NA
Singapore	0.05	0.30	0.44	0.83	0.04	0.20	NA
Taiwan	0.37	1.10	2.21	1.05	0.09	NA	0.08
Thailand	1.05	0.60	0.63	0.80	0.26	NA	NA
Latin America							
Argentina	0.60	1.01	0.25	0.21	0.90	0.20	NA
Brazil	2.80	2.47	1.00	0.83	0.66	0.84	NA
Chile	0.25	0.24	0.12	0.42	0.03	NA	NA
Mexico	1.64	0.90	0.39	0.51	1.15	0.09	0.17
Memo							
Germany	1.42	8.68	12.47	3.25	9.65	7.68	6.33
Japan	2.19	18.35	26.42	20.62	13.12	19.92	8.72
U.K.	1.02	3.97	8.86	7.91	8.09	2.41	2.97
U.S.	4.60	24.97	12.14	38.55	9.71	43.33	52.81
G-10[8]	12.48	73.78	79.30	82.53	68.23	91.67	87.14
EU[9]	9.33	51.39	74.53	46.36	67.24	52.49	43.40

Notes: [1]World Population: 5.7 billion.

[2]World GDP: 26,471 billion USD.

[3]World Banking Assets: 30,428 billion USD.

[4]World Equity Market Capitalization: 17,788 billion USD.

[5]World International Debt Securities: 2,803 billion USD.

[6]World Domestic Debt Securities: 24,878 billion USD. This total is based upon OECD countries plus selected emeging markets

[7]World Mutual Fund Assets: 5,341 billion USD.

[8]Group of Ten (G-10) countries include Belgium, Canada, France, Germany, Italy, Japan, the Netherlands, Sweden, Switzerland, the U.K., and the U.S. Switzerland became a full member in 1984, bringing the group to eleven members.

[9]European Union countries include Austria, Belgium, Denmark, Finland, France, Germany, Greece, Ireland, Italy, Luxembourg, the Netherlands, Portugal, Spain, Sweden, and the U.K.

Source: Milken Institute

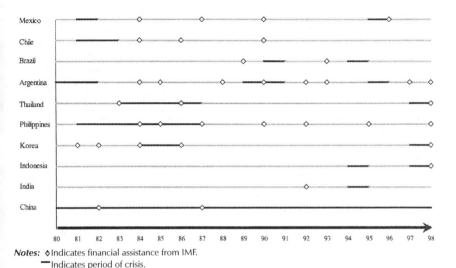

Notes: ◊ Indicates financial assistance from IMF.
━ Indicates period of crisis.

Figure 3. Bank Crises and IMF Financial Assistance: 1980 to Present

growth. If the access to foreign private savings comes in the form of direct investment, it will generally also entail access to skills and knowledge from abroad.

If, instead, the developing and emerging market countries of East Asia and other areas of the world attempt to rely predominantly on their own internal financial resources, or pay only lip service to integrating their financial systems with those of the rest of the world, they can expect to experience far lower paths of economic development and growth than they could otherwise achieve. Indeed, the economic development and growth that they can achieve if they focus on integrating their financial systems with those of the rest of the world could be significant by comparison.

With greater development of global financial markets there are also important potential benefits for the savers in countries with relatively well developed financial markets. To the extent that a greater flow of savings into other countries develops and finances productive investment projects, the greater will be the risk-adjusted return to the savers in the relatively well-developed nations. This follows from the fact that these savers have an expanded range of potentially productive investments over a wider geographical area into which to place their savings.

In order for an efficient and innovative global financial system to evolve, however, individual borrower countries' financial systems need some fundamental compatibility with those of individual lender countries. This is what one should be working toward: compatible and predominantly market-driven financial systems

Table 2. Bank Crises: 1980 to Present

	Crisis Years	Estimated Cost or Magnitude of Problem	Financial Assistance from the IMF (total amount agreed in billions of SDRs and specific years of agreement)
Asia			
China	1980s - present	Official estimates suggest 10-20% of bank loans nonperforming.	1.1 (1981, 1986)
Hong Kong	1982 - 1983	16 banks and other deposit-taking institutions failed.	0.0
India	1994 - 1995	Nonperforming domestic assets of the 27 public sector banks estimated at 19.5%	2.4 (1991)
Indonesia	1994	1.8% of GDP	7.3 (1997)
	1997 - present	Bank nonperforming loans estimated to be close to 50%.	
Korea	Mid - 1980s	Nonperforming loans of deposit money banks exceeded 7% of total assets in 1986.	1.8 (1980, 1981, 1983) 0.3 (1985)
	1997 - present	Bank nonperforming loans were 7.5% of GDP at end-September 1997.	15.5 (1997)
Malaysia	1985 - 1988 1997 - present	4.7% of GNP Bank Negara forecast non-performing loans at year-end 1998 to be 12%.	0.0
Philippines	1981 - 1987	3% of GDP	1.8 (1983, 1984, 1986, 1989) 2.6 (1991, 1994, 1998)
Singapore	1982	Nonperforming loans at domestic commercial banks wer 0.6% of GDP.	0.0
Taiwan	1983 - 1984 1995	NA	0.0
Thailand	1983 - 1987 1997 - present	1.5% of GDP Bank of Thailand reported nonperforming loans of commercial banks as 8.2% of loans, June 30th 1997.	0.3 (1982) 0.4 (1985) 2.9 (1997)

Latin America			
Argentina	1980 - 1982	55.3% of GDP	4.3 (1983, 1984, 1987, 1989)
	1989 -1990	Failed banks held 40% of financial system assets.	0.8 (1991)
			4.0 (1992)
	1995	45 institutions closed or merged.	2.8 (1996, 1998)
Brazil	1990	NA	1.1 (1988)
	1994 - 1995	5-10% of GDP	1.5 (1992)
Chile	1981 - 1983	41.2% of GDP	1.4 (1983, 1985, 1989)
Mexico	1981 - 1982	Government tood over troubled banking system.	4.8 (1983, 1986)
			3.7 (1989)
	1995	12-15% of GDP	12.1 (1995)
Memo			
Germany	None	NA	0.0
Japan	1990s	25% of GDP	0.0
U.K.	None	NA	0.0
U.S.	1984 - 1991	3.2% of GDP	0.0

Note: Indonesia: Wall Street Journal 4/23/98, Pg. A-15.

-IMF: Korea's request for stand-by arrangement 12/3/97, Pg. 3.

Malaysia: Euromoney April 1998, Pg. 46.

Thailand: The Banker, December 1997, Page 40

Source: Milken Institute

where the wealth of the developed world can find its way anywhere in the world based on market assessments of risk and return.

IV. LESSONS FROM RECENT BANKING PROBLEMS

Financial Assistance from the IMF and Other Trans-National Agencies

Figure 3, based on data presented in Table 2, provides information on banking problems in selected countries for the period 1980 to the present. The figure shows the time periods of the banking crises for ten of the currently 133 IMF member countries that have experienced banking crises or significant banking problems since 1980, and received IMF financial assistance. The countries include Indonesia, Korea, and Thailand—the recipients in 1997 of the largest financial assistance pledges in history from the IMF, the World Bank, the Asian Development Bank, and individual or groups of industrial countries.[12]

As Figure 3 reveals, among the selected countries that received IMF assistance over the period, there were or are continuing extended banking problems in China, India, Korea, Thailand and Argentina. Some of the countries, moreover, like Indonesia, Korea, Thailand, Argentina, Brazil and Mexico had more than one discreet period of crisis. These countries are a subset of 16 countries listed in Table 2 that experienced banking crises during the period. In six countries—Hong Kong, Malaysia, Singapore, Taiwan, Japan, and the United States—there were significant banking problems but no IMF financial assistance.

Over the 1980-1998 period, the ten countries shown in Figure 3 received separate assistance pledges from the IMF a total 36 times. An issue that arises is what should have been expected of the IMF and other trans-national agencies based upon such extensive involvement in countries experiencing financial problems. This applies to not only the recent crisis in East Asia, but also the crisis in Mexico in 1994 and perhaps even some of the crises that occurred earlier.

Were the IMF and other trans-national agencies caught off guard by both the Mexico crisis and the East Asian crises? Looking merely at Figure 3, has the performance by the IMF been acceptable given so many past problems, including several instances of multiple banking crises and corresponding IMF assistance in such countries as Mexico (1981-1982, 1995), Argentina (1980-1982, 1989-1990, 1995), Thailand (1983-1987, 1997), Philippines (1981-1987), and Korea (mid-1980s and 1997). Under the circumstances, would one not reasonably expect the IMF to be aware of the conditions leading to potential problems and to work with the countries to mitigate potential problems? In answering these questions, one must remember that the IMF lacks the enforcement powers necessary to impose its views on countries. Countries, moreover, may be unpersuaded by or resist entreaties to do what the IMF considers necessary to forestall problems. In

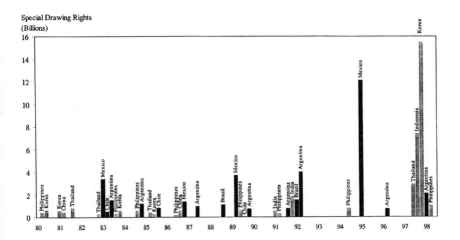

Figure 4. Financial Assistance from the IMF

view of this situation, should one reasonably expect the IMF to express its views about problems publicly?

A related issue arises in the context of Figure 4, again based on data presented in Table 2, that shows the dollar amount of IMF, and in some instances, related assistance agreed upon for the ten countries in Figure 3. Figure 4 shows, beginning with the Mexican assistance package in 1995, the amount of IMF assistance to recipients has generally increased sharply. The assistance provided to Korea in 1997 was substantially greater than that provided to Mexico, while IMF assistance provided to Thailand, Indonesia, and even Argentina exceeded amounts previously provided other recipients after financial crises.

With substantial experience with so many previous crises, what is the precise role of the IMF when countries experience financial difficulties? This is an important question because Michel Camdessus, IMF Managing Director, has stated that in Thailand, for instance, the costly developments " . . . were so preventable" (IMF, November 13, 1997). Stanley Fischer, IMF First Deputy Managing Director, has also stated that " . . . the Asian financial crisis may result in the IMF 'going public' when it has concerns about the economy of certain countries . . ." (IMF, February 23, 1998). If crises are indeed preventable and the public is not forewarned of impending crises, is the IMF forced by default to engage in forbearance and thereby to provide more financial assistance than would otherwise be necessary? And, if so, is this an acceptable role for the IMF?[13]

Inherent Difficulties Faced by the IMF

This discussion indicates that the IMF faces inherent difficulties and limitations given that it must deal with sovereign nations, and that it does not have statutory power to impose what it may consider to be appropriate remedies when financial difficulties initially begin to arise. Within a country, when financial difficulties are detected, domestic regulatory agencies have varying degrees of legal authority to impose by force what they consider to be appropriate remedies. The IMF has no such authority over the sovereign nations with which it must deal. As a result of its lack of statutory power, moreover, it cannot behind the scenes enforce changes to prevent or to mitigate financial crises that it might if it had such power. For the same reason, it is limited in its ability to cajole sovereign governments to do what the IMF might want them to do in response to what it perceives as impending difficulties.

The power that the IMF does have involves its ability to provide financial assistance. When it perceives that there are events occurring that may lead to subsequent financial crises, it may be able to effect what it considers to be appropriate remedies by either dangling or threatening to withhold future financial assistance. Even if indeed this is the case, the analysis above suggests that financial crises have nonetheless become more frequent and more costly.

As the East Asian crises highlight, the ability of the IMF to enforce what it considers appropriate remedies occurs to varying degrees after a full-blown crisis develops, when in exchange for a financial assistance pledge, it can make varying demands of sovereign governments. Thus, the ability of the IMF to effect change is largely associated with the conditions that it can negotiate with sovereign countries in return for financial assistance pledges.

It is this role that is often referred to as the IMF's role as the international lender of last resort. As is well known, however, beginning with the classic work of Bagehot (1873), there are three characteristics that a true lender of last resort possesses: infinite ability to provide liquidity, the ability to discern the difference between solvent and insolvent institutions—so as to lend only to solvent institutions—and the ability to lend at punitive interest rates.

It may be that in many cases the IMF possesses few of these characteristics. First, it certainly is not able to provide infinite liquidity.[14] Second, a domestic lender of last resort assesses the solvency of domestic financial institutions to which it might make liquidity available; the IMF provides liquidity to sovereign governments about which the issue of solvency may not be relevant. Third, the IMF has not charged, though it probably could charge, punitive rates of interest in exchange for liquidity.

It seems inappropriate to describe the IMF as a true lender of last resort. It appears more appropriate to describe it as a trans-national agency with no statutory power to enforce what it considers to be appropriate remedies on a sovereign government before a financial crisis develops. After a crisis develops, the IMF has a limited ability to negotiate conditions with sovereign countries in exchange for finite financial pledges. Thus, by its very structure the IMF faces severe limitations in its ability to effect what it may consider appropriate remedies before and even after a financial crisis develops.

Regarding whether the IMF should disclose its view about whether a crisis is likely in the future, according to Mr. Fischer, a difficulty is whether such a warning would " . . . precipitate a crisis that wouldn't otherwise have happened" (see Davis, 1998, p. A15). Perhaps more importantly, Mr. Camdessus states that, "The IMF deals with confidential information provided by a member country. It must respect the intentions of that country and cannot, without losing the country's confidence, publish information without the country's consent. The IMF also serves as a discreet advisor, particularly in times of stress. In no circumstances ... should the desire to disseminate undermine the IMF's relations with its member countries and its ability to help them do the right thing" (IMF, April 27, 1998, p. 125). Apparently, the IMF believes it cannot acknowledge difficulties it knows exist.[15]

The Issue of Moral Hazard and IMF Financial Assistance

Previous IMF financial assistance packages, moreover, may have created a serious moral-hazard problem in which the likelihood and severity of financial crises have worsened. The specific moral-hazard problem may be stated as follows. With many past crises, the IMF provided financial assistance. Given that such assistance had become somewhat predictable, it is possible that selected parties formed expectations that in future crises the IMF would once again provide financial assistance that would help bail them out.[16] Parties who might form these expectations include domestic lenders and investors in the countries that subsequently received assistance, and foreign lenders and investors. Governments in a situation to receive future IMF financial assistance might also have formed such expectations. As a result, within individual countries in a position to receive future IMF assistance, greater funds flowing into excessively risky activities may have occurred due to inappropriate incentives on the part of all concerned parties.

These incentives may have existed for some time and may have grown in recent years in tandem with the growth in both the IMF's financial resources and the financial assistance it has extended to countries. After all, if effective, the past conditions that have been imposed by the IMF on countries over a lengthy period of time in exchange for previous assistance should have lessened both the likelihood and the severity of future problems, and thereby have lessened both the likelihood and the amount of any future financial assistance. Neither, however, seems to have occurred. In reaction to the most recent crises, the IMF is seeking significant banking reform in selected countries.[17] Given the lengthy history of IMF involvement in financial crises around the globe, it seems clear that the reforms now being advocated were apparent earlier, and thus could have been implemented by countries to alleviate, if not prevent, the current crises. If this had been the case, it is

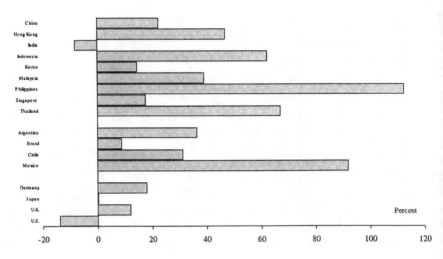

Figure 5.   Growth in Bank Credit to the Private Sector
Relative to the Growth of GDP: 1990-1996

unlikely that the IMF would now be seeking greater financial resources with which to be in a position to respond to even more crises.

The Moral-Hazard Problem and East-Asian Bank Lending

Information provided in Figure 5 is relevant to what the IMF knew or could have known before the East Asian crises of 1997, as well as what may have been the growing moral-hazard problem created by previous IMF financial assistance provided to nations experiencing banking crises. For selected countries for the period 1990 to 1996, including all of the countries involved in the East Asian crisis, the figure shows the growth in bank credit to the private sector relative to the growth of GDP. Thus, if a nation's bank credit grew at the same rate as the nation's GDP, the relative growth rate would be zero. In general, if a nation's bank credit grows substantially in excess of the growth of GDP over several years, it is an indication of excessive bank lending presaging future credit-quality problems.

As Figure 5 shows, a significant number of countries had bank credit growth rates that substantially exceeded GDP growth. In particular, Indonesia, the Philippines, Thailand, and Mexico had bank credit growth rates that exceeded the corresponding GDP growth rates by 60 percent or more. These bank credit growth rates are consistent with excessive and thus quite risky lending, and may reflect actions taken in response to incentives consistent with the moral hazard problem. Indonesia, Thailand, and Mexico, for example, were three of the four countries that have received the largest ever assistance pledges from the IMF and others.

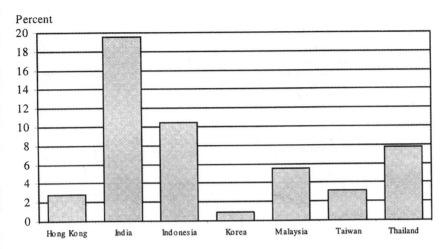

Figure 6. Bank Non-performing Loans/Total Loans-Asia: 1995

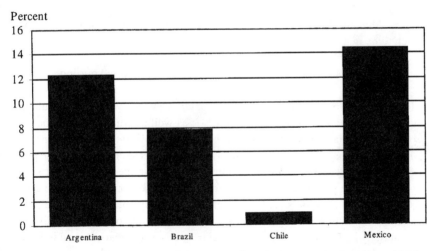

Figure 7. Bank Non-performing Loans/Total Loans-Latin America: 1995

Figure 5 also addresses the issue of whether the IMF and others had access to information that would have allowed them to be better prepared to anticipate and to react to crises more appropriately. The IMF and others presumably had access to data on the growth of bank credit to the private sector for several years before the culmination of the East Asian crisis in 1997. The IMF and others were undoubtedly aware that rapid bank credit growth could be associated with

Table 3.   Indicators of the Structure of the Banking Industry: 1994 (Percent)

	Bank Share in Financial Intermediation[1]	Share of State-owned Banks[2]	Operating Costs[3]/ Total Assets	Net Interest Margin[3]/ Total Assets	Non-performing Loans/ Total Loans	
					1994	(1995)
Asia						
China	74	100	NA	NA	NA	NA
Hong Kong	94	0	0.8[4]	1.6[4]	3.4[5]	2.8[5]
India	80	87	2.3	2.9	23.6[6]	19.5[6]
Indonesia	91	48	2.4	3.3	12.0	10.4
Korea	38	13	1.7	2.1	1.0	0.9
Malaysia	64	8	1.6	3.0	8.1	5.5
Philippines	NA	NA	NA	NA	NA	NA
Singapore	71	0	1.4	1.6	NA	NA
Taiwan	80	57	1.3	2.0	2.0[7]	3.1[7]
Thailand	75	7	1.9	3.7	7.5	7.7
Latin America						
Argentina	98	42	8.5	9.2	8.6	12.3
Brazil	97	48	8.3	10.0[4]	3.9	7.9
Chile	62	14	3.0	6.1	1.0	1.0
Mexico	87	28	3.9	5.1	10.5[8]	14.4[8]
Memo						
Germany	77	50	1.1	1.4	NA	NA
Japan	79	0	0.8	1.1	3.3[9]	3.3[9]
U.K.	NA	NA	NA	NA	NA	NA
U.S.	23	0	3.7	4.2	1.9	1.3

Notes: [1]Assets of banks as a percentage of the assets of banks and non-bank financial institutions.
[2]Percentage share of assets except for Argentina (share of deposits). For India 1993.
[3]Average of 1990 -1994.
[4]1992 -1994.
[5]Locally incorporated banks only.
[6]Public sector banks only.
[7]Past-due loans.
[8]Commercial banks only. The figure for 1995 incorporates the effects of special programs to deal with bad loans. Without such programs figure would have been 19.3.
[9]Fiscal year.

Source: Milken Institute

subsequent credit quality problems. The availability of the data indicate that there was enough "transparency" concerning bank credit growth rates, which indeed subsequently led to acknowledged and reported credit quality difficulties and to severe bank problems in several countries.

As shown in Figure 6, based on data in Table 3, for example, in 1995 the reported ratio of bank non-performing loans to total loans in Indonesia was 10.4

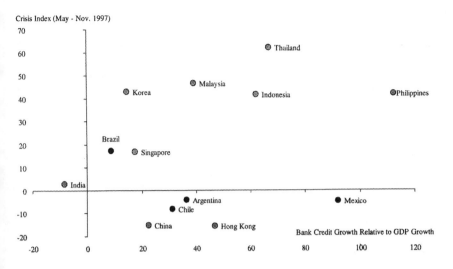

Figure 8. Bank Credit Boom: 1990-1996

percent and in Thailand it was 7.7 percent. Thus, two years before the East Asian banking crises there was evidence not only of rapid increases in bank credit, but presumably also evidence of significant deterioration in reported bank credit quality. As Figure 7 and Table 3 show, non-performing loans were a problem in Mexico in both 1994 and 1995. Accompanying the rapid expansion of bank credit discussed above, however, non-performing loans as a percentage of total loans actually grew steadily from approximately 2.5 percent in 1990 to 14.4 percent in 1995. This information on acknowledged poorly performing loans before the crises in Mexico and several East Asian countries are further indications that the IMF and others had sufficient information from which to conclude that significant difficulties might subsequently occur.

Indeed, Figure 8 presents evidence that the bank-lending boom of 1990-1996 contributed to the financial crises in several countries of East Asia in 1997. This figure correlates the growth in lending presented in Figure 5 for 1990-1996 with a crisis index for the period from May to November of 1997, when the full-blown crisis struck East Asia. The crisis index is the sum for each country of the depreciation rate minus the percentage change in international reserves.[18]

Notably, the countries with the highest rates of bank credit growth—Indonesia, Malaysia, the Philippines, and Thailand—had the highest crisis index ratings as well. Although Korea's index was also high, it was not associated with a high rate of growth in bank credit. This, as explained in more detail below, may reflect government-directed lending to a small number of large firms. Again, however, the government-directed bank lending in Korea as well as the rate of growth in bank credit in other countries was information that was readily available to the IMF and others well before the crises actually occurred.[19]

These findings suggest that the bank credit growth rates and indices of poorly performing loans were "leading indicators" of subsequent exchange rate and international reserve difficulties in selected countries in East Asia. The findings also suggest that the IMF had relevant information available to it to help anticipate crises that eventually developed. Regardless as to whether the IMF adequately anticipated the crises, it reacted clumsily after they developed.[20]

The issue of contagion is also addressed by the information provided in Figure 8. It has been argued that the financial crises in East Asia represented in some way a contagion, in which the currency difficulties of one country were like a communicable disease transferred to other countries. The information in Figure 8 is not fully consistent with this argument. All of the countries that suffered the most serious financial difficulties did so because there were real economic difficulties in their countries, associated in large part with excessive bank credit growth and subsequent bank loan and bank insolvency issues.

V.   THE ROLE OF REGULATORY ISSUES IN BANKING

Prevailing Views of the Cause of East Asian Bank Difficulties

If one were to summarize the view most often expressed about how the banks in East Asia reached their current condition, it would be that banks' lending policies reflected lax and inappropriate examination, supervision, and regulation by bank regulatory authorities, including inappropriate resolution policies for insolvent banks. It is also argued frequently that inadequate information, what has become known as a lack of "transparency" on banks' financial condition, is available. It is widely argued by some that a combination of these conditions contributed significantly to the financial difficulties in East Asia.

From this view, the prescription for bank reform that generally follows is to require a bank regulatory regime that generally includes some form of the following components:

- Impose internationally established capital requirements on all banks and pursue "prompt corrective action"[21] against troubled banks;
- Require more stringent bank examination and supervision;
- Require consolidated financial reporting with financial statements reviewed by independent auditors; and
- Establish an explicit deposit-insurance system, if one does not exit.

Table 4. Permissible Banking Activities, Bank-Nonbank Ownership Opportunities, and Other Related Information

Country and Bank Supervisor(s)	Securities[1]	Insurance[2]	Real Estate[3]	Bank Investment in Nonfinancial Firms	Nonfinancial Firm Investment in Banks	Depositor Protection Scheme	Other Information			
							External Audits Required	Global Consolidated Reporting Required	Capital Adequacy based on Basle Accord	Allowed Foreign Ownership
Asia										
CHINA People's Bank of China	Prohibited.	Prohibited.	Prohibited.	Prohibited.	Prohibited.	No	NA	NA	NA	NA
HONG KONG Hong Kong Monetary Authority	Unrestricted.	Permitted.	Permitted.	Restricted.	Permitted.	No	Yes	Yes	Yes	No limit
INDIA Reserve Bank of India and Board for Financial Supervision	Permitted.	Prohibited.	Restricted.	Restricted.	Restricted.	Yes, ex ante and compulsory	Yes	NA	Yes	24% of shares (20% for State Bank of India)
INDONESIA Bank Indonesia	Permitted.	Prohibited.	Prohibited.	Prohibited.	Unrestricted.	No	Yes	Yes	Yes	49% of shares
KOREA Bank of Korea	Permitted.	Permitted.	Permitted.	Restricted.	Restricted.	Yes, ex ante and compulsory (since June 1996).	Yes	Yes	Yes	NA
MALAYSIA Bank Negara Malaysia	Unrestricted.	Unrestricted.	Unrestricted.	Permitted.	Permitted.	No	Yes	Yes	Yes	30% of shares

(continued)

Table 4. (Continued)

Country and Bank Supervisor(s)	Securities[1]	Insurance[2]	Real Estate[3]	Bank Investment in Nonfinancial Firms	Nonfinancial Firm Investment in Banks	Depositor Protection Scheme	Other Information			
							External Audits Required	Global Consolidated Reporting Required	Capital Adequacy based on Basle Accord	Allowed Foreign Ownership
PHILIPPINES Central Bank of the Philippines	Unrestricted.	Permitted.	Permitted.	Permitted.	Permitted.	Yes, ex ante and compulsory	Yes	Yes	Yes	30% of shares (40% with special approval)
SINGAPORE Monetary Authority of Singapore	Permitted.	Permitted.	Permitted.	Restricted.	Permitted.	No	Yes	Yes	Yes	40% of shares
TAIWAN Ministry of Finance and Central Bank of China	NA	NA	NA	NA	NA	Yes, ex ante and voluntary.	NA	NA	NA	NA
THAILAND Ministry of Finance and Bank of Thailand	Permitted.	Permitted.	Permitted.	Restricted.	Restricted.	No, not a formal scheme, but Bank of Thailand provides some assistance if bank fails.	Yes	Yes	Yes	25% of shares

198

LATIN AMERICA

ARGENTINA Central Bank of Argentina	Restricted. Permitted. Permitted. Restricted.	Unrestricted.	Yes, ex ante and compulsory (effective April 1995)	Yes	Yes, since Sept. 1994.	Yes	NA
BRAZIL Central Bank of Brazil	Permitted. Permitted. Restricted. Restricted.	Unrestricted.	Yes, ex ante and compulsory (1995).	Yes	NA	Yes	NA
CHILE Superintendency of Banks and Other Financial Institutions	Permitted. Restricted. Prohibited.	Prohibited.	Yes, provided by the State and covers all banks.	Yes	No	No	NA
MEXICO National Banking and Securities Commission (an Agency of the Ministry of France)	Permitted. Permitted. Restricted. Prohibited.	Restricted.	Yes, ex ante and compulsory.	Yes	No	No	No more than 20% of a bank whose capital is greater than 6% of the entire banking system's capital.

(continued)

Table 4. (Continued)

Country and Bank Supervisor(s)	Securities[1]	Insurance[2]	Real Estate[3]	Bank Investment in Nonfinancial Firms	Nonfinancial Firm Investment in Banks	Depositor Protection Scheme	External Audits Required	Global Consolidated Reporting Required	Capital Adequacy based on Basle Accord	Allowed Foreign Ownership
MEMO										
GERMANY Federal Banking Supervisory Office and Deutsche Bundesbank	Unrestricted.	Restricted.	Permitted.	Unrestricted.	Unrestricted.	Yes, ex ante and voluntary.	Yes	Yes	Yes	NA
JAPAN Ministry of Finance (primary responsibility) and Bank of Japan	Restricted.	Restricted.	Prohibited.	Restricted.	Restricted.	Yes, ex ante and compulsory.	Yes	Yes	Yes	NA
UNITED KINGDOM Bank of England (prior to 1998)	Unrestricted.	Permitted.	Unrestricted.	Unrestricted.	Unrestricted.	Yes, ex ante and compulsory.	Yes	Yes	Yes	NA
UNITED STATES Federal Reserve System, Comptroller of the currency, Federall Insurance Corporation, and State Authorities	Restricted.	Restricted.	Restricted.	Restricted.	Restricted.	Yes, ex ante and compulsory.	Yes	Yes	Yes	No limit

Source: [1]Securities activities include underwriting, dealing and brokening all kinds of securities and all aspects of the mutual fund business.
[2]Insurance activities include underwriting and selling insurance as principal and as agent.
[3]Real estate activities include real estate investment, development and management.

Definitions: Unrestricted- A full range of activities in the given category can be conducted directly in the bank.
Permitted- A full range of activities can be conducted, but all or some must be conducted in subsidiaries.
Restricted- Less than a full range of activities can be conducted in the bank or subsidiaries.
Prohibited- The activity cannot be conducted in either the bank or subsidiaries.

These prescriptions are consistent with the general approach taken by several trans-national agencies well before the outset of the current crisis. The Basle Committee on Banking Supervision, the Bank for International Settlements (BIS) and the IMF have been moving for some time to develop international bank regulatory protocols including the components just mentioned.

In October 1996, for example, Mr. Camdessus said, "There are problems of banking soundness all over the world . . . We are doing a lot of work on improving banking systems; this is a big growth area for us." In December 1997, Mr. Camdessus also said, "We all have been troubled by developments in the Thai economy . . ." Among the problems, he noted were " . . . weak and overextended banking sectors, poor prudential supervision, and substantial short-term borrowing in foreign currency" (see *Financial Times*, December 19, 1997). Even more recently in April 1998, Mr. Fischer (IMF, April 6, 1998, p. 101) said that "...macroeconomic adjustment is not the main element in the programs of Indonesia, Korea, and Thailand; financial sector restructuring and other structural programs lie at the heart of each program. The problems they deal with—weak financial institutions, inadequate bank regulation and supervision, and the complicated and nontransparent relations among governments, banks and corporations—lie at the heart of the economic crisis in each country."

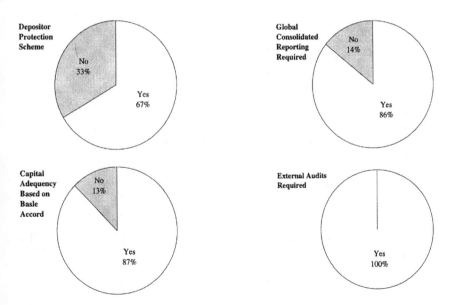

Figure 9a. Bank Activities in Selected Countries

Evidence from Around the World

At issue is whether there is evidence to support the conclusion that the banking crises in East Asia and elsewhere around the world in recent years are due to inadequate regulation and supervision. As one can see from Table 4, external audits, global consolidated reporting, and capital adequacy standards based on the Basle accord are required.

As a result, despite Mr. Camdessus' reference to "poor prudential supervision" and Mr. Fischer's reference to inadequate bank regulation and supervision, the Thai bank regulatory system had most of the components that the IMF and other trans-national agencies have been advocating. The difficulties experienced by Thailand, moreover, did not fundamentally stem from inadequate reporting requirements, either domestically or internationally. Indeed, Thailand reported, as depicted in Figure 5, that it had the second highest rate of growth in bank credit relative to GDP in East Asia—over 60 percent in 1990-1996. In addition, Thailand reported a significant ratio of bank non-performing loans to total loans of 7.5 percent in 1994, three years before the Thai financial crisis.

The Thai difficulties stemmed in large part from excessive bank lending that was apparently allowed not only by Thai bank regulatory officials but also tolerated in some manner by the IMF to whom data on bank lending presumably were

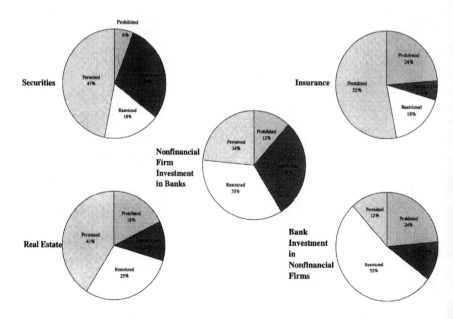

Figure 9b.   Bank Activities in Selected Countries (continued)

available. The apparent position of the IMF must be that even if a country has a fairly comprehensive bank regulatory, supervisory, and reporting system—including conveying available information to the IMF—excessive bank lending and associated loan quality problems can still occur.

As Figure 9a indeed shows, fairly comprehensive bank regulatory, supervisory, and reporting systems are the rule rather than the exception in most of the countries that have experienced recent banking difficulties. The figure is derived from information on the 18 countries in Table 4. As Figure 9a shows, the majority of the nations have explicit depositor protection schemes, require external audits, mandate global consolidated reporting, and impose capital adequacy standards based on the Basle accord. Thus, most of the nations already conform generally to the bank regulatory structure that the IMF and other trans-national agencies say is needed.

Table 4 and Figure 9b also provide information on the extent to which banks in these countries can engage in securities, insurance, and real estate activities, as well as invest in non-financial firms and vice versa. It may be seen that there is not a close association between bank crises and whether banks are allowed to engage in these particular activities or whether banks are allowed to own or be owned by non-financial firms. This lack of association is important because of the debate in the United States and elsewhere over whether to be more or less restrictive in theses areas. The IMF apparently provides financial assistance to countries on the condition their banking systems be reformed regardless of whether the reforms are consistent with prevailing practices in the United States.

It may be that when Mr. Camdessus referred to "poor prudential supervision" in Thailand that he was merely referring to "bad judgment" or "inappropriate implementation" or some other form of human failure. If so, those kinds of deficiencies cannot be addressed systematically over time by the IMF or other trans-national agencies. The fact remains that in East Asia and elsewhere in the world where banking crises have occurred, they did so in countries with fairly elaborate bank regulation and supervision regimes of the types that have been advocated by the IMF and other trans-national agencies for some time.[22]

The Case of the United States

The recent banking crisis in the United States forms an important backdrop in evaluating the general notion that government regulation and supervision can be effective in preventing banking crises or reducing the severity of such crises when they occur. Even before the 1980s, as one can see from Table 4, the United States had one of the most elaborate and restrictive regulatory regimes in the world.[23] Yet, throughout the 1980s and into the early 1990s, the United States experienced one of the lengthiest banking crises in the world that involved an unprecedented number of banking institution failures and costly resolutions.

Limitations on Allowable Activities: Government-Directed Lending

It is common in the United States to describe savings and loans at the beginning of the 1980s as among the most highly regulated firms in the United States. Although this is accurate, it does not fully convey the fact that the regulation largely involved a program of specific government-directed lending. Savings and loan institutions, for example, were primarily limited to making home mortgage loans, but essentially forbidden by law from offering adjustable-rate home mortgages. They could not make most loans that commercial banks could make, such as commercial real estate loans, commercial loans to businesses, and consumer loans. In short, until quite recently, savings and loans were mainly restricted to making long-term, fixed-rate home mortgage loans.[24]

The government-directed home lending program for the savings and loans was in fact the source of their difficulties. It is an example of how government-directed lending can effectively inhibit regulated firms from adapting to competitive markets in which there is rapid and substantial change.[25] At the same time, it is also an example of the way in which government intervention through regulatory forbearance can cause greater problems in the form of moral hazard and adverse selection when an entire industry is struggling to survive with inadequate private owner-contributed equity capital.

The extent of government-directed lending restrictions can vary dramatically. Savings and loans had extensive restrictions on their lending, leading this sector into extreme difficulties beginning in the late 1970s and extending into the early 1990s.[26] These restrictions can be seen as one point on a continuum in which at one end there are essentially no restrictions, and at the other end there is state ownership of firms. Although the United States likes to see itself and advertise itself as a market-based economy, the regulatory intervention in the business affairs of financial institutions—particularly banking institutions—has been so extensive and intrusive for so long that the United States moved far closer to the state-ownership end of the continuum than it would like to admit.

The Role of Private Owner-Contributed Equity Capital and Selected Forms of Government Intervention

Another important component of the savings and loan and banking crisis in the United States in the 1980s and early 1990s revolved around the role played by private owner-contributed equity capital. As Figure 10 shows, there have been several periods in which there have been noticeable increases or decreases in private owner-contributed bank equity capital relative to total assets. The ratio declined after the adoption of federal deposit insurance, increased from the early 1940s to the early 1960s, and decreased thereafter until rising again in the 1990s.

Percent

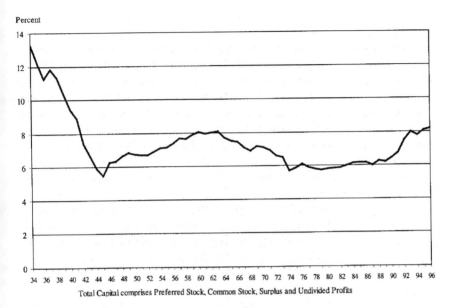

Total Capital comprises Preferred Stock, Common Stock, Surplus and Undivided Profits

Figure 10.   Capital-to-Asset Ratio for U.S. Insured Commercial Banks:
1934-1996

The most dramatic change followed the adoption of federal deposit insurance in
the United States in 1933 for commercial banks. The ratio of private owner-contributed bank equity capital-to-total assets fell from 13 percent to less than 6 percent between 1934 and 1945. When federal deposit insurance replaced private
owner-contributed equity capital as a buffer against losses to be borne by depositors, government discipline largely supplanted market discipline. Even with the
recent increases in bank equity capital relative to assets in the contemporary
period, the ratio of private owner-contributed equity capital-to-total assets today is
still substantially below the ratio that prevailed before the adoption of the federal
deposit-insurance system.

The creation of federal deposit insurance signified that risk bearing was being
shifted; after adoption of deposit insurance, taxpayers bore a greater risk and
insured depositors bore less risk for the cost of resolving bank failures. Deposit
insurance also created incentives that affected both the owners of private
owner-contributed equity capital and the deposit-insurance agencies. Deposit
insurance simultaneously conveyed a put option to the owners of private
owner-contributed equity capital and a call option to the deposit-insurance agencies.[27] In general in the United States, as the level of private owner-contributed
equity capital declines toward zero, the holders of privately contributed capital

may put the institution back to the deposit-insurance agency, or the deposit-insurance agency can exercise its call option and seize the institution.

Almost without exception, the relevant deposit-insurance agency should seize a banking institution that has become insolvent, for an appropriate resolution. The reason is in part due to the incentives created by insolvency. In general, as long as the institution is solvent, the put is out of the money and thus the value of the option is zero. When insolvent, however, the put is in the money, and its value is maximized by greater risk-taking as long as the institution remains open and operating. Private owner-contributed equity capital therefore is an important constraint on risk-taking.

Regulatory authorities can reduce the incentive to take greater risk in a number of ways. Appropriate examination and supervision, for example, can potentially detect and deter greater risk-taking behavior. The fear of subsequent legal enforcement and penalties for imprudent behavior can also deter greater risk-taking. In addition, the ownership form of an institution can affect risk-taking. The incentives to take risk have been found in general to be less in mutual-type versus stock-type institutions, for example. Adequate capital standards, of course, are essential in deterring excessive risk-taking behavior.

With deposit insurance, it is possible to have widespread banking institution insolvencies, and thus incentives to take greater risk, at the same time that a deposit-insurance agency's resources are insufficient to contain and resolve problems.[28] This happened in the United States in the 1980s and early 1990s with deposit-insurance agencies for both the savings and loans and commercial banks actually reporting insolvency for some years (Barth & Litan, 1997). First for the savings and loans and then for the banks, institution insolvencies mounted and their contemplated resolution forced the deposit-insurance agencies to report insolvency.

Under these circumstances, the incentive to take excessive risk on the part of some private owners of bank equity capital can occur when the deposit-insurance agency is unable to adequately supervise troubled institutions and unable to resolve institutions known to be insolvent. If the deposit-insurance agency is either unwilling or unable to obtain adequate funds to resolve insolvent institutions, there will be an incentive to forbear in resolving insolvent institutions, thereby exacerbating an already serious situation.

This occurred in both the savings and loan and banking crises in the United States in the 1980s and early 1990s. In the early 1980s, for example, virtually the entire savings and loan industry was insolvent when marked-to-market because rising interest rates had drastically reduced the value of their long-term, fixed-rate home mortgage portfolio. Based on the estimated market value of the industry's home mortgage portfolio, the industry insolvency was $110 billion in 1981. In the same year, the reported reserves of the deposit-insurance agency were only slightly more than $6 billion (see Brumbaugh, 1988).

At the time there was a "prompt corrective action" regime in place in which savings and loans were required by law and regulation to meet a 5 percent minimum capital requirement. If the capital ratio fell to 3 percent, the institutions were subject to strict supervisory control. If the capital fell to zero or less, institutions were to be seized by the appropriate regulatory authorities.

Growth in Bank Credit During the Crisis

Nonetheless, during the early 1980s when the savings and loan industry became insolvent, the prompt corrective action mechanism was converted to a delay mechanism rather than strictly enforced. Laws and regulations were simply changed so that institutions were subject to lower minimum capital requirements at the same time as there was a liberalization of the items that could count as capital, thereby providing institutions with the ability to grow in size. The overall effect was to allow institutions reporting negative capital on the basis of the stricter Generally Accepted Accounting Principles (GAAP) to remain open and operating. By 1986, for example, when the deposit-insurance agency for savings and loans itself reported insolvency, nearly 500 institutions reporting negative GAAP capital were open and operating. Eventually, the present-value cost of resolving all failed savings and loans from 1980 to 1996 was an estimated $154 billion (see Barth & Litan, 1997).

To deter excessive risk-taking with depleted capital, one would expect growth in assets of savings and loans to be relatively modest during the 1980s. Total assets at all savings and loans, however, doubled from $604 billion in 1980 to $1.2 trillion in 1986, 41 percentage points more than the growth of GDP over the same period. Such rapid growth in overall bank credit, and even more rapid growth by the insolvent institutions, would not have occurred in the absence of federal deposit insurance and in the presence of market discipline. Leaving aside the fact that without government-directed lending and with adequate private owner-contributed capital no industry would have developed with such overwhelming interest-rate risk, once capital was being depleted liability holders would not have tolerated any subsequent explosive growth of further lending.

A central issue is whether banking crises would be more or less likely to occur if there were more reliance on private owner-contributed equity capital, and less reliance on government determined minimum capital requirements and associated prompt-corrective-action rules, deposit insurance, regulation of allowable activities, and ownership and organizational restrictions. These regulatory functions were largely designed to overcome problems with various information asymmetries that could disrupt the credit system and payments mechanism, but as the examples above indicate, they create their own set of problems. Indeed, these problems may be of greater magnitude than the problems they were designed to address.[29]

As the following sections of the paper demonstrate, the U.S. banking crisis in the 1980s and early 1990s has much in common with the current crises in East Asia. The central similarities involve government-directed lending and inadequate private owner-contributed equity capital. In both the U.S. crisis and the East Asian banking crises there were different forms of government-directed lending. As with the U.S. case, despite banking institutions experiencing difficulties, there were extraordinary growth rates in bank credit relative to GDP growth in several East Asian countries. Again, as with the banks in the United States, these growth rates occurred in the absence of adequate private owner-contributed bank equity capital. Neither the bank credit growth rates nor the original targeted bank lending that caused the difficulties would have developed as they did if decisions had been based on the existence of adequate private owner-contributed bank equity capital.

VI. BANKING IN EAST ASIA

The Role of State-Owned Banks

Although there are many ways in which governments affect banking, it is help-ful to understand that to varying degrees the banks in several East Asian countries are state-owned. As shown in Figure 11, based on Table 3 , in East Asia a signifi-cant percentage of banks assets are in state-owned banks. Until very recently in China, 100 percent of the banks were state owned. For other East Asian nations the respective percentages are 87 percent for India, 57 percent for Taiwan, 48 percent for Indonesia, 13 percent for Korea, 8 percent of Malaysia, and 7 percent for Thai-land. As Figure 12, also based on information in Table 3, shows, the respective percentages for nations in Latin America are 48 percent for Brazil, 42 percent for Argentina, 28 percent for Mexico, and 14 percent for Chile.

For state-owned banks over which there is state control, it seems inappropri-ate to discuss their difficulties as a result of lax or inappropriate regulation and supervision. These banks' lending policies, accounting, disclosure, examination and supervision, and capital levels directly reflect state ownership of equity cap-ital. Prompt corrective action rules for inadequately capitalized banks also reflect direct state involvement in banking. In many countries, moreover, there is interaction between state-owned banks and state-owned or subsidized commercial enterprises.

In these countries, the issue becomes more one of the advisability of state own-ership of banks rather than lending determined by market participants in privately owned banks subject to some form of government regulation. Indeed, depending on the extent of state-owned banks in these country's banking sectors and related state involvement in commercial enterprises, the idea of bank regulation as one thinks of it in the United States does not apply.

Percent

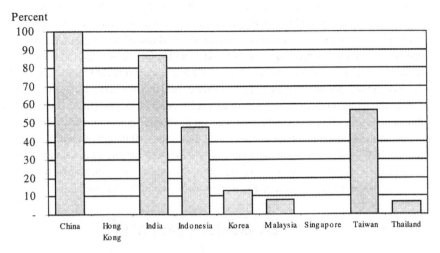

Figure 11.   State-Owned Banks' Share of Total Assets-Asia: 1994

Percent

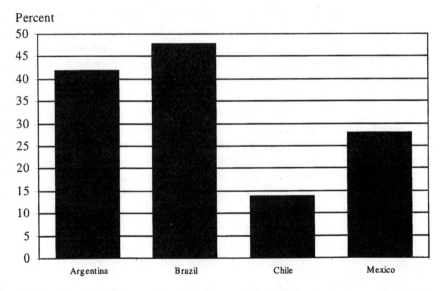

Figure 12.   State-Owned Banks' Share of Total Assets-Latin America: 1994

In addition, the incentives of bank directors, officers, and private owners of bank equity capital in privately owned banks are different than those of officials who run state-owned banks with taxpayer contributed capital. In privately owned banks, directors and officers are generally provided incentives to maximize the expected future net cash flows for the benefit of the private owners of equity capital. The owners of bank equity capital also have an incentive to monitor bank performance to be sure that the expected future net cash flows are indeed being maximized.

In contrast, state-owned banks are capitalized, at least in part, by government allocation of tax dollars. Taxpayers do not in general have the same ability to be sure that an adequate risk-adjusted return on their tax dollars is being earned as private owners of equity capital do regarding their private funds. It is also highly unlikely that law makers, government officials, or managers of state-owned banks can or even attempt to design remuneration systems that would successfully mimic incentives of private equity capital owners and their agents.

The economic theory of regulation suggests that the outcome would be substantially different. Broadly stated the economic theory of regulation states that there is a demand for regulation by those who would be regulated (see Stigler, 1971; Posner, 1974). Once regulated, regulatees can among other things use the coercive power of government to stifle competition. State-ownership of banks is in a sense the limit case of regulation providing politically well-connected individuals the incentive to gain access to bank funds, to limit or blockade entry of other borrowers, and to limit or blockade exit (in essence to gain forbearance) in the case of difficulties. The economic theory of regulation would suggest that "crony capitalism"—lending to a select number of individuals on favorable terms based at least partly on non-economic criteria—would be the expected result of state-ownership of banks regardless of the form of the government.

The Banking Market in Indonesia

Assets in Indonesian state-owned banks have been declining, and assets in private national banks, joint-venture banks with foreign involvement, and foreign bank assets have been correspondingly rising from approximately 46 percent in 1991 to approximately 57 percent by 1995 (IMF, September, 1997; Montgomery, 1997). This increase is frequently noted, and is an important change. Nonetheless, the Indonesian banking system is one still heavily influenced by state-owned banks. An important nuance, for example, is that the average size of the state-owned banks is approximately double that of private and joint and foreign banks.

In terms of relative efficiency, it is also interesting to compare nonperforming loans and profitability for state-owned banks in Indonesia relative to private banks. Nonperforming loans have been a substantially greater percentage of total credits for state banks relative to other banks in recent years. In 1995, for example, reported nonperforming loans at state-owned banks exceeded 15 percent in contrast to 5 percent for private banks. The return on assets in recent years of foreign banks in particular, but also joint banks, is substantially

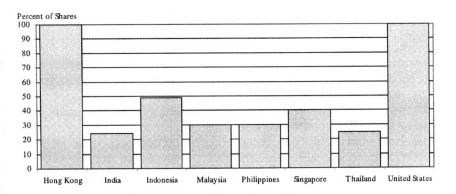

Figure 13. Allowed Foreign Ownership of Domestic Banks

greater than state-owned banks. In 1996, return on assets for foreign banks exceeded 400 basis points in contrast to state banks reporting less than 100 basis points (see Barth & Litan 1997). This indicates that despite the relative size and special benefits that accrue to state banks, privately owned banks nonetheless have outperformed state-owned banks in Indonesia.

As shown in Figure 13, based on information in Table 4, allowable foreign ownership of banks in the East Asian area is greatly limited. Based on allowable ownership of shares of stock in banks, only Hong Kong allows unlimited ownership, with Indonesia a distant second at 49 percent of shares. Thereafter, no country among India, Malaysia, the Philippines, Singapore, or Thailand allows more than 30 percent of shares to be owned by foreigners. This is an example of how these countries have adopted strategies that sometimes explicitly limit the type of foreign capital flow to their financial systems and the nature of competition.[30]

The recent Indonesian experience suggests that privately owned banks in nations with a heavy influence from state-owned banks may perform better than state-owned banks. This outcome is consistent with the idea that banks in which there is private owner-contributed equity capital are better at determining the allocation of funds than state-owned banks in which the incentives and decision making processes are likely to be quite different. The outcome is also consistent, for example, with evidence from the U.S. savings and loan crisis of the 1980s in which institutions resembled state-owned banks because of substantial government directed lending. This suggests that privately owned financial institutions are better able to adapt to changing conditions than are state-owned firm or firms subject to substantial government directed lending.[31]

VII. STATE INFLUENCE ON BANK LENDING: THE CASE OF KOREA

As discussed above, Korea reported only 1.0 and 0.9 percent bank non-perform-ing loans to total loans in 1994 and 1995, respectively, yet ended up requiring a large financial assistance pledge from the IMF. In addition, there are only two state-owned banks in South Korea, neither of which are in the top ten, and they hold only 13 percent of bank assets in Korea. There is, however, far more gov-ernment involvement in bank and non-bank lending than these figures would indicate.

A recent IMF publication notes the following for Korea. "Explicit govern-ment-directed lending (Industrial Rationalization Loans) has given way to directed lending of a different kind—for example, banks are required to allo-cate a certain proportion of marginal loans to the small and medium-sized enter-prise sector—while political influence on lending decisions appears to continue" (see IMF, November, 1997, p. 150). Thus, there is direct government lending in the form of Industrial Rationalization Loans, and although this kind of lending is diminishing, the government has moved to allocating more lend-ing through banks.

A footnote in the same publication referring to the Industrial Rationalization Loans notes that "The commercial banks still had W 4.5 trillion in policy loans (that is Industrial Rationalization Loans) on their books at end-1996, 56 percent of which were nonperforming." This is the outcome in Korea where government intervention in lending has developed without significant state ownership of banks.[32]

A report issued in November 1997, based upon an earlier internal IMF evalua-tion of Korea, concluded, "At present, the main risks to the banking system derive from the past practice of government intervention in banks' credit alloca-tion decisions" (see Davis, 1998, p. A15). The basic problem is that private sec-tor financial decisions were not being made on the basis of adequate private owner-contributed equity capital being put at risk, something which an appropri-ate regulatory system or market forces absent the expectation of bailouts would require.[33]

VIII. COMPOSITION OF FINANCIAL MARKETS IN EAST ASIA

Bank Assets, Bond Markets, and Equity Market Capitalization

As well as evaluating the performance of banks and the effect of the banks' per-formance on among other things the likelihood of a financial crisis, it is important to evaluate the composition of financial systems. In general the broader and deeper a financial system, the more stable it will be and the more efficient it will be in channeling funds from savers to investors, thereby promoting economic development and growth. With the exception of the Hong Kong, Malaysia, and Singapore equity markets, in all of the East Asian countries the banking sector is larger than either the bond or equity sectors.

As shown in Figure 14, derived from information in Table 5, bank assets as a percentage of GDP in China, Indonesia, Korea, Taiwan, and Thailand are greater and in some cases much greater than the nations' bond markets or capitalization of equity markets. For sake of comparison, as Figure 14 also shows, in the United States the banking sector is smaller than the both the bond and equity sectors.[34]

It is interesting to note that in China, Indonesia, Taiwan, and Thailand, the bond markets are extraordinarily rudimentary. Relative to bank assets and equity market capitalization, bond markets in Hong Kong, Malaysian, and Singapore are also relatively small. In China both the bond market and the capitalization of the equity market are extremely small relative to bank assets. It is also important to note that until relatively recently equity market capitalization in Indonesia was effectively insignificant as well, representing as little as 5.8 percent of GDP as recently as 1991.

Given the extent of relatively recent direct state-ownership of banks in East Asia and Latin America as well as the indirect involvement of governments in banking markets, the size of the banking sector relative to other components of the financial system can be of extreme importance. For a given level of state ownership of banks, for example, if the banking sector is large relative to the debt and equity sectors, non-bank, market-related financial firms may be at

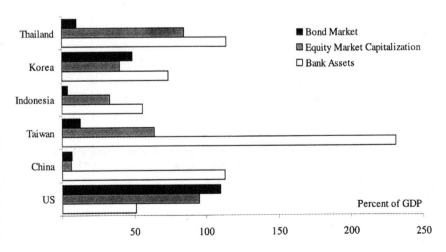

Figure 14. Relative Position of Bank Assets, Equity, and Bonds: 1995

Table 5. Relative Position of Bank Assets, Equity, and
Bonds: 1995 (Percent of GDP)

	Bank Assets	Equity Market Capitalization	Bond Market	Total
Asia				
China	113	6	7	126
Hong Kong	185	211	10	406
India	40	39	29	108
Indonesia	56	33	4	93
Korea	74	40	49	163
Malaysia	190	261	52	503
Philippines	63	79	36	178
Singapore	156	174	54	384
Taiwan	231	64	13	308
Thailand	114	85	10	209
Latin America				
Argentina	27	13	22	62
Brazil	44	21	32	97
Chile	55	110	57	222
Mexico	48	36	17	101
Memo				
Germany	157	24	83	264
Japan	144	72	68	284
U.K.	239	127	35	401
U.S.	51	95	110	256

Source: Milken Institute

a significant disadvantage relative to state-owned banks. Commercial firms may also have less access to non-bank and non-state-owned bank sources of funds. This is particularly important with respect to the financing of large industrial projects where individual banks are subject to loan-to-one-borrower limitations.

In addition, a financial system is going to be affected to a greater degree by bank difficulties if the banking sector is large relative to other sectors. Bank failure costs relative to GDP will tend to be higher. The effect of bank failures on economic development and growth will also be greater. Even in the absence of state involvement, a financial system is likely to be less efficient and less stable if it is dominated by one sector. All the sectors are complements, not substitutes, in affecting economic development and growth.

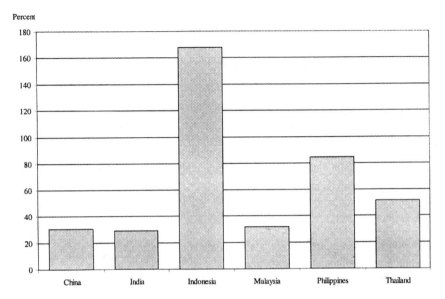

Figure 15. Short-Term Foreign Debt/Int'l Reserves-Asia: 1995

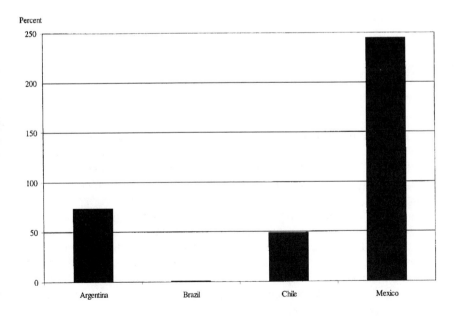

Figure 16. Short-Term Foreign Debt/Int'l Reserves-Latin America: 1995

Table 6. External Debt, Reserves and Money: 1995 Percent

| | Long-term Debt/Total Debt | Distribution of Long-term Debt | | | Short-term Debt/Reserves | Money/ Reserves | Money + Quasi-Money/Reserves |
		Multilateral	Bilateral	Private			
Asia							
China	81	17	21	62	30	407	965
Hong Kong	NA	NA	NA	NA	NA	NA	NA
India	92	35	31	34	29	324	903
Indonesia	79	23	37	40	168	153	709
Korea	NA	NA	NA	NA	NA	154	611
Malaysia	79	6	12	82	32	107	333
Philippines	85	25	41	33	85	119	586
Singapore	NA	NA	NA	NA	NA	26	105
Taiwan	NA	NA	NA	NA	NA	NA	NA
Thailand	68	8	20	71	52	43	369
Latin America							
Argentina	82	13	16	71	74	116	364
Brazil	81	7	15	78	1	70	421
Chile	73	15	4	81	49	41	180
Mexico	68	17	18	66	245	139	520
Memo							
Germany	NA	NA	NA	NA	NA	643	1802
Japan	NA	NA	NA	NA	NA	995	3185
U.K.	NA	NA	NA	NA	NA	921	2742
U.S.	NA	NA	NA	NA	NA	1633	5678

Note: [1]Based upon M0.

Source: Milken Institute

Percent

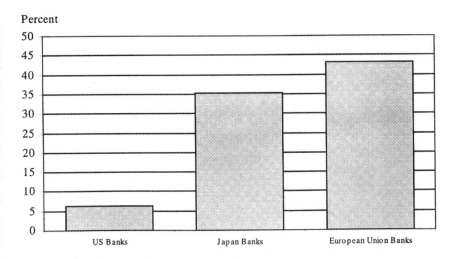

Figure 17. Relative Shares of Outstanding International Bank
Lending to East Asia: 1996

These issues are not limited to any one region of the world or any one stage
of economic development. As shown in Table 5, many Latin American nations
have financial systems that are relatively small percentages of GDP. In addition, highly developed nations like Germany and Japan have bank assets that
dominate both bond markets and the capitalization of equity markets. Many of
these "stylized" facts on the size and composition of financial systems reflect
laws, regulations, and taxes, not simply market forces. Such laws, regulations,
and taxes, in turn, by affecting financial systems, can enhance or impede
economic development and growth.

The Role of Short-Term Foreign Debt in the East Asian Crises

Figures 15 and 16, derived from data in Table 6, show short-term foreign
currency denominated debt to international reserves for selected East Asian
and Latin America countries in 1995. As the figures show, the ratio was 245
percent for Mexico and over 160 percent for Indonesia. These countries are
clearly outliers. The next highest ratios were for the Philippines at 85 percent
and Argentina at 74 percent. The remainder of the nations had relatively modest ratios ranging from a low of one percent for Brazil to 52 percent for
Thailand.

Those nations whose crises resulted in the largest financial assistance
pledges from the IMF were those with the most significant ratios of short-term
debt to international reserves—Mexico in 1995 and Indonesia, Argentina, and

Table 7.   Outstanding International Bank Lending to East Asia: 1996

	Total International Lending (Billions of U.S. dollars)	Percent of Total		
		US Banks	Japanese Banks	European Union Banks
China	55.0	5	32	47
Hong Kong[1]	207.2	4	42	42
Indonesia	55.5	10	40	38
Korea	100.0	9	24	34
Malaysia	22.2	10	37	41
Philippines	13.3	29	12	47
Singapore[1]	189.3	3	31	54
Taiwan	22.4	14	12	57
Thailand	70.2	7	53	27
Vietnam	1.5	13	13	67
East Asia total	736.6	6	35	43

Note: [1]The data for Hong Kong and Singapore reflect their roles as international financial centers.

Source: Milken Institute

Thailand in 1997. Clearly, those nations with the highest ratios were the ones with the greatest need for financial assistance in order to be able to both help repay the short-term foreign debt as it became due and to help replenish their international reserves.

As discussed above, these nations were also the ones whose bank loan growth relative to GDP was the highest in the 1990-1996 period—Mexico, Indonesia, and

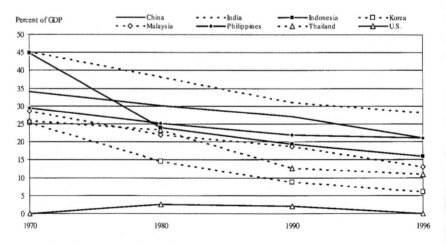

Figure 18.   Share of GDP-Agriculture: 1970-1996

Table 8. Sectoral Breakdown of Gross Domestic Product: 1970-1996

	1995 Nominal GNP per capita (U.S. dollars)	Distribution of GDP (percent)															
		Agriculture				Industry				Manufacturing				Services			
		1970	1980	1990	1996	1970	1980	1990	1996	1970	1980	1990	1996	1970	1980	1990	1996
Asia																	
China	620	34	30	27	21	38	49	42	48	30	41	34	38	28	21	31	31
Hong Kong	22,990	NA	1	0	0	NA	32	25	16	NA	24	18	9	NA	67	74	84
India	340	45	38	31	28	22	26	29	29	15	18	19	20	33	36	40	43
Indonesia	980	45	24	19	16	19	42	39	43	10	13	21	25	36	34	41	41
Korea	9,700	25	15	9	6	29	40	43	43	21	29	29	26	46	45	48	51
Malaysia	3,890	29	22	19	13	25	38	40	46	12	21	18	34	46	40	41	41
Philippines	1,050	30	25	22	21	32	39	34	32	25	26	25	23	39	36	44	47
Singapore	26,730	2	1	0	0	30	38	37	36	20	29	30	26	68	61	63	64
Taiwan	12,780	NA	8	4	4	NA	46	41	36	NA	NA	NA	NA	NA	47	55	60
Thailand	2,740	26	23	13	11	25	29	37	40	16	22	27	29	49	48	50	50
Latin America																	
Argentina	8,030	10	6	8	6	42	41	36	31	32	29	27	20	48	52	56	63
Brazil	3,640	12	11	10	14	38	44	38	36	29	33	26	23	49	45	51	50
Chile	4,160	7	7	9	8[2]	40	37	36	33[2]	25	21	NA	NA	53	55	55	59[2]
Mexico	3,320	12	8	8	5	29	33	30	26	22	22	22	20	59	59	62	68
Memo																	
Germany	27,510	3	2	2	1[3]	49	43	39	34	NA	NA	NA	24	47	55	60	65[3]
Japan	3,640	6	4	3	2	47	42	41	38	36	29	28	25	47	54	56	60
U.K.	18,700	3	2	2	2[1]	47	43	35	32[1]	35	27	23	21[1]	50	54	63	66[1]
U.S.	26,980	NA	3	2	2[1]	34	34	28	26[1]	NA	22	19	18[1]	NA	64	70	72[1]

Notes: [1] Reflects 1995 data.
[2] 1995 Estimates.
[3] Reflects 1994 data.

Source: Milken Institute

Thailand. Again, all of these data were available to the individual governments and the IMF and other trans-national agencies. Again, an issue that arises is whether the IMF essentially engaged in forbearance, thereby increasing the severity of individual country's crises and raising the cost higher than it would have been otherwise.

Another issue is raised by the disparity in risk exposure of lending by banks headquartered in different countries. As Figure 17 shows, based on Table 7 in the Appendix, only 6 percent of international bank lending came from U.S. banks, while 35 percent came from Japanese banks and 43 percent came from European Union banks. These differences raise an issue about who benefits from the financial assistance being provided to countries with financial crises, and who should ultimately pay for such assistance.

In reaction to the short-term borrowing issue some, most prominently Mr. Fischer, have suggested considering adoption of rules that would limit short-term borrowing from foreigners. The rationale for limiting this particular type of foreign capital flow is based on the view that the current crises could have been lessened significantly if East Asian banks and others had less access to short-term foreign currency loans.[35]

Size of the Banking Market and Economic Development

In general, the less developed the nation the more likely the nation's economy is going to be dominated by agricultural production, in contrast to industrial production and the provision of services. In turn, the more a nation relies

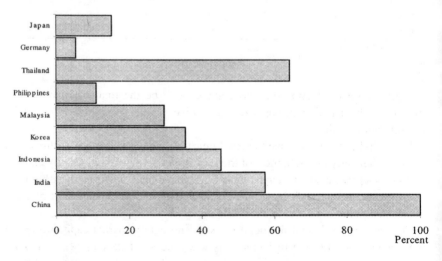

Figure 19. State Enterprise Bonds as Percent of State Enterprise and Corporate Bonds: 1995

Table 9.   Size and Composition of Bond Market: 1995

	Total (Billions of U.S. dollars)	Percent of Total			
		National Government	State Government	State Enterprises Central Bank	Corporates
Asia					
China	45.4	91	0	9	0	0
Hong Kong	14.6	0	0	0	52	48
India	103.4	65	10	14	0	11
Indonesia	8.3	0	0	17	61	20
Korea	190.0	16	2	23	18	42
Malaysia	41.6	70	0	9	0	21
Philippines	27.0	93	0	0	3	3
Singapore	46.3	94	0	0	0	6
Taiwan	36.4	NA	NA	NA	NA	NA
Thailand	16.8	10	0	57	2	32
Latin America					
Argentina	61.0	NA	NA	NA	NA	NA
Brazil	220.9	NA	NA	NA	NA	NA
Chile	38.2	NA	NA	NA	NA	NA
Mexico	42.5	NA	NA	NA	NA	NA
Memo					
Germany	2,870.3	36	4	3	0	56
Japan	3,784.1	58	3	6	0	33
U.K.	399.2	92	0	0	0	8
U.S.	8,007.4	32	13	30	0	25

Source: Milken Institue

on agricultural production the less complex will be the financial markets and the larger the banking sector will be relative to the bond market or equity market capitalization.

In that light, it is instructive to view Figure 18, based on Table 8. As the figure shows, as recently as 1970, most of the East Asian nations relied heavily on agriculture as a percentage of each nation's GDP. Since then, however, there has been a significant decline in each nation's reliance on agriculture, with offsetting gains distributed in the industrial and services sectors.

The implication is that the bond markets and equity market capitalization of these countries will tend to increase as this process of development continues with an accompanying greater need for large infrastructure projects and more external funds for larger commercial firms.[36] For comparison, Figure 18 also shows the percentage of GDP represented by agricultural production in the United States at approximately 2 percent. Thus, the United States and other fully industrialized nations have both the least amount of GDP represented by agricultural production combined with the most elaborate financial systems.

IX.   A LOOK INSIDE THE BOND MARKET

Even within the East Asian bond markets there are indications of government involvement that suggests state bond financing of commercial ventures. This can take the form of state enterprise bonds, or state bonds for commercial ventures. As shown in Figure 19, based on Table 9, in selected East Asian countries the portion of state enterprise bonds to the sum of corporate bonds plus state enterprise bonds is relatively high. In 1995 there were no corporate bonds in China. In India, Indonesia, and Thailand state enterprise bonds were more than 40 percent of all commercial enterprise bonds. Korea and Malaysia also had substantial state-enterprise bonds as a percent of state-enterprise and corporate bonds in 1995.

Again, the existence of state-enterprise bonds is another example of direct government involvement in the financial systems of the East Asian nations, as well as elsewhere. It is another indication that there are a large number of ways, directly and indirectly, in which governments can influence financial systems primarily through state-owned banks, direct government lending, government-mandated lending through private banks, regulation of products and prices of private banks, and state-sponsored commercial enterprises. In effect, this results in employing public-contributed equity capital rather than private owner-contributed equity capital for financial allocation decisions. This creates incentives in which financial decisions are not based strictly on economic criteria related to risk and return, but also on non-economic criteria based on bureaucratic myopia, corruption, nepotism, cronyism, and more.

X.   POLICY IMPLICATIONS AND CONCLUSIONS

Becker Versus Rubin: The Role of Government Intervention Versus Markets

As the following quotations indicate, there is a fierce rhetorical debate coinciding with the substantive debate. In February, the Nobel Laureate economist Gary Becker (1998, p. 22) was quoted as saying that " . . . obtrusive regulations and excessive government control over the financial sector are the weakest links in the economic superstructure of Indonesia, Malaysia, Thailand, and South Korea." Their governments, he said, "have regularly steered subsidies and other assistance to favored companies and bailed out those that got into financial difficulties. . . ."

In contrast, at about the same time, the United States' Secretary of the Treasury, Robert Rubin, was reported to have said that ". . . the Asian crisis demonstrates that markets cannot be trusted to correct their own excesses and [he] called on governments to step in and 'modernize the architecture' of international finance" (see Pearlstein, 1998, p. G1).

Becker might wish to re-paraphrase the Secretary, saying that the East Asian crisis demonstrates that governments cannot be trusted to correct their own excesses, but in the process of trying to obscure them they can be counted on to blame markets. The analysis presented in this paper, certainly, is not consistent with the hypothesis that the East Asian crisis is the direct result of market forces leading to instability.

In each of the East Asian countries experiencing severe banking problems, to varying degrees the banking sectors are significantly influenced by direct and indirect government intervention, including state ownership of banks. The bond and equity sectors are small relative to the bank sector. Even within the bond sector there is significant government influence on borrowing. In many countries, moreover, non-financial markets are significantly influenced by direct and indirect government intervention.

In such an environment, it appears inappropriate to claim that the recent difficulties have been caused by market forces. Rather individuals within countries experiencing difficulties have responded to a distorted incentive structure, based largely on inadequate private owner-contributed equity capital in banking and other enterprises that would serve as a constraint on risk-taking behavior. Individuals in other countries, moreover, have undoubtedly channeled funds into those countries based in part on the belief that the IMF, and others, would be standing by ready to provide financial assistance when the crisis struck.

It appears equally inappropriate to believe that a central remedy ought to be an attempt to focus more on international capital standards, examination and supervision regimes, activity limitations, ownership restrictions, and explicit deposit-insurance systems regarding the nations' banking sectors. In part this is the case because similar regulatory regimes were generally already in place, but did not prevent the difficulties.

To the degree that bank lending occurs with little or no private owner-contributed equity capital at risk, and hence little or no market evaluation of risk and return, the imposition of such policies can border on meaningless. It is clear that in far too many countries significant government intervention in what are often rudimentary financial systems is the rule rather than the exception.

The Appropriate Role of Government and Markets

Our analysis of the East Asian banking and more general financial crises suggests that the most important issue that needs to be addressed is the widespread and inappropriate intrusion of many of the region's governments directly and indirectly into the financial system. The inappropriate intrusion of government into the financial system has the effect of supplanting the important role played by private owner-contributed equity capital. The outcome is a structure of incentives resulting in widespread financial decisions being widely divorced from a more market-based analysis of risk and return.

As we have discussed in detail, in many countries government involvement extends to extensive state ownership of banks. It includes direct state involvement in corporate bond markets, state limitations on private and foreign involvement in financial systems, and state direction of lending of non-state owned financial institutions toward state-selected enterprises.

In our view, the remedies that should be emphasized are ones that in various countries to various degrees are already underway, but need to be dramatically accelerated. State ownership of most financial institutions should be phased out. Private and foreign ownership of financial institutions should be encouraged, especially when failed state banks are seized and reorganized. Expansion of what are now often insignificant bond and equity markets should be a primary goal as countries grow and mature.

Foreign investment of all types should be encouraged, not only by specifically encouraging it, but also by lowering huge transactions costs that are now embedded, for example, in corruption (sometimes official), in non-impartial judiciary systems and government civil services, and in inappropriate or non-existent accounting. In our view the emphasis should be on adequate private owner-contributed equity capital as the basis for making most decisions about the allocation of financial and real resources. This should be a central tenet of future IMF and other trans-national proposals regarding international banking and financial crises.

Designing Solutions: Experience in the Developed World

In designing solutions involving banks in developing East Asian economies, it may help to look at the unprecedented number of recent banking crises in developed countries. In some of these countries the difficulties have occurred despite elaborate restrictions on allowable activities, on form of ownership and organizational structure, and on location. Even countries that combined explicit deposit-insurance schemes, minimum capital requirements based upon the Basle accord and prompt corrective action rules, elaborate examination and supervision, and fairly high degrees of transparency did not avoid difficulties.

That is certainly true of Spain and Canada, which experienced banking problems from the late 1970s through 1985. Denmark and the United States experienced significant banking problems in the period 1987-1992. The savings and loan crisis in the United States extended from the early 1980s through the early 1990s. Six countries—Germany France, Italy, Finland, Sweden, and Switzerland—experienced banking problems for some number of years in the period 1987-1995. Finally, Japan has experienced significant banking difficulties since 1992.

Perhaps the best single window through which to examine these issues may be the savings and loan crisis in the United States in the 1980s and early 1990s. In 1980 the savings and loans in the United States had one of, if not the most, elaborate regulatory mechanisms in the world imposed on privately owned firms. There was federal deposit-insurance and a prompt-corrective-action mechanism for resolution of troubled and insolvent savings and loans. There was a statutorily mandated, relatively high minimum capital standard that most savings and loans met. There was an elaborate examination and supervisory apparatus. There was, moreover, no issue about an inadequate accounting system or more generally, a lack of transparency. In other words, there were all the regulatory attributes that now much touted by among others the IMF.

At the same time, however, as discussed above the government simultaneously required savings and loans to make fixed-rate, long-term home mortgages financed by shorter-term, more variable rate deposits. The government largely forbade the use of variable-rate mortgages and the use of futures and options markets to hedge interest-rate risk. Then the yield curve inverted, and the entire industry was deeply insolvent in 1981. In response to this dire situation, the Congress—with full knowledge of the extent of the problem—lowered capital standards and jettisoned prompt corrective action measures.

The problem was not the absence of an explicit deposit-insurance system, capital standards, prompt corrective action requirements, restricted activities, government examination and supervision, or a lack of transparency. The problem was that within this structure the government mandated what kind of loans could be made and how to price them. When in response to market forces the government-directed lending program fell apart, the appropriate incentive system was also permitted to fall apart. The government basically spent a decade making the situation worse and blaming others.

Our analysis above suggests that this is a remarkably similar pattern to what has happened in the contemporary East Asian banking and more general financial crises. Much of the deregulation and privatization came too late. And then when private owner-contributed equity capital was inadequate. Despite this situation a credit boom was tolerated, heavily funded with short-term foreign debt.

The Role of the IMF and other Trans-National Agencies

The Imposition of International Banking Protocols: A Central Goal of the IMF

It is certainly true that the IMF and the other trans-national agencies, for example, have called for greater "transparency" through improved accounting and less government secrecy. They have also lauded privatization of banks when it has occurred and encouraged it when it has not occurred. Likewise, they have encouraged increased foreign investment and ownership of banks. Yet, it does not appear that these are the central components of their proposed remedies for banking difficulties in East Asia, or that they are central to their analysis of the East Asian banking difficulties.

In addition to their continued role in providing financial assistance for international banking crises, a central goal of the IMF appears to be the imposition of international banking protocols, whose design and implementation would be heavily influenced by the IMF.[37] As the IMF has discussed widely, the banking protocols that are envisioned build upon the Basle accord on required international capital levels and complementary explicit deposit-insurance schemes.[38] The IMF has stated that banking crises around the globe have resulted because of inappropriate banking practices and regulatory regimes, and that their proposed reforms would help reduce the number and severity of bank crises.

As this paper has pointed out, however, depending on the degree of state influence in commercial ventures and bank lending, if the lending decisions prove inappropriate, the concept of "adequate regulation" may not apply at all. The banks in this kind of arrangement are instead instruments of government policy which can lead to politically favored lending to selected commercial entities. Likewise, the concept of adequate examination and supervision that in the United States applies to privately owned banks, for example, cannot be similarly applied to state-owned banks carrying out state policies.

Government-determined capital levels and decisions of how to handle insolvent state-owned banks cannot be compared to either market-based capital levels and bankruptcy proceedings or required minimum capital levels and prompt corrective action rules adopted by bank regulators in countries like the United States. This largely describes the nature of the banking markets in some of the East Asian countries in which there has been substantial direct and indirect government intervention in the financial systems.

In the absence of market-driven lending based on a market-evaluation of risk and return with adequate private owner-contributed equity capital as the backstop, such recommendations cannot be viewed as sufficient efforts at financial reform. To the contrary, these countries need assistance in eliminating the state-ownership of banks where it exists. Similarly, these countries need help in reducing, if not, eliminating state direction of lending either through state-owned banks, indirectly through influence on non-state-owned banks or through bond markets. State influence can either go through financial institutions or directly through government sponsorship of commercial ventures. The latter form of state influence can corrupt financial systems to such a degree that banks and non-bank financial institutions can be adversely affected. As a result, countries need help in minimizing these forms of government intervention in financial systems.

Furthermore, these countries need assistance in lowering the sometimes substantial transactions costs associated with among other things corruption, inadequate legal protection and enforcement of property and other legal rights, biased judicial and civil service systems, and flawed accounting systems. These are the kinds of reforms that can establish greater compatibility with the developed world's financial systems.

New Government Imposed Rules on Selected Types of Activities

As discussed above, some individuals have mentioned the possibility of new rules limiting certain forms of short-term foreign borrowing. The heaviest short-term foreign borrowing relative to international reserves occurred in nations whose financial systems are dominated by state-owned banks, and have significant government direct and indirect influence over financial and non-financial firms. The accumulation of the short-term foreign debt over time appears to have been reported publicly and was therefore known by the relevant governments, the IMF, and other trans-national agencies. Thus, if the accumulation of the short-term foreign debt did not directly reflect government policy, it was tolerated by the respective governments without significant concern expressed by the IMF and other trans-national agencies. This suggests that short-term foreign lending per se was a symptom but not the cause of the difficulties facing certain nations.[39]

As with the substantial growth rate of bank lending relative to GDP growth in these nations, the accumulation of short-term foreign debt relative to international reserves is relevant to the moral-hazard problem discussed above. The participants in these transactions—foreign lenders, regional banks, and regional governments—were aware of the risks that were being taken. Given the pattern of past IMF financial assistance, it became reasonable to expect future IMF financial assistance would be provided if new financial crises developed, thereby creating an incentive to take excessive risk with short-term debt, as well as with bank lending. The implication is that it may be more appropriate to curtail expectations of future IMF financial assistance in financial crises, rather than establishing rules regarding short-term foreign debt levels.

The IMF and Bank Regulation

The IMF would like to play a significant role in designing and implementing international bank regulatory protocols. In an address at the G-7 summit in Lyons in June 1996, for example, Mr. Camdessus said "The dissemination of a clear set of internationally accepted standards could provide the basis for the regulation and supervision of banking systems around the world." He added, " . . . the IMF, because of its legitimacy and universal responsibility for surveillance, has a role to play in facilitating this globalization of standards for bank supervision developed in Basle and put in practice in the G-10 countries."[40]

If these efforts are successful, the IMF will have new and expanded powers, potentially becoming a new form of international bank regulator. If so, such a position and the specific regulations that it advocates merit debate, especially given the

228   J. R. BARTH, R. D. BRUMBAUGH, JR., L. RAMESH, and G. YAGO

IMF's history of ineffective and potentially destabilizing actions in the recent crises in East Asia and elsewhere.

ACKNOWLEDGMENT

The authors are grateful to Jeremy Bolt and Tejaswini Chaudhari for excellent assistance in
preparing the paper.

NOTES

1.   See Barth and Litan (1997). For a more detailed analyses of the U.S. savings and loan and
banking problems of the 1980s and early 1990s, see Barth (1991), Brumbaugh (1988, 1993), Barth,
Brumbaugh, and Litan (1992), Carron (1982), Kane (1985, 1989), and White (1991).
2.   See Caprio and Klingebiel (1997, p. 80, 1996, p. 15), who provide the first and most extensive
compilation of data on bank insolvencies worldwide.
3.   For information on bank structure and regulation in the nineteen non-overlapping G-10 and
European Union countries, see Barth, Nolle, and Rice (1997).
4.   Indeed, in a study of 49 countries La Porta, Lopez-de-Silanes, and Shleifer and Vishny (1997,
p. 1132) conclude that there is ". . . strong evidence that the legal environment has large effects on the
size and breadth of capital markets across countries." Also, see Levine (1997, 1998), who concludes in
the more recent study that "Although changing legal codes and improving the efficiency with which
legal systems enforce laws and contracts is difficult, the economic returns to improving the legal environment appear very large" (1998, pp. 21-22).
5.   More generally, modern information technology, by increasing available information and lowering transactions costs, allows for a diverse range of financial products and services without as much
need for liquidity and maturity transformation services that have been traditionally provided by financial intermediaries. As a result, the traditional intermediaries are increasingly repositioning themselves
as asset managers and risk managers.
6.   In this regard, according to Borsuk and Casey (April 27, 1998, p. A19), "A new Indonesian
court to deal only with bankruptcy cases will open in August. But while foreign bankers applauded the
move, it's not certain that the court will give them what they want: an effective legal mechanism to
declare debtors bankrupt and deal with selling their assets...Indonesia's lack of a credible and efficient
legal mechanism for settling disputes between creditors and debtors is an old problem."
7.   For the classic statement of the role of such a lender, see Bagehot (1873), and as applied in an
international context, see Barth and Keleher (1984). For a good discussion of the general issue of systemic risk, see Kaufman (1995).
8.   Neither the lender of last resort nor a deposit-insurance system is designed to keep insolvent
institutions open. As long as runs cannot spread from insolvent institutions to solvent institutions, the
credit system and payment mechanism need not be disrupted when runs occur on the former. In the
U.S. savings and loan and banking crisis of the 1980s and early 1990s, deposit-insurance protection
was provided to depositors of institutions left open even though reporting insolvency. The reason was
that the deposit-insurance agencies, for a lengthy period of time, did not have and did not request the
necessary financial resources to resolve all insolvent institutions at the time of reported insolvency.
This was a manifestation of the moral-hazard and principle-agent problems. In the East Asian crisis of
1997 and 1998 in Indonesia, deposit insurance was implemented for depositors of insolvent banks after
they had been seized.
9.   For further discussion of these issues, see Barth and Brumbaugh (1994).

10.   The G-10 countries include Belgium, Canada, France, Germany, Italy, Japan, the Netherlands, Sweden, Switzerland, the United Kingdom and the United States. Switzerland became a full member in 1984, bringing the group to eleven members. Since 1984 the G-10 has included 11 countries.

11.   In a seminal study, King and Levine (1993, p. 540) conclude that "We find support for the core idea advanced in our model: better financial systems stimulate faster productivity and growth in per capita output by funneling society's resources to promising productivity enhancing endeavors." More generally, see Levine (1997) for an excellent survey of this literature.

12.   The total financing committed was $40 billion to Indonesia, $57 billion to Korea, and $17.2 to Thailand. See IMF (January 1998).

13.   The IMF itself admits that "There is neither point nor excuse for the international community to provide financial assistance to a country unless that country takes measures to prevent future such crises" (IMF, April 6, 1998, p. 101).

14.   As Barth and Keleher (1984, p. 66) state, "... the IMF must depend on the limited contributions from member countries for funds to lend. Once the IMF reaches this quota, its funds are exhausted; it cannot create either a world currency or the currencies of its members. Since the ability to create money is the chief feature distinguishing a lender of last resort, the IMF does not qualify fully for that role."

15.   According to Jeffrey Sachs (1997), Director of the Harvard Institute for International Development, "The secrecy ... makes it impossible to maintain broad public and professional scrutiny of IMF operations. ... In short, the IMF gets away with serious mistakes of judgement that never come to light."

16.   Mr. Camdessus (IMF, March 23, 1998, p. 89), for example, admits that "...it is true that some short-term creditors are being at least partly protected [when the IMF provides financial assistance]."

17.   In particular, according to Philippe Maystadt, Chairman of the Interim Committee of the Board of Governors of the IMF (IMF, April 27, 1998, p. 114), it is the intention of the IMF "To actively encourage members to adopt internationally agreed standards for strengthening banking regulation and supervision."

18.   This definition of crisis is based on Sachs, Tornell, and Velasco (1996).

19.   It is interesting to note that Mexico had a negative crisis index, reflecting the earlier resolution of its crisis. Despite a relatively high growth rate in bank credit, Hong Kong's crisis index was also negative, reflecting perhaps the existence of a currency board and a relatively high level of international reserves.

20.   According to Sanger (1998, p. A1) for example, "A confidential report by the International Monetary Fund on Indonesia's economic crisis acknowledges that an important statement of the IMF's rescue strategy backfired, causing a bank panic that helped set off financial declines in much of Asia." In addition, Sachs (1997) states that " The IMF has not stopped the panic, and arguably has added to it, both by its rhetoric (which underplays the role of panic and overplays the weaknesses in Asia) and by its draconian macroeconomic policy conditions."

21.   The term "prompt corrective action," (PCA), in general refers to increasing regulatory scrutiny and intervention as a banking institution's reported capital declines. For a recent summary of the provisions, see Barth, Nolle, and Rice (1997), Table 13. One recent empirical assessment of prompt corrective action concludes that the ". . . results raise doubts about whether PCA legislation will reduce BIF losses" (Gilbert, 1992, p. 20). Alice M. Rivlin (1996, pp. 5-6), Vice Chair of the Board of Governors of the Federal Reserve System, moreover, states that "Supervisory sanctions under Prompt Corrective Action were to be based on the bank's risk performance as measured by its levels of regulatory capital, in particular its leverage ratio and total risk-based capital ratio under Basle capital standards." Yet, "These standards now seem well-intentioned but rather outdated." The reason, according to Ms. Rivlin, is that "the scope and complexity of banking activities has proceeded apace during the last two decade or so, and standard capital measures, at least for our very largest and most complex organizations, are no longer adequate measures on which to base supervisory action."

22.   In the case of Indonesia, McLeod (1996, p. 29) states that "Frustration with the central bank's inability to enforce regulations against politically powerful bank shareholders (including the govern-

ment itself) is resulting in more and more prudential regulation, but little actual progress in improving prudential standards."

23.   The relevant banking laws largely evolved in the United States from the early 1930s following the Great Depression and involved government-mandated allocation of a significant proportion of financial services and products among banking institutions. In general, among banking institutions (commercial and mutual savings banks, savings and loans, and credit unions), who could offer what product at what price in which location, for example, was largely determined by the government. Although still heavily regulated, different types of banking institutions are now largely free to offer many of the same products and services wherever they wish. For more information comparing U.S. banks to banks in other industrial countries, see Barth, Nolle, and Rice (1997).

24.   Studies find that in the 1980s on average savings and loans could not profitably hold fixed-rate home mortgages in portfolio. See, for example, Carron and Brumbaugh (1991) and Passmore (1992). Yet, the first year that federally chartered savings and loans could make commercial loans was 1982. The first year that federally chartered savings and loans could make consumer loans or issue credit cards was 1980. The first year they could make construction or education loans was 1978. For more information on these and other restrictions on the activities of savings and loans, see Barth (1991) and Brumbaugh (1988).

25.   As recently as 1950, 65 percent of the total financial assets in U.S. financial intermediaries were in banking institutions. The percentage has declined steadily to less than 30 percent in 1997. In the process, there has been significant development of less regulated non-bank competition to which the heavily regulated banks have had to adapt.

26.   It is important to note that the problems of savings and loans were not associated with securities and insurance activities or investment in non-financial firms or visa versa.

27.   See Barth, Page, and Brumbaugh (1992) for an analysis of the importance of the put option to savings and loans in the 1980s.

28.   Importantly, in a study of thirty-one episodes of systemic banking crises in developing and developed countries, Demirgüç-Kunt and Detragiache (1997, p. 33) report that "Our regressions indicate rather unambiguously that the presence of an explicit deposit insurance scheme tends to increase the probability of systemic banking problems." Furthermore, Cull (1998, p. 19) concludes "... in countries that adopt deposit insurance to stop or delay a crisis (i.e., those with high financial instability), the program has been unsuccessful... ."

29.   Kaufman (1996, p. 18) states that it can be argued that ". . . the poor performance of banking experienced in almost all countries in the last two decades reflects primarily regulatory or government failures, rather than market failures. . . ." Also, Caprio (1996, p. 18) states that "If owners have more at stake...they can be expected to take greater measures to safeguard their bank than under the present system in most countries with limited liability, modest capital requirements, and some form of deposit guarantee."

30.   With respect to the particular type of limitations being discussed, Claessens, Demirgüç-Kunt, and Huizinga (1997, p. 18), in an interesting study of banking in 80 countries,find "that the overall welfare implications of foreign bank entry are positive."

31.   In a recent study of the financial sectors in East Asia, Claessens and Glaessner (1997, p. 35) state that "to achieve better banking systems, countries must . . . reconsider the state role in the financial sector."

32.   This is not to say that all such intervention is, or has been, inappropriate. Rather, as Korea and other countries develop and grow, greater reliance on market forces becomes crucial.

33.   This is consistent with Caprio and Klingebiel's conclusion, based upon a study of banking sector insolvencies in 29 countries, that ". . . the primary causes of bank insolvency are considered to be deficient management, faulty supervision and regulation, government intervention, or some degree of connected or politically motivated lending."

34.   The relative size of the banking sector in the United States to the bond market and equity market capitalization largely explains why the banking crisis of the 1980s and early 1990s did not disrupt

the U.S. financial system significantly as well as the real economy. Indeed, the estimated resolution cost for the savings and loan crisis was 3.5 percent of GDP (see Barth & Litan 1997).

35.   In this regard, Claudio Loser (1998, p. 67), Director of the IMF Western Hemisphere Department, states that ". . . controls—either on inflows or outflows--have been ineffective at best, if not useless, because such restrictions tend to be easily and quickly circumvented. Nevertheless, in the case of certain countries—Columbia and Chile, for example—the authorities have successfully introduced or maintained certain capital controls on inflows." Sebastian Edwards (1998, p. A19) stresses the limitations and costs of such controls, but states that "during the transition a scheme [of controls on short-term capital flows] similar to that used in Chile may be helpful."

36.   Furthermore, Black and Gilson (1998) argue that stock markets are more conducive to entrepreneurial activity and venture capitalists than bank-based financial systems.

37.   The IMF (March 26, 1997, p. 156) states that it "...is paying increasing attention to the quality of banking systems in its surveillance and its technical assistance ... [and in] advising its members on banking standards, the IMF will use the Basle Committee's new core principles wherever possible."

38.   It is worthwhile pointing out that at the same time within the United States under some circumstances official support of deposit insurance may be eroding. Thomas M. Hoenig (1996, p. 11), President of the Federal Reserve Bank of Kansas City, for example, has recently stated that "In light of the costs and difficulties of implementing prudential supervision for larger institutions who are increasingly involved in new activities and industries, the time may have come to sever the link between these institutions and the safety nets making it feasible to significantly scale back regulatory oversight of their operations".

39.   Lawrence Summers (1997), U.S. Deputy Treasury Secretary, states that "The speculative activity we saw in the weeks leading to the crisis was the result—not the cause—of Thailand's problems." He adds that he does "...not believe the openness of Thai financial markets was responsible for the crisis."

40.   See IMF (1996, p. 236). For a discussion of the role of the IMF as a potential international lender of last resort, see Barth and Keleher (1984). Other proposals for international agencies also exist. Noia (1995, p. 30), for example, states that "The problems of coordinating different countries DIAs (Deposit Insurance Agencies) are so big that they could be solved in various ways . . ." including ". . . the creation of a European DIA . . ." which ". . . could be something like a regional agency for Europe of an international deposit insurance corporation.

REFERENCES

Bagehot, W. (1962). *Lombard Street.* Homewood, IL: Irwin.

Barth, J. R. (1991). *The great savings and loan debacle.* Washington, DC: The American Enterprise Institute.

Barth, J. R., & Brumbaugh, Jr., R. D. (1994). Depository institution failures and failure costs: The role of moral hazard and agency problems. In G. G. Kaufman (Ed.), *Research in financial services: Private and public policies.* Greenwich: JAI Press.

Barth, J. R., & Brumbaugh, Jr., R. D. (1997). *Development and evolution of national financial systems: An international perspective.* Mexico: Latin American Studies Association.

Barth, J. R., & Brumbaugh, Jr., R. D. (1996). The changing world of banking: Setting the regulatory agenda. In D. B. Papadimitriou (Ed.), *Stability in the financial system.* London: Macmillan Press Ltd.

Barth, J. R., Brumbaugh, Jr., R. D., & Litan, R. E. (1992). *The future of American banking.* Armonk, NY: M. E. Sharpe, Inc.

Barth, J. R. , Gropper, D. M., & Jahera, Jr., J. S. (1998). A multi-country analysis of bank capital and earnings. In *Review of Pacific Basin Financial Markets and Policies.* Wold Scientific Publishing Company.

Barth, J. R., & Keleher, R. (1984). Financial crises and the role of the lender of last resort. *Economic Review.*

Barth, J. R., Nolle, D. E., & Rice, T. N. (1977). *Commercial banking structure, regulation, and performance: An international comparison. Office of the Comptroller of the Currency,* Economics Working Paper 97-6, March.

Barth, J. R., & Litan, R. (1997). *Preventing bank crises: Lessons from bank failures in the United States. Presented at a conference entitled Preventing Bank Crises: Lessons from Recent Global Bank Failures.* sponsored by the Federal Reserve Bank of Chicago and the Economic Institute of the World Bank, Chicago, Illinois.

Barth, J. R., Page, D. E., & Brumbaugh, Jr., D. R. (1992). Pitfalls in using market prices to assess the financial condition of depository institutions. *Journal of Real Estate Finance and Economics.*

Black, B. S., & Gilson, R. J. (1998). Venture capital and the structure of capital markets: Banks versus stock markets. *Journal of Financial Economics, 47*(3).

Becker, G. S. (1998). Asia may be shaken but it's no house of cards. *Business Week,* February 2.

Borsuk, R., & Casey, M. (1998). Indonesia overhauls bankruptcy process. *Wall Street Journal,* April 27.

Brumbaugh, Jr., R. D. (1988). *Thrifts under siege: Restoring order to American banking.* Cambridge, MA: Ballinger Publishing Company.

Brumbaugh, Jr., R. D. (1993). *The collapse of federally insured depositories: The savings and loans as precursor.* New York: Garland Publishing, Inc.

Caprio, G. Jr., & Klingebiel, D. (1996). *Bank insolvency: Bad luck, bad policy, or bad banking?* Annual Bank Conference on Development Economics, The World Bank.

Caprio, G. Jr. (1996). *Bank regulation: The case of the missing model.* The World Bank, Policy Research Working Paper 1574.

Caprio, G. (1996). *Bank insolvencies: Cross-country experience.* The World Bank, Policy Research Working Paper 1620.

Carron, A. S. (1982). *The plight of the thrift institutions.* Washington, DC: The Brookings Institution.

Carron, A. S., & Brumbaugh, Jr., D. R. (1991). *The viability of the thrift industry.* Housing Policy Debate, Federal National Mortgage Association, Summer.

Chote, R. (1996). Banking on a catastrophe. *Financial Times,* October 21, London Edition.

Claessens, S., & Glaessner, T. (1997). *Are financial sector weaknesses undermining the East Asian miracle?* Washington, DC: The World Bank.

Claessens, S., Demirgüç-Kunt, A., & Huizinga, H. (1997). *How does foreign entry affect the domestic banking market?* mimeo. The World Bank.

Cull, R. (1998). *How deposit insurance affects financial depth: A cross-country analysis.* The World Bank, Policy Research Working Paper 1875.

Davis, B. (1998). IMF debtors and creditors deadlock over disclosure. *Wall Street Journal,* March 4.

Demirgüç-Kunt, A., & Detragiache, E. (1997). *The determinants of banking crises: Evidence from industrial and developing countries.* The World Bank, Policy Research Working Paper 1828.

Gilbert, R. A. (1992). The effects of legislating prompt corrective action on the bank insurance fund. *Economic Review,* 3-22.

Hoenig, T. M. (1996). Rethinking financial regulation. *Economic Perspectives.*

International Monetary Fund. (1995). Much is at stake for G-7 in today's globalized world. IMF Survey, July 15, 229.

International Monetary Fund. (1988). Participation in the IMF is an investment in world stability and prosperity. *IMF Survey,* March 23.

International Monetary Fund. (1988). *IMF bail outs: truth and fiction,* January.

International Monetary Fund. (1998). Camdessus cites greater IMF transparency; urges Japan to pursue bank restructuring. *IMF Survey,* April 27.

International Monetary Fund. (1997). Indonesia—recent economic developments. *IMF Staff Country Report No. 97/75,* September.

International Monetary Fund. (1997). *International capital markets: Developments, prospects, and key policy issues*, November.

International Monetary Fund. (1998). *Morning Press*, February 23.

International Monetary Fund. (1998). Fischer outlines IMF policy prescription to minimize impact of Asian crisis. *IMF Survey*, April 6.

International Monetary Fund. (1997). Globalization calls for extending IMF's role. *IMF Survey*, March 26.

Kane, E. J. (1985). *The gathering crisis in federal deposit insurance.* Cambridge, MA: MIT Press.

Kane, E. J. (1989). *The S&L insurance mess: How did it happen?* Washington, DC: The Urban Institute.

Kaufman, G. G. (1996). Bank failures, systemic risk, and bank regulation. *Cato Journal, 16*(1).

Kaufman, G. G. (1995). Banking, financial markets, and systemic risk. In *Research in Financial Services* Greenwich, CT: JAI Press Inc.

King, R. G., & Levine, R. (1993). Finance entrepreneurship and growth, theory and evidence. *Journal of Monetary Economics.*

Levine, R. (1997). Financial development and economic growth: Views and agenda. *Journal of Economic Literature.*

Levine, R. (1998). *The legal environment, banks, and long-run economic growth.* The Thomas Jefferson Center for Political Economy, Discussion Paper 307, January.

Levine, R. (1997). *Law, finance, and economic growth.* The Thomas Jefferson Center for Political Economy, Discussion Paper 30, July 1997.

Lindgren, C. J., Garcia, G., & Saal, M. I. (1996). *Bank Soundness and Macroeconomic Policy.* Washington, DC: International Monetary Fund.

Loser, C. (1998). Interview on facing Asian crisis, Latin America and Caribbean demonstrate resiliency, potential for growth. *IMF Survey*, March 9.

McLeod, R. H. (1996). *Control and competition: Banking deregulation and re-regulation in Indonesia.* Australian National University, Working Paper.

Montgomery, J. (1997). *The Indonesian financial system: Its contribution to economic performance, and key policy issues.* IMF Working Paper, April.

Passmore, W. (1992). Can retail depositories fund mortgages profitably? *Journal of Housing Research 3*(1).

Pearlstein, S. (1998). On the table: Reform of the global financial system. *Washington Post,* January.

Posner, R. A. (1974). Theories of economic regulation. *Bell Journal of Economics and Management Science, 5.*

Rivlin, A. M. (1996). *Optimal supervision and regulation of banks.* Washington, DC: The Brookings Institution National Issues Forum.

Sachs, J. (1997). Letter to the editor. *Financial Times,* December 19.

Sachs, J., Tornell, A., & Velasco, A. (1996). Financial crises in emerging markets: The lessons for 1995. *Brookings Papers on Economic Activity, 1.*

Sanger, D. E. (1998). I.M.F. now admits tactics in Indonesia deepened the crisis. *New York Times,* January 14.

Stigler, G. J. (1971). The theory of economic regulation. *Bell Journal of Economics and Management Science,* Spring.

Summers, L. (1997). *Building a global financial system for the 21st century.* Congressional Economic Leadership Council, August 12.

White, L. J. (1991). *The S&L debacle: Public policy lessons for bank and thrift regulation.* Oxford: Oxford University Press.

AN EXAMINATION OF BANK REGULATORS' DECISIONS TO FAIL BANKS:
AN INTERNATIONAL PERSPECTIVE

Philip F. Bartholomew and Benton E. Gup

Bank failures occur throughout the world. Lindgren, Garcia, and Saal (1996) reported that over 131 of the 181 countries that are members of the International Monetary Fund had severe banking problems since 1980.[1] In 1997 and 1998, the financial crises in Southeast Asia brought with it a new wave of bank failures. Although the causes of bank failures have been researched extensively, relatively few deal explicitly with the bank regulators' decisions to fail banks.[2] The reality of the situation is that bank regulators resolve some problem banks swiftly, whereas it may take years to resolve others. What accounts for the differences in timing?

In most cases, banks and other depository institutions are regulated by the government, usually at the national level or with substantial national government involvement, and through government intervention, institutions deemed failures are handled by government authorities. Several factors involved in the regulatory

Research in Financial Services: Private and Public Policy, Volume 10, pages 235-257.
ISBN: 0-7623-0358-1

decision to fail a bank can be generalized to include insolvency, illiquidity, or operation in an unsafe and unsound manner. But the decision to close a bank and the manner in which closure is effected can differ over time and in different countries. Since closure may also involve the manner in which the failed institution is resolved or disposed of, the resolution strategy or set of strategies can affect the decision to close.

There is an extensive literature on early warning models that offers some insights on determinants of individual bank failure.[3] For example, Dimergüc-Kunt (1991) found that a bank's net value (capital plus insurance guarantees) was a good indicator of the likelihood of a failure decision. Thomson (1992) modeled bank regulator's decision to close banks as a call option whose value depends on the bank's charter, solvency and resolution costs. Cole and Gunther (1994) found differences in regulatory treatment helped large banks to avoid failure. In a later study Cole and Gunther (1995) concluded that the closure of large banks was not delayed relative to the closure of small banks. Freixas and Rochet (1997, pp. 281-287) reviewed a study by R. Repullo that used game theory, and concluded that bank closures should be made by the central bank when depositor withdrawals are small, and by the insurance fund when they are large. Mailath and Mester (1994) used dynamic game theory and to deal with the issue of when to close a bank that is near failure and invests in risky assets.

This paper does not address what causes banks and others depositories to fail. Rather, it extends the research on bank closures by: (1) examining the process of failure in an international context, and (2) examining factors related to resolving failed banks that may affect the regulators' decision to fail banks.

I. BANK FAILURE DEFINED

There is no universally accepted definition of bank failure. Failure is a regulatory or legal decision. Bank regulators fail a bank when they decide that it is unable to operate because it cannot meet its financial obligations, or it has violated certain rules, such as inadequate capital, or for other reasons.[4] In the United States, only state and federal bank chartering agencies have the authority to close a bank, and the FDIC can take control of a failing institution and operate it as a bridge bank. The authority close or control banks varies from country to country. In France, for example, Credit Lyonnais is a state-owned bank that the government is bailing out rather than close it.

To avoid confusion over the meaning of the term failure, many analysts resort to using the term "resolution." There is no legal definition of this term either, but it is fairly uniformly applied in the literature on the thrift crisis and the bank failures of the 1980s.[5] Whereas failure can mean that an institution has become insolvent or non-viable, or, it can mean that the regulator has closed or resolved it, resolution specifically refers to a regulatory action. This paper uses the GAO definition of a "resolution" to mean the regulatory action of "taking" an institution, determining its estimated present-value resolution cost, and committing to a strategy of liquidation or purchase and assumption.

If or when bank regulators fail a bank is a matter of judgement which is influenced by the economic condition of the bank and other factors that are explained below.

Principal Agent Problems

According to Kane (1989), there are principal agent problems that may give some bank regulators incentives to delay or not to close troubled banks. Cole (1989, 1993) found that agency conflicts between regulators and taxpayers helped to explain why some thrifts were closed and others were not. In contrast to principal agent problems, Kroszner and Strahan (1996) found that regulators lacked the cash to close insolvent thrifts; and they induced private investors to provide capital through mutual-to-stock conversions.

Financial Stability

Crockett (1997) argues that financial stability is an appropriate goal of public policy. Implementation of this policy requires the intervention of bank regulators to prevent runs, contagion, and to reduce the cost of resolution. An FDIC study, History of the Eighties (1997, Vol. 1, p. 42), concluded that "At various times and for various reasons, regulators generally concluded that good public policy required that big banks in trouble be shielded from the full impact of market forces and that their uninsured depositors be protected." The treatment of less-developed-country (LDC) loan losses at the nine largest banks and holding companies in the United States in the 1982 is one example. LDC loans were more than 288 percent of their capital and reserves (White, 1992, p. 56). The FDIC study (History of the Eighties, 1997, Vol. 1, p. 43) states that following the Mexican default on interest payments in 1982, "U.S. banking officials did not require that large reserves be immediately set aside for the restructured LDC loans, apparently believing that some large banks might have been insolvent and that an economic and political crises might have precipitated." It was not until 1987, that the affected banks began to recognize massive losses on their LDC loans that were carried at par on their books for more than a decade. Had they been required to reflect these losses earlier, the banks might have failed. Accordingly, the regulatory policies toward these banks reflected a preference for financial stability and public polices toward LDCs.

Size and Complexity of Crisis

Corrigan (1995) addressed the issue of how central banks manage a financial crisis. One point that he made concerned the size, financial condition, and complexity of troubled banks with foreign branches and subsidiaries. If the foreign establishments encounter large-scale deposit outflows, the complexities of managing the situation rise geometrically. The problem is exacerbated when internationally active corporations are made up of dozens of legal entities, many of which are subject to different regulatory and bankruptcy processes.

Too-Big-To Fail or Regulate

In 1984, bank regulators intervened in the case of Continental Illinois National Bank and Trust Company of Chicago because they feared that its failure might cause a systemic crisis. Comptroller of the Currency Todd Conover announced that the government would not let the 11 largest banks fail (Carrington, 1984). As applied to U.S. banks, the Too-Big-To-Fail doctrine means that the organization may continue to exist, but the stockholders, subordinated debt holders, managers, and some creditors may suffer financial losses. In the case of Continental Illinois, the FDIC assumed a large portion of the bank's bad assets and responsibility for its Federal Reserve liability in exchange for 80 percent ownership (Robertson, 1995, p. 226).

The Federal Deposit Insurance Corporation Improvement Act of 1991 limited the Too-Big-To-Fail doctrine in the United States. Under its Section 131 on prompt corrective action, FDICIA tied the intensity of supervision to an institution's capital position and established an explicit closure rule.[6] Some provisions of this section facilitate supervisory actions to limit risk-taking and encourage remedial actions by bank management of capital-deficient institutions.[7] Other provisions generally require regulators to close institutions when their capital falls below 2 percent. Supervisors can make exceptions to this rule, but they must justify and document their reasons, and the process for determining an institution "Too-Big-To-Fail" requires senior political concurrence.

Although U.S. government policy on this delicate subject seems codified, and its resort made exceptional, other countries have no explicit policy. Much popular sentiment is that other countries have a policy of Too-Big-To-Fail, but uncertainty exists over which institutions qualify. Moreover, it is unclear that such a policy, as is popularly characterized, does not involve forms of government intervention that does not require "resolution" or explicit public acknowledgment.

In the United States, the proposed or consummated mergers of Bank of America and Nations Bank, Chase Manhattan and Chemical, Citicorp and Travelers, First Union and Core States, Nations and Barnett, and Wells Fargo and First Interstate may result in trillion dollar institutions that once again raised the issue of too-big-to-fail, and maybe too-big-to-regulate. Former FDIC chairman L. William

Seidman, said that he doubts that regulators are ready to supervise Citigroup or the largest institutions (Seiberg, 1998). A *Business Week* article quotes William Isaac, another former FDIC chairman as saying "the market place is moving so fast that the government is unable to keep up with it"; and Arthur Rolnick, Director of Research of the Minneapolis Fed, stated that in the case of Travelers, "with the safety net starting to extend beyond banking, the potential taxpayer exposure has grown" (Foust, 1998).

Government Ownership

Government owned banks get special consideration when they are in financial distress. Credit Lyonnais was incorporated as a private bank in 1863 in France, and it was nationalized in 1946. It is the largest bank in France. Despite large loan losses in the early 1990s, Credit Lyonnais was not allowed to fail because it is government owned. Instead, the French government bailed it out (Commission Decision, 1995). The bailout and restructuring of the state-owned bank was still being debated and was expected to continue through the year 2000 (Jack & Tucker, 1997).

II.   BANK FAILURES IN NON-U.S. G-10 COUNTRIES

While there is an extensive literature on bank failures in the United States, less is written in the academic literature on bank failures in other countries. Prior to the mid-1990s, there was a popular opinion that banks rarely failed in other countries. Often this opinion was accompanied with the explanation that banks in most non-U.S. countries were not allowed to fail. Recent studies challenge this popular notion. Using data collected by the Office of the Comptroller of the Currency, Table 1 shows some information regarding failures in Canada, Germany, Italy, the United Kingdom, and the United States.

Gup (1998) and Bartholomew and Gup (forthcoming) surveyed publicly available information to ascertain the extent of bank failures in non-U.S. G-10 countries. They reported several findings. First, all countries in the G-10 have dealt with bank (i.e., depository institution or credit institution) failures. Second, in addition to the United States, Canada, Sweden, and Japan have been confronted with major problems involving significant numbers of failures. Third, of the failures surveyed in non-U.S., G-10 countries, about half were attributed to credit problems with one third of these associated with real estate finance. Slightly more than 10 percent were attributed to fraud—with these failures concentrated in smaller institutions. They were unable to find bank or depository institution failures since 1980 attributable to securities or insurance activities. This finding should be qualified slightly, however, since some failures or significant problems (i.e., near-failures) are attributable to derivatives activities or credit problems

Table 1. Bank Failures in Selected Countries

	1980	1981	1982	1983	1984	1985	1986	1987	1988	1989	1990	1991	1992	1993	1994	1995	1996
Canada	1	0	0	2	2	5	3	2	4	0	0	5	3	3	4	2	4
Germany	3	1	3	5	2	1	0	0	1	1	1	1	1	0	2	2	NA
United Kingdom	NA	NA	3	2	6	0	2	2	0	0	2	5	3	3	1	1	NA
U.S. Banks	10	10	42	48	78	120	138	194	200	206	168	124	120	41	13	6	5
U.S. thrifts	11	28	76	54	27	36	51	47	222	327	213	144	59	9	2	2	1

Notes: Numbers for Canada include only formal deposit insurance resolutions of chartered banks, trust companies and mortgage loan companies. Numbers do not include 18 insurance policy cancellations and/or institutions disolved. Numbers for Germany are for failures of credit institutions. Numbers for Italy include only formal liquidations. Numbers for U.S. banks include commercial and FDIC-insured savings banks.

Source: Office of the Comptroller of the Currency

where some form of securities activity was involved. Traditional securities and insurance underwriting or sales activities do not seem to have caused any bank failures in non-U.S., G-10 countries, but there have been some insurance company, investment company, and securities dealer failures.

Canada, Sweden, and Japan have all experienced significant numbers of bank or depository institution failure. The experiences of these three countries are characterized as crises because they involved substantial political involvement in the resolution process even though in some cases, as in Canada, the actual bank failures were relatively minor.

Closure and resolution of failures differs by country and situation. Most countries in the G-10 routinely do resolved failed institutions. In an environment of few bank failures, or faced with the failure of a small institution with few external ramifications, most governments close banks based on violations of law—typically, insolvency. But, most countries also use government intervention in a form that does not fit definitions of depository resolution used in analyses of the U.S. thrift crisis or banking problems of the 1980s. When faced with a substantial number of failures or a relatively large or important institution that may have external ramifications, banking authorities have resorted to special means of resolving the situation. Some countries have formally nationalized problem institutions; some have extended government credit with or without accompanying changes.in corporate control; some have arranged special private sector capitalization through sales or long-term lending.

According to German bank supervisory authorities, Germany has had 143 credit institution (i.e., bank) failures during the period 1950 through 1995. Between 1980 and 1992, they only had to deal with twenty-four. Except for the famous Herstatt bank failure of 1974, whose failure is attributed to foreign exchange activities and involved a relatively small institution, the Germans have not had to deal with a major failure in the post-war economy.

The Belgians have had a few routine failures mostly attributable to fraud. A surprising finding of the Bartholomew and Gup (forthcoming) study was that the Swiss banking authorities have closed mostly smaller, regional institutions on a routine basis. The Dutch had a significant number of minor failures in the early 1980s related chiefly to real estate finance, but without any systemic consequence. The United Kingdom has had few failures, but problems at BCCI (which were also experienced in other countries where BCCI had operations) and Barings were major events.

Italy has had some notorious failures involving gross negligence and fraud. Bartholomew and Gup (forthcoming) report that information on routine failures is less complete on Italian bank failures than for other countries, but there have been small failures. Table 1 shows Italian depositories, most if not all are mutual savings institutions, that were liquidated; a number of distressed larger institutions were resolved through merger with other credit institutions.

France also has a banking system with a high degree of direct and indirect government involvement. France has routinely closed several smaller institutions, most of which are foreign-owned. Problems at Credit Lyonnais require a special case study as it is substantially a government-owned institution. Recent estimates of its resolution cost suggest that expenditures of about $25 billion are required.

III. THE CAUSES OF LARGE SCALE BANK FAILURES

What causes large scale bank failures? Mondschean (1993) offers one model of banking crises:

> Banking crises have followed an all too familiar pattern in recent years. First, the seeds of the crisis are sown when financial institutions experience rapid growth in certain classes of loans and securities. Then, an economic shock, such as a decline in real estate prices or an increase in default rates among corporate borrowers, results in lowered net operating income, increased loss provisions, and reduced capital. If the losses render banks insolvent, government regulators may close or liquidate firms, merge them with healthy banks, take them over, or allow them to remain open in their weakened state. Finally, after the banking crisis occurs, a government may decide to 'reform' its system of bank regulations.

Another view is that failed institutions were victims of government policies or external shocks that were beyond their control. Benston and Kaufman (1997, p. 3) argue that the thrift crisis was caused initially and primarily by government policies: tight monetary policy in the late 1970s resulted in a sharp increase in interest rates that exacerbated the duration mismatch between S&L's assets and liabilities. Other institutional rigidities in the S&L industry included limits on rates that could be paid on deposits, and limits on investments.[8]

Still another view of the process is that banks have control over their own destinies. Greenspan (1993) said "Banks are in the business of managing risk. If done correctly, the bank will create economic value by attracting savings to finance investment. If done incorrectly, real resources will be misallocated, and the bank may fail." There is ample evidence from around the world that many of the banks that failed were engaged in excessive risk taking activities that were the proximate cause of their demise. If those banks taking excessive risks have "herd behavior," it is possible that they may fail en-masse.

There is merit to all of these views: some government policies, external shocks (i.e., speculative currency attacks, oil shocks, etc.), and excessive risk taking contribute to bank failures. Sometimes it is the combination of the two, government policies and banks taking excessive risks that result in failures. In Thailand, for example, government policies encouraged rapid economic growth (Greenwood, 1997; Moreno, 1997; Mydans, 1997). The government liberalized the financial system and let Thai banks and finance companies borrow in dollars and lend in the local currency (bahts). The end result was that government policies encouraged overvaluation of the baht and bank lending. Thai banks and finance companies made real estate loans that contributed to a speculative real estate bubble. In Bangkok, office vacancy rates exceeded 20 percent, and there was about a 3-year oversupply of housing. In addition, there was a currency crisis. Following speculative currency attacks and the bursting of the real estate bubble, the Bangkok Bank of Commerce, which had over $3 billion in bad loans was taken over by the government, and 58 of the countries real estate finance companies were suspended.

In South Korea, government directed investments and the relationships between banks and chaebols (family owned conglomerates) helped to produce strong economic growth for about three decades. Chaebols, such as Hanbo steel, Kia motors, and Halla shipbuilding, were the largest customers of some banks, and they could not or did not refuse extending additional loans, even though there was excess industry capacity. An editorial in *The Economist* (Asia, 1997) said that "fast growth had concealed, or encouraged, the existence of many poorly run and poorly regulated banks."

IV. THE SUPERVISORY DECISION TO FAIL A BANK

A major question confronted by bank supervisors is dealing with banks when they are financially troubled. Absent a bank supervisor, the market will decide when a bank fails. Should the market perceive that the soundness of a bank is questionable, creditors of the bank may call their loans to the bank. As most creditors of the bank are depositors, this means that depositors will withdraw their funds. Absent perfect information about the bank's soundness, depositors may withdraw funds from a bank if they see other depositors withdrawing their funds in a fashion other than in the course of normal business. This can create a liquidity problem for a bank, and the bank may be forced to sell non-monetary assets to cover the withdrawals. If the forced sale leads to bank loss in value, it may become insolvent.

One solution is for the bank to suspend payments to withdrawing depositors. Announcement of such a suspension typically further erodes depositor confidence. But, suspension can permit the orderly sale of assets in order that bank creditors receive all or as much as possible of the value of their deposits. Bankruptcy protection can afford some of the same benefits of suspension, but this can be a long process that also creates great uncertainty. Most governments have one or more banking authorities make the failure decision and handle the resolution of the failure.

A problem arises when the troubles or failure of one bank cause the public's confidence in the banking system to diminish. Because of information asymmetries, depositors, fearing financial loss and having poor information regarding the soundness of their bank, may withdraw funds from their bank merely because they are worried about the condition of all banks. This can lead to widespread runs. If these runs force many banks to sell-off assets at major losses, a serious disruption of the banking system can occur. This phenomena of widespread runs is called a contagion—problems at one institution are spread to others. It is a form of systemic risk.

Although the term systemic risk has been used fairly widely since the early 1980s, no works can be found addressing it specifically until the 1990s. Davis (1992), Bartholomew and Whalen (1995), Kaufman (1995), Mishkin (1995), Schwartz (1995), Eisenbeis (1997), and Bartholomew, Mote, and Whalen [forthcoming], Bartholomew (1993a, 1993b) present overviews of systemic risk, suggest alternative definitions of the term, and relate systemic risk to the more often discussed term financial crisis. What emerges from this literature, however, is that there is disagreement over its definition.

V. RECOGNITION OF FAILURE

As banks and other depositories are subject to government regulation, they are also monitored and supervised by government authorities. The supervising and monitoring authorities determine if a regulated institution should be subject to government intervention. These authorities may also administer the process of closing and resolving a failed institution. Often, however, the supervising and monitoring authorities may work in conjunction with other government authorities depending on the individual country's specific laws and practices.

The two most prevalent criteria for government intervention are illiquidity or insolvency. Other criteria, such as non-compliance with applicable banking or other depository statutes or regulations, may be used as well. In general, all of these criteria require some judgement on the part of the closing authority. Whereas laws and regulations may be viewed as relatively objective, measurement of the specific criteria can be subjective and involve regulatory discretion. Much is made in the economic and financial literature of the difference between book and market valuations in determining solvency. There is also some mention of the difficulty in applying standards to the criterion of operating in a safe and sound manner. Regardless of the varying discretion afforded closing authorities, some rules apply in a government regulated system of financial institutions. Two factors seem to influence the regulatory decision to close and resolve institutions in addition to the more straightforward criteria of insolvency.

First, the government intervention must be justified in law. The government action must be reasonable and subject to review by other government authorities or the courts. If the government authority charged with closing failed institutions feels its actions may be overturned subsequent to the action, the authority might have a disincentive to take action and delay action.

Second, the government intervention may be subject to a least-cost resolution strategy. This may be limited to the direct costs associated with resolution of failure, or it may involve the government authority taking account of the indirect consequences of closing or not closing the failed institution. When many banks fail, or if the failure is large with potential external ramifications, and indirect consequences are deemed significant, the process of dealing with the failure or group of failures has involved special treatment beyond the straightforward treatment afforded the closing authority.

VI. RESOLUTION TECHNIQUES IN THE UNITED STATES

Basically, there are two methods of resolving a failed bank. Typically, the distressed bank's chartering authority makes the decision to close the bank and take control of the institution. In the United States, resolution is handled by the deposit insuring authority. Since the 1930s, most FDIC-insured commercial banks are placed in FDIC receivership. In a decision generally made prior to closure, the FDIC resolves the institution through either its liquidation or its merger with another depository. Since the thrift crisis and banking problems of the 1980s, there are now several ways to achieve either of these general approaches, and some hybrid approaches have been introduced that do not exactly fit either one or both.

In a liquidation, the FDIC takes control (but not ownership) of the distressed institution. In a perfect world, it pays off insured depositors to the maximum of their coverage, disposes of the assets, and settles remaining creditor and other claims against the institution according to the prevailing legal hierarchy of the claims. Disposal of the assets can take between six to ten years. Since the authorities prefer to settle other claims in as orderly a fashion as possible, they often pay some or all of the claimants prior to full disposition of the assets. This can complicate resolution, make cost accounting problematic, and incur unnecessary costs. It can speed up the resolution process and may be considered necessary if there is a public confidence problem surrounding the failure.

A straight liquidation is probably the most expensive resolution technique available to the FDIC. It generally precludes benefits of bundling of assets, franchise value of the institution as an ongoing concern, and other savings from bulk disposal. During the thrift crisis, liquidations cost between 5 percent and 20 percent more than resolutions using a merger technique.[9] One modification of a strict liquidation introduced by the FDIC and the Resolution Trust Corporation was the Insured Deposit Transfer. Under this approach, bulk deposits were transferred to another depository institution. The FDIC or RTC was able to pay the acquiring institution less than the face value of the deposits because some franchise value was associated with the accounts.

Generally, it is cheaper to resolve a failed institution through selling it to another. The technique used by the FDIC is called a purchase and assumption, and their are many variants. Basically, the FDIC takes receivership of an institution and then sells its assets and transfers its liabilities to another depository. The

Number of Resolutions

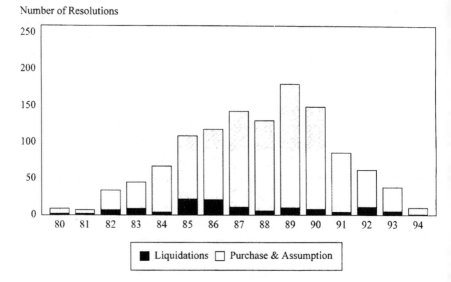

Figure 1. Resolutions for FDIC-Insured Commercial Banks by Type

acquiring institution "purchases" the assets and "assumes" its liabilities. The FDIC pays the acquiring institution the difference between the estimated value of the assets and liabilities. As this process is achieved through some form of bidding process, assuming more than one potential buyers, the amount the FDIC must pay to "fill the hole" should be less than if they had liquidated the institution. The difference between the liquidation cost and the cost of the purchase and assumption is attributable to franchise value of the failed institution as an ongoing concern. This franchise value may be associated with the failed institution's branching network, sales force, customer relationships, and other intangibles. The cost savings of a purchase and assumption may also be attributed to lower administrative costs associated with resolution and better rates of return on asset disposal achieved by the acquirer.

When the bank and thrift failure rate was low in the United States, the FDIC, the RTC, and other resolving authorities were able to make what were called "clean" purchase and assumptions. These transactions meant disposal of the entire institution to a single acquirer with the government authority retaining receivership for only minimal claims. As the caseload of resolutions increased, however, clean purchase and assumptions became a rarity.

In order to best effect resolution, closure and the decision of resolution technique must be made quickly and fairly concurrently. Prior to 1991, the resolving authorities claimed to use resolution strategies that would achieve lowest cost— since passage of FDICIA, they are explicitly accountable for "least-cost resolution." This is tricky since the choice of resolution strategy requires an *ex ante* estimation of resolution cost. As a purchase and assumption benefits from the presence of more than a single bidder, the timing of making such cost estimates and consummating sales becomes complicated.

Because of this, resolving authorities resorted to modifications of purchase and assumptions. One modification used by the Federal Savings and Loan Insurance Corporation was offering warrants or guarantees on the assets (and sometimes liabilities or off-balance sheet items) of the failed institution. Another strategy used by all resolving authorities was offering the option to the acquirer to put-back assets to the resolving authority at face or agreed value if the acquirer at a later date did not want the asset. These modifications of purchase and assumptions led to considerable criticisms of resolving authorities, but validation of their least-cost strategy was almost problematic because of limited data. One method of overseeing the resolution process was to have another government agency, in the United States this is the General Accounting Office, audit the transaction.

Table 2. Attribution Among Institutions Insured by the Federal Savings and Loan Insurance Corporation, 1980-1992
(Assets and costs in millions of dollars

| | Resolutions Requiring FSLIC or RTC Assistance | | | | | |
| | Liquidations | | | Mergeres and Other Types of Assisted Resolutions | | |
Year	Number	Total Assets	Total Cost	Number	Total Assets	Total Cost
1980	0	0	0	11	1,459	166
1981	1	89	30	27	13,818	730
1982	1	36	3	62	17,627	803
1983	5	262	60	31	4,368	215
1984	9	1,498	583	13	3,583	160
1985	8	1,752	549	23	4,614	477
1986	10	582	253	36	11,868	2,813
1987	17	3,045	2,276	30	7,619	1,428
1988	26	3,052	2,586	179	98,190	29,203
1989	30	2,202	1,533	7	8,606	4,380
1990	143	18,272	11,949	172	75,976	25,353
1991	67	17,156	9,625	165	58,791	24,881
1992	6	274	71	63	35,065	6,644

Notes: Costs are estimated present-value costs of resolution. Total assets after 1988 are based on gross assets reported by the Resolution Trust Corporation (RTC). Numbers have been rounded.

Source: Office of the Comptroller of the Currency using data from the Congressional Budget Office, Federal Home Loan Bank Board and the Office of Thrift Supervision.

Another modification of the purchase and assumption technique is a partial purchase and assumption. Under this approach, only a portion of the assets and liabilities are purchased and assumed by an acquirer. The remainder are liquidated by the resolving authority. This technique was a compromise between speed and cost savings.

Figure 1 shows FDIC resolutions using both basic types for the period 1980 through 1994. The purchase and assumption technique is by far the preferred approach. Table 2 shows the breakdown of liquidations versus purchase and assumptions for the thrift industry for the period 1980 through 1992. As can be seen, the purchase and assumption resolutions were less costly, as measured by cost to assets, than liquidations. It can not be concluded, however, that liquidations are always more costly than purchase and assumptions. For some failures, buyers could not be found. It may even be the case that liquidation may have been less costly by the resolving agency than another receiver or acquiring institution could have achieved.

Another difference between the liquidation technique and the purchase and assumption is the working capital associated with the transaction. In a strict liquidation, the resolving authority must front far more cash than in a modified liquidation or in a purchase and assumption. This is important to consider especially if cost savings associated with purchase and assumptions are marginal or negative. It is also important to know that the financial resources of the resolving agency are an important determinant for resolution strategy. When the FSLIC was faced with little cash resources, it was unable to resort to liquidation techniques and was forced to use non-cash incurring purchase and assumption techniques. FSLIC's lack of financial resources probably forced it to forbear and delay closure of hundreds of distressed thrifts and may have caused it to have higher costs of resolution than otherwise would have been the case.

VII.   RESOLUTION COST AS A DETERMINING FACTOR

As discussed above, the term resolution, as used here, refers to the actions taken by bank regulators to fail a distressed bank and deal with its assets, liabilities, and other claims. In theory, failure or closure occurs when a bank is insolvent.[10] The institution is technically insolvent when the value of its assets is worth less than the value of its liabilities.

The net worth of a depository institution can be expressed as:

$$\text{Net Worth} = \text{Assets} - \text{Liabilities} \qquad (1)$$

Since depository institutions report their financial condition using book values, it is useful to express net worth in market value terms. One simplified way to do this is:

$$\text{Net Worth} = (\text{Assets} - \text{Write down}) - (\text{Liabilities} - \text{Adjustments}) + \text{Franchise Value} \quad (2)$$

or,

$$NW = \alpha A - \beta L + F \quad (2.1)$$

where α and β are positive coefficients that reflect whether book values are above or below market values. It is important to understand that the values of α and β are variable over time and change based upon the valuation method employed. For example, a set of assets may be worth more or less to one holder than another. Moreover, the market value of that set of assets may differ if it is assumed that they are to be held to maturity or for a long period, or if they are to be liquidated at a fire sale price.

Franchise value (F) is introduced in Equations (2) and (2.1) in a manner specific to depository institution failure. It is considered the value of the institution or parts of the institution that have value to the enterprise as a going concern. Examples of franchise value include value associated with customer relationships, existing retail networks, and other intangibles. For simplicity of exposition, F is introduced to the net worth equation additively.

The net worth equation is useful for deriving a simple expression of resolution cost:[11]

$$\text{Cost of Resolution} = \beta L - \alpha A - F + \text{Administration Expense} \quad (3)$$

Assuming that administration expense of resolution is also associated with disposal of assets and liabilities, Equation (3) can be rewritten as[12]:

$$CR = (\beta + \sigma_L) L - (\alpha + \sigma_A) A - F + \sigma_G \quad (3.1)$$

From this simplistic expression of resolution cost, it can be seen readily that resolution cost is reduced if the resolving agency increases franchise value, reduces or eliminates administrative expense, reduces liabilities, increases assets, or increases recovery rates on assets (α).

VIII.   THE RESOLUTION DECISION AND FAILURE

In a bank regulatory environment that is highly transparent and accountable, the resolution strategy must be defended *ex post*. Considerable scrutiny was placed on

Table 3. Interbank Deposits in G-10 Countries

Country	Institutions	1989	1990	1991	1992	1993	1994
Interbank Deposits from Other Banks as a Percentage of Assets							
Belgium	All Banks	43.7	42.9	39.6	39.0	35.7	32.9
Canada	Large Domestic Banks	11.9	12.5	11.7	14.1	12.7	13.5
France	Commercial Banks	46.8	42.9	40.0	40.2	43.0	44.2
	Largest 5	37.1	33.5	31.0	30.7	35.2	35.9
Germany	Commercial Banks	27.7	27.1	25.5	26.6	24.3	28.5
	Largest 3	24.5	25.0	22.2	24.5	22.5	29.0
Italy	All Depositories	8.5	6.2	5.3	7.1	7.4	6.8
Netherlands	Commercial Banks	22.3	23.6	24.4	23.7	24.1	23.1
Sweden	Commercial Banks	39.2	41.7	33.9	26.1	22.0	21.9
Switzerland	Large Banks	23.7	24.0	23.3	22.5	25.5	23.5
U.S.	Commercial Banks	4.8	4.0	4.3	3.8	3.8	4.3
	100 Largest Banks	7.6	6.4	6.9	5.9	5.8	6.5
Japan	Commercial Banks	16.1%	13.4%	11.3%	10.2%	10.7%	9.9%
U.K.	Commercial Banks	16.1%	15.5%	15.0%	13.6%	14.9%	15.7%

Source: Office of the Comptroller of the Currency using data from the Organization of Economic Co-operation and Development.

the FDIC, RTC, and FSLIC to demonstrate it had chosen the best method of resolution, its asset recovery rates were high, and it tried to capture franchise value where possible.

Interestingly, the American system does not consider some alternative resolution strategies as are practiced elsewhere. As shown in the previous section, if administration costs are eliminated or reduced, the cost of resolution is reduced. One obvious way to do this is to not resolve the failed institution through a government process. The losses associated with the failure are then borne by the resolving agent. In some older banking systems, for example, the eighteenth century Scottish banking system, shareholders were responsible for losses at a failed institution up to some limit. In other banking systems, other banks resolved the distressed institution.

One common practice that results in failure resolution not incurring explicit government expense is use of a debt-equity swap. When an institution fails, certain creditors of that institution either assume or are instructed to assume that balances they held heretofore at the failed institution are converted to an equity stake. The regulators may or may not choose to impose a valuation procedure of this new equity stake at the acquiring institution that might ease the burden. As this practice does not require formal government acknowledgment of failure resolution, it is unclear how extensively it has been employed. However, as can be seen in Table 3, interbank claims due other banks are held in high proportion to assets in some countries outside the United States. One benefit of this practice is that it reduces explicit government expenditure. It may or may not be more efficient. It certainly is not transparent, and the loss sharing arrangement, either to acquiring banks or bank consumers who ultimately pay for those losses, is probably not well known.

IX. RESOLVING A SUBSTANTIAL FAILURE OR GROUP OF FAILURES

Regulatory intervention takes many different forms depending on its purpose. One purpose is to aid distressed organizations and maybe prevent failures. Other purposes include avoiding systemic crisis, reducing the cost of resolution, and protecting deposit insurance funds. In Japan, for example, Hokkaido Takushoku, one of the nation's largest city banks, had about 400 billion yen in bad loans when it was failed in November 1997. For several years it was known that the bank had loan problems. However, regulators delayed closing the bank because they feared that it might break the deposit insurance fund (Sapsford, 1997).

The intervention techniques used by bank regulators throughout the world can be grouped into six broad categories that are described below in alphabetical order.[13] Selected examples of each technique are presented.

Forbearance

Forbearance means not enforcing capital or other supervisory standards in banks that are financially troubled. Supposedly, this practice is reserve only for distressed institutions judged to be viable fundamentally. The delay in recognizing LDC debt exposure at large commercial banks in the United States in the early 1980s is one example of waiting that is considered by many to be successful. On the other hand, the deliberate policy of forbearance granted by thrift regulators early on during the thrift crisis, was unsuccessful. Such a strategy of forbearance is highly risky and can lead to future structural and regulatory problems. One problem with forbearance as a regulatory option in a situation of distress of a substantial portion of the financial industry is that it is the default strategy—and has a likelihood of high cost if inapplicable or inappropriately applied.

Recapitalization

So long as resources permit, governments could force shareholders of distressed institutions, other financial sector participants, or other sectors of the economy to recapitalize distressed institutions. If an institution fails to recapitalize, the government supervisor would resort to other means. Recapitalization is probably best applied before an institution becomes insolvent and supervisory actions would be mandatorily taken as an institution's capital deteriorated.

Long-term Investments

Long-term investments in problem banks can take a variety of forms. In the United States for example, the Source of Strength doctrine requires all commonly controlled banks to be liable for the losses of affiliated banks.[14] Open-bank assistance is another form of long-term investment.[15] Open-bank assistance includes the FDIC net worth certificate program for savings banks, the FDIC capital forbearance and loan amortization programs for agricultural and energy banks, and direct open-bank assistance.

In other countries, long-term investments may take the form of debt-equity swaps, long-term loans by other financial institutions, or equity investments. In Japan stronger companies help weaker ones. This is called the "convoy" method of intervention. For example, the Bank of Japan, commercial banks, and life insurance companies invested capital in the failing Nippon Credit Bank (Martin, 1997).

Good Bank/Bad Bank

The government could separate the bad loan portfolio from the rest of the troubled bank and sell each separately. This was done to some degree in the United States when the FDIC and RTC did what were called non-clean purchase and assumptions. But the term good bank/bad bank now seems to signify a notion of the government selling off the good portions of the distressed institution and retaining the bad portion in a government-capitalized institution. This was being tried in Sweden and Finland, but the governments initially were unable to find private investors. Canada has used this strategy recently with the good portions of failed near banks being sold to large chartered banks and the CDIC retaining the bad portions.

Foreign Capitalization

The government could seek foreign banks to merge with troubled institutions. According to Bartholomew (1993), the Canadians were successful with this strategy, but Scandinavian authorities were unsuccessful. This is often mentioned as a potential recapitalization strategy for emerging market banking systems that have become distressed recently. One argument favoring it is that the recapitalization comes not only in the form of finance but in terms of human capital. Unfortunately, the consequences of foreign capitalization have not all been studied and merit closer scrutiny.

Nationalization

Nationalization refers to government ownership. In the United States, the Reconstruction Finance Corporation held "preferred stock" in hundreds of banks in the early 1930s. Preferred stock is one form of equity interest. In 1984, the FDIC owned 80 percent of the stock in Continental Illinois Bank. Nationalization with subsequent privatization seems to have been successfully employed in the Norway, Sweden, and Finland.

X. CONCLUSION

Banks and other depository institutions are typically regulated by the government. In addition to the chartering, regulation, supervision, and monitoring this involves, government regulation also generally involves closure and resolution. Regardless of the theoretical considerations that should apply, the determination of failure is made through the government authority's action of closing an institution it has deemed a failure.

The action of failing an institution can involve objective or subjective criteria. Throughout the G-10 countries, criteria exist for government intervention on troubled or failing banks or other depositories. Whereas these criteria may be applied in straightforward situations, special circumstances, such as large scale failures in a system or the failure of a large or important institution with potential deleterious external consequences, has required special processes of closure and resolution.

As the manner in which failures are resolved affects both the direct and indirect costs of dealing with failures, different approaches to both closure and failure have been taken. Although this can be seen through examination of the determinants of explicit cost of resolution, a more generalized model of both direct and indirect costs is required to appropriately examine the regulatory closure rule and its various applications.

ACKNOWLEDGMENTS

The views expressed are those of the authors and do not necessarily reflect those of the Comptroller of the Currency or the Department of Treasury. The authors are indebted to Sarah C. Clark and Kori L. Egland for research assistance and Richard W. Nelson for comments on an earlier draft.

NOTES

1. See also World Bank (1989), Barth and Bartholomew (1992, pp. 1-25), and Caprio and Klingbiel (1997).

2.   The literature on bank failures is less extensive than that on thrift failures (see, for example, Bartholomew [1993] for a review of literature on the thrift crisis). Some important studies on bank failures include, for example, Barth, Brumbaugh, and Litan (1992), Bartholomew and Whalen (1996, 1995), Federal Deposit Insurance Corporation (1997), Gordon and Lutton (1994), Graham and Horner (1988), Kaufman (1994), O'Keefe (1990), and Randall (1993). There is also a considerable literature on the method and cost of resolving failed banks. Brown and Epstein (1992), Bovenzi and Muldoon (1990), Bovenzi and Murton (1988), Carns (1992), and James (1991) all provide useful detail on FDIC methods of a bank resolution.

3.   For a review of this literature, see for example, Hooks (1992). Also of interest are studies by Laviola and Trapanese (1997) and Cannari and Signorini (1994) which look at early warning models as applied to Italian non-financial firms and banks, respectively.

4.   An analogy to bank failure is that of a failing student. Regardless of how explicit the criteria for failure, or how hard the student tries to fail, the official failure decision rests with the instructor who assigns the failing grade.

5.   See Bartholomew (1990, 1993) and General Accounting Office (1991).

6.   See Bartholomew (1994a).

7.   For a discussion of prompt corrective action, see, for example, Benston et al. (1986) and Kaufman and Benston (1993).

8.   See Barth (1991) and Bartholomew (1996, 1993), Kaufman (1996), National Commission on Financial Institutions Reform, Recovery and Enforcement (1993), and White (1991) for a more detailed discussion of the several causes of the thrift crisis.

9.   See Bartholomew (1993).

10.   Under FDICIA, in the U.S., bank and thrift regulators are required to close an institution when its capitalization falls below 2 percent. Explicit closures rules differ in other countries, but most use solvency as the primary criteria for closure.

11.   See Carns and Nejezchleb (1992) for an excellent derivation of resolution cost.

12.   Equation (3.1) assumes that overhead administration expenses (σ_G) are fixed. More than likely, they are associated with the size of the institution or other factors. Unfortunately, due to likely, they are associated with the size of the institution or other factors. Unfortunately, due to the manner in which these expenses are accounted, they are indeterminant. Though some have reported estimates of the proportion of resolution costs to assets or other factors, because of the presence of franchise value and the embedded nature of administration expense in recoveries and payouts, estimation of administration expense or its proportion is indeterminant.

13.   See Bartholomew (1993), Berg (1993) and Freixas and Rochet (1997). Freixas and Rochet (1997, 280) report a 1993 study by C. Goodhart, and D. Schoenmaker. They classify resolution techniques in four categories: 1) Rescue package, 2) Acquisition, 3) Special treatment by government or insurance fund, and 4) Liquidation.

14.   The Source of Strength Doctrine was enacted into law in the Financial Institutions Reform, Recovery, and Enforcement Act of 1989.

15.   The Garn-St. Germain Depository institutions Act of 1982 amended section 13© of the Federal Deposit Insurance Act to grant the FDIC authority to provide financial assistance to selected banks.

REFERENCES

Asia and the Abyss. (1997). *The Economist*, December 20, p. 15.

Barth, J. R. (1991). *The great savings and loan debacle*. Washington, DC: American Enterprise Institute Press.

Barth, J. R., Brumbaugh, Jr., R. D., & Litan, R. E. (1992). *The future of American banking*. Armonk, NY: M. E. Sharpe, Inc.

Barth, J. R., & Bartholomew, P. F. (1992). *Emerging challenges for the international financial services industry.* Greenwich, CT: JAI Press.

Bartholomew, P. F. (forthcoming). Asian Contagion? In J. R. Barth & R. D. Brumbaugh, Jr. (Eds.), *Restructuring regulation & financial institutions.* Milken Institute.

Bartholomew, P. F. (forthcoming). Banking consolidation and systemic risk. *Brookings-Wharton Papers on Financial Services.*

Bartholomew, P. F. (1996). The thrift crisis revisited: A critique of the S&L commission's report. In G. G. Kaufman (Ed.), *Research in financial services and public policy* (Vol. 8, pp. 239-249). Greenwich, CT: JAI Press Inc.

Bartholomew, P. (1994a). FDICIA two years later. In G. Kaufman (ed.), *Assessing bank performance: FDICIA two years later.* The Center for Financial and Policy Studies, Loyola University of Chicago.

Bartholomew, P. (1994). Comparing depository institution difficulties in Canada, the United States, and the Nordic Countries. *Journal of Housing Research, 6*(2).

Bartholomew, P. (1993). *Resolving the thrift crisis.* Washington, DC: Congressional Budget Office.

Bartholomew, P. (1990). *Reforming federal deposit Insurance.* Washington, DC: Congressional Budget Office.

Bartholomew, P. F., & Gup, B. E. (forthcoming). Survey of bank failures in non-U.S. G-10 countries since 1980. In I. Finel-Honigman (Ed.), *European union banking issues: Historical and contemporary.* Greenwich, CT: JAI Press.

Bartholomew, P. F., & Whalen, G. W. (1996). Analysis of bank failure data: The case of de novo banks. Presented at the annual meetings of the Eastern Finance Association, Charlotte, NC.

Bartholomew, P. F., & Whalen, G. W. (1995). Analysis of bank failure data: Commercial bank resolutions 1980-1994. Presented at the annual meetings of the Eastern Finance Association, Hilton Head, SC.

Bartholomew, P. F., & Whalen, G. W. (1995). Fundamentals of systemic risk. In P. F. Bartholomew and G. G. Kaufman (Eds.), Research in financial services and public policy (Vol. 7, pp. 3-17). Greenwich, CT: JAI Press Inc.

Benston, G. J., Eisenbeis, R. A., Horvitz, P. M., Kane, E. J., & Kaufman, G. G. (1986). *Perspectives on safe & sound banking: Past, present, and future.* Washington, DC: MIT Press.

Benston, G. J., & Kaufman, G. G. (1993). The intellectual history of the federal deposit insurance corporation improvement act of 1991. In G. Kaufman & R. Litan (Eds.), *Assessing bank reform: FDICIA One year later.* Washington, DC: the Brookings Institution.

Benston G. J., & Kaufman, G. G. (1997). FDICIA after five years: A review and evaluation. Federal Reserve Bank of Chicago Working Paper (WP-97-1), July.

Berg, S. A. (1993). The banking crisis in the Scandinavian countries. In *Bank structure and competition.* Federal Reserve Bank of Chicago, (May).

Bhalla, A. S. (1995), Collapse of Barings Bank, case market failure. *Economic and Political Weekly,* 658-662.

Bovenzi, J. F., & Muldoon, M. E. (1990). Failure-resolution methods and policy considerations. *FDIC Banking Review, 3*(1).

Bovenzi, J. F., & Murton, A. J. (1988). Resolution costs of bank failures. *FDIC Banking Review, 1*(1).

Brown, R. A., & Epstein, S. (1992). Resolution costs and bank failures: An update of the FDIC historical loss model. *FDIC Banking Review, 5*(1).

Cannari, L., & Signorini, L. F. (1994). *AL'analisi discriminante per la previsione delle insolvenze delle micro-branche.* Banca d'Italia, mimeo.

Caprio, G., Jr., & Klingbiel, D. (1996). Bank insolvency: Bad luck, bad policy, and bad banking. In M. Bruno & B. Pleskovic (Eds.), *Annual bank conference on development economics.* The World Bank.

Carns, F. S., & Nejezchleb, L. A. (1992). Bank failure resolutions, the cost test and the entry and exit of resources in the banking industry. *Bank structure and competition*, Federal Reserve Bank of Chicago, (May).

Carrington, T. (1984). U.S. won't let 11 biggest banks in nation frail. *Wall Street Journal*, September 20.

Cole, R. (1990). Insolvency versus closure: Why the regulatory delay in closing troubled thrifts. Federal Reserve Bank of Dallas, Financial Industry Studies Working Paper No. 2-90, July.

Cole, R. (1993). A when are thrift institutions closed? An agency-theoretic model. *Journal of Financial Services Research*, 7, 283-307.

Cole, R., & Gunther, J.W. (1994). When are failing banks closed? Federal Reserve Bank of Dallas, *Financial Industry Studies*, 1-2.

Cole R., & Gunther, J. W. (1995). Separating the likelihood and timing of bank failure. *Journal of Banking and Finance*, 19, 1073-1089.

Commission Decision of 26 July 1995 giving conditional approval to aid granted by France to the bank Credit Lyonnais. (1995). *Official Journal of the European Communities*, English edition, December 21.

Core principles for effective banking supervision. (1997). Basle Committee on Banking Supervision, Basle, Switzerland, April.

Corrigan, E. G. (1995). How central banks manage financial crises. An address by E. G. Corrigan, Chairman, International Advisors, Goldman, Sach & Co., Shanghai, China, October 25. www2.gs.com/about/speeches/shanghai.html

Crockett, A. (1997). Why is financial stability a goal of public policy? *Economic Review*, 82(4), 5-22.

Dimergüc-Kunt, A. (1989). Deposit-institution failures: A review of empirical literature. *Economic Review*, 2-16.

Dimergüc-Kunt, A. (1991). Principal-agent problems in commercial-bank failure decisions. Federal Reserve Bank of Cleveland, Working Paper 9106, April.

Federal Deposit Insurance Corporation. (1997). *History of the eighties: Lessons for the future: An examination of the banking crises of the 1980s and early 1990s*, 1. Washington, D.C.

Federal Deposit Insurance Corporation. (1997). *The FDIC quarterly banking profile*, Second Quarter.

Federal Deposit Insurance Corporation. (1984). *The first fifty years B A history of the FDIC 1933-1983*, Washington, DC: Federal Deposit Insurance Corporation.

Folkerts-Landau, D., & Ito, T. (1995). *International capital markets: Developments, prospects, and key policy issues*. Washington, DC: International Monetary Fund.

Foust, D. (1998). If this safetey net snaps, who pays? *Business Week*, pp. 38-39.

Freixas, X., & Rochet, J.C. (1997). *Microeconomics of banking*. Cambridge, MA: MIT Press.

Graham, F., & Horner, J. (1988). Bank failure: An evaluation of the factors contributing to the failure of national banks. In *Bank structure and competition*, Federal Reserve Bank of Chicago, (May).

Gordon, P., & Lutton, T. J. (1994). *The changing business of banking: A study of failed banks from 1987 to 1992*, CBO Study. Washington, DC: Congressional Budget Office.

Greenspan, A. (1993). Remarks by Alan Greenspan, Chairman, Board of Governors of the Federal Reserve System. *Bank structure and competition*. Federal Reserve Bank of Chicago, (May).

Greenwood, J. (1997). The lessons of Asia's currency crises. *Wall Street Journal*, A22.

Gup, B. E. (1998). *Bank failures in the major trading countries of the world: Causes and remedies*. Westport, CT: Quorum Books.

Hooks, L. M. (1992). What do early warning models tell us about asset risk and bank failures? *Financial Industry Studies*, Federal Reserve Bank of Dallas, (August).

Jack, A., & Tucker, E. (1997). Paris pressed on credit lyonnais. *Financial Times*, p. 2.

James, C. (1991). The losses realized in bank failures. *Journal of Finance*, 46, 1223 B1242.

Kane, E. J. (1989). *The S&L insurance mess: How did it happen?* Washington, DC: The Urban Institute.

Kaufman, G. G. (1995). The U.S. banking debacle of the 1980s. *The Financier*, 9-26.

Kaufman, G. G. (1996). What is good and what is bad in the national commission report. *Research in Financial Services and Public Policy,* 8, 239-249.

Kroszner, R. S., & Strahan, P. E. (1996). Regulatory incentives and the thrift crises: Dividend, mutual-to-stock conversions, and financial distress. *Journal of Finance,* 51, 1285-1319.

Laviola, di Sebastiano, and Mauricio Trapanese (1997), APrediction of Corporate Insolvencies and Banks' Loan Quality: A Statistical Analysis. *Temi di Discussione del Servizio Studi,* Banca d'Italia, No. 318, (September).

Leeson, N., & Whitley, E. (1996). Rouge trader: How I brought down barings bank and shook the financial world. Boston: Little Brown and Company.

Lindgren, C., Garcia, G., & Saal, M. I. (1996). *Bank soundness and macroeconomic policy.* Washington, DC: International Monetary Fund.

Mailath, G., & Mester, L. (1994). A positive analysis of bank closure.

Martin, N. A. (1997). Japan's turn. *Barrons,* 18-20.

Mondschean, T. 1993. *Banking crisis: A global perspective.* Paper summarizing the Annual Conference on Bank Structure and Competition, Federal Reserve Bank of Chicago.

Moreno, R. (1997). Lessons from Thailand. *Economic Letter,* Federal Reserve Bank of San Francisco, No. 97-33, November.

Mydans, S. (1997). 56 Troubled lenders closed by Thailand. *New York Times,* December.

Nakamura, L. I. (1990). Closing troubled financial institutions: What are the issues? *Business Review,* (May/June), 15-24.

National Commission on Financial Institutions Reform, Recovery and Enforcement. (1993). *Origins and causes of the S&L debacle: A blueprint for reform.* A report to the President of the United States, Washington, DC.

O'Keefe, J. (1990). The Texas banking crisis: Causes and consequences, 1980-1989. *FDIC Banking Review,* 3(2).

Randall, R. E. (1993). Safeguarding the banking system from financial cycles. In R. E. Randall (Ed.), Safeguarding the banking system in an environment of financial cycles. Proceedings of a Symposium Held in November 1993, Federal Reserve Bank of Boston, Conference Series No. 37.

Robertson, R. M. (1995). *The comptroller and bank supervision: A historical appraisal.* Washington, DC: Office of the Comptroller the Currency.

Sapsford, J. (1997). Fears grow that Japan's bank woes could bust its deposit-insurance fund. *Wall Street Journal,* December 3.

Seiberg, J. (1998). In an era of new megabanks, oversight efforts debated. *Amercian Banker,* p. 2.

Thomson, J. B. (1992). Modeling the bank regulator's closure option: A two-step logit regression approach. *Journal of Financial Services Research,* 6, 5-23.

U.S. General Accounting Office. (1991). Letter to Congressman Bruce F. Vento from Craig A. Simmons, Director, Financial Institutions and Market Issues. Washington, DC., February 4.

White, E. N. (1992). *The comptroller and the transformation of American banking, 1960-1990.* Washington, DC: Office of the Comptroller of the Currency.

White, L. J. (1991). *The S&L debacle: Public policy lessons for bank and thrift regulation.* New York: Oxford University Press.

World Bank. (1989). *World development report 1989.* New York: Oxford University Press.

DOES THE PUBLICATION OF SUPERVISORY ENFORCEMENT ACTIONS ADD TO MARKET DISCIPLINE?

R. Alton Gilbert and Mark D. Vaughan

I. INTRODUCTION

Bank supervisors use enforcement actions to bring banks into compliance with consumer regulations and standards for safe and sound banking. Enforcement actions can take one of two forms: informal agreements between banks and their supervisory agencies and more formal actions, enforceable in the courts. Informal agreements between supervisors and banks have historically been treated as confidential, but since 1990, supervisors have been required to publicly announce most of the formal enforcement actions.

In principle, the publication of safety and soundness related enforcement actions could strengthen market discipline. Depositors, once armed with the knowledge that their bank is engaged in unsafe or unsound practices, may withdraw their funds or demand a substantial increase in deposit rates. Such behavior would then prompt bank management to address the problems that triggered the

Research in Financial Services: Private and Public Policy, Volume 10, pages 259-280.
Copyright © 1998 by JAI Press Inc.
All rights of reproduction in any form reserved.
ISBN: 0-7623-0358-1

enforcement action. Publication of enforcement actions related to safety and soundness could, therefore, add market pressure to the supervisory pressure on a bank to mend its ways.

To assess the effects of publicizing enforcement actions, we examine the impact of 90 Federal Reserve announcements on bank deposit levels and deposit rates in the 1990s. We find no evidence of deposit declines after announcements of safety and soundness related enforcement actions. We do find that deposit rates at banks subject to the publicly announced actions climbed in the wake of the disclosures. The increases, however, were not discrete. Instead, deposit rates began rising well before the public announcements and continued to rise as overall conditions deteriorated at the sample banks. The results suggest that public announcements of enforcement actions provide little additional information to depositors and, therefore, add little to market discipline.

II.   A PRIMER ON ENFORCEMENT ACTIONS

In safety and soundness supervision, the term "enforcement action" loosely refers to a broad range of powers used to address the suspect practices of domestic depository institutions, foreign institutions operating in the United States, and/or institution-affiliated parties.[1] Enforcement actions are typically imposed after an on-site exam has unearthed adverse information, but they can also be triggered by deficient capital levels under the prompt corrective action guidelines of the FDIC Improvement Act of 1991 (FDICIA).[2]

Enforcement actions can be informal or formal. Informal actions—the far more common type—are voluntary agreements between supervisors and banks to correct suspect banking practices. Supervisors resort to informal actions when problems are considered less severe and when management is expected to take the necessary corrective steps. These actions are not enforceable through the courts. Moreover, violation of an informal action cannot serve as a basis for assessing civil money penalties, for initiating actions to remove bank officers or directors, or for prohibiting bank officers or directors from involvement in the affairs of any other federally insured bank. Informal actions do not have to be disclosed to the public.

Board resolutions and memoranda of understanding are the most common forms of informal enforcement actions. For example, between 1990 and 1997, 52 percent of informal actions imposed by the Federal Reserve were board resolutions, while 31 percent were memoranda of understanding. Board resolutions generally represent a number of commitments made by the institution's directors that have also been incorporated into the organization's corporate minutes. The institution's directors are then requested to provide a signed copy of the corporate resolution with their examination response letter. Memoranda of understanding are bilateral agreements signed by the regulatory agency and the institution's board of directors. They are highly structured written—but informal—agreements that are generally used when regulators determine that an institution suffers from multiple problems. Although, as noted, informal agreements are generally not publicized, the Securities and Exchange Commission (SEC) may require disclosure that a memoranda of understanding is in effect.

Enforcement actions are generally implemented in a graduated manner, with informal actions typically preceding formal actions. Supervisors resort to formal actions only when violations of laws or regulations continue, or when unsafe and abusive practices occur. Formal actions are legally enforceable and must generally be disclosed to the public. Cease and desist orders, written agreements, prohibition and removal orders,[3] civil money penalties, and prompt corrective action directives are all formal actions that must be disclosed to the public. Of these, written agreements and cease and desist orders are the most common. Between 1990 and 1997, for example, the Federal Reserve announced 265 final, formal enforcement actions. Of this total, 180 (68%) were written agreements, and 62 (23%) were cease and desist orders.

A cease and desist order requires a depository institution or person subject to the order to: (1) cease and desist from the practices or violations; or (2) take affirmative action to correct the violations or practices. An affirmative action could, for example, require returning the institution to its "original condition"—the condition it was in before the practice or violation. Other affirmative actions include: restrictions on growth, debt and dividends; disposition of certain loans or assets; rescission of agreements or contracts; or terminating the employment of certain officers or employees. Unlike cease and desist orders, written agreements are typically employed when an institution's problems warrant a less severe form of formal supervisory action.

Between 1990 and 1997, the Federal Reserve imposed 1,611 enforcement actions against bank holding companies and state-member banks (Table 1). Of this total, 1,346 (84%) were not disclosed to the public. The number of enforcement actions issued by the Fed declined rapidly between 1990 and 1997, largely as a result of improving economic conditions and the tighter capital standards established by the Financial Institutions Reform, Recovery, and Enforcement Act of 1989 (FIRREA) and FDICIA. In 1990, for example, the Fed issued 242 public and nonpublic enforcement actions. This number rose to 364 in 1992, before dropping to 42 in 1997. The most common form of public action—written agreements—jumped from 27 to 51 between 1990 and 1992, then tumbled to 2 in 1997.

III. THE DEBATE OVER DISCLOSURE OF ENFORCEMENT ACTIONS

FIRREA and the Bank Fraud Act (BFA), enacted in November 1990, initiated or extended many of the supervisory agencies' enforcement powers. In particular,

Table 1.   Public Versus Private Supervisory Actions[1], 1990-1997

Action	1990	1991	1992	1993	1994	1995	1996	1997
Non-Publicly Disclosed Actions[2]								
Board Resolutions	90	129	123	130	79	67	60	26
Commitments	1	0	0	0	1	0	1	4
Memoranda of Understanding	69	84	113	60	38	27	11	9
Temporary Cease & Desist Orders	1	2	0	0	0	1	0	0
Orders of Investigation	0	0	0	0	0	1	4	0
Other Non-Publicly Disclosed Actions[3]	44	59	52	34	14	6	6	0
Total non-public supervisory actions	205	274	288	224	132	102	82	39
Publicly Disclosed Actions[4]								
Cease and Desist Orders	8	17	20	11	10	0	1	1
Civil Money Penalties	2	2	5	2	2	0	0	0
Prompt Corrective Actions	0	0	0	2	1	0	1	0
Written Agreements	27	44	51	26	9	13	8	2
Total public supervisory actions	37	63	76	41	22	13	10	3
Total Supervisory Actions	242	337	364	265	154	115	92	42

Notes: [1]Table includes data only for banking institutions supervised by the Federal Reserve System.
[2]Non-publicly disclosed actions include informal supervisory actions, such as Board Resolutions, Commitments, and Memoranda of Understanding, as well as non-final formal actions, such as Temporary Cease-and-Desist Orders and Orders of Investigation.
[3]The category "Other Non-Publicly Disclosed Actions" includes other informal actions initiated by Federal and state regulatory agencies to correct supervisory issues. This includes "formal" actions implemented by state agencies that are not enforceable under Section 8 of the Federal Deposit Insurance Act.
[4]Publicly disclosed actions include all final formal enforcement actions. In addition to those listed in the table, the subset of publicly disclosed actions also includes Prohibition and Removal Orders. However, such actions are issued exclusively against institution-affiliated parties which are not included in this study.

Source: National Information Center Database

provisions of FIRREA and BFA required bank supervisory agencies—for the first time—to publicly disclose final, formal enforcement actions and any modifications or terminations of them. Prior to the passage of FIRREA, only depository institutions with publicly traded stock subject to SEC regulation were required to disclose enforcement actions. In addition, the Office of the Comptroller of the Currency—on a very limited case-by-case basis—publicly disclosed the facts surrounding its enforcement actions (U.S. Congress 1988, p. 88).

Congress called for public disclosure of formal enforcement actions to level the playing field among federal regulators. House Report No. 101-54(I), which explains the legislative intent of FIRREA, noted that bank supervisors were alone among federal regulators in keeping civil enforcement actions confidential (U.S.

Congress, 1989, p. 470). The report concluded, moreover, that preserving the confidentiality of enforcement actions perpetuated banker misconduct and contributed to the worsening problems of financial institutions. The House based this conclusion on the October 1988 Government Operations Committee report, which specifically recommended legislation to require the banking agencies to publicly disclose all formal civil enforcement actions and any modifications to, or terminations, them of (U.S. Congress, 1989, p. 470). The recommendation came after the committee learned that the number of formal enforcement actions against institutions and individuals was declining, even though the number of significant criminal referral filings was rising.

Bank supervisory agencies responded to the House by arguing that the disclosure of disciplinary actions against depository institutions and their officers would inflict additional damage on troubled institutions (U.S. Congress, 1988, p. 89). The Committee rejected this argument, noting that it could find no example of a bank or thrift run following indictment and prosecution of a bank official or owner (U.S. Congress, 1988, p. 89)

Congress went on to argue that increased disclosure would serve the public interest in several additional ways. First, it would inform taxpayers about the effectiveness of the bank regulatory system. Second, it would provide depository institutions with information on the types of conduct that would not be tolerated. Third, it would alert the financial community to problems at particular institutions, enabling it to exercise prudence when purchasing loans from those institutions or hiring persons allegedly involved in abusive practices or misconduct at those institutions. In the end, Congress concluded that any potentially harmful short-run effects of disclosure were outweighed by the long-term benefits of the public knowing how banking agencies operate and of the deterrent effect on insider abuse and misconduct (U.S. Congress, 1988, p. 89)

IV. MARKET DISCIPLINE AND ENFORCEMENT ACTIONS: A SURVEY OF THE LITERATURE

As is commonly known, underpriced deposit insurance creates moral hazard (Merton, 1977). Depository institutions can play a "heads I win, tails the FDIC loses" game, pursuing high-risk ventures, confident that they will capture the rewards in the good state and that the FDIC will bear the losses in the bad state. Four forces constrain the ability of banks to maximize the value of this put option: hands-on supervision (e.g., Shadrack & Korobow, 1993), market discipline by liability holders (e.g., Flannery & Sorescu, 1996), market discipline by equity holders (e.g., Keeley, 1990), and managerial risk aversion (e.g., Saunders, Strock, & Travlos, 1990).

Much recent academic attention has focused on the degree of substitutability between the market and supervisors. This issue is important because it could influence the future of supervisory policy. If, for example, the market and supervisors have similar objective functions, and the market imposes adequate penalties on a bank's appetite for risk, then supervisors could rely on the market—rather than on capital requirements and hands-on surveillance—to reduce the likelihood of bank failures. If the market disciplined some types of banks adequately but not others, supervisors could use resources more efficiently by focusing their attention on the subset of the banking sector not subject to market penalties (Flannery, 1994).

Recent work indicates that bank claimholders and supervisors have slightly different objective functions, suggesting that markets are not perfect substitutes for hands-on government supervision. Hall, Meyer and Vaughan (1997) found that supervisors focus on the asset quality, liquidity and capital of publicly traded holding companies, while stockholders focus only on asset quality. In a follow-up study, Hall, King, Meyer and Vaughan (1998) determined that supervisors care about the asset quality, liquidity and capital of nonpublicly traded institutions, but that certificate of deposit holders care only about asset quality and liquidity.

Evidence on the strength of market discipline suggests that bank claimholders do provide some incentives for depository institutions to maintain safety and soundness. Gilbert (1990) surveyed the early literature and concluded that, prior to the 1990s, bank equity prices reflected risk, but certificates of deposit and subordinated debt often did not, perhaps because of "too big to fail" guarantees. More recently, Flannery and Sorescu (1996) found that, between 1983 and 1991, subordinated debt yields were sensitive to bank risk and that the sensitivity increased as the government withdrew de facto insurance coverage from uninsured liabilities. In a survey of the more recent literature, Flannery (1998) concluded that "the evidence supports the proposition that market investors and analysts could reasonably provide a greater proportion of corporate governance for large, traded U.S. financial firms."

Despite the large literature on the efficacy of market discipline in general, only a few studies have explored the specific effects of enforcement actions on that discipline. A recent FDIC study (Curry, 1997) concluded that formal enforcement actions had about the same effects on the behavior of problem banks as informal actions. This work, however, contains a number of problems that render its conclusions suspect (Gilbert, 1997). In a series of papers exploring the impact of supervisors on credit availability, Peek and Rosengren (1995a, 1995b, 1996)

Table 2.   Occurrences of Enforcement Actions at Sample Banks

Type of Action	Number of Banks	Percentage of Sample
Written Agreements	62	68.9%
Cease and Desist Orders	28	31.1%

presented evidence suggesting that formal enforcement actions reduce bank assets and loans significantly. We are not aware of papers that estimate depositor reaction to publicly announced enforcement actions. Estimating these reactions is the contribution of this study.

V. THE DATA

Our sample includes only those safety and soundness related enforcement actions imposed by the Federal Reserve. We limited the sample to safety and soundness related actions because we believe that the announcement of actions dealing with consumer affairs problems reveals little or no adverse information about bank condition. We confined our analysis to Federal Reserve actions for two reasons. First, using Federal Reserve announcements enables clearer identification of event dates since the Fed announces each action in a separate press release at the time the action is imposed. The Comptroller of the Currency and the FDIC, in contrast, announce all actions in monthly press releases, even though the actions have various effective dates during the months. Second, as Fed employees, we are privy to confidential supervisory information that allowed us to better understand the context of the Fed-imposed enforcement actions.

We obtained our sample by reading the press releases for every enforcement action imposed by the Federal Reserve in the 1990s. We identified only those actions that were clearly related to individual bank condition and, hence, would be interpreted by depositors as bad news about the condition of their banks. The text of the sample enforcement actions included some common provisions, including prohibitions on paying dividends and requirements to raise capital ratios. Sixty-nine percent of the enforcement actions in the sample were written agreements, while the remaining 31 percent were cease and desist orders (Table 2). These percentages correspond roughly to the breakdown of all Federal Reserve enforcement actions in the 1990s.

Table 3 presents summary information about the 90 enforcement actions in the sample. Each enforcement action was imposed on a different bank. The 90 banks were located in 25 states, representing each of the nine U.S. Census regions except the Pacific Northwest. Most of the actions were imposed on small banks; 68 of the 90 public enforcement actions were imposed on banks with less than $250 million in assets. The enforcement action announcements were concentrated in the years 1991-1994. The small number of sample enforcement actions after 1994 reflects the recent improvement in the condition of banks.

When studying the impact of enforcement actions on deposit rates and levels, it is important to separate the effects of actions by supervisors from the effects of actions by depositors. If an enforcement action were imposed close to the time a bank's CAMEL score was downgraded, for example, an observed decline in deposits might reflect a supervisory mandate to boost the capital

Table 3.   Sample of Banks Subject to Enforcement Actions

Year	Number of banks
Number of Banks by Year	
1990	6
1991	20
1992	34
1993	13
1994	11
1995	4
1996	1
1997	1
Size of Banks	
Range of deposits[1] (millions of dollars)	*Number of banks*
$0 to $25	0
$25 to $50	10
$50 to $75	20
$75 to $100	10
$100 to $250	28
$250 to $500	7
$500 to $1,000	7
$1,000 to $2,000	4
$2,000 to $5,000	4
Over $5,000	0
Location of Banks	
Region	*Number of banks*
New England	
Connecticut	3
Maine	1
Massachusetts	3
Rhode Island	1
Vermont	3
Middle Atlantic	
New Jersey	9
New York	3
Pennsylvania	5
South Atlantic	
Florida	6
Georgia	1
Maryland	3
South Carolina	1
Virginia	5

(continued)

Table 3   (Continued)

Region	Number of banks
Location of Banks	
East South Central	
Kentucky	2
West South Central	
Arkansas	2
Oklahoma	1
Texas	4
East North Central	
Illinois	3
Indiana	1
Ohio	4
West North Central	
Iowa	1
Kansas	3
Missouri	8
Pacific Northwest	
None	NA
Pacific Southwest	
California	14
Colorado	3

Notes: [1]Total deposits as of the week just prior to the announcement.

Table 4.   Percentage of Banks Rated CAMEL 3, 4, or 5 in
Periods Prior to Dates of Enforcement Actions

Period	Number of banks in sample (90 total)	Percentage of banks in sample
90 days or more	83	92.2%
180 days or more	78	87.6%
365 days or more	60	66.6%

ratio, rather than depositor-initiated withdrawals. For most of the banks in the sample, this separation is not a problem. Table 4 classifies the 90 banks by the time elapsed between the downgrade to problem status (a CAMEL rating below 2) and the enforcement action.[4] Supervisors downgraded 92 percent of the sample banks 90 or more days before the dates of the publicly announced enforcement actions. The periods between CAMEL downgrades and the announcement of enforcement actions were 180 or more days for 87 percent of the banks. Thus, for the vast majority of the banks, supervisors recognized the

Table 5. Distribution of Banks by Measures of Financial Strength in the Quarter Prior to Announcement of Enforcement Actions

Measure of financia strength	Number of banks in sample (90 total)	Percentage of banks in sample
Equity as a percentage of total assets		
Capital Strength		
Above 10%	6	6.7%
8 to 10	12	13.3%
7 to 8	20	22.2%
6 to 7	23	25.6%
5 to 6	9	10.0%
4 to 5	12	13.3%
2 to 4	6	6.7%
Below 2	2	2.2%
Net income as percentage of total assets		
Earnings		
Over 1%	17	18.9%
0.5% to 1	13	14.4%
0.0 to 0.5	18	20.0%
Negative	42	46.7%
Asset Quality		
Nonperforming loans as percentage of total assets[1]	Number of banks in sample (88 total)	
Less than 1%	13	14.8%
1 to 2	17	19.3%
2 to 3	13	14.8%
3 to 4	8	9.1%
4 to 5	11	12.5%
5 to 6	9	10.2%
6 to 7	7	8.0%
Over 7	10	11.4%

Note: [1]A loan is classified as "nonperforming" if it is 90 days or more past due or in nonaccrual status. Two banks are excluded from this analysis of nonperforming loans because in the relevant quarters they did not report these items.

problems and demanded remedial action at least several months before the enforcement actions were announced.

Table 5 presents information about the financial condition of the banks based on call report data in the quarter just prior to the enforcement actions. Depositors at these banks would have had access to this information before the dates of the enforcement actions. Most of the banks had relatively high capital ratios. Banks with equity capital greater than or equal to 6 percent of total assets are generally considered adequately capitalized; about two-thirds of the banks met this standard in the quarter prior to the announcement of their enforcement actions. These banks did, however, have relatively low earnings. Only about 18 percent of the banks met the industry benchmark which calls for net income to exceed 1 percent of total assets. Net income was negative at about 45 percent of the banks. Asset quality was suspect at a large portion of the sample banks.[5] Over 42 percent of the banks reported nonperforming loans in excess of 4 percent of total assets, and over 11 percent reported nonperforming loans in excess of 7 percent of assets.

VI. ENFORCEMENT ACTIONS AND DEPOSIT LEVELS

If depositors learn that the condition of their bank has deteriorated markedly, they can discipline the bank in one of two ways: moving their funds to another, sounder bank, or demanding a higher interest rate. The prospect of scrambling for funds or facing a higher cost of funds would, in turn, provide an incentive to the bank to address the problems.

To estimate the disciplining effects of enforcement actions, we first looked for evidence of deposit run-offs following the announcement of a safety and soundness related enforcement action. To do this, we compared deposit growth rates before and after the announcement dates using weekly data for four classes of deposits: transactions deposits, savings deposits, small denomination time deposits (accounts of $100,000 or less), and large time deposits. We compared growth rates over three intervals: four weeks before the announcement to four weeks after the announcement, 13 weeks before the announcement to 13 weeks after the announcement, and 26 weeks before the announcement to 26 weeks after the announcement.

To control for seasonal and geographic influences on deposit growth, we identified at least three healthy, comparably sized peer banks that were located in the same Census region and examined their deposit growth, again using weekly data. (See Table 3 for region specification.) We used only "healthy" banks-those rated CAMEL 1 or 2-as peer banks because assets and deposits tend to decline sharply around the time supervisors downgrade their ratings to problem bank status (Gilbert, 1994).

We measure the effects of enforcement actions on deposit growth with the equation below. To illustrate this measure of relative deposit growth, suppose we choose as the relevant period the 13 weeks before and after the announcement of an enforcement action. D_0 is deposits of the bank subject to the announcement in the week just prior to the announcement, and D_{13} is deposits of that bank 13 weeks later. D^p is the sum of deposits for the peer banks. The relevant measure of deposit growth is as follows:

$$Relative\ growth\ rate\ =\ \frac{D_{13}}{D_0} - \frac{D_{13}^P}{D_0^P} - \left[\frac{D_0}{D_{-13}} - \frac{D_0^P}{D_{-13}^P}\right]$$

A negative value for the relative growth rate implies that deposit growth was slower at the sample banks relative to the peer banks in the 13 weeks after the announcement (compared with the 13 weeks before the announcement). We would interpret the negative growth rate as evidence that the announcement of the enforcement action induced depositors to withdraw their funds.

Table 6 presents evidence about the relative growth rates of bank deposits around the time the Fed announced that the banks were subject to enforcement actions. The means of the relative growth rates did not differ significantly from zero for any of the 12 groups (four categories of deposits, with growth rates measured over three periods before and after the announcements). This evidence is not consistent with the hypothesis that announcements of enforcement actions induce depositors to withdraw their deposits from banks.

Publicly announced enforcement actions will induce deposit withdrawals, however, only if the actions reveal new information about a bank's condition. One reason the means of the relative deposit growth rates in Table 6 do not differ significantly from zero may be that depositors knew about the problems before the announcements. The details of the enforcement actions may have been more of a surprise to the depositors of banks that appeared to be financially strong prior to the announcements. We tested the hypothesis that the relative growth rates of deposits were lower for banks that appeared financially stronger prior to the announcements of enforcement actions by dividing the sample into the following groups, based on the information described in Table 5:

• Those with ratios of equity to assets above and below 6 percent;
• Those with positive and negative net income; and
• Those with nonperforming loans above and below 4 percent of total assets.

For each pair of banks, we compared means of relative growth rates for the four categories of deposits, over the three time periods in Table 6 (results not reported). Using the ratio of equity to assets and net income as indicators of financial condition, means of relative growth rates were significantly different at the 5 percent level for some categories of deposits and time periods before and after the announcements. The signs of the differences in growth rates, however, were not consistent with the hypothesis tested in this section; indeed, the means of the relative growth rates were actually higher for banks with relatively high ratios of equity to total assets and positive net income. Using nonperforming loans as an indicator of financial condition, none of the 12 pairs of means for relative growth rates were significantly different at the 5 percent level. Taken together, the evi-

Table 6.   Relative Growth Rates of Deposits Around
the Announcement of Enforcement Actions

Category of deposits	Period before and after the announcements	Mean of relative growth rates[1] (t-statistics in parentheses)	
Transactions deposits	4 weeks	0.0177	(1.4883)
	13 weeks	0.0041	(0.2052)
	26 weeks	−0.0378	(1.3799)
Savings deposits	4 weeks	−0.0045	(0.4811)
	13 weeks	0.0014	(0.0859)
	26 weeks	−0.0518	(1.7695)
Small denomination time deposits	4 weeks	0.0057	(1.2484)
	13 weeks	0.0053	(0.4350)
	26 weeks	−0.0005	(0.0182)
Large time deposits	4 weeks	−0.0217	(1.0770)
	13 weeks	−0.0107	(0.3482)
	26 weeks	−0.2666	(1.3604)

Notes: D_0 is deposits of the bank subject to the announcement in the week just prior to the announcement, and D_{13} is deposits of that bank 13 weeks later. D^P is the sum of deposits for the peer banks. The relevant measure of deposit growth, called the "relative growth rate," is as follows:

$$Relative\ growth\ rate\ =\ \frac{D_{13}}{D_0}\ \frac{D_{13}^P}{D_0^P}-\left[\frac{D_0}{D_{-13}}\ \frac{D_0^P}{D_{-13}^P}\right]$$

dence does not support the hypothesis that depositors were more likely to withdraw their funds from banks that appeared to be in stronger financial condition prior to the enforcement actions.[6]

Finally, depositors of banks of different size may react differently to information in formal enforcement actions. For instance, depositors of relatively large banks may be more confident that the government will keep their banks in operation. To test this hypothesis, we calculated the statistics in Table 6 excluding the eight banks with total deposits in excess of $1 billion at the time of the enforcement actions. The result was that one of the 12 measures of the relative growth rate had a negative sign and was significantly different from zero at the five percent level—the relative growth rate of savings deposits over 26 weeks before and after the enforcement actions. With this one exception, adjusting for bank size did not change our conclusion that enforcement actions had little or no effect on the growth of bank deposits in our sample.

VII.   ENFORCEMENT ACTIONS AND DEPOSIT YIELDS

The evidence does not reveal a general tendency for depositors to withdraw their funds after the announcement of safety and soundness related enforcement actions. It is possible, however, that depositors discipline banks by demanding higher deposit rates when alerted to safety and soundness related problems by enforcement actions.

To test this hypothesis, we used call report data to compute the average rates paid on deposits by both our 90 sample banks and the peer banks. Deposit rates were calculated as interest paid on deposits in a given quarter, divided by the average level of deposits in that quarter. We calculated six deposit rates:

- NETYLD - the average yield on all deposits, net of deposit charges
- GROSYLD - the average yield on all deposits (not adjusting for deposit charges)
- JUMYLD - the average yield on jumbo (> $100,000) CDs
- SMALYLD - the average yield on time deposits under $100,000
- TRANYLD - the average yield on transactions deposits
- SAVYLD - the average yield on savings deposits

For each category of deposits, we computed the spread between the average rate paid by the sample banks and the peer banks. We, then, examined this spread in the quarter during which the enforcement actions occurred (time t), as well as in the quarter immediately preceding the quarter of the action (time $t - 1$), and one quarter after the action (time $t + 1$). Finally, we performed difference of means tests on the spreads to determine whether the difference between the average spread in any two quarters was statistically different from zero. If the announcement of enforcement actions caused depositors to demand higher yields, the tests should reveal a significant positive difference between the spreads before and after the announcement. That is, the sample banks should have increased deposit rates relative to their peers.

Finding evidence that spreads increased significantly after the announcement of the enforcement actions, however, does not demonstrate that depositors demanded higher yields *because* of the announcement. Perhaps depositors were demanding higher yields because of a general deterioration in the condition of the institutions, and the enforcement actions—though announced during the time the spreads were increasing—were not *itself* responsible for the increase. One way of distinguishing between these two possibilities is to look at the trend in the spreads over a longer period of time. If the spreads were growing before the enforcement actions and did not rise faster after the announcements, the case for attributing the rise in the spread to enforcement actions would be weak.

We examined the quarter-by-quarter changes in the six spreads beginning a year before the quarter of the action (time $t - 4$) through a quarter after the quarter of the

Table 7. Deposit Rate Spreads (Sample Bank-Peer Bank)

Variable	Obs	$t+1$ Mean	Std Dev	Obs	t_0 Mean	Std Dev
NETYLD	556	0.43%	1.29%	555	0.36%	1.37%
GROSYLD	556	0.49%	1.02%	555	0.41%	1.12%
JUMYLD	555	0.62%	2.40%	554	0.59%	2.36%
SMALYLD	555	0.32%	1.21%	554	0.06%	4.46%
TRANYLD	547	0.28%	0.96%	546	0.20%	1.12%
SAVYLD	552	0.41%	1.60%	551	0.36%	1.59%
		$t-1$			$t-2$	
NETYLD	550	0.14%	1.35%	546	−0.15%	1.36%
GROSYLD	550	0.18%	1.13%	546	−0.08%	1.21%
JUMYLD	549	0.26%	2.61%	544	−0.02%	2.36%
SMALYLD	549	−0.22%	6.77%	545	−0.20%	1.37%
TRANYLD	541	−0.03%	1.20%	538	−0.24%	1.19%
SAVYLD	546	0.17%	1.56%	542	−0.08%	1.61%
		$t-3$			$t-4$	
NETYLD	549	−0.41%	1.42%	530	−0.65%	1.46%
GROSYLD	549	−0.35%	1.28%	530	−0.59%	1.34%
JUMYLD	547	−0.18%	2.65%	529	−0.41%	2.72%
SMALYLD	548	−0.46%	1.46%	530	−0.77%	1.79%
TRANYLD	541	−0.45%	1.11%	525	−0.67%	1.07%
SAVYLD	545	−0.36%	1.63%	529	−0.55%	1.62%

Note: t_0 is the quarter of the enforcement action.

Key:
NETYLD	=	the average yield on all deposits, net of deposit charges.
GROSYLD	=	the average yield on all deposits (not counting deposit charges).
JUMYLD	=	the average yield on jumbo (> $100,000) CDs.
SMALYLD	=	the average yield on deposits under $100,000.
TRANYLD	=	the average yield on transactions deposits.
SAVYLD	=	the average yield on savings deposits.

action (time $t + 1$). As detailed in Table 7 and Figure 1, the spreads did not change discretely around the announcement quarter. Rather, the increases in all six spreads were gradual and continued over the entire period. Moreover, the changes in these spreads were strongly significant between every pair of quarters (see Table 8), except the quarter of the action (time t) and the quarter after the action (time $t + 1$). The spreads on the jumbo CDs (JUMYLD) and the small deposits (SMALYLD) exhibited only marginally significant growth in some quarters, but across periods of two or three quarters, even they showed a strongly significant upward trend.[7]

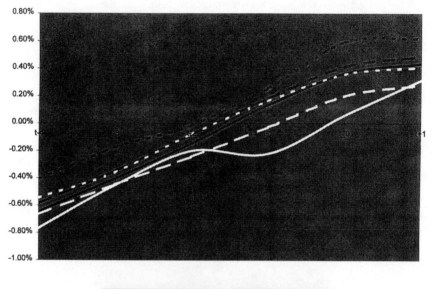

Figure 1.   Deposit Rate Spreads

As in the analysis of deposit growth rates, we also tracked the changes in spreads for smaller banks and for banks that appeared to be in sound condition according to their latest call reports. The results mirrored those obtained with the full sample. In short, the rise in the interest rates paid on deposits at banks subject to publicly announced enforcement actions appears to reflect the general deterioration of the institutions, not the enforcement actions themselves.[8]

VIII.   WHY DON'T DEPOSITORS DISCIPLINE BANKS SUBJECT TO PUBLIC ENFORCEMENT ACTIONS?

The evidence indicates that publicly announced enforcement actions did not cause deposit run-offs or discrete changes in deposit rates at the banks subject to the actions. There are two possible explanations for the lack of depositor reaction. First, local and regional newspapers did not report the information released by the supervisors; hence, depositors were unaware of the enforcement actions. Second, depos-

Table 8. Changes in Deposit Rate Spreads

	Variable	t+1 Mean	t-stat	t₀ Mean	t-stat	t-1 Mean	t-stat
		$t+1$		t_0		$t-1$	
	Variable	Mean	t-stat	Mean	t-stat	Mean	t-stat
$t+1$	NETYLD	0.00%	-				
	GROSYLD	0.00%	-				
	JUMYLD	0.00%	-				
	SMALYLD	0.00%	-				
	TRANYLD	0.00%	-				
	SAVYLD	0.00%	-				
t_0	NETYLD	0.07%	0.878	0.00%	-		
	GROSYLD	0.07%	1.120	0.00%	-		
	JUMYLD	0.03%	0.182	0.00%	-		
	SMALYLD	0.26%	1.307	0.00%	-		
	TRANYLD	0.08%	1.250	0.00%	-		
	SAVYLD	0.05%	0.516	0.00%	-		
$t-1$	NETYLD	0.30%***	3.753	0.23%***	2.798	0.00%	-
	GROSYLD	0.30%***	4.677	0.23%***	3.409	0.00%	-
	JUMYLD	0.36%**	2.384	0.33%**	2.227	0.00%	-
	SMALYLD	0.54%*	1.845	0.28%	0.819	0.00%	-
	TRANYLD	0.31%***	4.685	0.23%***	3.263	0.00%	-
	SAVYLD	0.24%**	2.550	0.19%**	2.041	0.00%	-
$t-2$	NETYLD	0.58%***	7.290	0.51%***	6.244	0.28%***	3.463
	GROSYLD	0.57%***	8.443	0.50%***	7.074	0.27%***	3.762
	JUMYLD	0.63%***	4.409	0.61%*	4.262	0.27%*	1.816
	SMALYLD	0.52%***	6.637	0.26%	1.310	-0.02%	(0.071)
	TRANYLD	0.53%***	8.005	0.45%***	6.356	0.22%***	2.966
	SAVYLD	0.49%***	5.018	0.44%**	4.530	0.24%***	2.539
$t-3$	NETYLD	0.84%***	10.309	0.77%***	9.210	0.54%***	6.485
	GROSYLD	0.84%***	12.010	0.76%***	10.555	0.53%***	7.313
	JUMYLD	0.79%***	5.218	0.77%***	5.083	0.43%***	2.735
	SMALYLD	0.77%***	9.557	0.52%	2.573	0.23%	0.787
	TRANYLD	0.73%***	11.614	0.65%***	9.633	0.42%***	5.995
	SAVYLD	0.77%***	7.892	0.72%***	7.421	0.53%***	5.457
$t-4$	NETYLD	1.08%***	12.913	1.01%***	11.774	0.78%***	9.120
	GROSYLD	1.07%***	14.917	1.00%***	13.397	0.77%***	10.234
	JUMYLD	1.03%***	6.606	1.00%***	6.483	0.67%***	4.111
	SMALYLD	1.08%***	11.718	0.83%*	3.973	0.54%*	1.791
	TRANYLD	0.95%***	15.298	0.87%***	12.986	0.64%***	9.165
	SAVYLD	0.96%***	9.762	0.91%***	9.303	0.71%***	7.363

(continued)

Table 8 (Continued)

	Variable	t+1 Mean	t-stat	t-3 Mean	t-stat	t-4 Mean	t-stat
t-2	NETYLD	0.00%	-				
	GROSYLD	0.00%	-				
	JUMYLD	0.00%	-				
	SMALYLD	0.00%	-				
	TRANYLD	0.00%	-				
	SAVYLD	0.00%	-				
t-3	NETYLD	0.26%***	3.075	0.00%***	-		
	GROSYLD	0.27%***	3.540	0.00%	-		
	JUMYLD	0.16%	1.059	0.00%	-		
	SMALYLD	0.25%***	2.966	0.00%	-		
	TRANYLD	0.21%***	2.941	0.00%	-		
	SAVYLD	0.28%***	2.881	0.00%	-		
t-4	NETYLD	0.50%***	5.784	0.24%***	2.736	0.00%	-
	GROSYLD	0.50%***	6.480	0.24%***	2.973	0.00%	-
	JUMYLD	0.39%**	2.534	0.23%	1.421	0.00%	-
	SMALYLD	0.56%***	5.827	0.31%***	3.139	0.00%	-
	TRANYLD	0.42%***	6.100	0.22%***	3.252	0.00%	-
	SAVYLD	0.47%***	4.767	0.19%*	1.892	0.00%	-

Notes: t_0 is the quarter of the enforcement action.
*indicates significance at the 90% level.
**indicates significance at the 95% level.
***indicates significance at the 99% level.

Key:
NETYLD	=	the average yield on all deposits, net of deposit charges.
GROSYLD	=	the average yield on all deposits (not counting deposit charges).
JUMYLD	=	the average yield on jumbo (> $100,000) CDs.
SMALYLD	=	the average yield on deposits under $100,000.
TRANYLD	=	the average yield on transactions deposits.
SAVYLD	=	the average yield on savings deposits.

itors were aware of the enforcement actions, but believed that the increase in expected losses due to the announcement was less than the transactions costs and interest penalties associated with moving their deposits.

To examine the first possibility, we searched several news data bases for articles about the banks subject to enforcement actions. The data bases included articles from 127 major regional newspapers and business publications as well as several publications with national distribution.[9] We looked for articles about each bank or its holding company beginning two months before the announcement of the enforcement action and ending two months after the announcement. The search revealed articles about 34 of the 90 enforcement actions in the sample. Articles mentioned financial problems at three additional banks in the sample, but the articles did not specifically mention the enforcement actions affecting these banks. The 34 banks with enforcement actions cited in the press were larger, on average, than the 56 banks not cited in the search, and the percentage located in metropolitan areas was higher for the 34 banks cited in the press than for the other 56 banks in the sample. Of the 34 enforcement actions cited in the press, 15 were reported in the *American Banker*, a daily trade newspaper with national circulation directed at the banking industry. Most of the other articles appeared in large regional newspapers.

If bank customers rely on the press for information about the actions, we might expect deposit declines around the dates of actions to be larger for banks whose actions were cited in the press. To explore this possibility, we compared the relative growth rates of deposits at the 34 banks cited in the press with the growth rates for the other 56 banks using the four categories of deposits and the three time windows employed in the section above. For these 12 comparisons of means of relative growth rates, the t-statistic was negative and significant in only one case— growth of small time deposits 26 weeks before and after the action. However, the 34 banks with enforcement actions cited in the press actually experienced faster growth of their small time deposits than the 56 banks not cited in the press.

The data did not show any tendency for yield spreads to rise faster, or more discretely, for the banks reported in the press. Indeed, the yield spreads of the banks whose enforcement actions were reported in the press generally rose at a slower pace than the rest of the sample. The average deposit rate spread (net of income from deposit charges), for example, climbed 62 basis points over the five-quarter sample period for the banks with press-reported actions. By comparison, the five-quarter change for the entire sample was 108 basis points. Furthermore, the statistical significance of spread changes among banks with press-reported actions was much lower than for the full sample.

Another potential reason why depositors did not react to enforcement actions is that they believed the increases in expected losses due to the announcements would have been less than the transactions costs and interest penalties associated with moving deposits. Deposits less than $100,000 are fully insured. The cost of failure to a depositor at this level is merely the inconvenience of delayed indemnification. Deposit insurance coverage may, therefore, explain why a given depositor did not withdraw his funds or demand a higher interest rate. Depositors holding more than $100,000, however, have an incentive to carefully monitor bank conditions since a portion of their funds is at risk. That said, the evidence does not show a propensity for depositors to withdraw funds or demand higher interest rates in such circumstances. Perhaps large depositors did not react to the enforcement actions because the announcements provided no new information. As noted, deposit rates began rising before the announcement of enforcement actions, as the condition of the banks deteriorated. Another possibility is that the announcements did not offer enough explanation since Federal Reserve enforcement actions are disclosed through short press releases with no accompanying information. Moreover, the Fed does not answer questions about publicly announced enforcement actions. Large depositors, then, may simply view the enforcement actions as noise.

IX. CONCLUDING REMARKS

We examined depositor reaction to public announcements of safety and soundness related bank enforcement actions. The evidence suggests that banks slapped with formal enforcement actions did not suffer deposit run-offs after public disclosure. Moreover, we found no evidence of discrete changes in implicit or explicit deposit rates at the banks subject to the publicly announced enforcement actions at the time of the announcements. Apparently, the public announcement of an enforcement action reveals no useful or new information to depositors. If the public announcement of formal enforcement actions adds to market discipline, the effect does not come through the actions of depositors.

ACKNOWLEDGMENTS

We thank Cathy Hohl, as well as seminar participants at the Federal Reserve Bank of Dallas and Federal Reserve Bank of St. Louis, for their useful comments. We also thank Boyd Anderson, Winchell Carroll, Tom King and Rob Webb for excellent research assistance. All errors and omissions are our own. The views expressed in this paper do not necessarily reflect official positions of the Federal Reserve Bank of St. Louis, the Board of Governors or the Federal Reserve System.

NOTES

1. "Institution-affiliated parties" include officers, directors, employees, controlling shareholders, consultants, joint-venture partners, attorneys, appraisers and individuals required to file change-in-control notices.

2. FDICIA introduced prompt corrective action (PCA). PCA guidelines impose mandatory and progressively more severe regulatory restrictions on banks that fail to meet specified capital levels. By providing an objective and automatic trigger for enforcement actions, PCA guidelines limit regulatory forbearance, an oft-cited cause of the banking crisis of the late 1980s and early 1990s. For a critique of FDICIA, see Benston and Kaufman (1997).

3. Prohibition and removal orders apply only to institution-affiliated parties and, therefore, are not represented in the sample of banks in this study.

4. Based on exam findings, supervisors assign CAMEL scores to reflect their assessment of a bank's safety and soundness in five areas: "C" for capital adequacy, "A" for asset quality, "M" for management strength, "E" for earnings, and "L" for liquidity. Each category is graded on a 1 (best) through 5 (worst) scale. Banks receiving a composite CAMEL rating of less than 2 are considered problem institutions. In recent years, the most common composite score has been a 2. Individual bank CAMEL scores are not publicly disclosed. In our analysis, downgrade dates are the opening dates of examinations that ultimately led to an increase in (deterioration of) the bank's composite CAMEL rating.

5. The ratio of nonperforming loans to total assets is a good measure of asset quality. Results in Gilbert (1992) can be used as a standard for interpreting this ratio. In 854 banks that failed in the years 1985-1990, nonperforming loans exceeded 4 percent of total assets eight quarters prior to failure, and exceeded 7 percent of total assets three quarters prior to failure.

6. Release of information in enforcement actions may have also triggered runs by bank creditors other than depositors, creating liquidity crises at the banks subject to these announcements. One way

to detect liquidity crises in banks is to determine whether they borrowed at the discount window. There is evidence that, among banks with serious financial problems, those with the more rapid declines in deposits made greater use of credit from the discount window (Gilbert, 1995).

Only a few of the banks subject to public announcements of enforcement actions borrowed from the discount window around the time of the announcement. Of the 90 banks subject to announcements, 21 borrowed from the discount window at some point during the year before or the year after the announcements. Of these 21, only seven borrowed after the announcements, and three of these seven borrowed during just one week after the announcement. One bank in the sample, however, borrowed for 25 consecutive weeks after the announcement of its enforcement action. Borrowings by this bank during 22 of the 25 consecutive weeks were seasonal borrowings. (For a description of the Fed's seasonal borrowing program, see Clark, 1992). In addition, this period of continual borrowing began 22 weeks after the announcement of the enforcement action. The evidence does not indicate that the public announcement of enforcement actions forced banks to the discount window to deal with liquidity problems.

7. Interestingly, the deposit rates paid by the sample banks were below those paid by the peer banks up until roughly two quarters before the announcements of the enforcement actions. One possible reason for this is supervisory pressure on the sample banks after CAMEL downgrades. Put another way, the sample banks may have kept deposit rates below peer rates as a means to raise capital ratios and comply with supervisory directives. Later, however, the sample banks would have been forced to raise deposit rates relative to peer rates to stem the outflow of deposits.

8. In fact, the increase in most spreads appears to have slowed after the quarter of the supervisory action. This phenomenon may be a market reaction to supervisors stepping in to curtail the bank's unsafe or unsound practices.

9. The publications with national circulation include: *The New York Times, The Washington Post, The Christian Science Monitor* and *American Banker.*

REFERENCES

Benston, G. J., & Kaufman, G. G. (1997). FDICIA after five years. Journal of Economic Perspectives, 11(3), 139-158.

Clark, M. A. (1992). Are small rural banks credit-constrained? A look at the seasonal borrowing privilege in the eighth federal reserve district,. Federal Reserve Bank of St. Louis Review, 52-66.

Curry, T. (1997). Chapter 12, bank examination and enforcement. In Federal Deposit Insurance Corporation, History of the Eighties, Lessons for the Future (Vol. 1, pp. 421-475). Washington, DC: Federal Deposit Insurance Corporation.

Flannery, M. J. (1998). Using market information in bank prudential supervision: A review of the U.S. empirical evidence. Journal of Money, Credit and Banking, forthcoming.

Flannery, M. J. (1994). Corporate finance, market discipline, and bank supervision. Pp. 313-330 in The declining role of banking. Proceedings of a Conference on Bank Structure and Competition. Chicago: Federal Reserve Bank of Chicago.

Flannery, M. J., & Sorescu, S. (1996). Evidence of bank market discipline in subordinated debenture yields: 1983-1991. Journal of Finance, 50, 1347-1377.

Gilbert, R. A. (1997). Comment on examination and enforcement. In Federal Deposit Insurance Corporation, History of the Eighties, Lessons for the Future (Vol. II, pp. 5-10). CITY: PUBLISHER.

Gilbert, R. A. (1995). Determinants of Federal Reserve lending to banks that failed. Journal of Economics and Business, 397-408.

Gilbert, R. A. (1994). The benefits of annual bank examinations. In G. G. Kaufman Research in financial services: Private and public policy (Vol. 6, pp. 215-248). Greenwich, CT: JAI Press.

Gilbert, R. A. (1992). The effects of legislating prompt corrective action on the bank insurance fund. Federal Reserve Bank of St. Louis Review, 3-22.

Gilbert, R. A. (1990). Market discipline of bank risk: Theory and evidence. The Federal Reserve Bank of St. Louis Review 72(1), 3-18.

Hall, J.R., King, T. B., Meyer, A. P., & Vaughan, M. D. (1998). Do certificate of deposit holders and bank supervisors view risk similarly? A comparison of the factors affecting CD default premiums and CAMEL scores. Supervisory Policy Analysis Working Paper, Federal Reserve Bank of St. Louis.

Hall, J. R., Meyer, A.P., & Vaughan, M. D. (1997). Do equity markets and regulators view bank risk similarly? An investigation of the factors influencing market-based risk measures and regulators' BOPEC scores. Supervisory Policy Analysis Working Paper, Federal Reserve Bank of St. Louis.

Keeley, M. C. (1990). Deposit insurance, risk, and market power in banking. American Economic Review 80, 1183-1198.

Merton, R. C. (1977). An analytic derivation of the cost of deposit insurance and loan guarantees: An application of modern option pricing theory. Journal of Banking and Finance, 1, 3-11.

Peek, J., & Rosengren, E. S. (1995a). Banks and the availability of small business loans. Working Paper No. 95-1, Federal Reserve Bank of Boston, January.

Peek, J., & Rosengren, E.S. (1995b). Bank regulation and the credit crunch. Journal of Banking and Finance, pp. 679-692.

Peek, J., & Rosengren, E. S. (1996). Bank regulatory agreements and real estate lending. Real Estate Economics, 24, 55-73.

Schadrack, F. C. (1993). Overview of supervisory elements. In F. C. Schadrack & L. Korobow (Eds.), The basic elements of bank supervision. Federal Reserve Bank of New York.

Saunders, A., Strock, E., & Travlos, N.G. (1990). Ownership structure, deregulation, and bank risk. Journal of Finance 45, 643-654.

U.S. Congress, House Committee on Government Operations. (1988). House report 100-1088, Combating fraud, abuse, and misconduct in the nation's financial institutions: Current federal efforts are inadequate. Washington, DC: U.S. Government Printing Office.

U.S. Congress. (1989). House report No. 101-54(I), financial institutions reform, recovery, and enforcement act. Washington, DC: U.S. Government Printing Office.

CENTRAL BANKS, ASSET BUBBLES, AND FINANCIAL STABILITY

George G. Kaufman

With the rapid disappearance of product (goods and services) inflation as a major policy concern for central banks in many countries over the last decade, asset price inflation (bubbles) and financial stability have increasingly become important concerns. A recent survey by the International Monetary Fund (IMF) reported serious banking and financial market problems in more than 130 of its 180 plus member countries since 1980, and that was before the most recent round of financial crises in Asia (Lindgren, Garcia, & Saal, 1996). The cost of resolving these crises is high. The transfer costs from the use of public (taxpayer) funds to finance the negative net worths of insolvent banks and at times of other financial institutions resulting from the shortfall of the market value of the institutions' assets from the par value of their deposit and other liabilities, which are explicitly or implicitly protected from loss by the government, exceeded 10 percent of GDP in a significant number of countries.

The overall cost of the problems is increased further by the costs from any unused labor and capital resources as well as the misallocation of employed resources that reduce GDP, from the depreciation of the domestic currency (which

Research in Financial Services: Private and Public Policy, Volume 10, pages 281-315.
Copyright © 1998 by JAI Press Inc.
All rights of reproduction in any form reserved.
ISBN: 0-7623-0358-1

is frequently translated into a higher rate of inflation), and from increased uncertainty that both fuels speculation and shortens investment time horizons and contributes to slower macroeconomic growth. As a result, financial instability is an important cause of macroeconomic instability and poor performance. The costs can also spillover to other countries either because of reductions in the values of cross border financial claims or because downturns in macroeconomic activity or depreciations of local currencies cause slowdowns in imports from other countries. Moreover, industrial countries are often called upon to provide direct financial as well as technical assistance to less industrial countries experiencing serious banking difficulties.

On the other hand, evidence also suggests that macroeconomic instability is an important cause of financial instability. In particular, inflation in either or both product prices and asset prices reduces the efficiency and endangers the survival of financial institutions. Although central banks have a long history of targeting and affecting product inflation and both the strategies used and their abilities to do so have been analyzed in depth, the role of central banks in targeting asset prices is less well chartered and considerably more controversial.[1]

This paper (1) reviews the evidence on the causes and implications of financial instability, in particular the role of asset price bubbles, (2) discusses the potential role of central banks in preventing financial instability, and (3) describes a prudential regulatory scheme and strategy that could help central banks insulate financial institutions from asset price bubbles and reduce disruptions to the macroeconomy.

I. FINANCIAL INSTABILITY

Andrew Crockett, the General Manager of the Bank of International Settlements (BIS) has defined financial stability as "stability of the key institutions and markets that make up the financial system." He continues that:

> Stability in financial institutions means the absence of stresses that have the potential to cause measurable economic harm beyond a strictly limited group of customers and counterparties....[S]tability in financial markets means the absence of price movements that cause wider damage...[S]tability requires (1) that the key *institutions* in the financial system are stable, in that there is a high degree of confidence that they can continue to meet their contractual obligations without interruption or outside assistance; and (2) that the key financial *markets* are stable, in that participants can confidently transact in them at prices that reflect fundamental forces that do not vary substantially over short periods when there have been no changes in fundaments (Crockett, 1997, pp. 9-10).

This paper focuses primarily on financial institutions, although institutions and markets are closely interrelated. A major cause of bank instability is instability in financial markets in the form of asset price bubbles. Conversely, bank instability feeds back onto financial markets, reducing their stability.

In market oriented economies, financial institutions mobilize savings and channel them to the most potentially productive uses. The more efficient this transfer, the more efficiently are real resources allocated and the greater is the aggregate welfare of the economy. Financial institutions also assist in monitoring the performance of the borrowers for the lenders and in policing corporate governance. Recent empirical evidence supports the theoretical arguments that banking matters, namely that the more developed is the financial sector in a country, the faster is real per capita macroeconomic growth. (The evidence is reviewed in Levine, 1997a and Rajan & Zingales, 1998.) Moreover, countries that have both developed banking markets and liquid capital markets appear to grow faster, on average, than countries that have only one developed market, which in turn grow faster than countries in which neither banks nor capital markets are very well developed (Levine, 1997b).

Although the evidence suggests that the behavior of banks importantly affects the macroeconomy for both good and bad, the predominant focus to date has been on the bad—breakdowns in banking spreading to breakdowns in the macroeconomy. A large number of studies report that the frequency of bank failures in industrial countries is inversely correlated with the stage of the business cycle—rising during recessions and falling during expansions—although the relationship appears stronger in the United States. (A review of the literature appears in Benston & Kaufman, 1995; Bordo, 1986; Kaufman, 1994; Mishkin, 1997.) For example, the correlation between annual changes in the number of bank failures and industrial production between 1875 and 1919 in the United States was -0.42 and in only two periods of sharp increases in bank failures did industrial production fail to decline (Benston et al., 1986). The studies differ on how banking crises begin—whether bank problems exogenously ignite the macroeconomic problems or are ignited by the macroeconomic or other exogenous forces and, in turn, feedback on the macroeconomy and intensify the magnitude and duration of the macro problem.

Among more contemporary economists, Hyman Minsky (1977) and Charles Kindleberger (1985 and 1996) are the major proponents of banks exogenously igniting problems that spread first throughout and then beyond the banking and financial sectors. Like most economic agents, banks get caught up in the euphoria of budding economic expansions and expand credit rapidly to finance the increase in economic activity, particularly in areas subject to the greatest increase in demand and consequently in prices, for example, stock market and real estate. Moreover, the credit is often collateralized by the assets purchased. The credit expansion fuels and accelerates the economic expansion, accelerates asset price increases, and encourages additional speculation. Both lenders and borrowers fall victim of "irrational exuberance." Through time, borrowers become more highly leveraged and turn increasingly to shorter-term debt. Their margin of safety in covering their debt service payments from operating revenues or continued increases in asset prices declines and approaches zero. Increasingly, debt servicing is financed out of new debt (in Minsky's terms—Ponzi finance). Given the high leverage, any slight decline or even slowdown in expected revenues, no less the bursting of asset price bubbles, and even moderate increases in interest rates can cause defaults. The financial system crashes off its own weight. This leads to a self-feeding sequence of distress-selling, fire-sale losses, further defaults, business failures, bank runs, and bank failures and the expansion turns into a macroeconomic downturn. Bank problems precede macroeconomic problems.

Most contemporary analysts, however, view the bank problems during macro-economic downturns to be caused primarily by the accompanying increase in busi-ness failures and rising unemployment, which in turn are often caused by some exogenous shock, including government policies that reduce aggregate bank reserves and therefore the money supply and the bursting of asset price bubbles (Bordo, Mizrach, & Schwartz, 1998 and articles included in Hubbard, 1991). Increased business failures and unemployment and sharply lower asset prices increase defaults on bank loans and also the perceived risk of performing bank loans. The banking problems make it increasingly difficult for depositors to eval-uate the financial health of their banks and to differentiate financially healthy from sick institutions (Mishkin et al., 1995). As a result, in the absence of deposit insur-ance, they are encouraged to run from deposits at their banks into currency outside the banking system, rather than to other "safe" banks. Unless the accompanying loss in aggregate bank reserves is offset by a central bank lender of last resort, a multiple contraction in money and credit is ignited (Kaufman, 1988). This, in turn, feedbacks onto the macroeconomy, transmitting and magnifying the initial down-turn. Kaminsky and Reinhart (1996) have recently examined 25 banking crises worldwide between 1970 and the early 1990s and developed a series of stylized facts. These are shown in Figure 1. Note that, on average, the banking crises are dated a number of months after declines in both aggregate output and the stock market and increases in real domestic credit and bank deposits. Kaminsky and Reinhart conclude that "recessionary conditions characterize the periods preced-ing...banking...crises" (Kaminsky & Reinhart, 1997, p. 15).

Asset price bubbles have received particular attention in recent years as evi-dence has accumulated that they contributed importantly to banking problems in many countries, for example, bubbles in real estate and energy in the United States in the mid and late-1980s; bubbles in real estate and stock prices in Japan in the early 1990s; and bubbles in real estate and stock prices in Korea and South-east Asia in the mid-1990s.[2] Financial institutions are particularly sensitive to abrupt asset price declines because many of them engage in asset-based lending in which the institutions finance the acquisition of assets, which are pledged as collateral. If asset prices decline abruptly, the institutions must either require additional collateral or sell the assets to repay the loans. If the asset sales are not quick enough, the banks may generate insufficient funds to retire the outstanding amount of the loans and the banks will suffer losses and, if large enough, may be driven into insolvency.

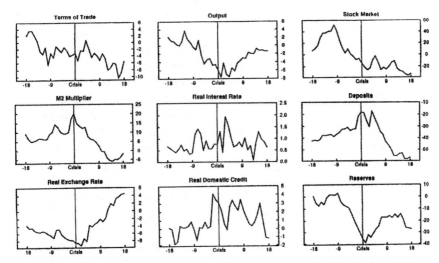

Note: The real exchange rate and the real interest rate are reported in levels while all other variables are reported in 12-month changes. All of them are relative to "tranquil" times. The vertical axes are in percent and the horizontal axes are the number of months.

Source: Kaminsky and Reinhart (1996, p. 28).

Figure 1. Empirical Regularities During Banking Crises

Capital impaired banks are likely to cutback on their new lending until their capital is replenished. Moreover, abrupt price declines increase general uncertainty. In such an environment, even solvent banks encounter difficulties in evaluating the value of risky assets and ventures and are likely, in the absence of deposit insurance and other guarantees, to reshuffle their loan portfolios towards safer projects; the more so, the closer the bank is to insolvency. Combined with the cutbacks in total bank lending, this behavior creates a "credit crunch" that makes it more difficulty to ignite and/or sustain recoveries in macroeconomic activity.

As Anna Schwartz has frequently and eloquently argued, financial institutions, and banks in particular, do not do well in periods of uncertainty and macroeconomic instability (Schwartz, 1988). To a great extent these institutions effectively deal in forward contracts. They commit themselves to pay sums of money on deposits and collect sums of money

on loans in the future at prices (interest rates) determined today. In the process, they assume a number of risks, including:

- credit risk - risk that all future payments are not made in full or on time
- interest rate risk - risk that interest rates change differently than expected
- foreign exchange risk - risk that exchange rates change differently than expected

- liquidity risk - risk that assets cannot be sold or liabilities replaced quickly at equilibrium prices
- operational risk - back office and general management risk
- legal risk - risk that priorities in default change
- regulatory/legislative risk—risk that regulations or legislation change
- fraud risk

Banks undertake some or all of these risks because they believe that they can manage them better than others, that is, because they believe that they have a comparative advantage arising from greater knowledge and expertise in both measuring and managing the risks involved. This involves forecasting interest rates, prices, exchange rates, income, and economic activity in the relevant market areas, as well as more specialized factors, such as political stability. As a result, the banks believe that they can sell their risk-taking services for more than the expected losses and generate a positive return on average. But to do so, their forecasts must be right. If they are wrong, any excess losses suffered are charged to capital. Because banks tend to be highly leveraged and have low capital-to-asset ratios, sufficiently large losses, which may appear relatively small to nonbanks that are less highly leveraged, may drive banks into insolvency. On the other hand, if the banks do not engage in any risks, they cannot expect to earn more than a risk-free return on their equity. To fulfill their economic role, banks must manage not eliminate risk taking.

The more volatile the economic, political, or social environment, the greater are the risks assumed in unhedged forward contracts and the greater must be the risk premiums charged in order to avoid losses. Empirical evidence suggests that, although banks fancy themselves as experts in risk management, their record is not exemplary. Their losses are occasionally substantial. Bank failures are highly correlated with volatility in product prices, asset prices, and interest rates. Michael Bordo (1997) has plotted the bank failure rate in the United States since 1870 with the rate of product inflation. This is shown in Figure 2. It is evident that, with the primary exception of the post-FDIC period through the late 1970s, bank failures peak after product inflation peaked and prices slowed sharply or declined. For S&Ls in the United States in the 1980s, the failure rate is effectively pushed forward some 10 years to when product inflation first accelerated sharply, pushing up interest rates unexpectedly abruptly at a time the institutions were heavily asset—long, and then slowed equally sharply.

Asset inflation plays a similar role. Many analysts have blamed the large increase in U.S. bank failures during the 1929-1933 Great Depression on the collapse in stock prices following a sharp run up, which they believed was fueled by excessively liberal bank credit. Earlier studies of banking problems in other countries as well as the United States have also identified collapses or bubbles in asset prices as a major culprit (Kindleberger, 1996; Friedman & Schwartz, 1963; Schwartz, 1988). In only two of the eight periods of sharp increases in bank fail-

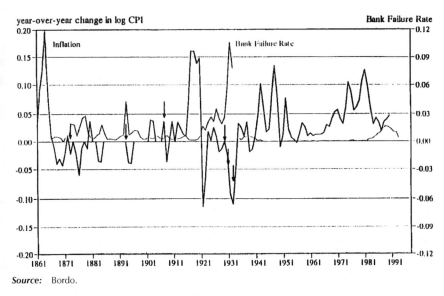

Figure 2. U.S. CPI Inflation Rate and Bank Failure Rate

ures in the United States before the Great Depression of the 1930s did the stock market not decline and the correlation between bank failures and the annual S&P stock index was −0.53 (Benston et al., 1986). More recently, as noted, asset price bubbles have played a major role in producing large banks losses and widespread bank insolvencies in many countries.

In the United States, a large number of the S&Ls and banks that failed in the 1980s and early 1990s experienced large losses from the bursting of energy prices, particularly in the Southwest, and real estate prices, primarily in the Southwest and New England. The institutions had lent heavily to finance both the acquisition of these assets and ventures based on projected increases in these asset prices. When the bubbles burst, defaults increased sharply both directly as the value of the collateral declined and indirectly as economic activity spurred by the asset price runups slowed. The banks victimized included the very large Continental Illinois Bank (the eight largest bank in the country at the time), the Bank of New England (Boston), and seven of the largest 10 banks in Texas (Kaufman, 1995). Kindleberger summarizes more than 30 banking and financial crises throughout Western Europe and the United States from the early 1600s through 1990, starting with the Thirty Years' War in Europe in the 1620s, Tulipmania in Holland in the 1630s, and the South Sea Bubble in England in the 1720s. In almost all of these, he identifies peaks in asset speculation (asset price bubbles) as preceding the crisis (Kindleberger, 1996, Appendix B).

Bank Fragility

Banks are widely perceived as particularly vulnerable to excessive risk taking because they are perceived to be more structurally fragile than other firms and therefore more likely to fail. Their perceived fragility arises from three sources:

- Low cash-to-assets ratio (fractional reserve banking)
- Low capital -to-assets ratio (high leverage)
- High demand debt (deposit)-to-total debt (deposit) ratio (high ability to run).

Each one of these sources by itself is perceived to reflect fragility, but all three in combination are perceived as particularly fragile and dangerous. At the first signs of doubt about the ability of their banks to be able to redeem deposits in full and on time, demand and other short-term depositors can run on the banks in order to be first in line and withdraw their funds without loss. Because they hold cash equal to only a fraction of their deposits, the banks are likely to have to sell some earning assets quickly to accommodate all fleeing depositors. In the process, they are likely to suffer fire-sale losses, the more so the more opaque are the assets. These losses, in turn, may exceed the small capital base of the banks and drive them into insolvency.

Not only were banks perceived to fail more frequently than other firms, but their failures were perceived to be more detrimental and costly to the economy for a number of reasons. Among other things, the failures would:

- Reduce deposits and thereby the aggregate money supply and hamper trade,
- Reduce the most liquid wealth holding of a large number of lower and middle income households,
- Reduce the availability of the major source of credit to households, business enterprises, and governments, and
- Give rise to fears that the failures would spread to other banks and beyond to the financial system as a whole, the macroeconomy, and other countries, that is, produce systemic risk.

But fragility per se does not necessarily imply breakage or failure. Rather, it implies "handle with care." And, when encouraged to do so, the market does so. As a result, the breakage rate for fine wine glasses and china is likely to be lower than for ordinary drinking glasses and dishware. And the same is true for banking. U.S. experience in this area is useful for a number of reasons. Reasonably long and accurate historical data is available. The United States has had a large number of privately owned banks. Until recently, most were particularly fragile because narrow restrictions on geographic and product-line expansion hindered them from reducing their risk exposures through diversification as much as otherwise. In addition, with the exception of the repudiation of gold contracts in 1933, the U.S. Government did not expropriate or devalue deposits and, with the exception of the South after the Civil War, the United States did not experience changes in governments where the new government repudiated the debt (money) of the old government or confiscated bank balances.[3] This permits us to analyze the performance of the U.S. banking system over a sufficiently long uninterrupted period of time to derive a meaningful number of observations both before and after the introduction of the safety-net. The U.S. experience also permits us to analyze the effects of imposing government guarantees on a previously basically uninsured banking system.[4]

From after the Civil War in 1870 through 1995, the average annual failure rate for banks in the United States was greater than for nonbanks (Kaufman, 1996b). But all the difference is attributable to the large number of bank failures during the Great Depression from 1929 to 1933, when nearly 10,000 banks failed. In the absence of this period, the annual bank failure rate was about the same as the rate of nonbank failures. Indeed, for the period 1870 to 1914, before the establishment of the Federal Reserve System and the beginning of the federal government safety net under banks, the annual bank failure rate was lower than that for nonbanks.[5,] [6] However, for all periods, the variance in the annual bank failure rate was greater; banks failures were clustered in a small number of years. Such clustering is consistent with the presence of bank contagion and systemic risk and contributes to the widespread public fear of bank failures.

Moreover, more thorough analysis of the numerical values of the three bank ratios that are widely perceived to reflect fragility indicates just the opposite, particularly in the period before the bank safety-net. These values were determined by the market place. Despite the perception, bank cash ratios were not lower than for other firms nor were or are their earning assets necessarily more opaque. Although demand deposits facilitate runs on banks, the very fact that they do serves as a powerful form of market discipline on bank management to curtail risk taking (Calomiris & Kahn, 1991.) That is, while runs may be detrimental to bank stability, the ex-ante threat of runs serves to enhance stability by making management more cautious.

The low capital ratios before deposit insurance (even after adjustment for double liability) could only have existed if the market perceived banks to be less risky rather than more risky than other firms. Indeed, the evidence suggests that in the United States in this period, not only was the bank failure rate lower than for nonbanks, but insolvent banks were resolved more quickly with less loss to depositors or creditors than insolvent nonbanks (Kaufman, 1992, 1994, 1996a). In the United States, insolvent banks are resolved by their chartering regulatory agency. They do not go through the regular corporate bankruptcy process. In the absence of deposit insurance, depositor runs on perceived insolvent banks quickly produced liquidity problems and forced the banks to suspend operations. Bank examiners determined whether the bank was experiencing a liquidity or solvency problem. If they concluded the bank was insolvent, it was resolved by the regulators through recapitalization by existing shareholders, merger, sale, or liquidation. The bank did not have much opportunity to operate while insolvent and increase its losses, as could happen after federal government provided deposit insurance was introduced and the need for depositors to run and force resolution was reduced. The decision to resolve insolvencies and the timing were effectively transferred from the market place to the regulatory agencies. In contrast, nonbank insolvencies are resolved through the bankruptcy process, which both before and after the safety-net is much slower and, in the United States, less favorable to creditors. Thus, creditors demand higher capital ratios at these firms to protect themselves from failures, which are associated with relatively larger losses.

It should be noted that the runs before deposit insurance and the accompanying liquidity problems were largely the result and not the cause of the bank insolvencies. That is, with rare exception, the solvency problems caused the liquidity problems, rather than the liquidity problems, causing the solvency problems (Kaufman, 1996a). An analysis of the causes of some 3,000 national bank failures before deposit insurance by J.F.T. O'Conner (1938), who served as Comptroller of the Currency from 1933 through 1938, reported that runs accounted for less than 10 percent of all causes listed for these failures (some failures had multiple causes) and were a cause in less than 15 percent of all failures.

Despite this evidence on the small number and low cost of bank failures on average before deposit insurance, the clustering of large numbers of bank failures in a few years was scary when they occurred and gave rise to fears of systemic risk. The failures were widely perceived to represent serious market failures. This led to calls for improvements. In response, the government imposed a government provided safety net under the banks, first in the form of a discretionary Federal Reserve lender of last resort and then, when this failed to prevent the severe banking crisis of the early 1930s (less than 20 years after it was introduced), in the form of less discretionary, at least on the downside, deposit insurance by the FDIC.

Gerald Corrigan, former President of the Federal Reserve Bank of New York, has stated that:

> More than anything else, it is the systemic risk phenomenon associated with banking and financial institutions that makes them different from gas stations and furniture stores. It is this factor—more than any other—that constitutes the fundamental rationale for the safety net arrangements that have evolved in this and other countries (Corrigan, 1991, p. 3).

When the government provides deposit insurance, it has, like any insurer/guarantor, a financial stake in the financial condition of the bank and will act to protect its interest through regulating prices and/or rules. Government provided deposit insurance by necessity begets government regulation.

II. GOVERNMENT REGULATION AND FINANCIAL STABILITY

By guaranteeing the par value of deposits, government provided deposit insurance (and other parts of the safety net under banks) changed the banking landscape greatly. Because it relieves some or all depositors of the need to be concerned about the financial health of their banks, deposit insurance, like all insurance, reduced the market discipline that the insured depositors previously exerted. But, unlike private insurance, it generally did not either price or increase regulatory discipline sufficiently to offset the market relaxation. As a result, banks engaged in moral hazard behavior and increased their risk exposures by increasing their asset and liability portfolio exposures to credit, interest rate, and other risks and lowering their capital—asset ratios. Moreover, governments were able to use banks to help pursue their economic and political objectives regardless of the increase in risk imposed on the banks. For example, to foster home ownership, the government in the United States in the 1960s and 1970s persuaded the S&L industry to extend progressively longer fixed-rate mortgages funded by short-term insured deposits, which greatly increased their interest rate risk exposure, and, to support its foreign policy, persuaded large money center banks in the late 1970s to make loans to less developed countries (LDCs). Without deposit insurance, it is highly unlikely that depositors would not have run on these risky institutions and discouraged them from participating in these activities. As it turned out, both policies resulted in large losses. Nor is it likely that Hong Kong and Southeast Asian banks would currently have as large portfolios of real estate and stock market loans in the absence of perceived government guarantees.

In addition, with insurance and little fear of depositor runs, the government regulators became less vigilant than their private counterparts in imposing sanctions on troubled institutions and, particularly, closure on economically insolvent institutions in order to minimize losses to the healthy banks, that contributed premiums to the insurance fund, and to the taxpayers, who are the ultimate guarantors of the fund. That is, the regulators became poor agents for their healthy bank and taxpayer principals. Regulators frequently tend to be motivated by political forces, such as friendships, bestowing favors, succumbing to pressures from powerful bankers or bank customers, and maintenance of personal reputations, as much if not more than by economic forces. Excessive moral hazard behavior by banks and poor agency behavior by regulators is, however, not inherent in government provided deposit insurance. Rather, it is only a likely outcome as governments tend to economically misprice and misstructure many of their services, including deposit insurance.

The evidence from almost each and every country in recent years is that some government provided deposit insurance, be it explicit or implicit, direct or indirect (backup to private insurance), and on all depositors or on only some depositors, is a political reality. Except for foreign owned banks in small countries, only governments are perceived to have the financial resources to stem a loss of confidence in large banks or the banking system as a whole, at least in terms of domestic currency. The evidence also suggests that it is best to provide such insurance explicitly, so that the rules are known in advance and the coverage not fought out ex-post on the political battlefield.

Thus, the solution to the deposit insurance and bank safety-net problem is to maintain some government provided protection, but to structure it in such a way that it is based on economic considerations and restricts both bank moral hazard behavior and regulator poor agent behavior to that that would exist if private firms provided the insurance. This is the objective of a scheme of structured early intervention and resolution (SEIR), which in large measure was enacted in weakened form in the United States in the prompt corrective action (PCA) and least cost resolution (LCR) provisions of the FDIC Improvement Act (FDICIA) of 1991, which was adopted at the depth of the banking and thrift crises. The particulars of SEIR, its history, and the experience to date have been discussed elsewhere and there is little need and even less room to review them again in any detail here (Benston & Kaufman, 1997, 1998; Kaufman, 1997a). Suffice it to say that this structure attempts both to: (1) supplement government regulation, required by the limited and explicit government deposit insurance provided, with market regulation and (2) structure the government regulation to mimic private market regulation. In the process, SEIR introduces explicit regulatory sanctions on financially troubled banks that become both progressively harsher and progressively more mandatory as a bank's performance deteriorates and it approaches insolvency. The major provisions are shown in Table 1.

In addition, and probably most importantly, SEIR introduces a mandatory "closure" rule, through which banks are resolved by recapitalization, merger, sale, or liquidation before their capital is fully dissipated, say, when their capital declines to some small but positive percentage of their assets.[7] In theory, if a bank could be resolved at such a point, losses are confined to shareholders and do not affect depositors. Deposit insurance is effectively redundant. Moreover, if losses from bank failures can be eliminated or at least minimized, fears either of a competitive banking system, which encourages the failure of individual inefficient banks, or of systemic or contagion risk, which occurs only when losses are sufficiently large to wipe out a bank's capital and the resulting large negative net worths cascade from bank to bank wiping out the next counterparty's capital, are no longer warranted. Unlike other insurance companies, which can limit but not eliminate all losses, for example, fire and automobile insurance, a government deposit insurance agency can effectively eliminate its losses completely by monitoring and strictly enforcing its closure rule at no lower than zero economic capital. That is, except for major fraud, losses from bank failures are effectively under its own control.

The incentive for banks to engage in excessive moral hazard behavior is restrained by copying the constraints that private insurance companies impose through insurance contracts and creditors on debtors through covenants. Risk exposure is priced by risk-based insurance premiums. The ability of the bank to

Table 1. Summary of Prompt Corrective Action Provisions of The Federal Deposit Insurance Corporation Improvement Act of 1991

Zone	Mandatory Provisions	Discretionary Provisions	Capital Ratios (percent)		
			Risk Based		Leverage
			Total	Tier 1	Tier 1
1. Well capitalized			>10	>6	>5
2. Adequately capitalized	1. No brokered deposits except with FDIC approval		>8	>4	>4
3. Undercapitalized	1. Suspend dividends and management fees 2. Require capital restoration plan 3. Restrict asset growth 4. Approval required for acquisitions, branching, and new activities 5. No brokered deposits	1. Order recapitalization 2. Restrict inter-affiliate transactions 3. Restrict deposit interest rates 4. Restrict certain other activities 5. Any other action that would better carry out prompt corrective action	<8	<4	<4
4. Significantly Undercapitalized	1. Same as for Zone 3 2. Order recapitalization* 3. Restrict inter-affiliate transactions* 4. Restrict deposit interest rates* 5. Pay of officers restricted	1. Any Zone 3 discretionary actions 2. Conservatorship or receivership if fails to submit or implement plan or recapitalize pursuant to order 3. Any other Zone 5 provision, if such action is necessary to carry out prompt corrective action	<6	<3	<3
5. Critically undercapitalized	1. Same as for Zone 4 2. Receiver/conservator within 90 days* 3. Receiver if still in Zone 5 four quarters after becoming critically under-capitalized 4. Suspend payments on subordinated debt* 5. Restrict certain other activities		<2		

Note: * Not required if primary supervisor determines action would not serve purpose of prompt corrective action or if certain other conditions are met.

Source: Board of Governors of the Federal Reserve System.

293

shift its losses to its creditors or insurance firms is reduced by imposing increasingly harsher and broader sanctions as insolvency approaches. The use of multiple performance zones or tranches, measured by capital-asset ratios or such, permits the sanctions to be graduated in strength rather than increased sharply and abruptly. This increases the credibility of regulators imposing the sanctions and decreases the incentive for the institution to increase its risk exposure as its performance deteriorates to near the bottom of a particular zone. To supplement the sanction sticks, carrots in the form of additional powers, fewer and faster examinations, and so on, are specified to encourage banks to perform well.

Regulatory discipline is reinforced by market discipline exerted by uninsured larger depositors and other creditors, who both may be reasonably assumed to be informed or at least informable creditors and make credit quality decisions regularly in the normal course of their business. They may be expected to charge higher interest rates as the financial condition of a bank deteriorates and/or run from these to safer banks. In contrast, small depositors are less likely to be very knowledgeable in credit evaluation procedures and efforts to force them to do so would be inefficient and represent a dead weight loss to the economy. In addition, small depositors are the only depositors who can operate with currency and therefore are likely to run into currency instead of other, safer banks and to drain reserves from the banking system as a whole. The definition of "small" depositors is as much political as economic. It may be defined as those depositors to whom any loss from bank failure represents a significant loss in their wealth and who are likely to take to the political battlefield to protest the loss and gain the sympathy of the country in the struggle.

Evidence from the United States and Canada before deposit insurance strongly indicates that at least many larger depositors are able to differentiate financially strong from weak banks (e.g., Calomiris & Mason, 1997; Kaufman, 1994; Carr, Mathewson, & Quigley, 1995). Likewise, a comparative analysis of deposit behavior during the 1994-1995 banking crises in Argentina, which had limited deposit insurance, and in Mexico, which guaranteed all deposits, showed that deposits declined more at banks with progressively greater nonperforming loans in Argentina but not in Mexico (Moore, 1997). This is shown in Figure 3.

SEIR restrains the incentive for regulators to delay and forbear in imposing sanctions in response to political pressures or other agendas by specifying loss minimization from bank insolvencies as effectively the sole objective of prudential regulation and imposing explicit and visible rules that mandate sanctions, including resolution, when banks fail to respond to earlier discretionary sanctions. The sanctions become progressively more mandatory as the performance of a bank deteriorates. The threat of mandatory sanctions increases the credibility and effectiveness of discretionary sanctions and serves to supplement rather than to replace the discretionary sanctions. The mandatory sanctions also increase certainty, treat all banks equally, and help free regulators from political pressures. Identifying insolvency loss minimization as the objective of prudential regulation establishes

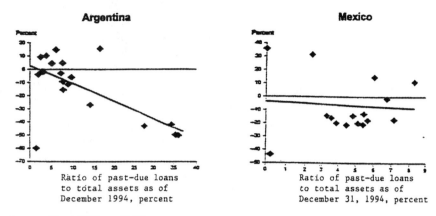

Argentina   **Mexico**

Ratio of past-due loans
to total assets as of
December 1994, percent

Ratio of past-due loans
to total assets as of
December 31, 1994, percent

Source: Moore (1997, pp. 18-19).

Figure 3.   Real Deposit Growth and Bank Asset Quality
in Argentina and Mexico December 1994-June 1995

the same objective as private insurers and creditors have. By aligning the objectives and achieving objective compatibility, deposit insurance becomes incentive compatible, so that all players—private and government—will row in the same direction. At the same time, increased transparency enhances regulatory agency compliance and accountability. While SEIR should reduce the number of bank failures, it is particularly designed to reduce, if not to eliminate, the costs of bank failures. The exit of banks that fail through either bad management or bad luck is required to attain and maintain an efficient banking industry.

To date, the PCA and LCR structure in FDICIA appears to have been successful in the United States. However, because the combined effects of the prolonged recovery of the U.S. economy, the virtual elimination of product inflation, the avoidance of asset price bubbles in energy and real estate (where U.S. banks are big lenders), and an upward sloping yield curve have enhanced the recovery of banks and thrifts from the debacle of the 1980s to their healthiest level since the 1960s, the precise contribution of FDICIA is difficult to isolate. But both the rapid build up in bank capital ratios through the sale of new shares in the early 1990s to the highest levels since the 1960s before bank profitability was established and the imposition of shared losses on uninsured depositors at resolved banks in almost all resolutions in which the FDIC suffered a loss, indicates strongly that market discipline had been awakened (Benston & Kaufman, 1997, 1998). On the other hand, because no major money center bank has failed since 1992 or even deteriorated sharply in performance, a true test of too big to fail—TBTF (or, more accurately, too big to impose pro-rata losses on uninsured deposits)—has not yet occurred.

It is important to note, however, that TBTF has become substantially more difficult for the regulators to impose. With one exception, the FDIC is prohibited from protecting uninsured depositors at insolvencies where doing so will increase its losses. In order to protect uninsured deposits at such insolvent institutions, a determination must be made in writing by two-thirds of the FDIC directors and the Board of Governors of the Federal Reserve System and by the Secretary of the Treasury in consultation with the President of the United States that not protecting the uninsured depositors "would have serious adverse effect on economic conditions or financial stability" and that protecting these depositors would "avoid or mitigate such adverse effects." If afterwards the protection results in a loss to the FDIC, a special assessment must be levied on all banks based on their total assets. Thus, most of any cost would be borne by other large and likely competitor banks, who may be unenthusiastic about using their monies to keep an insolvent competitor in operation. In addition, the documentation underlying the decision must be provided by the Secretary of the Treasury to the Congress and reviewed by the General Accounting Office. This requirement should discourage aggressive use of the TBTF exception. Moreover, TBTF would be invoked only if a very large bank had been unresponsive to the series of PCA sanctions that had been imposed on it earlier to prevent it from failing. If the sanctions were imposed on a timely basis, few if any banks should be in a position to require such protection.

It is also important to understand how prorata losses could be imposed on uninsured deposits without affecting the economy adversely. As noted earlier, in the United States, insolvent banks are resolved by federal regulators without going through the bankruptcy courts. The FDIC generally also acts as receiver. Insured depositors have full and complete access to their funds on the next business day at either the bank that assumed these deposits or at the bank in receivership until liquidated. Because, under FDICIA's PCA requirements, regulators become increasingly involved with a troubled institution before it requires resolution in an attempt to turn it around, including identifying and notifying other banks that may be potential bidders of the possible insolvency of the bank, the FDIC has the opportunity to value its assets before resolution. Thus, at the time of resolution, it is in a position to make a reasonably accurate estimate of the recovery value of the assets and of the loss it will incur in protecting insured depositors. It then provides an advanced dividend of the prorata, albeit conservative, estimated recovery value to the uninsured depositors available the next business day. In effect, the uninsured depositors will have immediately available funds equivalent to the par of their deposits amount less the prorata estimated loss, which under FDICIA should be relatively small. If such provisions were not in place, it is likely that long delays would result in uninsured depositors receiving their funds, substantial unnecessary economic harm may occur, and pressure to protect uninsured deposits fully become too strong to resist.

SEIR has a large number of advantages over other prudential regulatory structures that also makes it desirable for countries other than the United States (Kaufman, 1997b). These include:

- Maintains existing banking structure
- Maintains insurance for "small" depositors only
- Reduces number of failures
- Reduces losses from failures (makes deposit insurance effectively redundant)
- Reduces bank insurance premiums and incorporates risk-based premiums
- Reduces probability of systemic (contagion) risk
- Reduces too big to fail (protection of uninsured depositors)
- Encourages market discipline from "large" depositors to supplement regulatory discipline
- Reduces moral hazard behavior by banks
- Reduces agency problem for regulators
- Provides for carrots as well as sticks to improve bank performance
- Permits wide range of product powers for well-capitalized banks
- Reduces regulatory micro-management of banks
- Treats all banks equally

But, because countries differ in significant ways, it is important to tailor the structure to the particular economic, political, social, legal, and cultural characteristics of the country (see Working Party on Financial Stability, 1997). To be effective, SEIR depends on the abilities of both the regulators and the market place to impose sufficient discipline to curtail bank risk taking and losses, of bankers to manage their operations in a way to maximize value to both shareholders and the economy, and of governments to accept loss minimization in insolvencies as the primary goal of bank regulation. If these parties can agree to these preconditions, SEIR may be modified to be effective in the particular countries. The more important modifications required depend on the country's:

- Macroeconomic instability
- Political instability
- Strength of private market and tradition of market discipline
- Structure of banking, including solvency and the importance of SOBs and SCBs.
- Sophistication of bankers
- Sophistication of bank regulators, supervisors, and examiners
- Sophistication of market participants
- Credit culture
- Equity culture
- Bank control of nonbanks and nonbank control of banks
- Loan concentration in banks

- Quality of accounting information and disclosure
- Bankruptcy and repossession laws
- Bank reliance on foreign currency deposits

More specifically, the following features need to be tailored carefully to the country:

- Values of the tripwires for PCA and LCR
- Types of regulatory sanctions
- Division between regulatory rules and discretion
- Definition of "small" depositors
- Regulation of foreign currency exposure
- Bankruptcy (resolution) process for insured banks

The greater the macro and political instability in a country, the higher need be the numerical values of the tripwires for the PCA and LCR tranches, particularly for resolution of potential insolvencies. If these zones are stated in terms of capital asset ratios, it is important to note both that assets must include both on—as well as off-balance sheet activities and that the Basle capital ratios are minimum requirements for large, international banks in industrial countries with relatively high macroeconomic and political stability. For most other banks and countries, the capital ratios for each zone need to be considerably higher. These values need also be higher, the poorer is the quality of accounting information. Although poor quality accounting information may either overstate or understate the true information, incentives are to overstate. Thus, banks almost universally under reserve for loan losses and find additional ways of at least temporarily hiding losses. Because the value of the final tripwire for resolution determines the potential for losses to the insurance agency, assigning a value that is too low to prevent or minimize losses can defeat the objective of SEIR.

What is the appropriate capital ratios for banks in a particular country? Because deposit insurance insulates banks from full market discipline, the market solution in an insurance environment implicitly incorporates a provision for loss sharing and therefore understates the private capital ratio that the market would require in the absence of the insurance. A proxy for this value may be obtained in each country by observing the ratio the market requires of noninsured bank competitors, for example, independent finance companies, insurance companies, and so on. In most countries, these ratios are significantly higher. Thus, increasing bank capital ratios to these levels does not increase their costs unfairly, but primarily removes a subsidy. Moreover, because capital is effectively any claim that is subordinated to the insurance agency, it can consist of such subordinate debt, which in some countries has tax advantages over equity. Resolving a bank before its capital becomes negative does not represent confiscation. Current shareholders are given first right to recapitalize the institution. It is only if they prefer no to do so, most likely because they believe that the bank's true capital position is even worse than the reported position, that resolution through sale, merger, or liquidation proceeds. Any proceeds remaining after resolution are returned to the old shareholders.

It also follows that the values of the tripwires for each zone need to be higher, the weaker the credit and equity cultures in a country; the less sophisticated the bankers, regulators, and market participants; the more concentrated bank loan portfolios; the larger the definition of "small" depositor; and the greater bank reliance on foreign currency deposits. Likewise, these conditions also suggest greater emphasis on regulatory rules than on regulatory discretion.

Foreign currency denominated deposits are particularly important in smaller, open economies. Exchange rate (currency) problems and banking problems are often interrelated and easily confused. Foreign currency problems can spillover and ignite banking problems. Banks that offer deposits denominated in foreign currencies assume exchange rate risk, unless offset by foreign currency denominated assets or hedged otherwise. And the shorter term the deposits—the "hotter" the money—the greater the risk. Banks are particularly tempted to raise funds in foreign currencies when domestic interest rates greatly exceed those on the foreign currencies. Economic theory, however, indicates that in equilibrium such rate differences should be matched by equal differences in the opposite direction between spot and forward exchange rates. This condition is referred to as interest rate parity.[8]

Any downward pressure on the country's exchange rate will impose losses on unhedged banks and, if large enough, may cause banking problems in previously strong banking systems or exacerbate problems in weak banking systems, such as in many Asian countries in the past year. In addition, downward pressure on the exchange rate in a country with a financially strong banking system may encourage depositors in domestic currency to run into deposits in foreign currencies, possibly even at the same "safe" banks. This is a run on the domestic currency, not on banks. The run exerts downward pressure on the country's exchange rate. If the country attempts to protect its exchange rate (maintain fixed exchange rates), it needs to sell foreign reserves. This reduces aggregate bank reserves.[9] Unless this decrease is offset by infusions of reserves from other sources by the central bank, which would be difficult in these countries without intensifying the problem, it will ignite a multiple contraction in money and credit. This is likely to impair the financial solvency of the banks and may possibly ignite bank runs.

Such a scenario is visible in the stylized facts on banking and balance of payments crises compiled by Kaminsky and Reinhart. As shown in Figure 1, foreign reserves begin to decline before the banking crises. The banking impact, however, is offset temporarily by increases in the money (deposit) multiplier that permit both deposits and credit to continue to increase. At some point, the banking crises occurs and sets in motion the series of adverse effects. In some countries, there is evidence that the rapid increases in deposits and credit before the banking crisis were fueled by increased bank reserves resulting from large capital inflows and government policies of maintaining fixed exchange rates, which required purchasing the foreign currency.

Conversely, if a country with a strong foreign currency position but a financially weak banking system experiences depositor runs to domestic currency deposits at "safe" banks or into domestic currency, the banking problem will not spread to foreign currency (exchange rate) problems. But, if the runs are from domestic currency deposits to foreign currency deposits even at the same "safe" banks, downward pressure will be exerted on the exchange rate and ignite an exchange rate problem. Thus, exchange rate problems can cause banking problems and banking problems can cause exchange rate problems.[10] But, because the causes differ, the solutions also differ.

Banking problems require first the recapitalization of insolvent or undercapitalized banks and then the introduction of SEIR-like deposit insurance provisions. Because state owned banks (SOBs) and at times also state controlled banks (SCBs) are perceived to have complete government protection, they provide unfair competition to other private banks and are likely to prevent these banks from gaining or even maintaining market share, unless equal protection is provided them either explicitly or implicitly. Indeed, it is difficult to have a system of limited deposit insurance in a banking system that includes major SOBs or SCBs.

Major SOBs and SCBs should be completely privatized with sufficient capital to be both economically solvent and politically independent. Because their insolvencies or negative net worth are likely to be greater than their going concern or franchise values, it is unlikely that private parties will bid on these banks unless the capital deficits are reduced. This requires the use of public (taxpayers) funds. Because the sale will change bank management and ownership and value will not accrue to the old shareholders, such a use of public funds is necessary and appropriate and differs significantly from the inappropriate use of public funds to prop up existing shareholders and managers as is being practiced in a number of countries including Japan.[11] Permitting well-capitalized foreign banks to purchase SOBs in competitive bidding is desirable for at least four reasons. One, in some countries, the foreign banks will be relatively small units of much larger and well capitalized organizations that may be perceived to be able to protect their small affiliates more securely than the domestic government can protect deposits at domestically owned banks through deposit insurance. Two, foreign banks are likely to bid a higher premium for insolvent or barely solvent institutions in order to get a toehold in the country, thereby reducing the need for any public funds to lower the negative net worth position of insolvent institutions to a level that domestic private parties are willing to absorb. Three, the foreign banks are likely to enhance competition and encourage a more efficient domestic banking system, particularly in countries which are dominated by a few large domestically owned banks. Four, large international banks are likely to be better diversified than smaller domestic banks and will reduce the vulnerability of the banking sector to adverse shocks.[12]

Foreign currency problems generally reflect macroeconomic problems with which central banks have traditionally dealt. The solution does not require changes in prudential bank regulations, although the scheme discussed in this paper is helpful if governments permit these problems to deteriorate into banking problems.

III. CENTRAL BANK POLICIES TO ENHANCE FINANCIAL STABILITY

As discussed earlier in this paper, financial instability is often ignited by instability in product and asset prices. Stabilizing product prices is a time honored, traditional central bank operation that most banks appear to have achieved successfully in recent years, at least temporary. Affecting asset prices is a less well traveled path for central banks. Indeed, although the harm both to financial institutions and markets and to the macroeconomy from instability in asset prices has been well documented, the theoretical and policy links between the central bank and asset prices have only rarely been developed.

This is not to argue that central banks have not had a long standing interest in asset prices and preventing asset price bubbles. The uncertainty focuses on when asset price changes become undesirable and what should and could central banks do about them when they to occur. In the late 1920s, the Federal Reserve became greatly concerned about the rapid increase in stock prices in the United States and directed policy actions at slowing the increase (Friedman & Schwartz, 1963). The discount rate was increased to increase the cost of credit used in the stock market and to reduce its amount. Some analysts have blamed these actions for the severity and long duration of the subsequent Great Depression. They argue that, while stock prices may have been rising rapidly, the rest of the economy was not overheated and the Federal Reserve's restrictive actions were unwarranted and dangerous. More recently, again in response to rapidly rising stock prices, Federal Reserve Chairman Alan Greenspan has attempted to "talk-down" any potential bubble by cautioning market participants about the possibility of "irrational exuberance" and the unstainability of the current rate of price increases. However, unlike in the 1920s, the Federal Reserve did not take any specific policy actions directed at the stock market and , after briefly dipping in response to the comments, market prices have continued their upward spiral to date.

The recent Japanese experience resembles the U.S. experience of the 1920s and 1930s, at least in terms of monetary policy and asset bubbles. As shown in Figure 4, stock prices and real estate prices both surged rapidly in the mid-and late-1980s to far above their trend values. At first, the Bank of Japan did not respond, in part because product inflation was moderate. Moreover, the asset price increases and in particular the land prices were believed to be fueled by sharp increases in bank credit following liberalization of bank deposit rates and

GEORGE G. KAUFMAN

Semi-annual data, observations at the ends of March and September each year.
Trend line is the exponential of the fitted values from the following regression:

$\ln(X) = \alpha + \beta - t$; X = original asset price; Period: 1975:01-1985:01

Stock Price Index (TOPIX)

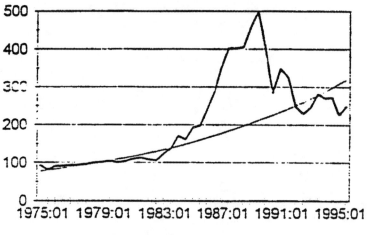

Land Price Index

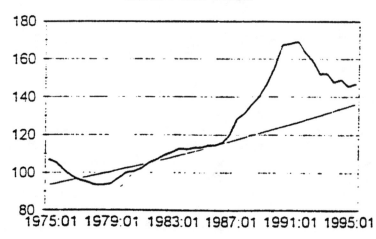

Stock: TOPIX (the average of the 1st section. Tokyo stock exchange)
Land: Land Price Index of Cities (Japan Real Estate Institute) (Both series are nominal and are normalized in the way that 1980:01 = 100.)
Source: Bordo, Ito, and Iwaisako.

Figure 4. Japanese Stock and Land Prices

portfolio restrictions. Only when product inflation started to accelerate in early 1989, did the Bank tighten policy (Bordo, Ito, & Iwaisako, 1997). It increased its discount rate sharply from 2.5 percent to 6 percent and restricted bank credit extensions to real estate. At least in partial response, both stock and land prices started their sharp and prolonged declines. However, the real economy remained strong for another year or two, before it weakened, and monetary policy remained restrictive over that period.

In its *1997 Annual Report,* which devotes considerable attention to the issue of asset prices and financial stability, the BIS lists three reasons why central banks may wish to respond to sharp movements in asset prices. Such changes: (1) may lead to financial instability, (2) play a major role in the transmission mechanism for monetary policy by being a major component of changes in aggregate wealth, and (3) contain valuable information about expectations of future prices, income, and policies, for example, the yield curve on Treasury bonds.

But the BIS is nevertheless uncertain about what central banks can or should do with this information. "While asset prices may be useful indicators, gearing policy directly to them could give self-validating asset price movements" (BIS, 1997, p. 75). Unlike product inflation, which experience has shown must be targeted to be low and the harm caused by not constraining it has been amply verified, appropriate targets for asset inflation have not been developed and the harm caused by asset inflation before prices bubbles burst has not been demonstrated. Asset price bubbles are recognized only after they occur—ex-post. While asset prices are rising— bubble? What bubble? One person's bubble is another's equilibrium price based on solid fundamentals. Current asset prices to a large extent reflect future asset prices or future prices of the goods or services generated by the assets. Without knowing the future and disagreeing with it, it is difficult for a central bank to argue that the current asset prices are either too low or too high, that is, that the stock market or real estate are either over-or under-valued. Nor do asset prices necessarily move in high correlation with product prices. Although the energy-price bubble of the early 1980s in the United States occurred simultaneously with the sharp acceleration in product inflation, the real estate bubbles in the energy belt and New England in the mid- and late-1980s occurred while product inflation was slowing. Likewise, as noted, the sharp runup in real estate and stock prices in Japan in the late-1980s occurred in a period of slow product inflation, as did the real estate and stock market bubbles in Southeast Asia in the late 1990s.

Although central banks may not target asset prices directly, their actions directed at product prices and other targets affect asset prices. Decreases in interest rates increase asset prices and increases in interest rates decrease asset prices. At times, conflicts may arise between central bank polices required to achieve product price and macroeconomic stability and to achieve asset price and financial/ banking stability. For example, in periods after asset price bubbles have contributed to both a weakened banking system and a macroeconomic recession, central banks pursue expansive monetary policies. But undercapitalized banks are constrained from expanding lending and likely even to curtail it. To stimulate lending and energize its expansive measures, central banks may be tempted to ease prudential standards before the commercial banks have recovered. In contrast, in periods of accelerating product inflation and income growth, the central bank needs to pursue restrictive polices, but may be constrained by fear that the accompanying higher interest rates might induce sharp reductions in asset prices and financial instability. Thus, it is likely, that the strategy of relatively low interest rates to avoid choking off the current macroeconomic expansion in the United States in light of the low rate of product inflation may be contributing to the very acceleration in stock prices that disturbs Chairman Greenspan, as well as accelerating the budding rise in real estate prices. The conflicts and pitfalls facing central banks at times of asset price bubbles are well summarized in the following two statements by long-time students of monetary policy. In reviewing recent central bank policy in Japan, Bordo, Ito, and Iwaisako write:

> In the second half of the 1980s, partly preoccupied by the exchange rate fluctuations, Japanese monetary policy ignored the speculation in domestic asset markets. After mid-1989, containing the asset price boom became an objective for the monetary authorities. Admittedly, many economists were supportive of the Bank of Japan in its policy toward stopping a bubble during this period. However, both Japanese monetary authorities and academic economists may have underestimated the effects of asset deflation on the Japanese economy. So we learned an old lesson once again in a hard way: the monetary authority should pay regard to the asset markets, but stopping short of including asset prices as one of the objectives policy....[As a result] the Japanese monetary authorities repeated the mistake the U.S. authorities made; using monetary policy to end speculation in asset markets carries a risk of subsequent deflation (Bordo, Ito, & Iwaisako, 1997 pp. 12, 29).

Likewise, based on his analysis primarily of the United Kingdom and United States, economies, Goodhart concludes that:

> [M]acro-policy has been systematically mishandled.... This was partly because they [central banks] were concentrating on a limited index of inflation, current service flow prices, and ignoring the message about inflation given by asset prices...The monetary authorities, therefore, share responsibility, along with the commercial banks, for the recent asset price/banking cycle.

> There is an inbuilt conflict...between the imposition of generalized prudential regulations and macro-monetary stability, since the former, almost by definition, must bite harder at times of (asset price) deflation, and hence must, to some extent, aggravate the accompany credit contraction. But it would make a mockery of such regulations, and negate their impact, if they were to be regularly relaxed at such times; though I would advocate that Central Banks should have a, carefully restricted, right of override of these regulations at times of severe, unforeseen shocks. Faced with this conflict, the correct response for the Central Banks is to take more aggressive expansionary action during such deflations, while still using their traditional rescue policies, to prevent systemic panics, in the time-honored fashion (Goodhart, 1995, p. 294).

Insulating Banks from Price Bubbles

In the absence of agreement on stabilizing asset prices to avoid financial instability, central banks can protect the financial sector and thereby the macroeconomy from asset bubbles by adopting a version of SEIR and increasing the
numerical values of all capital-asset tripwires to provide greater protection against
losses from the increased risk exposures of banks when asset inflation accelerates.
Because capital absorbs losses before they are charged to depositors and other
creditors, the higher the ratios, the less likely is the probability of bank insolvency.
Excessive leverage has been identified as a major cause of failure in most banking
debacles, particularly in the recent Asian banking crises. However, its is unlikely
and undesirable to raise required capital ratios for all banks to levels that would
absorb all shocks and prevent all insolvencies. But, as discussed earlier, government provided deposit insurance and other forms of the safety-net encourage
banks to substitute public for private capital and to hold smaller private capital-asset ratios than either the market requires of noninsured bank competitors or
that is consistent with the degree of instability in the macroeconomic in the
absence of deposit insurance. Thus, increases in private capital ratios to these levels would not be inappropriate.

The higher capital ratios would not impose an unfair competitive disadvantage
on banks nor reduce their potential return on equity below that of comparable noninsured firms. Rather, the increases reduce any subsidy that banks may be deriving
from underpriced deposit insurance or would be matched by decreases in insurance premiums if the probability of failure and losses are reduced. Nor would the
higher capital requirements necessarily encourage banks to increase their risk
exposures unduly. To the extent the higher requirements match the requirements
the market would impose in the absence of insurance, the risk exposures should
also be comparable (see Esty, 1998 for historical evidence). Moreover, the banks
remain subject to the SEIR sanctions when losses from any greater risk taking
occur and their capital deteriorates through the multizones. In addition, the regulators could subject excessively risky banks to harsher and/or earlier sanctions.
Last, as long as the performance of the banks can be monitored by the regulators
on a reasonably accurate and timely basis and in the absence of large abrupt
declines in asset values (jump processes), the severe penalty of resolution at no
less than zero economic capital also serves to constrain bank risk taking behavior.

At least until the theory and practice of central bank intervention in asset prices
is better developed, increasing capital ratios is a relatively costless but effective
way of insulating banks and the macroeconomy from the bursting of asset price
bubbles that are associated with larger losses and defaults than otherwise.

Unfortunately, many banks and bank regulators have a strong aversion to
requiring additional private capital of banks, despite the overwhelming evidence
of recent years that insufficient capital was a major cause of the widespread bank
failures in effectively every country. Indeed, regulators appear schizophrenic on

the issue. On the one hand, ex-post, they identify insufficient capital as an important factor in almost every banking crisis. On the other hand, ex-ante, they oppose increasing it. As argued above, banks currently maintain private capital ratios well below those that would be required in a nonsafety-net environment. Part of the hostility may be due to a misunderstanding of the cost of bank capital. Basic finance theory tells us that, in the absence of mispriced deposit insurance, taxes, and other institutional details, the overall cost of bank funding is independent of the source of the funding. The lower the proportion raised through capital, the higher is the cost of debt financing and vice versa. With fairly priced deposit insurance, the premiums paid should approximate the reduction in interest rates paid on deposits, as the risk is shifted from the depositor creditor to the insurance agency. Again, the total cost of funds to the bank remains basically unaffected. Only if deposit insurance were underpriced for the protection provided, would reductions in capital reduce the total cost of funds and lead to higher returns on equity than otherwise.

Under SEIR, sufficient capital is required to validate that a strictly enforced closure rule at some low positive capital ratio that would, at best, eliminate or, at worst, minimize losses to depositor creditors. The stronger the validation, the lower would be the insurance premiums charged on insured deposits and the interest rates on uninsured deposits and other funds.

Capital is sometimes confused with assets or number of banks, particularly in discussions of excess capacity in banking. Because deposit insurance and other government guarantees to banks permit insolvent banks to continue to operate and thus prevent exit from the industry through failure, there are more assets in the banking industry in some countries than can earn a competitive return and than would exist without these guarantees. But this "overbanking" does not imply that there is also too much private capital in banking. Indeed, the presence of insolvent banks in such environments indicates that there is too little capital. Requiring additional private capital would encourage exit by banks that cannot generate a competitive return. This distinction is also missed by others. A recent article in the prestigious *Economist* argued that the problem with the Japanese banking system was too much, rather than too little, capital (*Economist*, 1998). Nor does the presence of such overbanking suggest that there are too many banks. Reducing the number of banks without reducing the amount of aggregate banking assets will only reduce the intensity of competition and be counterproductive and dangerous public policy.

Another reason that increases in capital are opposed is that capital is perceived to be a flawed measure of the health of a bank. Many banks that failed had high reported capital ratios.[13] But this reflects primarily problems with the measurement of capital rather that the concept of capital per se. Reported capital often differs significantly from economic capital, or the capital that is available to absorb losses before they must be charged to depositors. Regulators frequently permit banks to under-reserve for loan losses and underreport nonperforming loans.

Adjustments frequently are not made for loans made to the holders of a bank's capital (bank owners), or "connected credit." Such credit needs to be subtracted from the bank's capital in order to obtain a measure of the net funds that capital providers have at risk. Losses (and gains) in securities due to increases (decreases) in interest rates are also generally not recorded in accounting measures of capital, so that market values of capital differ from book or historical values of capital (Benston, 1990).[14]

Moreover, in many countries, regulators permit, if they do not outright encourage or require, reported capital to be inflated by accounting trickery, to deliberately project a misleading image of a stronger than actual banking system to ease public fears of a banking crisis and/or the need for public (taxpayer) funding support. Such trickery includes capitalizing loan losses and amortizing them slowly over time, recording guarantees of support by the government as assets, and recording upward adjustments for increases in the market values of bank buildings or securities but not requiring reporting of comparable losses, that is, reporting the higher of market or book values. A description of the fast footwork practiced during the 1980s by U.S. regulators to increase the reported official capital ratios of S&Ls is reviewed by Kane (1989) and Barth (1991) and of banks by Barth, Brumbaugh, and Litan (1992). Bank regulations in Japan are currently promoting such accounting trickery, as well as using government funds to purchase bank stock. Neither strategies are likely to fool many anymore and only postpones and very likely increases the cost of the ultimate resolution.

Some reduction in the meaningfulness of reported capital is brought about by the regulators themselves. The amount of capital a private noninsured firm is required to hold by the market place is determined by the market's evaluation of its risk exposure. The riskier the market evaluates the operation of a firm, the greater will be the capital demanded by its creditors to preserve a given level of credit risk. In recent years, bank regulators in industrial countries have attempted to mimic the market and require capital adjusted for, at least, the bank's credit risk. Major banks in industrial countries that prescribe to the Basle Accord are subjected to a minimum 8 percent risk-adjusted capital requirement. Similarly risk-adjusted capital-to-asset ratios are used to partially define the capital zones for PCA under FDICIA. But while worthy in objective, the Basle risk-based capital measures are badly flawed and possibly counterproductive in implementation. The risk categories and weights assigned to each asset by the regulators are determined not by the market, but by relatively arbitrary and broad classifications and political pressure. The less risky regulators classify a particular activity relative to the market assigned risk, the lower is the regulatory required capital relative to the market determined capital and the more profitable is it for banks to extend credit for the activity. The potential distortions have been described in the literature by Grenadier and Hall, (1995), Kane (1995), and Williams (1995), among others. Until better, more objective risk measures are developed by regulators, on which they are currently working, risk-adjusted capital measures are less useful for regulatory purposes than simple market value and even book value (adjusted for off-balance sheet entries) capital-to-asset leverage ratios that may be interpreted more easily. FDICIA requires that the performance zones be defined by both unadjusted and risk-adjusted capital measures.

Basle regulators also divide capital between that which is permanently provided, basically equity (Tier 1), and that which has a maturity date and needs to be repaid (Tier 2). Tier 1 is rated higher than Tier 2. But this division not only fails to recognize the basic function of capital and is inconsistent with any accepted financial theory, but discourages the use of an efficient type of capital in the form of subordinated debt. The basic function of capital is to absorb losses to avoid charging them against other higher priority claims. What serves as capital depends on the legal rank of a particular claimant in insolvency. The more senior the claim, the more other types of claims serve as protection or capital (Kane, 1992; Benston, 1992; Kaufman, 1992; Miller, 1995). From the vantage point of bank regulators, capital should be any financial claim that is junior to the government's claim through deposit insurance, regardless of whether it is equity or debt with the exception that the debt must have a sufficiently long remaining maturity, say two years, so that it cannot run and disappear at times of trouble and that interest payments may not be made if they reduce remaining capital below the resolution tripwire value.

In countries that have developed capital markets, such subordinated debt is a particularly useful type of capital for a number of reasons. Knowing its junior standing and its inability to participate in the bank's upside earnings potential beyond the amount of the coupons, holders of the debt will monitor the issuing bank carefully and sell the debt if they perceive undesirable increases in risk taking. This reaction increases interest rates on the debt and signals other participants and the regulators. In the United States, FDICIA prohibits critically undercapitalized banks from making any payment of principal or interest on their subordinated debt after sixty days from the date of their being so classified. The market discipline so induced will supplement and reinforce regulatory discipline. In addition, to the extent the debt is not perpetual and is issued in staggered maturities, the bank must refinance it periodically and any difficulties encountered in doing so would be visible to the market and the regulators. In response to its banking crisis of 1994 and 1995, Argentina required all banks to issue subordinated debt equal to 2 percent of their deposits. At least in the United States, failure to give full regulatory weight to subordinated debt discourages banks from holding as much capital as otherwise as interest on the debt is tax deductible while dividends on equity is not. Thus, subordinated debt is a cheaper but just as effective source of capital for banks in some countries for protecting the insurance agency as is equity.[15]

At times, regulators also appear to lose sight of the fundamental role of capital—to absorb losses—and view it only as a high cost source of funds to penalize banks. In the Unitrd States, for example, they appear to be wedded to the numerical values for the FDICIA capital zones that they set in 1992, regardless of the changes in conditions since. It may credibly be argued that the values set in 1992 were set deliberately low in order not to identify too many banks as poorly capitalized in a period in which the industry was still in crisis. But now that the industry is healthier. Almost all banks are not only classified as "well-capitalized" but are maintaining capital well in excess of this criterion. Nevertheless, the regulators are still hesitant to increase the tripwire values, even though it would downgrade few banks. At the same time, reductions in the capital ratios of large banks are beginning to be reported as a concern in the press (Padgett, 1998).

Regulators need not be concerned about all losses in banking, even losses that may periodically exceed a or a few banks' capital and threaten insolvency. Indeed, market discipline requires periodic losses to remind participants of the penalties for being wrong and to encourage them to operate prudently. Periodic small losses are the best deterrent to large losses and market failures in the future that are likely to give rise to calls to replace market regulation with government regulation. If the market does not enforce proper corporate governance of financial institutions and markets, governments will and many countries will find themselves back in the periods of broad government intervention and subsequent regulatory failures from which they are now trying to escape through financial liberalization.

In many countries, financial deregulation or liberalization is being introduced at the same time as deposit insurance reform and for the same reasons. The two reforms are not independent of each other. Because SEIR retains some government provided deposit insurance, it retains the need for some government regulation, in particular for government supervision and examination to be able to monitor banks on an adequate basis. Deregulation does not imply desupervision.

Indeed, supervision may need to be intensified as many banks, after laboring for years under a repressed system, are often ill prepared to suddenly operate in a market structure with penalties as well as rewards. In particular, they are likely to have weak if any credit cultures and engage in insufficient credit analysis and monitoring. Moreover, many borrowers have also been protected and are not used to either operating profitably on an unsubsidized basis or repaying loans promptly. Thus, bank risk exposures and subsequent losses are likely to virtually explode following a sudden changeover from financial repression to financial liberalization, unless the liberalization is structured correctly (Working Party on Financial Stability, 1997). Unfortunately, this was not recognized sufficiently in many countries, including both in the United States in the early 1980s and in Japan in the late 1980s, and was an important cause of the banking debacles. Banking liberalization must be phased in or sequenced in such a way that at any one time regulatory discipline is not reduced by more than market discipline is reasonably able to replace. The weaker is the sum of market and regulatory discipline, or total discipline, on banks, the higher need be the required private capital ratios to achieve the same degree of stability.

Other Short-Term Assistance

Although the role of central banks in targeting asset prices is both largely unchartered and controversial, its role in preventing the adverse effects of a bursting of asset price bubbles is better chartered and less controversial, although not entirely without controversy. This role has been explored, at least in industrial countries, even before Bagehot in 1873 (Humphrey, 1989; Kaufman, 1991). As discussed earlier, burstings of important asset price bubbles are highly disruptive to both the financial system and the macroeconomy. Not only do the sudden and sharply falling prices trigger losses and defaults, but they destroy valuable price information necessary for economic agents to allocate resources efficiency and to be willing to trade in financial markets. If price information becomes too uncertain and unreliable, agents increasingly tend to make their portfolio adjustments in quantities (withdrawals and runs) rather than in prices. It is better to be safe than sorry at almost any price until conditions settle! This further reduces liquidity and reinforces the tendency for price declines to temporarily overshoot their new lower equilibrium levels and increase fire-sale losses. Information processing and decision making are not instantaneous, even in the current high tech world, and the more uncertain the environment, the longer the delays. In addition, trade clearing and settlements systems also slow when price information becomes less reliable and both delivery and payment fails increase.

As is well recognized, at such times, central banks need to act as active or standby lenders of last resort, injecting sufficient liquidity into the markets to avoid trading stalls. However, this is not straightforward for three reasons. One, central banks are unlikely to know the new lower equilibrium prices and thus how much liquidity support to provide. Although they may reasonably be expected to err on the side of too much rather than too little liquidity, they should not attempt to support the old prices. In addition, excessive liquidity to slow or offset the asset price declines carries the risks of both igniting product inflation and misallocating resources. Any excess liquidity needs to be withdrawn quickly (Mishkin, 1997).

Two, at least in developed countries with viable money and capital markets, central banks are unlikely to know the financial condition of individual institutions better than the market does. Thus, any liquidity assistance in these countries should be provided to the market as a whole through open market operations rather than directly to individual institutions through the discount window (Kaufman, 1991). That is, in developed economies the lender of the last resort and the discount window can and should be separated. Bagehot was writing in a very different environment. In countries with less developed financial markets, the discount window remains as the primary channel for lender of last resort funding. As a result, the central bank incurs the risk of misallocating resources through error or political pressure.

Three, central banks have unlimited capabilities of providing liquidity only in their own domestic currency. As discussed earlier in the paper, in smaller, open economies, banking and foreign currency problems are often interconnected, so that the bursting of asset price bubbles could require liquidity support in both domestic and foreign currencies. However, sufficient foreign currency support is unlikely to be provided by the domestic central bank and is likely to require multinational agreement or an international lender of last resort. This is a highly complex, controversial, and charged issue and will not be discussed in this paper.

IV. SUMMARY AND CONCLUSIONS

Financial stability is a prerequisite for macroeconomic stability in market economies. Recent experiences in many countries, differing widely in economic, political, legal, and cultural characteristics, have clearly demonstrated the high cost of bank crises both to the countries themselves and often also to other countries. Asset price bubbles have increasingly been a cause of banking crises. In contrast to product price stability, which is widely accepted as a legitimate goal of central bank policy and whose attainment is reasonably well known, asset price stability is clouded in controversy. Disagreement surrounds its definition, its causes, the role of central banks in targeting it, and the mechanism by which the central bank can affect asset prices, if indeed the bank wished to do so, without triggering major disruptions to the macroeconomy. To date, central banks have not been very successful in containing the damage from asset price bubbles. This paper argues that central banks can protect the financial system and the macroeconomy from much of the adverse effects of asset price bubble bursts through appropriate prudential and lender of last resort policies.

Commercial banks are particularly susceptible to asset price bubbles as their primary ongoing reason for being is the management of risk. The ability to manage bank risk successfully becomes more difficult, the less stable is the price and income environment. Ironically, government attempts to stabilize banking in the form of safety nets under the industry have unintentionally released powerful destabilizing forces that have to date rarely been held in check and have been counterproductive at least as frequently as they have been productive.

This paper examines the sources of these counterproductive forces and recommends a scheme for prudential regulation of banking that curtails these forces and promises to produce a more efficient and safer banking system. The scheme was recently enacted in the United States, following its banking crisis of the 1980s, and with relatively minor changes appears adaptable to other countries. The scheme permits the regulators to protect both the banking system and the macroeconomy from the full adverse effects of asset price bubbles by focusing on bank capital sufficient to absorb the greater losses and defaults that typically arise when asset price bubbles burst. The particulars of this strategy are dependent on a number of important characteristics of the country to which it is applied and may be expected to vary across countries. Nevertheless, higher ratios of economic capital to total bank assets represent a relatively costless and effective means of neutralizing asset price bubbles until effective strategies are developed for asset price stabilization by central banks.

Finally, central banks need to act as lenders of last resort, if sudden asset price declines appear to overshoot their new lower equilibrium levels. But, as central banks are unlikely to know these new levels and likely to err on the side of excessive ease, this policy could result in misallocating resources and igniting product inflation. It would be best to avoid asset price bubbles beforehand, if only we knew how!

ACKNOWLEDGMENT

This paper was prepared for presentation at the Fourth Dubrovnik Conference of Transitional Economies in Dubrovnik, Croatia on June 24-26, 1998, sponsored by the Croatian National Bank and is reprinted with permissio from Mario I. Blejer and Marko Skreb, eds. *Major Issues in Central Banking, Monetary Policies and the Implications for Transition Economies* (Kluwer Academic Press, 1999). It was also presented at the annual meeting of the Western Economic Association in Lake Tahoe, CA. June 29-July 1. I am indebted to the participants at both conferences and, in particular, to the assigned discussants, John Bonin (Wesleyan University) and Richard Nelson (Wells Fargo Bank), for their helpful comments and suggestions.

NOTES

1. Economists have only recently devoted much attention to either incorporating asset prices into measures of the general price level theoretically (Goodhart, 1995) or even to measuring aggregate asset price indexes. (Borio, Kennedy, & Prowse, 1994).

2. This BIS has estimated that after the bursting of property price bubbles in industrial countries in recent years commercial property traded at near 30 percent of its values and residential property at near 70 percent in real terms (BIS, 1998).

3. Much fear of bank failures in many countries appears to stem from government actions that devalued deposits and often also currency in some way, even though the banks may have been healthy.

4. Nonfederal government provided deposit insurance schemes had been introduced in a number of states before 1933 and national bank notes issued by nationally chartered banks were required to be fully collateralized and any deficit paid by the U.S. Treasury Department. Thus, early national banks had some of the characteristics currently proposed by proponents of "narrow banks" (Calomiris, 1989; Kaufman, 1987).

5. The low bank rate appears to have existed even before the Civil War. Alan Greenspan, Chairman of the Board of Governors of the Federal System as recently observed that:

[T]he very early history of American banking was an impressive success story. Not a single bank failed until massive fraud brought down the Farmers Exchange Bank in Rhode Island in 1809 (Greenspan, 1998, p. 2).

6. Schwartz (1988) reports similar evidence for other countries.

7. Liquidation or physically closing and liquidating insolvent banks should evidence for other countries, be employed only rarely when the demand for banking services at the locations involved appears insufficient to promise competitive returns.

8. Before the recent crisis, banks in a number of Asian countries were borrowing heavily in short-term foreign currencies (primary dollars) at low interest rates and lending in domestic currency much higher rates in amounts that may have suggested that they were operating under the illusion that their governments could and did repeal the law of interest rate parity. The BIS recently estimated that nearly 60 percent of the international interbank borrowing by banks in Indonesia, Korea, Malaysia, the Philippines, and Thailand in 1995 and 1996 were dominated in dollars and most of the rest in yen. Two-thirds had a maturity of less than one year (BIS, 1998).

9. The same effect is encountered if the run on the domestic currency takes the form of a run from bank deposits demoninated in domestic currency to currency, which is then shipped to banks in foreign countries for redeposit into foreign currency deposits.

10. Kaminsky and Reinhart (1997) find that banking crises predict balance of payments (exchange rate) crises, but balance of payments crises do not predict banking crises.

11. The use of taxpayer funds in supporting banks is often misunderstood. See, for example Working Party on Financial Stability (1997, p. 41).

12. As some countries break up into smaller countries, the ability of banks to diversify geographically domestically is reduced further.

13. The BIS, for example, notes that many Asian banks had much higher reported capital ratios before the crisis than required by the Basle Accord (BIS, 1998).

14. Because of the difficulty in measuring and monitoring capital correctly, some countries, particularly developing and transitional economies, partially shift prudential emphasis to cash reserves, which are easier to measure and monitor. The larger is the percentage of cash reserves required, the less important is capital, although banks could attempt to offset the loss in earnings from high reserve requirements by selecting riskier earnings assets. Problems of connected lending may also be reduced by requiring arms-length types of transactions between the bank and the owners' entities. But caution still suggests that the amounts lent be excluded from regulatory capital.

15. Recently, some Basle and other industrial countries have permitted large banks to use additional subordinated debt with a minimum maintained maturity of two years as a newly added Tier 3 capital against market risk in trading accounts.

REFERENCES

Bank for International Settlements. (1997). *67th Annual Report.* Basle: Switzerland.
Bank for International Settlements. (1998). *The transmission of monetary policy in emerging market economies* (BIS Policy Papers No. 3). Basle, Switzerland: Bank for International Settlements.
Bank for International Settlements. (1998). *68th Annual Report.* Basle, Switzerland.
Barth, J. R. (1991). *The great savings and loan debacle.* Washington, DC: American Enterprise Institute.
Barth, J. R., Brumbaugh, R. D. Jr., & Litan, R. E. (1992). *The future of American banking.* Armonk, NY: M.E. Sharpe.
Basle Committee for Banking Supervision. (1997). *Core principles for effective banking supervision.* Basle, Switzerland: Bank for International Settlements.
Benston, G. J. (1990). Market-value accounting by banks: Benefits, costs and incentives. In G. Kaufman (Ed.), *Restructuring the American financial system.* Boston: Kluwer Academic.
Benston, G. J. (1992). The purposes of capital for institutions with government-insured deposits. *Journal of Financial Services Research,* 369-384.
Benston, G. J., Eisenbeis, R. A., Horvitz, P. M., Kane, E. J., & Kaufman, G. G. (1986). *Perspectives on safe and sound banking.* Cambridge, MA: MIT Press.

Benston, G. J., & Kaufman, G. G. (1995). Is the banking and payments system fragile? *Journal of Financial Services Research*, 209-240.

Benston, G. J., & Kaufman, G. G. (1997). FDICIA after five years. *Journal of Economic Perspectives*, 139-158.

Benston, G. J., & Kaufman, G. G. (1998). Deposit insurance reform in the FDIC improvement act: The experience to date. *Economic Perspectives*, 2-20.

Bordo, M. (1986). Financial crises, banking crises, stock market crashes and the money supply: Some international evidence 1870-1933. In F. Capie & G. E. Wood (Eds.), *Financial crises and the world banking system*. New York: St. Martin's Press.

Bordo, M. D. (1997). *Financial crises and exchange rate crises in historical perspective*. Working Paper, Rutgers University, August.

Bordo, M.D., Ito, T., & Iwaisako, T. (1997). *Banking crises and monetary policy: Japan in the 1990s and U.S. in the 1930s*. Working Paper, University of Tsukuba (Japan).

Bordo, M. D., Mizrach, B., & Schwartz, A. J. (1998). Real vs. pseudo international systemic risk: Some lessons from history. *Review of Pacific Basin Financial Markets and Policies*, 31-58.

Borio, C. E. V., Kennedy, N., & Prowse, S. D. (1994). *Exploring aggregate asset price fluctuations across countries* (BIS Economic Papers No. 40). Basle, Switzerland: Bank for International Settlements.

Calomiris, C. W. (1989). Deposit insurance: Lessons from the record. *Economic Perspective*, 10-30.

Calomiris, C. W., & Kahn, C. M. (1991). The role of demandable debt in structuring optimal banking arrangements. *American Economic Review*, 497-513.

Calomiris, C. W., & Mason, J.R. (1997). Contagion and bank failure during the great depression: The June 1932 Chicago banking panic. *American Economic Review*, 863-883.

Caprio Jr., G., & Klingebiel, D. (1996). *Bank insolvency: Bad luck, bad policy, or bad banking*. Working Paper, World Bank.

Carr, J., Mathenson, F., & Quigley, N. (1995). Stability in the absence of deposit insurance: The Canadian banking system 1890-1966. *Journal of Money, Credit, and Banking*, 1137-1158.

Corrigan, E. G. (1991). The banking-commerce controversy revisited. *Quarterly Review*, Spring, 1-13.

Crockett, A. (1997). Why is financial stability a goal of public policy. In *Maintaining financial stability in a global economy*. Kansas City Federal Reserve Bank.

Esty, B. (1998). The impact of contingent liability on commercial bank risk taking. *Journal of Financial Economics*, 189-218.

Friedman, M. and Schwartz, A. (1971). *A monetary history of the United States, 1867-1960*. Princeton, NJ: Princeton University Press.

Goodhart, C. A. E. (1995). Price stability and financial fragility. In C.A.E. Goodhart (Ed.), *The central bank and the financial system* (pp. 263-302). Cambridge, MA: MIT Press.

Greenspan, A. (1998). *Remarks*. Washington, DC: Board of Governors of the Federal Reserve System, May 2.

Grenadier, S. R., & Hall, B. J. (1995). *Risk-based capital standards and the riskiness of bank portfolios: Credit and factor risk*. Working Paper No. 5178, National Bureau of Economic Research.

How to Waste $250 Billion. (1998). *The Economist*, January 24, p. 16.

Humphrey, T. M. (1989). Lender of last resort: The concept in History. *Economic Review*, 8-16.

Kaminsky, G. L., & Reinhart, C. M. (1996). *The twin crises: The causes of banking and balance of payments problems*. International Finance Discussion Papers (No. 544). Washington, DC: Board of Governors of the Federal Reserve System.

Kane, E. J. (1989). *The S&L insurance mess*. Washington, DC: Urban Institute Press.

Kane, E. J. (1995). Difficulties in transferring risk-based capital requirements to developing countries. *Pacific Basin Finance Journal*, 193-216.

Kaufman, G. G. (1987). The federal safety net: Not for banks only. *Economic Perspectives*, 19-28.

Kaufman, G. G. (1988). Bank runs: Causes, benefits, and costs. *Cato Journal*, 539-587.

Kaufman, G. G. (1991). Lender of last resort: A contemporary perspective. *Journal of Financial Services Research,* 95-110.

Kaufman, G. G. (1992). Capital in banking: Past, present, and future. *Journal of Financial Services Research,* 385-402.

Kaufman, G. G. (1994). Bank contagion: A review of the theory and evidence. *Journal of Financial Services Research,* 123-150.

Kaufman, G. G. (1995). The U.S. banking debacle of the 1980s: An overview and lessons. *The Financier,* 9-26.

Kaufman, G. G. (1996a). Bank failures, systemic risk, and bank regulation. *Cato Journal,* 17-45.

Kaufman, G. G. (1996b). *Bank fragility: Perception and historical evidence.* Working Paper Series (96-18). Chicago: Federal Reserve Bank of Chicago.

Kaufman, G. G. (1997a). *Banking reform: The whys and how to's.* Working Paper, Loyola University Chicago.

Kaufman, G. G.(1997b). Lessons for transitional and developing economics from U.S. deposit insurance reform. In G. M. von Furstenberg, (Ed.), *Regulation and supervision of financial institutions in the NAFTA countries and beyond.* Boston: Kluwer Academic.

Kindleberger, C. P. (1985). Bank failures: The 1930s and 1980s. In *The search for financial stability: The past fifty years.* San Francisco: Federal Reserve Bank of San Francisco.

Kindleberger, C. P. (1996). *Manias, panics, and crashes: A history of financial crises* (3rd ed). New York: Wiley.

Levine, R. (1997a). Financial development and economic growth: Views and agenda. *Journal of Economic Literature,* 688-726.

Levine, R. (1997b). Stock markets, economic development, and capital control liberalization. *Perspective (Investment Company Institute),* 1-7.

Lindgren, C. J., Garcia, G., & Saal, M. I. (1996). *Bank soundness and macroeconomic policy.* Washington, DC: International Monetary Fund.

Miller, M. H. (1995). Do the M&M propositions apply to banks? *Journal of Banking and Finance,* 483-489.

Minsky, H.P. (1977). A theory of systematic financial fragility. In E. Altman & A. Sametz (Eds.), *Financial crises: Institutions and markers in a fragile environment* (pp. 138-152). New York: Wiley.

Mishkin, F. S. (1995). *The causes and propagation of financial instability: Lessons for policy makers In Maintaining financial stability in a global economy.* Kansas City: Federal Reserve Bank of Kansas City.

Mishkin, F. S. (1995). The monetary transmission mechanism. *Journal of Economic Perspective,* 3-96.

Moore, R. R. (1997). Government garantees and banking: Evidence from the Mexican peso crisis. *Financial Industry Studies,* 13-21.

O'Conner, J.F.T. (1938). *The banking crisis and recovery under the Roosevelt administration.* Chicago: Callaghan and Co.

Padgett, T. (1998). Capital slide could spur big banks to debt market. *American Banker,* 1-2.

Rajan, R. G., & Zingales, L. (1998). Financial dependence and growth. *American Economic Review,* 559-586.

Schwartz, A. J. (1988). Financial stability and the federal safety net. In W. S. Haraf & R. M. Kushmeider (Eds.), *Restructuring banking and financial services in America.* Washington, DC: American Enterprise Institute.

Williams, M. G. (1995). *The efficacy of accounting-based bank regulation: The case of the Basel accord.* Working Paper No. 95-9. Santa Monica, CA: Milken Institute.

Working Party of Financial Stability in Emerging Market Economies. (1997). *Financial stability in emerging market economies.* Basle, Switzerland.

COMMENT

Richard W. Nelson

This paper addresses the role of government in causing or resolving banking failures or crises. In doing so, it develops three major theses: (1) that banking crises generally result from economic or financial shocks that are systematically missed a priori by private market participants and governments alike; (2) that the performance of government regulation in preventing or ameliorating the impact of banking crises depends crucially on the behavior of government officials, which in turn is tied to the political process; and (3) hope for a more effective government process partially lies in increased public accountability of government and regulatory officials.

The paper draws upon four papers presented elsewhere in this volume which focus on different phases of the bank failure process. Barth, Brumbaugh, Ramesh, and Yago (1998), focus on the government's role in precipitating banking crises. Gilbert and Vaughan (1998), analyze enforcement actions by the government regulatory agencies, prior to declarations of insolvency. Kaufman (1998) likewise is interested in early intervention and restructuring of banks by government regulators and the operation of a lender of last resort, both of which occur late in the failure/banking crisis process. Bartholomew and Gup (1998) address alternative resolution methods after failure has occurred. With the exception of Gilbert and

Research in Financial Services: Private and Public Policy, Volume 10, pages 317-322.
Copyright © 1998 by JAI Press Inc.
All rights of reproduction in any form reserved.
ISBN: 0-7623-0358-1

Vaughn, all are broad essays that survey previous work and integrate international comparisons with analysis of United States experience during the latter part of the twentieth century. All of these papers are important for the perspectives that they develop on banking crises and the political process involved in dealing with them.

A brief first point is to ask what can be gleaned from the international record about the causes of banking crises and how effectively government deals with them. In any one country, banking crises are historical events that tend to extend over a number of years but occur infrequently. As a result, it is tempting to look to international comparisons to provide some comparative analysis. However, although they eliminate changing institutional contexts associated with time, international crises reveal very different institutional contexts associated with political and economic systems and culture. As a result, analysis of banking crises, whether within a country or from an international perspective, tends to proceed case by case and is better suited to inventing hypotheses about the political process in banking than really testing them. Within this context, it is quite reasonable, then for Kaufman (1998) and Barth et al. (1998) to come to different interpretations. Were data available, it would be nice to see some direct comparisons relating, for instance, the extent of bank powers to failure rates, the regulatory approach to dealing with failure to resolution costs, and the impact of the political system on the magnitude of the crises. However, even in the absence of a way to test alternative hypotheses scientifically, developing alternative hypotheses regarding banking crises is a useful step in thinking through the public policy issues.

A second important introductory point concerns the role of economic and financial shocks in precipitating bank failures and banking crises. Kaufman (1998), for instance, points out that "the frequency of bank failures in industrial countries is inversely correlated with the stage of the business cycle" (p. 4) and that "financial institutions are particularly sensitive to abrupt asset price declines because many of them engage in asset-based lending . . . ." (p. 6). Nelson (1988) came to similar conclusions.

Governments need to know the nature of the risks that banks face if they are to have a constructive effect in preventing or ameliorating bank failures and banking crises. Much analysis simply assumes that risks are known and can be quantified in advance, and that failures result from management making the wrong tradeoffs. Whereas this situation certainly characterizes many individual bank failures, it is not clear at all that it is relevant in the systemic failures that constitute or lead to banking crises. Thus, looking backwards, it was excessive interest rate risk that led to S&Ls demise in the first phase of the United States' Great Savings and Loan Debacle (Nelson, 1993). Yet S&Ls were not the only economic agents who failed to give much likelihood to the possibility that interest rates might rise as high as they did during the 1979-1982 period. Insurance companies were similarly hard hit, as was the social security trust fund which was largely invested in long-term, fixed rate government securities.

Price shocks (including interest rate shocks) are by definition not anticipated or even envisioned to occur with any significant likelihood, and are thus underappreciated by both banks and government regulators, alike. Because they are systematically missed in advance throughout the system, they are likely to translate into systemic failures and thus banking crises. But it is important to recognize that such shocks are equally unlikely to be anticipated by government regulators as by private banks. Thus studies of banking crises may best be thought of as studies as to how economic agents and government react to systematically unexpected events (Nelson, 1988).

What, then, should be the role of government regulation in banking? Here, Kaufman seems to come to very different conclusions than do and Barth, Brumbaugh, Ramesh, and Yago. Kaufman argues that we should perfect regulation by extending internationally the U.S. system of SEIR (Structured Early Intervention and Restructuring) combined with an effective lender of last resort. On the other hand, Barth et al. point out that intervention by international lending organizations, both with regard to support for troubled institutions and the conditions/regulations they impose to avoid them, has not been very effective and may actually have created incentives which exacerbate the problem.

The real difference in these two views lies not so much in the logic of the arguments but rather in some implicit assumptions about how government processes actually work. The lender of last resort, for instance, is a concept that developed historically as a prescription for public policy but which has rarely been perfectly implemented. The debate over the "too big to fail" concept in the United States is an excellent example. Classical lender of last resort theory calls for the central bank to act in a banking crisis by providing unlimited liquidity to sound institutions upon good collateral. Nowhere does it envisage lending to insolvent institutions or protecting their shareholders or creditors from loss. And even were the lender of last resort limited to the classical theoretical concept, it still would risk the danger of creating moral hazard in the markets collectively were it used too frequently or too predictably.

The question, then, arises as to why "too big to fail" thinking developed in the United States rather than the classical lender of last resort concept. Lending to insolvent institutions in the United States probably reached its apex during the Great Savings and Loan Debacle, where most of the institutions were not large by the largest commercial bank standards but were collectively very significant. Dissatisfaction with the Federal Reserve's lender of last resort policies led to a legislative tightening of the groundrules in FIDICIA in 1991, but the effectiveness of this legislative fix in face of a major crisis remains to be tested. Turning to the international sector, critics of the international lending institutions, including Barth et al., also maintain that the current practice of these agencies is to bail out insolvent institutions, contravening the classical lender of last resort theory. Classical lender of last resort policy may, consequently, be an effective solution which the political process is incapable of implementing.

In contrast to the concept of lender of last resort, SEIR is a concept that was articulated relatively recently, by George Kaufman in the late 1980s and early 1990s. However, like the concept of lender of last resort, SEIR is an ideal prescription for public policy, calling for regulators to intervene in the bank failure process well before a bank fails. SEIR establishes a precisely structured set of rules tied to the capital position of financial institutions, beginning with early intervention to encourage existing management to take appropriate steps when capital falls below a certain point and culminating, if deterioration proceeds sufficiently far, in a regulator-arranged change in ownership of the institution.

Just as the classical lender of last resort is a concept that has rarely been practiced by the political process, classical SEIR also has not been subjected to a real test since its articulation in the last ten years. Bartholomew and Gup (1998), however, point out in their paper that elements of SEIR have been in place previously but were abandoned during crises. Thus, the Federal Home Loan Bank Board had well defined and structured capital rules prior to the S&L debacle that would have required closure of many institutions during the early 1980s, prior to the acceleration of the crisis in the mid to late 1980s. Yet the FHLB chose to alter its regulations rather than to enforce them, in effect granting forbearance that gutted their effect.

Both classical SEIR and classical lender of last resort theory thus are promising policies to address banking crises. But at issue is whether governments are likely to implement these concepts in their classical form. Answering this question calls on broader traditions of political economy rooted also in theories of government, and the conclusions given our current state of knowledge are probably somewhat fuzzy. In the democratic United States, the answer clearly hinges on both the quality of politicians and the underlying desires of the electorate. In developing countries, both Kaufman and Barth et al. recognize that legal and political institutions are important infrastructure to effective government action. The different prescriptions that they seem to favor, thus, may lie more in their relative optimism/pessimism about the emergence or persistence of a supporting political infrastructure than in analytical differences about the pure economic model.

Although the jury is still out concerning the effectiveness of the political process in the United States, a pessimistic view is not unreasonable. Such a view would hold that the populace is poorly informed about banking issues and national politicians are unprepared or unlikely to step up to the plate to provide leadership in this area. More fundamentally, it would trace the problem to roots in current cultural attitudes emphasize short-run, self-interested materialism, causing politicians to be more concerned with distributing income to constituents than to addressing long-term issues of economic efficiency.

SEIR also must confront one technical issue relating to the nature of the process that generates capital deterioration and failure. If this process is not a continuous one where banks weaken gradually but rather a jump process where economic shocks very quickly cause systemic insolvencies, then the SEI (structured early intervention) in SEIR may be impractical, leaving only prompt restructuring as an alternative. As previously argued, this situation was essentially that which did occur in the early S&L debacle between 1979 and 1982, leaving the FHLB with the choice of closing many institutions or adopting its policy of forbearance (Nelson, 1992, 1993). That is to say, the conditions that caused the FHLB to depart from SEIR were conditions that made the process impractical and simultaneously raised the political, income distribution considerations to very significant proportions. Further, it is not at all clear whether a well established policy of SEIR prior to the S&L debacle would have caused S&Ls to reduce their interest rate exposure to manageable proportions, particularly since capital rules had been in place and many nonbank financial participants took similar risk.

Openness and accountability is another dimension of the political process that is very relevant in discussions of banking policy. In the United States, legislation of the late 1980s and early 1990s required disclosure of supervisory information that regulators had previously resisted. Regulators were required to make public the existence of enforcement actions against banks, actions during the early stages of SEIR prior to restructuring. One argument for such a policy was that it would enhance market discipline, prompting private economic agents to restrict debt availability and thus complementing regulators' actions.

In a very careful analysis of actual announcements during the 1990s, subsequent to the new legislation, Gilbert and Vaughn (1998) come to the conclusion that disclosure of enforcement actions has very little impact on availability or terms of deposits to affected banking institutions. However, this leaves a number of other, very important questions about openness and accountability that Gilbert and Vaughn do not investigate. For instance, the effectiveness of regulatory enforcement actions is directly relevant to the debate concerning SEIR. What were the effects of enforcement actions taken under the policy of SEIR? Although they had little effect on market discipline, did they in and of themselves save banks, avoiding their failure or reducing the costs of resolution? Or did then represent a form of forbearance similar to that which was characteristic of the middle to late phases of the S&L debacle?

Even more interesting are several additional issues regarding disclosure. It has long been argued by some analysts and regulators that disclosure of regulatory actions, and possibly even the act of closing banks, itself, is not practical owing to their possible destabilizing impact on the banking system. In contrast, critics have argued that such arguments have prevented regulators from taking effective action to deal with weakening or failing banks. Gilbert and Vaughn's results support the view of the critics in that they show little market reaction to supervisory actions.

Finally, it can be argued that public disclosure is an important element in the political process required to make SEIR more effective in the future than the past record supports. One view of the S&L debacle, for instance, is that regulators and politicians were able to act contrary to the electorate's wishes because the public had insufficient information about what was going on. To the extent that government has not been effective in dealing with banking crises, it may well be that increased public accountability would improve the situation immeasurably. This view probably is not applicable to less democratic countries, but is plausible in context of the United States. Thus more disclosure by government agencies concerning their actions relating to banking crises probably is part of the solution to the issues discussed in this essay.

ACKNOWLEDGMENTS

This paper reflects the views of the author and does not necessarily represent the views of Wells Fargo Bank. The author wishes to thank Professor George Kaufman, Loyola University Chicago, for his continued encouragement.

REFERENCES

Barth, J. R., Brumbaugh, R. D. Jr., Ramesh, L., & Yago, G. (1998). *The role of governments and markets in international banking crises: The case of East Asia.* In G. G. Kaufman (Ed.), *Research in financial services: Private and publicy.* Greenwich, CT: JAI Press.
Bartholomew, P. F., & Gup, B. E. (1998). *An examination of bank regulators' decisions to fail banks: An international perspective.* In G. G. Kaufman (Ed.), *Research in financial services: Private and publicy.* Greenwich, CT: JAI Press.
Gilbert, R. A., & Vaughan, M. D. (1998). *Does the publication of supervisory enforcement actions add to market discipline.* In G. G. Kaufman (Ed.), *Research in financial services: Private and publicy.* Greenwich, CT: JAI Press.
Kaufman, G. G. (1998). *Central banks, asset bubbles, and financial stability.* In G. G. Kaufman (Ed.), *Research in financial services: Private and publicy.* Greenwich, CT: JAI Press.
Nelson, R. W. (1988). Management vs. economic conditions as contributors to the recent rise in bank failures. In *Financial risk: Theory, evidence, and implications.* Boston: Kluwer Academic Publishers.
Nelson, R. W. (1996). Supervision and the great deposit insurance debacle. In D. B. Papadimitriou (Ed.), *Stability in the financial system.* London: Macmillan Press.
Nelson, R. W. (1993). Regulatory structure, regulatory failure, and the S&L debacle. *Contemporary Policy Issues*, 108-115.
Nelson, R. W. (1992). The financial institutions reform, recovery, and enforcement act: Reshaping the U.S. depository institutions' regulatory structure. In J. R. Barth & P. F. Bartholomew (Eds.), *Emerging challenges for the international financial services industry.*Greenwich, CT: JAI Press.

JAI Press Inc.
Ablex Publishing Corp.

Research in Finance

Edited by **Andrew H. Chen,** *Edwin L. Cox School of Business, Southern Methodist University*

Volume 15, 1997, 360 pp. $78.50/£49.95
ISBN 0-7623-0259-3

CONTENTS: Why Do Firms Undertake Intra-Firm Exchange Offers?, *Kshitij Shah.* Indirect Financial Distress and Sales Performance, *G.M. Chen, J.K. Cheung,* and *L. J. Merville.* Multinational Firm and Strategic Trade Policy, *Manabendra DasGupta and Seung -Dong Lee.* The Role of Fundamental Data and Analysts' Earnings Breadth, Forecasts, and Revisions in the Creation of Efficient Portfolios, *John B. Guerard, Jr. Mustafa Gultekin, and Bernell K. Stone.* Earnings Forecasts, Revisions, and Momentum in the Estimation of Efficient Market-Neutral Japanes and U.S. Portfolios, *John Blin, Steve Bender, and John B. Guerard, Jr.* The Noise Trader Hypothesis: The Case of Closed-End Country Funds, *C. Sherman Cheung, Clarence C.Y. Kwan, and Jason Lee.* Stock Market Volatility and the Business Cycle, *Hany Shawky and Selcuk Caner.* An Empirical Study of the Behavior of Futures Prices, *Andrew H. Chen, Marcia Million Cornett, and Prafulla G. Nabar.* Pricing and Informational Efficiency of the Nikkei Futures Options, *Kian-Guan Lim and Christina Teo.* Determinants of Banks' Deposit Insurance Liabilities: Exogenous vs. Managrial Influences, *Jin-Chuan Duan and C.W. Sealey.* Coinsurance and Private-Public Partnership in Deposit Insurance, *Van Son Lai and Stephan Warywoda.* An Option-Based Analysis of Income-Equtiy Participation Loans, *Wm. Steven Smith.* Power Over Gamma: Curved Option Payoffs, *Garry de Jager and Joseph K. Winsen.*

Also Available:
Volumes 1-14 (1979-1996)
  + Supplements 1-2 (1984-1996) $78.50/£49.95 each

100 Prospect Street, P. O. Box 811, Stamford, CT 06904-0811
Tel: (203) 323-9606   Fax: (203) 357-8446
http://www.jaipress.com

JAI Press Inc.
Ablex Publishing Corp.

Advances in International Banking and Finance

Edited by **Sarkis Joseph Khoury,** *Graduate School of Management, University of California, Riverside*

Volume 3, In preparation, Spring 1999
ISBN 0-7623-0317-4   Approx. $73.25/£47.00

TENTATIVE CONTENTS: Editorial Board. Note on the Fribf. Foreword. The Changing Role of Banks and the Changing Value of Deposit Guarantees, *Peter Ritchken, James Thomson, Ivilina Popova.* International Equity Markets Integration and Settlement and Clearing Procedures, *Kyung-Won Kim and Joseph E. Finnerty.* The Relative Cost of Financial Distress in the International Firm, *David M. Reeb.* Fitting the Term Structure of Nominal Interest Rates with an Extended Vasicek Model, *Chen Guo.* Loan Sales: Pacific Rim Trade in Non-Tradable Assets, *Joseph G. Haubrich and James B. Thomson.* Mixed Currency Contracts of International Bank Loans, *Swapan Sen and Robert Peszek.* Policy Issues. Regulatory Design and Sharemarket Ownership in New Zealand, *Mark A. Fox and Girdon R. Walker.* Foreign Banks in the United States: Entry Strategies and Operations, *Sarkis J. Khoury.*

Also Available:
Volumes 1-2 (1995-1996) $73.25/£47.00 each

100 Prospect Street, P. O. Box 811, Stamford, CT 06904-0811
Tel: (203) 323-9606   Fax: (203) 357-8446
http://www.jaipress.com

JAI Press Inc.
Ablex Publishing Corp.

Research in Financial Services
Private and Public Policy

Edited by **George Kaufman,** *School of Business Administration, Loyola University of Chicago*

Volume 9, 1997, 320 pp. $73.25/£47.00
ISBN 0-7623-0301-8

CONTENTS: Introduction. U.S. BANKING SINCE FDICIA. The OCC and FDI-CIA, *Eugene A. Ludwig.* FDICIA: WHAT HAS WORKED AND WHAT HAS NOT. The FDICIA Improvement Act of 1991: What Has Worked and What Has Not, *Richard S. Carnell.* Evaluating FDICIA, *Frederic S. Mishkin.* FDICIA after Five Years: What Has Worked and What Has Not, *George G. Kaufman.* EVAL-UATING THE PROMPT CORRECTIVE ACTION AND LEAST COST RESO-LUTION PERFORMANCE OF THE REGULATORS. Evaluating the Prompt Corrective Action and Least Cost Resolution Performance of the Regulators: The Watchdog Perspective, *James L. Bothwell.* Contracting for Improved Su-pervisory Performance from Federal Banking Regulations, *Edward J. Kane.* BANKING PROBLEMS AND SOLUTIONS IN FOREIGN COUNTRIES. Safe and Sound Banking in Developing Countries: We're not in Kansas Anymore, *Gerard Caprio, Jr.* An International Baking Standard: The Time is Ripe, *Morris Goldstein.* Main Features of Banking Problems and Solutions in Japan, *Masaru Yoshitomi.* Financial Sector Reform: A Look Ahead. Optimal Supervision and Regulation of Banks, *Alice M. Rivlin.* INTERNATIONAL SETTLEMENTS: A NEW SOURCE OF SYSTEMIC RISK? Central Banks' Approach to Dealing with Settlement Risk in Foreign Exchange Transactions, *Christopher J. Mc-Curdy.* International Settlements: A New Source of Systemic Risk?, *Robert A. Eisenbeis.* International Settlements: A New Source of Systemic Risk?, *Nor-man R. Nelson.* THE NEXT FIVE YEARS IN BANKING: A PROPOSED AGEN-DA FOR THE NEW ADMINISTRATION AND CONGRESS. What's New after FDICIA?, *Robert E. Litan.* The Firrea Next Time: Consumer Debt and Congres-sional Action, *Karen Shaw Petrou.* The Next Five Years in Banking: A Proposed Agenda for the New Administration and Congress, *David Vitale.* FDICIA: The Unfinished Business, *William S. Haraf.* The Future Agenda: A Deposit Insurer's Perspective. The FDIC and FDICIA, *Ricki Helfer.*

Also Available:
Volumes 1-8 (1989-1996) $73.25/£47.00 each

100 Prospect Street, P. O. Box 811, Stamford, CT 06904-0811
Tel: (203) 323-9606   Fax: (203) 357-8446
http://www.jaipress.com

JAI Press Inc.
Ablex Publishing Corp.

Advances in Working Capital Management

Edited by **Yong H. Kim,** *University of Cincinnati*

Volume 3, 1996, 201 pp. $73.25/£47.00
ISBN 1-55938-576-6

CONTENTS: Preface, *Yong H. Kim.* PART I. VALUATION FRAMEWORK AND LIQUIDITY. The Value of Short-Term Cash Flow Forecasting Systems, *Tom W. Miller and Bernell K. Stone.* Liquidity and the Financing Policy of the Firm: An Empirical Test, *Esmeralda O. Lyn and George J. Papaioannou.* PART II. TRADE CREDIT: EFFICIENT MARKET, IMPERFECT INFORMATION, AND AN INTERNATIONAL PERSPECTIVE. A Role for Trade Credit in an Efficient Market, *Robert E. Rouault, Jr. and Daniel J. Kaufman, Jr.* Unbiased Trade Credit Decisions Under Imperfect Information, *David R. Fewings.* An International Accounts Receivable Management Model, *Pekka Ahtiala and Yair E. Orgler.* PART III. MANAGING CASH: BEHAVIORAL AND INTERNATIONAL PERSPECTIVES. Behavioral Relations and the Optimal Cash Discount, *William Beranek.* Optimum Cash Balances for International Firms, *Jongmoo Jay Choi, Dilip K. Ghosh, and Yong H. Kim.* Determination of Multicurrency Cash Balances: Strong Versus Weak Dollar Cycles, *Luc A. Soenen and Jeff Madura.* Swaps as a Cash Management Tool, *John F. Marshall, Vipul K. Bansal, and Alan L. Tucker.* A Test of One-Way Arbitarge in the Canadian/U.S. Dollar Commercial Paper Markets, *Mohsen Anvari and Alfred H.R. Davis.*

Also Available:
Volumes 1-2 (1988-1991) $73.25/£47.00 each

100 Prospect Street, P. O. Box 811, Stamford, CT 06904-0811
Tel: (203) 323-9606   Fax: (203) 357-8446
http://www.jaipress.com